McQuail's Reader in Mass Communication Theory

McQuail's Reader in Mass Communication Theory

Edited by

Denis McQuail

SAGE Publications
London • Thousand Oaks • New Delhi

First published 2002

Apart from any fair dealing for the purposes of research or
private study, or criticism or review, as permitted under the
Copyright, Designs and Patents Act, 1988, this publication
may be reproduced, stored or transmitted in any form, or by
any means, only with the prior permission in writing of the
publishers, or in the case of reprographic reproduction, in
accordance with the terms of licences issued by the Copyright
Licensing Agency. Inquiries concerning reproduction outside
those terms should be sent to the publishers.

SAGE Publications Ltd
6 Bonhill Street
London EC2A 4PU

SAGE Publications Inc
2455 Teller Road
Thousand Oaks, California 91320

SAGE Publications India Pvt Ltd
32, M-Block Market
Greater Kailash – I
New Delhi 110 048

British Library Cataloguing in Publication data

A catalogue record for this book is available from the
British Library

ISBN 0 7619 7242 0
ISBN 0 7619 7243 9 (pbk)

Library of Congress Control Number is available

Typeset by SIVA Math Setters, Chennai, India
Printed in Great Britain by The Alden Press, Oxford

contents

acknowledgements

The authors and publishers wish to thank the following for permission to use copyright material. Every effort has been made to trace all the copyright holders, but if any have been inadvertently overlooked, the publishers will be pleased to make the necessary arrangement at the first opportunity.

Kluwer Academic/Plenum Publishers for 'Media Sociology: the dominant paradigm' by Todd Gitlin, from *Theory and Society*, 6.

Taylor and Francis Ltd (http://www.tandf.co.uk/journals) for 'The Propaganda Model: a retrospective' by Edward Herman from Journalism Studies 1, 1; 'A Cultural Approach to Communication' by James Carey from *Communication 1–22* (1975); 'Streamlining Television Audiences' from *Desperately Seeking the Audience* by Ien Ang (1991); 'Fandom as Pathology' by Joli Jenson from *The Adoring Audience* by Lisa Lewis (1992).

Oxford University Press, Inc. for THE POWER ELITE, NEW EDITION by C. Wright Mills, copyright - 1956, 2000 by Oxford University Press, Inc.; NO SENSE OF PLACE by Joshua Meyrowitz, copyright – 1985 by Joshua Meyrowitz. Used by permission of Oxford University Press, Inc.

Palgrave for Alvin W. Gouldner, 'The Communications Revolution: news, public and ideology' from *The Dialectic of Ideology and Technology,* (1976) Macmillan, reproduced with permission of Palgrave.

Council of Europe for 'The Television Discourse: encoding and decoding' by Stuart Hall from *Education and Culture*, Number 25 (Summer 1974).

Verso for 'The Ideal Romance' in *Reading the Romance* by I Radway (1984).

Elihu Katz for 'Publicity and Pluralistic Ignorance: notes on the spiral of silence' from *Public Opinion and Social Change* (an anniversary edition for Elisabeth Noelle-Neumann), Westdeutscher Verlag (1981).

NORDICOM, Göteborg University, for 'Children and Television Violence in the United States' from *Children and Media Violence. Yearbook from the Unesco International Clearinghouse on Children and Violence on the Screen* (1998).

Lawrence Erlbaum Associates for 'Entertainment as Media Effect' by Dolf Zillmann from Media Effects, Bryant and Zillmann (1994).

sources

Chapter 1 First published in *Theory and Society*, 6, 205–253, Kluwer Academic/Plenum Publishers (1974) as 'Media Sociology: the dominant paradigm'.

Chapter 2 First published in *Communication, 2*, 1975: 1–22, Gordon & Breach Publishers (1975) as 'A Cultural Approach to Communication', pp. 1–10, 17–21.

Chapter 3 First published in *Feminist Media Studies*, L. van Zoonen, Sage Publications (1994) as 'A New Paradigm?', pp. 29–42.

Chapter 4 First published in *Journalism Studies 1, 1*, Taylor and Francis Ltd. (2000) as 'The Propaganda Model: a retrospective', pp. 101–111.

Chapter 5 First published in *The Power Elite*, C.W. Mills, Oxford University Press (1959) as 'The Mass Society', pp. 302–316.

Chapter 6 First published in *The Dialectic of Ideology and Technology*, A.W. Gouldner, Macmillan (1976) as 'The Communications Revolution: news, public and ideology', pp. 91–102.

Chapter 7 First published in *Media Events*, D. Dayan & E. Katz, Harvard University Press (1992) as 'Defining Media Events', pp. 4–23.

Chapter 8 First published in *No Sense of Place*, J. Meyrowitz, Oxford University Press (1985) as 'Missing Behavior: a missing link', pp. 13–23.

Chapter 9 First published in *Intermedia 14, 1*, International Institute of Communications (1986) as 'Towards a New Classification of Tele-Information Services', pp. 16–21.

Chapter 10   First published in *New Media and Society, 1, 1*, Sage Publications (1999) as 'Artifacts and Paradoxes in New Media, pp. 24–32.

Chapter 11   First published in *Journal of Communication 46, 1*, Oxford University Press (1996) as 'The Internet as Mass Medium, pp. 39–50.

Chapter 12   First published in *The Internet and Society*, J. Slevin, Polity (2000) as 'The Internet and Forms of Human Association, pp. 90–100.

Chapter 13   First published in *Enduring Issues in Mass Communication*, E.E. Dennis, A. H. Ismach and D.M. Gillmor, St. Paul, MN: West Publishing Company (1978) as 'The Press and the Public Interest: a definitional dilemma, pp. 327–340.

Chapter 14   First published in *Democracy and the Mass Media*, J. Lichtenberg, Cambridge University Press (1990), as 'Foundations and Limits of Freedom of the Press', pp. 102–115.

Chapter 15   First published in *Last Rites: revisiting four theories of the press*, J. C. Nerone, University of Illinois Press (1995), as On Social Responsibility Theory', pp. 77–100.

Chapter 16   First published in *Television and the Public Sphere*, P. Dahlgren, Sage Publications (1995), pp. 7–12.

Chapter 17   First published in *Television and the Public Interest*, J.G. Blumler, Sage Publications (1992), as New Roles for Public Service Television, pp. 206–215.

Chapter 18   First published in *The Globalization of News,* O. Boyd-Barrett and T. Rantanen, Sage Publications (1998), as 'Theorizing the News Agencies', pp. 6–12.

Chapter 19   First published in *Cultural Imperialism*, J. Tomlinson, Pinter (1991), as 'The Discourse of Cultural Imperialism', pp. 19–28.

Chapter 20   First published in *Communication: an introduction*, K.E. Rosengren, Sage Publications (2000), pp. 184–190.

Chapter 21   First published in *European Journal of Communication, 7*, Sage Publications (1992), as 'The Mythology about Globalization', pp. 69–93.

Chapter 22   First published in *Gatekeeping*, P. Shoemaker, Sage Publications (1991), as 'A New Gatekeeping Model', pp. 70–77.

Chapter 23   First published in *Making News: time and typicifcation*, G. Tuchman, Free Press (1978), pp. 45–58.

Chapter 24   First published in *Market-Driven Journalism: let the citizen beware*, J. H. McManus, Sage Publications (1994), pp. 85–91.

Chapter 25   First published in *The Hollywood TV Producer. His work and life*, M.G. Cantor, Basic Books (1971), pp. 189–209.

Chapter 26   First published in *Image, Music, Text: essays selected and translated by Stephen Heath*, Roland Barthes, Fontanta (1967), as 'Rhetoric of the Image', pp. 32–45.

Chapter 27   First published in *Decoding Advertisements*, J. Williamson, Marion Boyars (1978), as 'Introduction: Meaning and learning', pp. 11–14.

Chapter 28   First published in *Education and Culture* (Council of Europe), Number 25, Summer 1974, as 'The Television Discourse: encoding and decoding', pp. 8–15.

Chapter 29   First published in *Reading the Romance,* J. Radway, Verso (1984), as 'The Ideal Romance', pp. 131–152.

Chapter 30   First published in *Rethinking the Media Audience*, P. Alasuutari, Sage Publications (1999), as 'Three Phases of Reception Studies', pp. 1–8.

Chapter 31   First published in Desperately Seeking the Audience, I. Ang, Routledge (1991), as 'Streamlining 'television audience', pp. 60–67.

Chapter 32   First published in *The Adoring Audience*, Lisa A. Lewis, Routledge (1992), as 'Fandom as Pathology: the consequences of characterization', pp. 9–23.

Chapter 33   First published in *Children and Television*, R. Brown, Collier-Macmillan (1975), as 'The Functions Served by the Media', pp. 94–105.

Chapter 34   First published in *The Future of the Mass Audience*, W.R. Neumann, Cambridge University Press (1991), as 'The Future of the Mass Audience', pp. 164–171.

Chapter 35   First published in *Public Opinion and Social Change: for Elisabeth Noelle-Neumann*, H. Baier, H.M. Kepplinger and K. Reumann, Wiesbaden: Westdeutscher Verlag, as 'Publicity and Pluralistic Ignorance: notes on the spiral of silence', pp. 28–38.

Chapter 36   First published in *Journal of Communication, 43,4*, Oxford University Press, as 'Framing Towards Clarification of a Fractured Paradigm', pp. 51–58.

Chapter 37   First published in *Children and Media Violence*, Yearbook from the UNESCO Clearinghouse on Children and Media Violence on the Screen, E. Wartella, A Olivarez and N. Jennings, NORDICOM: Goteborg University (1998), as 'Children and Television Violence in the United States, pp. 57–61.

Chapter 38   First published in Media Effects, J. Bryant and D. Zillmann, Hillsdale, NJ:Erlbaum (1994) as 'Entertainment as a Media Effect', pp. 447–459.

Pertti Alasuutari is Professor of Sociology at the University of Tampere. His publications include *Rethinking the Media Audience* (editor) (London: Sage, 1999).

Ien Ang is Professor at the University of Western Sydney. Her publications include *Desperately Seeking the Audience* (London: Routledge, 1991) and *Watching Dallas*: *Soap Opera and the Melodramatic Imagination* (London: Methuen, 1985).

Roland Barthes (1915–1980). Formerly Directeur D'Etudes at the Ecole Pratique des Hautes Etudes, University of Paris. His books include *Elements of Semiology* (1964) and *Mythologies (1967)*.

Jay G. Blumler is Emeritus Professor, University of Leeds and University of Maryland. Author (with M. Gurevitch) of *The Crisis of Public Communication* (London: Routledge, 1995) and editor of *Television and the Public Interest* (London: sage, 1991).

Jan L. Bordewijk is Emeritius Professor at the Technical University, Delft. Author (with Ben van Kamm) of *Allocutie* (Baarn: Bosch and Keuning, 1982).

Oliver Boyd Barrett is Professor at the Polytechnic State Technical University, Poloma, California. His publications include *International News Agencies* (London: Constable, 1982) and *The Globalization of News* (with Terhi Rantanen) (London: Sage, 1998).

Jennings Bryant is Professor and Director at the Institute for Communication Research, University of Alabama and author of many works on media audiences and media effects.
Muriel Cantor (died 1994) was formerly Professor of Sociology at American Univer-

sity, Washington DC. She wrote *The Hollywood Television Producer* (New York: Basic Books, 1971), *Prime-Time Television* (Beverly Hills: Sage, 1984) and other works on media sociology.

James Carey is Professor in the School of Journalism, Columbia University, New York; formerly the Dean of the School of Communication, University of Illinois. His many publications on journalism and mass media include *Communication and Culture* (Boston, MA: Unwin Hyman, 1988).

Peter Dahlgren is Professor in the Department of Sociology and Communication, University of Lund and author of *Television Sphere* (London: Sage, 1995).

Daniel Dayan is Fellow, Centre National de Researche Scientifique, Paris. Author (with Elihu Katz) of *Media Events: the Live Broadcasting of History* (Cambridge, MA: Harvard University Press, 1992).

Everette E. Dennis is Distinguished Professor in Fordham University Business School, Lincoln Center, New York. Formerly Dean of the School of Journalism, University of Oregon and Executive Director of the Gannet Center for Media Studies (Freedom Forum), Columbia University, New York. Author of numerous books, including *Reshaping the Media: Mass Communication in the Information Age* ((Beverly Hills: CA, 1989) and *Of Media and People* (Beverly Hills: Sage, 1992).

Robert Entman is Professor in the Department of Communication, North Carolina State University, Raleigh NC. He is author, *inter alia*, of *Democracy Without Citizens: Media and the Decay of American Politics* (New York: Oxford University Press, 1989) and *The Black Image in the White Mind: Media and Race in America* (Chicago: Chicago University Press, 2000).

Celia von Feilitzen is Scientific Co-ordinator of the UNESCO Clearinghouse on Children and Violence, University of Goteborg. She has written widely on children and media.

Marjorie Ferguson (died 1999) taught in the Department of Sociology, London School of Econimics and was later Professor in the College of Communication, University of Maryland, Washington DC. Her publications include *Forever Feminine* (London: Heinemann, 1982), *Public Communication: the New Imperatives* (London: Sage, 1990) (editor) and *Cultural Studies in (Question* (editor with Peter Golding) (London: Sage, 1997).

Todd Gitlin is Professor in the Department of Media Ecology, New York University. He has published widely on media matters. Major publications include *The Whole World is Watching: Mass Media and the Making and Unmaking of the New Left* (Berkely CA: University of Californlia Press, 1980) and *Inside Prime-Time* (1983).

Alvin V. Gouldner (1920–1981). Formerly Professor of Sociology at the University of Amsterdam and at Washington University, St. Louis. Author of *The Coming Crisis of Western Sociology* (1970) and *The Dialectic of Science and Technology* (London: Macmillan, 1976).

Stuart Hall is Emeritus Professor, Open University; formerly Director of the Centre for Contemporary Cultural Studies, University of Birmingham and author of numerous publications on media, culture and society.

Edward S. Herman is Emeritus Professor of Finance at the University of Pennsylvania and author (with Noam Chomsky) of *Manufacturing Consent: the Political Economy of Mass Media* (New York: Pantheon, 1988).

Wolfgang Hoffmann-Riem is Professor of Constitutional and Administrative Law at the University of Hamburg and formerly Director of the Hans Bredow Institute for Radio and Television. He is author of *Regulating the Media* (New York: Guilford, 1996).

Joli Jensen is Professor at the University of Tulsa Oklahoma, Faculty of Communication. She has written on country music and communication technology and her publications include *Redeeming Modernity* (Beverly Hills, CA: Sage, 1990).

Ben van Kaam is a writer and researcher, formerly of the Press Institute, University of Amsterdam. Author (with J.L. Bordewijk) of *Allocutie* (Baarn: Bosch and Keuning, 1982).

Elihu Katz is Trustee Professor at the Annenberg School of Communication, University of Pennsylvania, Emeritus Professor of Sociology at the Hebrew University of Jerusalem and Scientific Director of the Guttman Institute of Applied Social Research. Author of numerous works on mass media, beginning with *Personal Influence* (with P.F. Lazarsfeld) (Glencoe, IL: Free Press, 1955).

Judith Lichtenberg is Professor in the Institute for Philosophy and Public Policy, University of Maryland, Washington DC. She edited *Democracy at the Crossroads* (Cambridge: Cambridge University Press, 1990).

John McManus is Professor at St. Mary's College, Mountain View, CA. He is author of *Market-Driven Journalism* (Thousand Oaks, CA: Sage, 1994).

Denis McQuail is Emeritus Professor, Department of Communication Science, University of Amsterdam and author of a number of works on mass media beginning with *Television and the Political Image* (with Joseph Trenaman) (London: Methuen, 1961) and most recently *McQuail's Mass Communication Theory* (London: Sage, 2000).

Joshua Meyrowitz is Professor of Communication at the University of New Hampshire, Durham NH. Author of *No Sense of Place: the Impact of Electronic Media on Social Behavior* (New York: Oxford University Press, 1985).

C. Wright Mills (1916–1962). Formerly Professor of Sociology, Columbia University, New York. He was an influential and radical social critic, author of *White Collar* (1953), *The Power Elite* (1956) and *The Sociological Imagination* (1959), all published by Oxford University Press.

Merrill Morris is Assistant Professor in the Department of Journalism, University of Memphis. She graduated Ph.D. from the University of Indiana after long professional media experience.

John C. Nerone is Professor in the Institute of Communications Research at the University of Illinois, Urbana-Champaign. He edited and contributed to *Last Rights: Revisiting Four Theories of the Press* (Urbana, IL: University of Illinois Press, 1995).

W. Russell Neuman is Professor in the School of Communication, University of Michigan, Ann Arbor. Numerous publications include *The Future of the Mass Audience* (Cambridge: Cambridge University Press, 1991).

Christine Ogan is Professor at the School of Journalism, University of Indiana. She has written widely on journalism and mass communication and is author of *Communication and Identity in the Diaspora* (Lanham: Lexington Books, 2001).

Janice Radway is Professor of American Civilization, University of Pennsylvania. Her publications include *Reading the Romance: Women, Patriarchy and Popular Literature* (Durham, NC: University of North Carolina Press, 1984).

Terhi Rantanen is at the London School of Economics after teaching at the University of Helsinki. She has published widely on news agencies and Russian media and is editor (with Oliver Boyd Barrett) of *The Globalization of News* (London: Sage, 1998).

Ronald E. Rice is Professor, School of Communication, Information and Library Studies, Rutgers University, Brunswick NJ. Author of *The New Media* (Beverly Hills, CA: Sage, 1983).

Karl Erik Rosengren is Emeritus Professor, Lund University, Sweden. His many publications in the communication field include *Media Matter* (with S. Windahl) (Norwood, NJ: Ablex, 1989) *Communication* (London: Sage, 2000).

Pamela Shoemaker is Professor at the S.I. Newhouse School of Public Communication, Syracuse University. She is author (with S.D. Reese of *Mediating the Message* (New York: Longman, 1991) and *Agenda-Setting* (Thousand Oaks, CA: Sage, 1997).

James Slevin is Associate Professor in the Amsterdam School of Communication Research, University of Amsterdam. Author of *The Internet and Society* (London: Polity, 2000).

John Tomlinson is Professor at Nottingham Trent University and Director of the Centre for International Communication and Culture. Publications include *Cultural Imperialism* (London: Pinter, 1991) and *Globalization of Culture* (Cambridge: Polity, 1999).

Gaye Tuchman is Professor in the department of Sociology, University of Connecticut, Storrs. She is author of *Making News: a Study in the Construction of Reality* (New York: Free Press, 1978).

Ellen Wartella is Dean of the College of Communication and Walter Cronkite Regents Chair at the University of Texas in Austin. She has published widely on issues to do with children and television and is author (with L. Grossman and D.C. Whitney) of *Media Making: the Mass Media in a Popular Culture* (Thousand Oaks, CA: Sage, 1999).

Judith Williamson is a writer and filmmaker. Her publications include *Decoding Advertisements* (London: Marion Boyar, 1978) and *Consuming Passions: the Dynamics of Culture,* 1986).

Dolf Zillmann is Professor in the College of Communication, University of Alabama. His many publications on the psychology of media audiences include *Media Effects* (editor with Jennings Bryant) (Hillsdale, NJ: LEA, 1994).

Liesbet van Zoonen is Professor in the Amsterdam School of Communication Research and Director of the Centre for the Study of Popular Culture at the University of Amsterdam. She is author of *Feminist Media Studies* (London: Sage, 1994) and other works.

T his selection of readings has been made in loose association with *McQuail's Mass Communication Theory*, to the extent that it follows the same structure in dividing up the field, and shares the same view of 'mass communication' as a concept and of the way it has been theorized and researched. Perhaps most important, it adopts the same view of what counts as theory for the purposes of a publication of this kind. The field of study of mass media is not rich in theory in the sense of precisely formulated propositions that can adequately describe in a formal way, explain or predict phenomena. The subject area is too diffuse and disparate to allow this and does not fall within any single discipline, with a shared theoretical framework and body of concepts. It is also an open terrain in which there is a wide public interest and much amateur theorizing and speculative assertions. A bridge to public debate has been provided by including a category of 'normative theory', that is, general ideas and concepts that relate to how mass media *ought* to perform in society.

Under these circumstances, the choice of entries has been guided by two main criteria. Firstly, the publication concerned should fall within the accepted canon of what can now be approximately labelled as 'media and communication studies' (although it has different names). Secondly, each contribution should be either the outcome of serious scholarship or research, or have a potential to contribute in this way. The ideas expressed or concepts developed in the readings should all contribute to an understanding of 'what is going on' in the complex interplay of media, communication and society.

Beyond this, the task of selection has turned out to be more difficult than anticipated, and not for lack of potential candidates. While the theoretical character of entries in the sense just mentioned is the most important criterion and also a necessary condition for selection, other factors have been taken into account. Most important and also most limiting has been the aim of achieving a balance across the various sub-topics of the field, even though these are not all equally developed theoretically. Secondly, I have attempted to recognize the great diversity of disciplines, approaches and quite fundamental differences of philosophy and purpose that characterize this field. This diversity cannot be adequately represented, but it is important to emphasize that there is no single correct way to apprehend the phenomenon of 'mass communication'. Thirdly, the selection seeks to provide some historical background to concerns about mass media, without simply being a collection of 'classic' writings (or writers). In fact, the majority of chapters have been published since 1990 and all have contemporary relevance. Finally, the selection has been made with a view to accessibility to non-specialists and suitability for anthologizing, avoiding technicalities and details of argument and evidence that cannot be adequately dealt with in the limited space available.

Denis McQuail
Chandlers Ford, Hampshire, UK

ORIGINS AND DEVELOPMENT OF THE FIELD OF STUDY

general introduction

EARLY BEGINNINGS

The concept of mass communication first appeared during the 1930s, to capture the essence of the dominant means of public communication of the early twentieth century, especially the 'new media' of the day. Although the newspaper press already had a long history, it was only towards the end of the nineteenth century that newspapers escaped from the constraints of localism, elitism or sectionalism (political or religious) and became a medium 'for the masses', although these were still mainly large urban populations. The formal study of the newspaper has its main roots in German universities early in the twentieth century under the heading of *Zeitungswissenschaft* (Hardt, 1979; Rosengren, 2000).

Theorists of society on both sides of the Atlantic (including, in America, William Sumner, Albion Small and Robert Park, and, in Europe, Ferdinand Tonnies, Georg Simmel, Gabriel Tarde, Max Weber and Albert Schaffle, among others) emphasized the intimate connection between the development and functioning of modern industrial societies and the newspaper press. The latter was found indispensable to modern democratic politics, economic life and the formation of public opinion. We can say that the impulse towards theorizing about mass media had its origins in a consciousness of the changed character of society. The particular function of the press was to provide the 'social cement' and the 'nervous system' of society (Hardt, 1979) that compensated for the decline of communal ties and the socially disruptive consequences of migration (across frontiers and into cities).

The newspaper press and the 'mass media' that supplemented it (film, radio, phonograph and, later, television) were, however, not primary topics for sociology when it developed as an independent social science and became institutionalized in university teaching and research from the 1940s onwards. The reasons for this marginal position are not obvious, although part of the explanation may be that the 'mass media' did not offer a sufficiently 'serious' subject matter to justify special attention. Sociology focused mainly on social 'problems' such as crime, deviance, poverty, race relations, and social and family dislocation.

The near global catastrophe of two world wars separated by the Great Depression also interrupted the flow of thought about the media, especially in Europe (although it also introduced new themes for theory). By comparison, the 'problems' presented by 'mass media' did not seem very significant. At worst, the media were viewed as an obstacle to cultural and educational advance, a potentially bad influence on children and young people and a source of misleading propaganda. When a theoretical interest in mass communication was revived (in Europe at least) after the Second World War, it tended to be driven either by a critical and normative spirit or by a fascination with the effects of communication technology.

Despite the relative neglect of theorizing in the first era of media expansion and innovation, a small core of theorists (including Paul Lazarsfeld, Harold Lasswell, Carl Hovland and Wilbur Schramm), mainly working in the United States, put together an essential body of theory about 'mass communication' that served the first generation of post-war research and teaching. The key ideas were encapsulated in the ideal-type concept of *mass communication*. This referred to the simultaneous transmission from a single or centralized (and organized) sender to all or most of a population of a recurring and standardized set of messages (news, information, fiction, entertainment and spectacle), without there being much possibility of responding or answering back.

The concept invokes associations with industrial mass production and the idea of a factory: assembly lines making standardized products and a disciplined workforce that might fancifully extend to include the audience. Mass communication enabled the symbolic and informational dominance of a whole society by those with control of the means of dissemination. It offered to individuals the means of sharing (mentally at least) in the collective life of society while retaining autonomy in the sphere of private behaviour. Mass communication brings about or facilitates the existence of mass audiences, consensus on opinions and beliefs, mass consumer behaviour, mass politics and other features of the so-called mass society. This depiction of a theory of mass communication for the purposes of initial presentation has been relatively neutral, simply extrapolating certain logical consequences arising from the operation of a system of public communication with the given characteristics.

The further story of mass communication theory makes it clear that the view outlined is far from an agreed one and may never have been agreed. It rests on a number of questionable (and questioned) assumptions, especially concerning the centralization of control at the source, the uniformity of content as sent and received, the power to influence, and the passivity and 'atomization' of audiences. The concept of *mass communication* is no more than an ideal type of some value in directing inquiry, but departing to a greater or lesser degree from the reality as much then as now. As a paradigm for theory and research about public communication, it has largely been replaced by new ideas, although not by any single, overarching alternative concept.

However, the *system* of communication media that initially gave rise to the concept is, in many respects, as much with us today as it was a century ago, albeit in more highly developed forms. The number of media channels has multiplied, their reach is greater and more effective, and the scale of media operations has transcended national societies to realize global communication. For the most part, the new technical possibilities for 'feedback' (interactive media) and for avoiding the whole system (via personalized information and entertainment supply) have not made much difference to the overall pattern of public communication. For these reasons, it is still worthwhile to follow the sometimes complex twists and turns of the theory of 'mass media' and to continue to apply earlier ideas to contemporary and future developments, even if the notion of 'mass communication' may have a diminished specific resonance and relevance.

SCHOOLS AND APPROACHES

The absence of a fixed disciplinary base during much of the history of mass communication theory has held back the development of a body of substantive theory, but it has promoted change and diversity of theoretical approaches. Not surprisingly, however, these largely reflected the currents of thought and the conflicts affecting the social sciences more generally. Rosengren (1983) mapped out the main types of media theory according to a classification originally developed for schools of sociological theory. For this purpose, the main dimensions were two polarities, one relating to assumptions about science, and the other to assumptions about the nature of society. The first dimension contrasted a 'subjective' with an 'objective' approach; the second distinguished 'radical change' from 'regulation'. When cross-classified, this gives rise to four types or 'paradigms' (of sociology and also communication theory): 'functionalist' (objective-regulation), 'interpretive' (subjective-regulation), radical humanist (subjective-radical change), and 'radical structural' (objective-radical change).

This scheme is equally helpful in mapping out the main alternative approaches to media theory and research, which have been seriously divided by their chosen method-ologies and priorities, as well as by their degree of commitment to radical change. The equivalent communication science 'paradigms' (if such they really are) to the four indi-cated above are as follows. Firstly, there is a 'functionalist' approach that emphasizes the 'positive' contribution of media to the existing social order and favours empirical, quantitative research. This has sometimes been called the 'dominant paradigm' (see Gitlin, Chapter 1 in Part II). Secondly, there is an approach that focuses on cultural issues (of quality and meaning in content) and uses mainly qualitative methods. Thirdly, there is a critical-cultural approach that uses interpretative methods to expose the ideo-logical working of mass media or to explore the implications for dissident groups in society, based on class, race, gender, etc. Fourthly, media are also examined critically as a material (mainly political-economic) force in society, open to objective analysis.

Underlying this set of divisions is a more basic division between 'media-centric' and 'socio-centric' theories. Media-centric theory not only attributes a strong causative role to each medium as a particular vehicle or carrier of meaning, but also places more emphasis on culture (of media as well as the society) and on texts and meanings. By contrast, socio-centric theory views technology and culture as dependent on more fundamental social forces.

Theoretical assessments of the significance of the mass media vary widely, and it is not helpful to describe media theory only in terms of these various paradigms, espe-cially since actual schools of theory or research draw elements from more than one. The fuller picture of media theory is more complex because there are cross-currents from other disciplines and other streams of thought. These include alternative ideas about democracy, technological determinism in one form or another, feminism, various branches of cultural theory, and information theory. These remarks are intended to emphasize the separate identity (from sociology) of contemporary theorizing about mass media, despite shared intellectual origins.

THE 'DOMINANT PARADIGM': FUNCTIONALIST AND EMPIRICAL

The term 'dominant paradigm' is generally associated with a critique of what it refers to (see Gitlin, 1978; Hall, 1989). The key features, whether favoured or not, are as follows: some version of functionalist theory, in which recurring processes and phenomena are taken to have some essential purpose for 'society'; an assumption that communication works in a more or less linear or transmission mode to deliver meaning 'as sent'; and a set of research methodologies and techniques that are believed to yield the best chance of reliable answers to questions asked. Arguably, the 'dominant paradigm' also involves a fundamental assumption (essentially an ideology) that the apparently successful forms of society (capitalist, liberal, secular and democratic by their own definition) are the best forms available at the current stage of social evolution (even if not perfect).

Research within this theoretical framework has lent support to the view that mass media tend to facilitate existing social organizations and goals, and thus the prevailing structures of power and social relations. They contribute to the work of other social institutions, including politics and the economy, by providing channels of communication, motivation and mobilization along with information about events and social circumstances. Their primary effects could be seen as promoting social cohesion and harmony, distributing symbolic rewards and punishments according to prevailing social norms, and defusing conflict. There was also scope for considering certain 'dysfunctional' aspects of mass media (e.g. the possible harmful effects of portrayals of sex and violence). However, the broad line of theorizing attributed 'positive' outcomes to the various uses and satisfactions derived from media by their audiences by way of their voluntary acts of choice. On the whole, the 'dominant paradigm' supported a view of society as voluntaristic and self-directed, rather than being manipulated or controlled by the media.

The 'paradigm' has been assaulted from all sides during the last 50 years. The functionalist sociology current during the 1950s was largely rejected because of fundamental theoretical vacuity, inconsistency with the new critical spirit of the 1960s and the subsequent appeal of new theories. Nevertheless, the underlying vague assumption that in many ways the mass media contribute (by their 'effects') to this or that 'positive' (functional) or 'negative' (dysfunctional) outcome for 'society' is still widely found in research into mass media, and there is even a revival of system theory, given support by information-technocratic thinking, that explicitly refers to the 'functions' of mass media (e.g. Luhmann, 2000). Meeting the demand for the useful information needed by the burgeoning communication industries (media, advertising, public opinion, public relations, information management) sits quite comfortably with functionalist and system thinking. The typical methods and research results (data) most adapted to the same needs are essentially those of the original 'dominant paradigm'. Within the institutions of social scientific research, status and funds are still routinely (perhaps more than ever) inclined to follow and lead the kind of research (and thus theorizing) that belongs to this tradition.

These remarks reflect something of the 'critique', as noted above. It does need to be acknowledged, even so, that the survival (even good health) of certain components of the 'dominant paradigm', long after its deconstruction and exposure, is due not only to the support of commercial and material interests. A belief in powerful 'effects' (or consequences) from media communication is still widespread, albeit more diversely and less crudely conceived than in early 'transmission' formulations. Without such a belief there would be little reason to take the media seriously, to distinguish between better and worse media systems and conduct, to trouble about media ethics, policy and regulation, or to care about who owns or controls the media. Theoretical ideas still need to be tested according to principles that embody assumptions about an observable reality and the possibility of finding empirical answers to some questions at least.

EARLY CRITICAL THEORY

Critical views of the influence of mass media are as old as the media themselves, and the grounds of complaint have not changed very much. Much criticism has related either to consequences that might be unintentionally harmful to society (such as diverting children from homework, misleading advertising, 'teaching' techniques of crime, or presenting a 'distorted' view of reality) or to an intrinsic lack of cultural or moral quality in the content distributed. A more fundamental critique has, from the earliest days, focused on the relation between media and the power structure of society. In the 'new democracies' of the early twentieth century, based on universal suffrage and still riven by conflicts between capital and labour, the mass media were largely interpreted by social critics as weapons in the hands of the ruling (capitalist) class, employed either to control and guide the masses by propaganda or to narcotize and divert them from effective opposition by escapist fantasies and consumerist dreams.

Marxist theory provided a clear theoretical statement to this effect, and Marxist cultural theorists of the Frankfurt school became eloquent critics of the insidious working of mass media and the 'cultural industries' (see, for instance, Adorno and Horkheimer, 1947; Marcuse, 1964). In post-war America, C. Wright Mills (Chapter 5 in Part III) expounded a theory of 'mass society' which echoed much contemporary thinking about the discontents of a 'modern industrial society' which dehumanized and disempowered the citizen, reducing him or her to a cog in the machine run by and for the new 'power elite' of the military-industrial complex. The media were assigned a special role ('function' perhaps) as the mechanism of persuading individuals voluntarily to suspend their true interest and identity (see also Marcuse, 1964) and lose their autonomy.

To some degree, this is a reverse image of the dominant paradigm described above, depicting a dystopian vision of modern society, held together by subtle means of compulsion, and drawing on some shared assumptions about the power of the media and shared formulations about how societies work. The examples of totalitarian societies of the first half of the twentieth century, especially Nazi Germany and the Stalinist Soviet Union, where the mass media were consciously and expertly controlled for the ends of the state, helped to give credibility to the fears of mass society theorists, despite the relative tolerance of the liberal-democratic regimes. Gramsci's (1971) notion of 'hegemony' rather than total control was helpful in bridging the gap between the two very different forms of 'mass society'.

LATER CRITICAL THEORY

From the 1960s onwards, the appeal of both classical Marxism and mass society theory waned, but the critical spirit was renewed under new banners and with new aspirations. It was promoted by new movements and new causes, especially opposition to war and militaristic policy (nuclear weapons), anti-imperialism and feminism, as well as by a demand for greater individual freedom and diversity within all the institutions of social life. Capitalism remained the enemy, but a socialist revolution was not seen by many as the answer. Criticism of the media focused on their subservience and service to the established 'authorities', on their stifling conformity, and on their centralization and regulation, as much by public bureaucracy as by capitalist owners. The demand was for free, diverse and subversive media, using the growing number of new technologies as well as liberating the old ones (Enzensberger, 1970). The elite cultural assumptions of some media controllers, as well as the crass commercialism of others, were under attack.

It is difficult to summarize 'later critical theory' by any single term or according to agreed central features. The spirit was vaguely 'neo-Marxist', but also 'liberal' in its search for 'liberation' from what was perceived as an outdated political and social order in Western society as well as in the Communist East. In its working out in research, this version of critical theory involved a number of practices. These included a concerted attempt to expose the way in which media organizations routinely operate to perpetuate a very limited view of 'social reality', not for some conscious 'ideological' purpose but for pursuit of their own organizational (and ultimately economic) goals, and as an expression of their professional ideology (especially that of journalistic 'objectivity'). Many works of the 1970s referred to news in particular as being 'manufactured', 'made' or artificially 'constructed'. The media were depicted as operating according to their own 'logic', subordinating the intentions of other would-be communicators to the consequences of this logic. On the whole, the pursuit by the media of their own goals was seen as a contribution to maintaining the 'status quo' rather than helping to promote social change. In addition, critical theory focused on the struggle over media meanings, not only in the textual practices but also in the encounter between 'reader' and 'text' at the point of reception. New critical theory favoured the view that all meaning has to be negotiated and that any 'text' is open to multiple and even opposed readings, depending on the circumstances and perception of the 'reader'. Critical theory cannot be fully appreciated independently of other theoretical advances, some aspects of which are described in this Introduction.

POLITICAL ECONOMY THEORY

This has much the same origins as Marxist theory of media and shares some of the same assumptions, although not that of historical determinism. It is, even so, a materialist theory, and its basic premise is that between them the economics of the media and the economic base of social power largely account for the main features of mass media development and the essential character of mass media systems and their content. The media are a form of property and an industry operating in several different markets in pursuit of profit. These facts of the case account for the recruitment of mass audiences and the mechanisms used to manage them (research, marketing, publicity). They are the fundamental cause of the particular way in which new communication technology is developed (as opposed to social and cultural explanations). They are the reason why the media develop monopoly tendencies, nationally and globally. They account for the skewed selection and standardization of media content and audience behaviour. In short, it is the logic of capitalistic economic and political forces, as exercised by owners and controllers, that accounts for the main features of mass communication perhaps better than does technology or the 'logic of media culture' itself.

There are alternative lines of analysis stemming from this broad perspective that can be applied to phenomena beyond actual structure and organization. For instance, the contents of the media can be understood as 'commodities' to be sold to consumers rather than forms of cultural expression. The hegemonic ideological tendencies attributed by critics to much media content can be explained by the logic of the market that finds it unprofitable to appeal to minority or deviant views, thus accentuating consensus and marginalizing opposition. Even audiences can be considered as products of the media, harvested by the appeal of popular commodities and sold to advertisers by the thousand according to their purchasing power. In the same vein, audiences can be viewed as 'working' for advertisers when they watch their 'free' television (Smythe, 1977). In general, the explanatory power of market forces in relation to the growing and increasingly commercialized media cultural industries seems quite strong.

The political-economic approach seems well suited as a framework for analysing the operation of global media, and especially those involving the new information technologies that, because of their immense economic and industrial potential, cannot be left to the vagaries of cultural preference. It is already apparent that the Internet is being powerfully shaped more by the possibilities for economic exploitation than by the intrinsic capacities of the net or the dreams of its founders. Even so, the elevation of political-economic explanations, however powerful, can lead to neglect of cultural analysis and overestimation of the significance of the forms of financing of media phenomena, as against their significance to their 'consumers'.

TEXTUAL AND LINGUISTIC THEORY

A new impetus was given to theory from the late 1960s by scholars mainly in the critical tradition and applying initially the concepts and methods of linguistic analysis derived from structuralism and semiology. Theoretical origins may be found in the work of Ogden and Richards (1923), Peirce (1931–5) and de Saussure (1915/1960), but specific applications to the texts of mass media were first made by continental theorists (including Roland Barthes, A.J. Greimas, Violette Morin and Umberto Eco). Initially, the main contribution to theory was to explicate the way in which media 'texts' (the symbolic content in physical form) work by way of meanings 'encoded' in linguistic and pictorial 'sign-systems'. This provided tools for uncovering 'latent' as well as 'overt', or surface, meanings, tools which made it possible to describe the underlying 'ideology' of media content (both in news and fiction) as well as to expose the processes by which advertising works. These developments were especially useful to theorists critical of the mass media.

The influence of linguistic ideas was much more extensive than this. When media texts are analysed in this way, their recurring patterns and structures strongly support the view that the mass media tend to offer us a 'preferred' reading of 'social reality' along with inbuilt cultural assumptions that are related to the distribution of power in economic, cultural, ethnic and gender terms. The media can be said to 'construct' social reality. This awareness makes it possible to contest such 'readings' and opens the potential for challenge to media hegemony. In the work of Hall (1989) and others, a central theoretical formulation suggests that our cultural and social circumstances impel us towards either accepting or rejecting dominant or consensual meanings. Alternative readings, leading to resistance and change, are always possible. This view of the hegemonic condition of society is both enlightening and more optimistic than the dystopian vision of early critical theory. Where resistance and the impetus to alternative reading will come from is an open question. Earlier critics of society saw it in education and political action. The new school of cultural theorists were more likely to see it in the liberating potential of popular culture and the undermining of hegemony by this route (see below).

The linguistic 'turn' of theory began by emphasizing the power of the 'text' as 'encoded', assuming its meaning to be more or less fixed according to the operation of objective sign-systems. However, it ended by advancing and reinforcing the view that the creation of meaning lies at least equally, if not more, with the manner of 'decoding', under the influence of experience, circumstances, desires and perceptions. Meaning and thus the basis for individual and social action are both constructed and (differentially) decoded, according to a complex process of 'negotiation' in which 'messages' are chosen to be interpreted according to the perspective of the receiver. During the 1970s and later, there emerged in media theory a more or less consensual coming together of linguistic theory and phenomenology, a school of sociology that emphasized voluntary action by individuals responding to their environment, making choices and solving problems in an active (and meaning-giving way).

This emerging consensus on the 'interactivity' and 'intersubjectivity' of media use and processes of influence found expression especially in 'reception theory', which strongly emphasized the 'role of the reader' (see Eco, 1977). In contrast with traditional audience research, which confined itself largely to describing audience 'choice behaviour' according to conventional industry-derived and fixed categories of content, reception research sought to understand in depth the personal and cultural significance of particular genres for particularly situated sets of audience members that could be characterized as 'interpretative communities'. This expression implies some shared view of the meaning and value of media experience as well as shared circumstances and outlook. Research in this theoretical mode often develops a common discourse to give an account of audience experience and media 'content'. It is more or less axiomatic that a 'media text' is complete only when it includes 'decoded' meanings as well as those 'encoded' (Fiske, 1987).

MEDIA CULTURAL THEORY

Some of the ideas already presented belong under this heading, but its specific purpose is to draw attention to the parallel and overlapping development of cultural and mass media theory. In this context, the origins of 'cultural theory' lie mainly in aesthetic, moral and normative judgements about cultural value. As applied to the mass media, these judgements were initially inclined to damn the 'culture of the media' as inferior in quality, degrading in tendency or politically exploitative in encouraging a docile labour force at a low price (see above). Other early strands of cultural theory supported not only the traditional 'high culture' of the cultivated classes but also the 'authentic' cultures of the 'folk', especially those with regional or (sub-) national identifications.

The critique of 'mass culture' gradually gave way from the 1960s onwards, under the liberating influences described above, to re-evaluations of popular culture, especially in the form of the new musical genres enjoyed by youth and the multiple cultural inventions developed for television and other new media. Even entrenched cultural critics of the traditional school found it hard to locate much of the new audiovisual culture of the mass media within the framework of conventional judgemental views. Many observers and theorists of the luxuriant fauna and flora of the media cultural landscape simply abandoned old perspectives as irrelevant and useless, and sought to make sense of cultural production and experience in their own terms, in general by linking media experience with the life experience of young people (mainly) in many sub-cultural contexts.

One school of critical theory (see McGuigan, 1992) adopted a cultural populism according to which new popular culture could be interpreted as a valid expression of 'resistance' to the dominant order (whether racial, patriarchal or class), even a 'revolt of the masses'. Popular culture was valued and celebrated for its own intrinsic meanings and values for its creators, performers and audiences. This approach to popular culture fitted very well with theories of 'postmodernism' when these became current during the 1980s. Postmodernism abstains from and undermines all absolutist theories of aesthetic or ethical value and treats all expressions of the human spirit and creative urge as equal. It celebrates the ludic and the ephemeral, making a definitive break with the early beginnings of 'cultural theory' as depicted above.

An important break with the functionalist-empirical tradition was signalled by the rejection of the linear 'transmission' model of communication that lent itself to the quantitative study of media effects in favour of an alternative 'cultural model' (see Carey, Chapter 2 in Part II). The basis for this view already existed in literary theory and in symbolic interactionism, and at its essence was a view of communication as 'expression' or 'ritual'. Much human communication is not utilitarian or practical and has no measurable outcome. It is engaged in for its own sake, as an expression or act of belonging to a particular 'community', or to mark some special occasion, such as celebration or mourning. The early study of mass communication was too often appropriated for commercial, educational or propagandist interests, in effect diverting attention from the essence of many forms of mass communication, including much 'entertainment'. The seeming 'purposelessness' of much communication was baffling to those who sought to measure 'effects' and 'effectiveness', and new approaches and methods were needed to take account of ritual and expressive communication uses.

This is not the whole story of cultural theory as far as the mass media have been concerned. Several strands of theory did not abandon the 'modernistic' approach that allocates differential value to various forms of cultural practice and experience. A prominent exception is the critique of 'cultural imperialism' and of 'globalization' (see Tomlinson, Chapter 19 in Part VI). It is hard to escape the fact that much, if not most, media popular culture is 'Western' in origin and expression, and also one of the main products of the global media industrial complex that has a dominant influence in world media systems and performance. It is not easy to reconcile the celebration of Western popular culture as a socially liberating and subversive force with a reasoned critique of global media industries, the exploitation of economically underdeveloped societies and the unrestrained export of a global consumer culture. These cultural phenomena do not seem compatible with the autonomous growth of cultural values and forms that are true to the traditions and experience of other societies.

This inconsistency cannot simply be dismissed, although there are some defences, aside from the argument that Western cultural forms may indeed be liberating in a certain sense if they undermine the hold of regimes and ideologies that are repressive and reactionary in Western eyes. More convincing is the pragmatic (rather than theoretical) view that exported cultures do not simply replace and destroy existing cultures when they 'invade'; they may simply have no great significance or effect, or, where they do, they are also subject to the process of negotiation of meanings mentioned above, whereby they acquire quite a different significance for other cultures. The pre-existing cultures are not simply 'traded in' for novel forms, but the latter are added to the repertoire of cultural possibilities. In addition, there is much evidence of adaptation and the formation of hybrid cultural forms combining native with imported elements. In a minor way, these tendencies have been observed to occur in the many different national cultures of Europe, in the face of a supposed wave of 'Americanizing' media cultural influences.

A footnote to this section is called for in order to recognize the development of what can be called a specific 'media culture'. The mass media are probably now the most productive cultural institution, and what they produce reflects the imperatives, working assumptions and practices of the media institution (and its workforce), exhibiting some common features worldwide. The main imperative on the media institution, stemming mainly from commercial motives, is for each channel to maximize the attention it receives under conditions of relentless competition (for audience and advertising income). The working assumption of media is that attention is best gained by appealing to sensation and human interest. The grooming of media 'stars' and 'personalities', on the one hand, and, on the other hand, the intense focus on prominent human beings and dramatic or exciting events and spectacles are the agreed means to gain attention. This can be expressed in terms of a more or less universal 'media logic' that is applied to all genres and topics of media content. The global character of media operation leads to continuous imitation and borrowing, and the reinforcement of similar occupational ideologies and codes of professional practice. It is arguable that significant 'effects' from mass media stem not from 'mass persuasion' but from the fact that many key public communicative transactions are mediated through a distorting prism of media-centric ideas and routine practices.

MEDIA TECHNOLOGY AND ITS EFFECTS

It could be argued that the very essence of mass communication theory is a simple but all-embracing expression of technological determinism, since the essential features depend on what certain technologies have made possible, especially the following: communication at a distance, the multiplication and simultaneous distribution of diverse 'messages', the enormous capacity and speed of carriers, and the limitations on response. There is no escaping the implication that public communication as practised in modern societies is profoundly shaped by these general features. The question remains, even so, as to whether particular technological means, as applied, have particular tendencies of influence that can be observed. It is of particular pertinence at a moment in the development of the media when new telecommunication and computer-based means of communication are being applied to the purposes previously dominated by print and broadcasting, changing the potential for diversity of forms, speed, capacity, access and interactivity.

The first theories relating to the influence of media technology were formulated by Harold Innis (1950, 1951), tracing a long history from early empires and forms of inscription to radio, and finding a logical correspondence between social formations and dominant means of communication. More specifically, theory then focused on the effects of printing, as introduced in Europe in the mid-fifteenth century. Again, many aspects of the rise of modern society and culture have been found to depend in some degree on the uses made of printing (Eisenstein, 1978; Febvre and Martin, 1984; Johns, 1999; McLuhan, 1962). When it came to television, imaginative speculation about its supposed effects by McLuhan (1964) and more reasoned analysis by Meyrowitz (Chapter 8 in Part III) supported the general idea that we are in an era much influenced by the form of the 'dominant' means of communication.

At specific moments in history, a single technology does seem to have had a major direct and specific influence, such as those of the electric telegraph in the mid-nineteenth century, which led to world news agencies, and the telephone somewhat later, which facilitated new architectural and work-organizational forms. In our own time, the computer is still having an even wider and deeper impact. More comprehensive assessments of communication technology developments (e.g. by Beniger [1986] and Winston [1986]) have stressed the extent to which technology is developed according to the needs of the dominant social order, suppressing more revolutionary potential for change, and reinforcing order.

These various theoretical efforts have all been largely vitiated by the enormous complexity of the questions being tackled and by the fact that the uses of any technology (and the technology itself) continually change and also vary between one society and another, despite some common 'media-cultural' features, as noted above. A theoretical analysis by Thompson (1995) avoids distinguishing between different technologies, and instead focuses on the significance in general of the mediation of experience and interaction of communication technologies, as opposed to face-to-face interaction or direct experience.

This is more promising intellectually and it offers a better grip on assessing the potential influence of new, more interactive means of communication, but there is no real escape from the fact that technologies are subordinate to cultural meanings, social definitions, actual uses and many other influences, making it impossible to isolate them as an 'independent variable'. We cannot go much further than more or less convincing interpretations applied to more or less specific situations. The effects of any technology are in the first instance their uses, and these uses often have observable effects as a matter of historical fact. The implication may be that we need histories of technology (effects) rather more than theories. Even so, it is unlikely that the appeal of following the technology trail will diminish.

FEMINIST MEDIA THEORY

Since the 1970s, in line with the general development of women's studies and feminist theory generally, a flourishing and independent body of knowledge has been accumulated about the relation between the media and women (and gender more widely). The significance of the media for women was initially seen to lie in the socializing role of the media for all young people (and adults), especially through the repetitive depiction of different gender roles and reinforcement stereotypes. Media representation was believed (and usually found) to emphasize the place of women in the home and their subordination generally in nearly all spheres of life.

As the scope of feminist theory widened, so feminist media theory also extended to embrace the view that female experience in society – historically, culturally and actually – is sufficiently different to suppose that women have fundamentally different interests and capacities. Their making of the media is or would be different, and similarly their experiencing and understanding of the media, even though the reality of media systems is such that most media can be observed to be controlled by men, produced by men and directed predominantly at men, or, if not, at audiences of women as largely envisaged by men.

This basic point has fundamental implications for following up the insights of other theories, for imagining effects and for working towards alternatives. It is not sufficient simply to identify 'women' as a demographic category more systematically in theory and research. Each branch of research, directed variously at the structures and control of the media, advertising and marketing, news and entertainment production, the selection and meaning of content, the interpretations and choices of audiences and many kinds of 'effects', has to be in principle reconsidered, probably, although not exclusively, by women theorists. Not all outcomes or reformulated theories will necessarily be different, but the priorities for theory and research and the specific infilling are likely to change under the influence of feminist theory. So far, most of the influence of feminist media theory can be observed in relation to studies of media culture and media reception, but the range is extending.

NORMATIVE MEDIA THEORY

Normative media theory refers to systematically worked-out sets of ideas about how the media *ought* to operate if they are to fulfil a wide range of expectations about their contribution to society. Most media in modern democratic states are free from positive obligations to provide particular services (there are exceptions, as in public broad-casting), and otherwise have much the same rights, freedoms and obligations as any citizen. At the same time, they often operate according to certain ethical and norma-tive principles formally by their own choice but also in response to requests and pres-sures and by agreement with agents of other social institutions. The democratic political system is the prime example, since its communication needs can only be fully met in cooperation with the mass media. There are historical precedents and long-established conventions that enable the media and political institutions to work together without compromising essential media freedoms.

Most formulations of normative media theory in fact turn on the tension between, on the one hand, media claims to freedom of publication that have their roots in early struggles for freedom and democracy and, on the other hand, various claims that the media ought also to serve the public interest and accept responsibility for their actions. Normative theory thus supports the idea of public policy for the media and for media regulation, and offers guidance for the forms such policy might take. The impulse to propose obligations for the media is rooted in a widely-held belief that public communication is too important to be left to chance or the market, and that the operation of the media always touches on matters that are politically, morally or ethically sensitive, and that are also matters for public opinion. Resistance to policy and regulation is usually based on libertarian or free market theory. The driving force for theory development on behalf of either control or freedom is continually renewed by changes in the nature of media technology and also by changes in the socio-cultural climate and political culture.

META-THEMES OF THEORY

Despite their differences, the schools and approaches described have all, in their distinctive ways, dealt with many of the same themes of mass communication, and it is worthwhile summarizing these, if only to restore some sense of the common origin and interconnection of the approaches. This commonality derives from the basic assump-tions about the character of mass media systems outlined at the start.

It is logical to start with the theme of *medium* theory, encompassing all ideas about the consequences of different communication technologies and especially the complete technological system that allows the few to distribute messages to the many with such apparent efficiency. Medium theory has often concentrated on the particular forms of the separate media that constitute the mass media (print, film, music, radio, television, multimedia, etc.) rather than on the 'mass media as such', but the logic of theorizing is much the same in each case. The main elements of the underlying logic are that newly invented communication technologies make possible more efficient production and distribution of symbolic content, and that the application of the technologies (including the forms of organization involved) inevitably leads to new uses and forms of communication, as well as to more communication. This also changes the relations between 'senders' and 'receivers'. Those who are predominantly 'receivers' of communication also experience a change in the balance and content of information they possess. New media mean new kinds of sense experience and media use behaviours. Just as important, new media change the power relations between different 'communicators' and between them and other agents of power in the society. These propositions are all significant in respect of their consequences and are quite plausible, even difficult to reject at some level of validity. As a result, they continue to provide fertile soil for speculation and enquiry in an age of 'information technology'.

The theme of *dominance through mass media* is in some respects dependent on 'medium theory', since it arises because of the alleged consequences of a society-wide form of communication which came to expose all members of a society to much the same degree and type of 'centrally' provided content. Centralization was a matter of both national and 'metropolitan' control, but also of the concentration of production and distribution information and culture in the hands of a few large, bureaucratic-industrial units. It is arguable whether the technology of mass communication has driven the emergence of the 'system' and its uses, or whether a centralized and nationalistic form of society adapted the technology to its purposes. In the case of the more recent innovations of communication technology, especially distribution by satellite and telecommunications, all based on computers, the pressure of technology (really from industrial and governmental backers) is clearly very strong.

For the further theoretical working out of the consequences for human society, it may not matter which came first. The central issue is the degree to which the flow of communication in society is unitary or diverse and the degree to which members of society are either *dependent* on this flow or susceptible to its influence on their own outlook and actions. Especially at issue is whether there is some dominant ideology or coherent portrayal of an alleged 'social reality' that is purveyed with or without some coherent plan. Within the scope of this theme are to be found lines of theory that reject the basic premise of subordination through mass communication, advancing arguments on behalf of the human capacity to resist unwanted or useless ideas and to render 'propaganda' counter-productive. The very notion of one-way communication can well be regarded as an expression of communication 'illiteracy', given the essentially interactive and intersubjective character of human communication. There is also a sociological illiteracy in the belief that flows of 'messages' determine the most important patterns of human social interaction.

A third theme that has some independence from the foregoing concerns aspects of *social and cultural identity and cohesion*. It arises initially not from a consideration of mass media but from ideas about social life. One aspect has to do with the essential conditions for desirable forms of society under conditions of freedom and social justice that promise a tolerated diversity of values and ways of life, as well as cooperation for common ends of the society and those of the global community. The part played by communication is important in these matters, and that of 'mass communication' is of especial importance in ensuring the framework of wider coexistence, the sharing of some common concerns, the interconnection of diverse microsocial and cultural environments, and in enabling an awareness of shared global interests.

Theoretical propositions have been advanced to argue that the mass media (universally shared channels and some 'content') are an essential support for a sense of common identity (national or cultural), although critical views of the media have long expressed the view that the more massive (and commercial) the media, the more they undermine the non-media (social and cultural) basis for social integration, and the more debilitating they are for active social participation. These ideas are connected with the predominantly pessimistic early theory of mass society and (perennially renewed) moral panics about the harmful and desocializing effects of mass media on children.

On balance, attention in mass communication theory has shifted to a concern with the potential subordination or marginalization of cultural and social minorities and the opportunities for communication multiplicity. In this respect, it is generally recognized that the limits of what can be achieved by way of the mass media (and they are quite restricted) have probably been reached, and that the long-heralded 'decline of the mass media' offers more hope for communication freedom and diversity.

The fourth main theme of theory can be summarized under the heading of *public interest*, bringing together all kinds of political, normative and ethical concerns arising from the development of a new social institution that is both essential to meeting the needs of society and also to a large extent outside direct public control in liberal-capitalist states. Here, as with other themes of theory, a certain degree of 'Western' bias is evident, and not all societies are restricted by their ideology from directing their media to fulfil their own version of the good of society. There are also differences within the 'liberal-democratic' category of nations. At the most basic level, there is a permanent debate in most countries about the potential social benefit or harm that can be obtained or expected from the mass media, and about how to achieve the one and avoid the other by policy, regulation or skilful planning and bargaining.

The question of what constitutes the public interest in the way a mass media system operates sometimes problematizes the very notion of identifying a 'public interest'. Either this turns out to be the sectional interest of those with power to impose a definition, or it leads to a suppression of the forces for change in society and in the media. Social change calls for a continuous redefinition of what is for the general good. At worst, the pursuit of a public interest is seen as a device for suppressing freedom.

The disputed character of the idea, let alone its institutional expression, has not suppressed or even diminished calls for the media to respond to their alleged responsibilities, and they have nowhere escaped all forms of accountability, ranging from legal and regulatory restrictions to some degree of direct public control, as in some broadcasting systems. For the most part, normative theory draws on ideas about the mass media that have already been presented, calling for limits on any monopoly of ownership and control, whether private or public, and for diversity and quality of content. Aside from law, public pressure from outside and professional aspirations within the mass media work towards greater public accountability. In the global arena, shared threats from armed conflict and ecological or economic disaster operate in the same direction. Normative concerns are often expressed positively, in terms of the more universal availability of communication systems and the opening of channels to greater access of all kinds. Anxieties about the media, aside from the issues of alleged harmful effects already mentioned, often include a reference to the supposed 'digital divide', once known as the 'information gap', that opens up between the 'information rich' and the 'information poor'. The cultural and informational benefits of communication technology are not universally available but are differentially distributed according to wealth and skills, leading to a more unequal society and a more divided world.

THE FUTURE OF MASS COMMUNICATION THEORY

The future of theory will clearly depend on the future of mass communication itself. Although 'new media theory' (represented in some degree in Part V) does open the way for the decline or end of mass communication, it has not really introduced any fundamentally new issues of communication theory. Unless there is a sudden and unexpected end to the mass press, television, music and related industries, the constant changes in the media and their use will continue to be examined within existing frameworks, using many of the concepts and associated methods that are represented in this collection of papers that spans the last 50 years.

REFERENCES

Adorno, T. and Horkheimer, M. (1947/1972) *The Dialectic of Enlightenment*. New York: Herder and Herder.

Beniger, J.R. (1986) *The Control Revolution*. Cambridge, MA: Harvard University Press.

de Saussure, F. (1915/1960) *Course on General Linguistics*. London: Peter Owen.

Eco, U. (1977) *The Role of the Reader*. Bloomington: University of Indiana Press.

Eisenstein, E. (1978) *The Printing Press as an Agent of Change*. New York: Cambridge University Press.

Enzensberger, H.M. (1970) 'Constituents of a theory of the media', *New Left Review*, 64: 13–36.

Fiske, J. (1987) *Television Culture*. London: Methuen.

Febvre, L. and Martin, H.J. (1984) *The Coming of the Book*. London: Verso.

Gitlin, T. (1978) 'Media sociology: the dominant paradigm', *Theory and Society*, 6: 205–53.

Gramsci, A. (1971) *Selections from the Prison Notebooks*. London: Lawrence and Wishart.

Hall, S. (1989) 'Ideology and communication theory', in B. Dervin, L. Grossberg, B.J. O'Keefe and E. Wartella (eds), *Rethinking Communication*, Vol. 1. Newbury Park, CA: Sage. pp. 40–52.

Hardt, H. (1979) *Social Theories of the Press*. Beverly Hills, CA: Sage.

Innis, H. (1950) *Empire and Communication*. Oxford: Clarendon Press.

Innis, H. (1951) *The Bias of Communication*. Toronto: University of Toronto Press.

Johns, A. (1999) *The Nature of the Book*. Chicago, IL: Chicago University Press.

Luhmann, N. (2000) *The Reality of the Mass Media*. Cambridge: Polity Press.

McGuigan, J. (1992) *Cultural Populism*. London: Routledge.

McLuhan, M. (1962) *The Gutenberg Galaxy*. Toronto: University of Toronto Press.

McLuhan, M. (1964) *Understanding Media*. London: Routledge and Kegan Paul.

Marcuse, H. (1964) *One-Dimensional Man*. London: Routledge and Kegan Paul.

Meyrowitz, J. (1985) *No Sense of Place*. New York: Oxford University Press.

Ogden, C.K. and Richards, I.A. (1923) *The Meaning of Meaning*. London: Routledge and Kegan Paul.

Peirce, C.S. (1931–5) *Collected Papers*. Cambridge, MA: Harvard University Press.

Rosengren, K.E. (1983) 'Communication research: one paradigm or four?', *Journal of Communication*, 33 (3): 187–207.

Rosengren, K.E. (2000) *Communication: An Introduction*. London: Sage.

Smythe, D.W. (1977) 'Communications blindspot of western marxism', *Canadian Journal of Political and Social Theory*, 1: 120–7.

Thompson, J.B. (1995) *The Media and Modernity*. Cambridge: Polity Press.

Winston, B. (1986) *Misunderstanding Media*. Cambridge, MA: Harvard University Press.

II

CONCEPTUAL ISSUES AND VARIETIES OF APPROACH

This selection of chapters as a whole locates the study of mass communication securely within the rather broad framework of the social sciences. As a result, the development of the field, its general direction and various twists and turns, has followed much the same path as other social sciences, more particularly sociology, with which it shares most common ground. The story might have been written differently if a unified 'science of communication' had succeeded in making its own independent way. In that eventuality, the field would have ranged across all kinds of communicative relationships and institutionalized communication practices, and been much less dominated by one institution – that of mass media. These remarks are meant as a reminder to the reader that there is more diversity and also controversy about concepts and definitions relating to communication than is represented in the selection that follows. The latter is distinctly 'socio-centric', turning mainly on questions concerning the exercise of power in society, with a limited recognition of conceptual problems about communication itself.

Gitlin (Chapter 1) describes a post-war 'dominant paradigm' of empirical social science from a radically critical perspective. Despite its polemical character, it does very clearly summarize the main features and potential limitations of an approach that has inspired continued application as well as much counter-thinking. The revolt against the 'linear information transmission' model of the dominant approach is signalled with equal eloquence by Carey (Chapter 2). Its especial importance lies in emphasizing a concept of communication that may be unsuited to the practice of 'scientistic' research but which probably captures more of the significance of mass communication than does the dominant model. Carey can usefully be read in conjunction with the work of Dayan and Katz (Chapter 7 in Part III). The main alternative approach to mass communication research has emphasized its cultural significance for audience and society rather than its controlling, manipulative potential for whatever 'power that be'. It leads away from measurement and towards interpretation, both in ways of thinking and in methods of research.

The strengths of the alternative approach (although it is not exclusively alternative) are illustrated by van Zoonen's (Chapter 3) overview of the field of mass communication defined from a feminist perspective. It is alternative not only in its cultural emphasis but also in its view of the source and working of symbolic forms of power, as stemming from gender as well as from class and other material factors. In general, feminist media theory has successfully combined 'idealist' with 'materialist' approaches. With Herman (Chapter 4) we return to a more traditional critical view of how big media serve to uphold the interests of state and big business, as a result of various features of the media system that filter out dissent. It is a view that implicitly credits the mass media with a good deal of political influence.

media sociology: the dominant paradigm

TODD GITLIN

The dominant paradigm in media sociology, what Daniel Bell has called the 'received knowledge' of 'personal influence,'[1] has drained attention from the power of the media to define normal and abnormal social and political activity, to say what is politically real and legitimate and what is not; to justify the two-party political structure; to establish certain political agendas for social attention and to contain, channel, and exclude others; and to shape the images of opposition movements. By its methodology, media sociology has highlighted the recalcitrance of audiences, their resistance to media-generated messages, and not their dependency, their acquiescence, their gullibility. It has looked to 'effects' of broadcast programming in a specifically behaviorist fashion, defining 'effects' so narrowly, microscopically, and directly as to make it very likely that survey studies could show only slight effects at most. It has enshrined short-run 'effects' as 'measures' of 'importance' largely because these 'effects' are measurable in a strict, replicable behavioral sense, thereby deflecting attention from larger social meanings of mass media production. It has tended to seek 'hard data,' often enough with results so mixed as to satisfy anyone and no one, when it might have more fruitfully sought hard questions. By studying only the 'effects' that could be 'measured' experimentally or in surveys, it has put the methodological cart ahead of the theoretical horse. Or rather: it has procured a horse that could pull its particular cart. Is it any wonder, then, that thirty years of methodical research on 'effects' of mass media have produced little theory and few coherent findings? The main result, in marvelous paradox, is the beginning of the decomposition of the going paradigm itself.

In the process of amassing its impressive bulk of empirical findings, the field of mass media research has also perforce been certifying as normal precisely what it might have been investigating as problematic, namely the vast reach and scope of the instruments of mass broadcasting, especially television. By emphasizing precise effects on 'attitudes' and microscopically defined 'behavior,' the field has conspicuously failed to attend to the significance of the fact that mass broadcasting exists in the first place, in a corporate housing and under a certain degree of State regulation. For during most of civilized history there has been no such thing. Who wanted broadcasting, and toward what ends? Which institutional configurations have been generated because of mass broadcasting, and which going institutions – politics, family, schooling, sports – have been altered in structure, goals, social meaning, and how have they reached back into broadcasting to shape its products? How has the prevalence of broadcasting changed the conduct of politics, the texture of political life, hopes, expectations? How does it bear on social structure? Which popular epistemologies have made their way across the broadcasting societies? How does the routine reach of certain hierarchies into millions of living rooms on any given day affect the common language and concepts and symbols? By skirting these questions, by taking for granted the existing institutional order, the field has also been able to skirt the substantive questions of valuation: Does the television apparatus as it exists fulfill or frustrate human needs and the social interest? But of course by failing to ask such questions, it has made itself useful to the networks, to the market research firms, to the political candidates.

First published in *Theory and Society*, 6, 205–253, Kluwer Academic/Plenum Publishers (1974) as 'Media Sociology: the dominant paradigm'.

THE DOMINANT PARADIGM AND ITS DEFECTS

The dominant paradigm in the field since the Second World War has been, clearly, the cluster of ideas, methods, and findings associated with Paul F. Lazarsfeld and his school: the search for specific, measurable, short-term, individual, attitudinal, and behavioral 'effects' of media content, and the conclusion that media are not very important in the formation of public opinion. Within this whole configuration, the most influential single theory has been, most likely, 'the two-step flow of communications': the idea that media messages reach people not so much directly as through the selective, partisan, complicating interpolation of 'opinion leaders.' In the subtitle of *Personal Influence*, their famous and influential study of the diffusion of opinion in Decatur, Illinois in the mid-Forties, Elihu Katz and Lazarsfeld were concerned with 'the part played by people in the flow of mass communications.'[2] One technical commentator comments with due and transparent qualification: 'It may be that few formulations in the behavioral sciences have had more impact than the two-step flow model.'[3] Daniel Bell, with his characteristic sweep, calls *Personal Influence* 'the standard work.'[4]

As in all sociology, the questions asked and the field of attention define the paradigm even before the results are recorded. In the tradition staked out by Lazarsfeld and his associates, researchers pay most attention to those 'variables' that intervene between message-producers and message-receivers, especially to the 'variable' of interpersonal relations. They conceptualize the audience as a tissue of interrelated individuals rather than as isolated point-targets in a mass society. They see mass media as only one of several 'variables' that influence 'attitudes' or voting choices, and they are interested in the measurable 'effects' of media especially in comparison with other 'variables' like 'personal contact.' They measure 'effects' as *changes* over time in respondents' attitudes or discrete behaviors, as these are reported in surveys. In a sequence of studies beginning with *The People's Choice*,[5] Lazarsfeld and his associates developed a methodology (emphasizing panel studies and sociometry) commensurate with their concern for mediating 'variables' like social status, age, and gregariousness. But in what sense does their total apparatus constitute a 'paradigm,' and in what sense has it been 'dominant'?

I want to use the word loosely only, without history-of-science baggage, to indicate a tendency of thought that (a) identifies as important certain *areas* of investigation in a field, (b) exploits a certain *methodology*, more or less distinctive, and (c) produces a set of *results* which are distinctive and, more important, come to be recognized as such. In this sense, a paradigm is established as such not only by its producers but by its consumers, the profession that accords it standing as a primary outlook.

Within the paradigm, Katz's and Lazarsfeld's specific theory of 'the two-step flow of communication,' the idea that 'opinion leaders' mediate decisively between mass communicators and audiences, has occupied the center of scholarly attention. In any discussion of mass media effects, citations of *Personal Influence* remain virtually obligatory. As the first extended exploration of the idea – 'the two-step flow' appears only as an afterthought, and without much elaboration, at the end of the earlier *The People's Choice* – *Personal Influence* can be read as the founding document of an entire field of inquiry. If the theory has recently been contested with great force on empirical grounds, the paradigm as a whole continues to be the central idea-configuration that cannot be overlooked by critics. Joseph T. Klapper's *The Effects of Mass Communication* (1960) is the definitive compilation of the field's early stages; but the Decatur study, spread out as it is in detail, seems to me a better testing-ground for a reexamination of the whole paradigm. By having the power to call forth citations and critiques at its own level of generality, it remains central to the field. For twenty years replicating studies have proliferated, complicating and multiplying the categories of the Decatur study, looking at different types of behavior, different types of 'news function' ('relay,' 'information,' and so on), some of them confirming the two-step flow on a small scale,[6] but most of them disconfirming or severely qualifying it. All these studies proceed from the introduction into an isolated social system of a single artifact – a product, an 'attitude,' an image. The 'effect' is always that of a controlled experiment (such, at least, is the aspiration), but the tendency is to extrapolate, without warrant, from the study of a single artifact's 'effect' to the vastly more general and significant 'effect' of broadcasting under corporate and State auspices. Whatever the particular findings, the general issues of structural impact and institutional change are lost in the aura, the reputation of the 'two-step flow.'

Perhaps Paul Lazarsfeld's looming presence throughout recent sociology is a 'personal influence' that helps account for the dominance of his paradigm, even beyond what were at times his own relatively modest claims for it. But one man's charisma, however routinized, cannot be the whole story. It cannot explain, for example, how the 'personal influence' paradigm finds its way, uncritically accepted, into a critical book like Anthony Giddens's *The Class Structure of the Advanced Societies*:[7]

> The influence of the mass media, and the diffusion of 'mass culture' generally, is usually pointed to as a primary source of the supposed 'homogenisation' of patterns of consumption, and of needs and tastes. But research on the 'two-step flow of communication' shows that formally identical content, as disseminated in the mass media, may be interpreted and responded to in quite different ways. Far from being eradicated by the uniform content of the media, existing forms of differentiation in social structure may be actively reinforced by it, as a consequence of such selectivity of perception and response.

Of course the issue for class structure may be neither its eradication (a straw man) nor its 'simple' reinforcement (as if reinforcement were simple), but its transformation *in a patterned way* through the possibility of alternate, and hierarchically preferred, 'readings' of any given media material.[8] But my point is that the Katz-Lazarsfeld theory still in 1973 had the power to compel enthusiasm in a theorist otherwise unsympathetic to their approach.

As Melvin L. DeFleur[9] and Roger L. Brown[10] have stressed, the course of mass media theory has to be understood as a historical process, in which theorists confront not only social reality but also the theories extant. Theorists, of course, respond to the going theories in the languages of social research then current, that is, within a social-scientific worldview now 'normal,' or becoming 'normal,' or contesting for 'normalcy.' They respond, explicitly or not, in the light or darkness of history of new, salient forces in the world: social, political, and technological. There are thus three meta-theoretical conditions shaping any given theoretical perspective: the nature of the theory or theories preceding (in this case, the 'hypodermic' theory); the 'normal' sociological worldview now current, or contesting the ideological field (in this case, behaviorism); and actual social, political, technological conditions in the world. The theory of the two-step flow, and the specific approach to 'effects' in which the theory is embedded, are generated by a behaviorist worldview which makes itself decisive – and invisible – in the form of methodological microassumptions. The dominant paradigm has to be understood as an intersection of all these factors.

In the critique that follows, I am concerned with *Personal Influence* as both buttress and instance of the larger, more general 'normal' approach to questions of mass media 'effects'; I want to identify the flaws in one particular theory, but more, to inquire into what they might imply for the whole field of communications research.

The 'Hypodermic' Theory

The 'personal influence' paradigm is itself located within a critique of the earlier 'hypodermic' theory, which is in turn both a theory of society and a theory of the workings of mass media within it.[11] In the 'hypodermic' model, society is mass society, and mass communications 'inject' ideas, attitudes, and dispositions towards behavior into passive, atomized, extremely vulnerable individuals. Katz and Lazarsfeld, who first named the 'personal influence' paradigm, codified it, and brought it to the center of the field, were explicitly aiming to dethrone the 'hypodermic' theory:[12]

... the media of communication were looked upon as a new kind of unifying force – a simple kind of nervous system – reaching out to every eye and ear, in a society characterized by an amorphous social organization and a paucity of interpersonal relations.

This was the 'model' – of society and of the processes of communication – which mass media research seems to have had in mind when it first began, shortly after the introduction of radio, in the 1920s. Partly, the 'model' developed from an image of the potency of the mass media which was in the popular mind. At the same time, it also found support in the thought of certain schools of social and psychological theory. Thus, classical sociology of the late 19th century European schools emphasized the breakdown of interpersonal relations in urban, industrial society and the emergence of new forms of remote, impersonal social control.

During the Twenties, the 'popular mind' of which Katz and Lazarsfeld spoke was recoiling from the unprecedented barrage of nation-state propaganda during the First World War, and the first wide-scale use of radio. The 'schools of social and psychological theory' to which they referred were those governed by the relatively simple stimulus-response psychology.[13] It was this 'hypodermic' model which Katz and Lazarsfeld proposed to dislodge by drawing attention to the social milieux within which audiences received media messages. As a corrective to overdrawn 'hypodermic' notions, as a reinstatement of society within the study of social communication, the new insistence on the complexity of the mediation process made good sense.

Behaviorist Assumptions and Damaged Findings

But the 'personal influence' theory was founded on limiting assumptions, so that its solid claims would be misleading even if substantial. Indeed, as it happens, the theory does not even hold up in its own terms; the Decatur study, taken on its face, fails in important ways to confirm the theory it claims to be confirming. Moreover, the anomalies themselves help us grasp the theory's social context; the anomalies mean something. For now I want to isolate the theoretical assumptions of the entire paradigm, and to see how they were applied in *Personal Influence*. In the discussion that follows, I center on the theory's limiting *assumptions*, some empirical *discrepancies*, and – a larger matter even if we set these aside – the theory's *limits in time*.

[...]

But all disclaimers aside, the method of the *Personal Influence* study, and that of its precursors and successors, stands as a perspective of its own. Not only did a generation of successors work with the personal influence model, but Katz himself[14] and many later commentators wrote on it as a self-contained hypothesis. The model by itself is meant to be more than preliminary; it is of a piece; it stands separate from the wished-for general model that never materialized. It demands its own critique, beginning with its taken-for-granted assumptions.

Assumption I

Commensurability of the Modes of Influence: The exercise of power through mass media is presumed to be comparable to the exercise of power in face-to-face situations.

'People' 'play a part' in the 'flow of mass communications.' The links in 'the general influence chain' are all of the same order; the relations between their influences can be characterized as 'greater' or 'lesser.' This was assumed rather than explicitly stated in *Personal Influence*, although there are points in the text (for example, p. 96) where the assumption lay relatively close to the surface. Discussing the two 'forms of influence' in the same breath, as functional equivalents or commensurables, is what made for the general effect.

This reduction of structurally distinct social processes to commensurables can be recognized as a cardinal operation in the behaviorist canon. But what is distinct about the two processes, of course, is that everyone has the opportunity to exercise 'personal influence' directly on someone else, albeit informally, and generally the relation is reciprocal, whereas the direct influence of mass media belongs routinely and professionally to the hierarchically organized handful who have access to it. The very image of a chain is reminiscent of the medieval Great Chain of Being, in which everyone, indeed everything, is in its duly and divinely appointed place. Language of this sort reveals the silent premise of the work.

Assumption 2

Power as Distinct Occasions: Power is to be assessed in case studies of discrete incidents. Katz and Lazarsfeld discussed and rejected two other possible criteria of influence: The reputational method, for one, (a) fails to reveal the frequency of influences, and (b) may elicit the names of prestigious individuals who have not actually directly influenced the respondent. Second, the counting of face-to-face contacts might let the decisive encounters through the sieve. Instead of these alternatives, they decided to ask respondents to recall 'incidents of influence exchange,' and the specific influentials involved therein.[15] In particular, they would ask respondents how they had changed their minds in each of four issue areas; then they would interview the next link in the chain. The occasion of influence was the face-to-face encounter in which individual A commended attitude *a* or behavior *b* to individual B. Those who exercised influence on such occasions were defined as 'opinion leaders.'

[...]

Assumption 3

The Commensurability of Buying and Politics: The unit of influence is a short-term 'attitude change' or a discrete behavior; or, more exactly, the report of such 'change' or behavior by a respondent, and one which the respondent can attribute to some specific intervention from outside. Katz and Lazarsfeld were concerned with 'four arenas of everyday decisions: marketing, fashions, public affairs and movie-going.' *These areas were to be assimilable within a single theory.*

[...]

So in two of the four issue-areas, the concern was explicitly with changes in consumer behavior; in the third, with another discrete behavior in the realm of consumer choice; and in the fourth, with change in the opinion expressed. These issue-areas were taken to be comparable, and the presumed comparability of political ideas and product preferences distorted some of the actual findings. But more: the blithe assumption of the commensurability of buying and politics, never explicitly justified, never opened up to question, hung over the entire argument of *Personal Influence* like an ideological smog.

Assumption 4

'Attitude Change' as the Dependent Variable: More deeply, more tellingly, the microscopic attention to 'attitude change' was built on a confining approach to the nature of power. In *Personal Influence*, power was the power to compel a certain behavior, namely buying: or, in the case of 'public affairs,' it was the power to compel a change in 'attitude' on some current issue. Respondents were asked if they had recently changed their attitudes on a current issue; if they had, they were asked who had influenced them.[16] *If they had not changed their attitudes, they were assumed not to have been influenced.*

Now there are two ways in which this sense of influence is inadequate. First, it is possible that a respondent had begun to 'change her mind' on a given issue, only to be persuaded back to the original position by personal influences or, directly, by mass media. More important still are the ways in which attitudes failed to change at all. If one does not take invariance for granted, but as something to be explained, how are we to understand the resulting 'nondecisions?' For there is no compelling reason why constancy of attitude, in the capitalist age, must be taken for granted. Indeed, what in the modern age is called a constancy of attitude would have been inconstancy itself in previous times. Fickleness of loyalties is a prerequisite of capitalist society, where private property routinely yields to the claims of wealth and accumulation.[17] In the phase of high-consumption capitalism especially, when 'new' is the symbolic affirmation of positive value and 'old-fashioned' an emblem of backwardness, 'changing one's mind' about products is a routine event. And in the realm of public life generally, one is frequently confronted with new political agendas (ecology, say), not to mention technological inventions, social 'trends,' celebrities and cultural artifacts, on which one is provoked into having opinions in the first place. Shifting policies of state routinely call for the mobilization and shift of public opinion.

In this historical situation, to take a constancy of attitude for granted amounts to a choice, and a fundamental one, to ignore the question of the sources of the very opinions which remain constant throughout shifting circumstances. Limiting their investigation thus, Katz and Lazarsfeld could not possibly explore the institutional power of mass media: the degree of their power to shape public agendas, to mobilize networks of support for the policies of state and party, to condition public support for these institutional arrangements themselves. Nor could they even crack open the questions of the sources of these powers.

[...]

Assumption 5

Followers as 'Opinion Leaders': Katz and Lazarsfeld took as given, definitive, and fundamental the structure and content of the media. The close attention they paid to 'opinion leaders' not only automatically distracted from the central importance of the broadcast networks and wire services, *it defined 'opinion leading' as an act of following* without the awareness – indeed, the amusement – that such confusion should have occasioned. They were looking at the process of ideas moving through society through the wrong end of the telescope.

Specifically, the Decatur women were asked to nominate 'opinion leaders' *in relation to the externally defined news.* To tell who was an 'opinion leader,' Katz and Lazarsfeld asked them 'for their opinions on a variety of domestic and international problems *then current in the news*, e.g., on Truman's foreign policy, on demobilization policy for the army, etc.' Then the women were asked if they had 'recently changed their opinions' and whether they had been asked for advice.[18] 'Experts,' meanwhile – those whose general public-affairs influence overflowed the boundaries between issues – were defined as those nominated in response to this question: 'Do you know anyone around here who keeps up with the news and whom you can trust to let you know what is really going on?'[19] In what sense, then, did an 'opinion leader' actually lead? What was an 'expert' expert in, and who decided the content of certified expertise?

The problem, to use the official language of sociology, is that the administrative mentality exaggerates the importance of 'independent variables' that are located closest in time and space to the 'dependent variables' under investigation.[20] Only their administrative point of view prevented Katz and Lazarsfeld from taking seriously the obvious: that their 'experts' were dependent for their expertise on a 'variable' explicitly ruled out of the scope of analysis. Respondents were being asked to name as influential those individuals who they thought were most tuned in to the mass media. Katz and Lazarsfeld were taking for granted the power of mass media to define news; and they were therefore discovering not 'the part played by people in the flow of mass communications,' but the nature of the *channels* of the flow.[21] Vague language (indeed, a vague concept of power) masked a crucial distinction. It is as if one were studying the influence of streets on mortality rates during an enormous flood. A street is a conduit, not a cause of drowning. But the distinction is lost in bland language. When they came to address the issue, Katz and Lazarsfeld skirted the issue of institutionalized news this way.[22]

> Compared with the realm of fashions at any rate, one is led to suspect that the chain of interpersonal influence is longer in the realm of public affairs and that 'inside dope' as well as influencing in specific influence episodes is much more a person-to-person affair.

The suspicion of a 'longer chain of influence' is an evasion of institutionalized relations between broadcasters and audiences.

But an administrative point of view is likely, from the outset, to confuse a report of a certain sort of influence with originating power, since the institutional origin, by being more distant both conceptually and in time and space, will inevitably 'leak' in transmission. In the process of asking *how* decisions are made at the bottom of the influence structure, it cannot ask *why* the occasion for deciding exists in the first place. It asks, in other words, the questions an administrator asks, or, in this case, the questions a marketer asks.

NOTES

1 Daniel Bell, 'The end of American exceptionalism', *The Public Interest* (Fall 1975), p. 218.
2 Elihu Katz and Paul F. Lazarsfeld, *Personal Influence: The Part Played by People in the Flow of Mass Communications* (New York: Free Press, 1955).
3 J. Arndt, 'A test of the two-step flow in diffusion of a new product', *Journalism Quarterly*, 47 (Autumn 1968), pp. 457–65.
4 Bell, loc. cit.
5 Paul F. Lazarsfeld, Bernard Berelson, and Hazel Gaudet, *The People's Choice*, 2nd edn (New York: Columbia University Press, 1948).
6 F.Z. Rosario, 'The leader in family planning and the two-step flow model', *Journalism Quarterly*, 48 (Summer 1971), pp. 288–97, in particular. Joseph T. Klapper, *The Effects of Mass Communication* (New York: Free Press, 1960).
7 Anthony Giddens, *The Class Structure of the Advanced Societies* (New York: Harper Torchbooks, 1975), p. 222.
8 Stuart Hall, 'Encoding and decoding in the television discourse', mimeographed paper, Centre for Cultural Studies, University of Birmingham, 1973; and Raymond Williams, *Marxism and Literature* (New York: Oxford University Press, 1977), pp. 121–7.
9 Melvin L. DeFleur, *Theories of Mass Communication*, 2nd edn (New York: McKay, 1970), pp. 112–54.
10 Roger L. Brown. 'Approaches to the historical development of mass media studies', in Jeremy Tunstall (ed.), *Media Sociology: A Reader* (Urbana: University of Illinois Press, 1970), pp. 41–57.
11 For more on 'personal influence' theory as a critique of the earlier 'hypodermic' theory, see Elihu Katz, 'Communication research and the image of society:

convergence of two traditions', *American Journal of Sociology*, 65 (March 1960), p. 113, and DeFleur, op. cit., pp. 112–17.

12 Katz and Lazarsfeld, op. cit., pp. 16–17.

13 See DeFleur, loc. cit.

14 Elihu Katz, 'The two-step flow of communication: an up-to-date report on an hypothesis', *Public Opinion Quarterly*, 21 (Spring 1957), pp. 61–78.

15 Katz and Lazarsfeld, op. cit., p. 146.

16 Ibid., p. 271, n. 2.

17 See Hannah Arendt, *The Human Condition* (Garden City, NY: Anchor, 1958).

18 Katz and Lazarsfeld, op. cit., p. 271n. Emphasis added.

19 Ibid., p. 276n.

20 Thanks to David Matza for putting this point to me in conversation.

21 Even at that, as we shall see on pages 219–20, the Katz-Lazarsfeld findings on 'public affairs influence' are the weakest in the book *on their face*, and do not warrant the exorbitant claims later made in their name. Nor did Katz and Lazarsfeld seem interested in the distinction between marketing and public affairs 'flows.' The differences might have spoken to the difference between consuming and politics.

22 Ibid., p. 319.

2

a cultural approach to communication

JAMES W. CAREY

Whereas I decided some years ago seriously to read the literature of communications, a wise man suggested I begin with John Dewey. It was advice I have never regretted accepting. While there are limitations to Dewey—his literary style was described by William James as damnable—there is a depth to his work, a natural excess common to seminal minds, that offers permanent complexities, and paradoxes over which to puzzle—surely something absent from most of our literature.

Dewey opens an important chapter in *Experience and Nature* with the seemingly preposterous claim that 'Of all things communication is the most wonderful.' What could he have meant by that? If we interpret the sentence literally, it must be either false or mundane. Surely most of the news and entertainment we receive over the mass media is of the order that Thoreau predicted for the international telegraph: 'the intelligence that Princess Adelaide had the whooping cough.' A daily visit with the *New York Times* is not quite so trivial, though it is an experience more depressing than wonderful. Moreover, most of one's encounters with others are wonderful only in moments of excessive masochism. Dewey's sentence, by any reasonable interpretation, is either false to everyday experience or simply mundane if he means only that on some occasions communication is satisfying and rewarding.

In another place Dewey offers an equally enigmatic comment on communication: 'Society exists not only *by* transmission, *by* communication, but it may fairly be said to exist *in* transmission, *in* communication.'[1] What is the significance of the shift in prepositions? Is Dewey claiming that societies distribute information, to speak rather too anthropomorphically, and that by such transactions and the channels of communication peculiar to them, society is made possible? That is certainly a reasonable claim but we hardly need social scientists and philosophers to tell us so. It rather reminds me of Robert Nisbet's acid remark that if you need sociologists to inform you whether or not you have a ruling class, you surely don't. But if this transparent interpretation is rejected, are there any guarantees that after peeling back layers of semantic complexity anything more substantial will be revealed?

I think there are, for the body of Dewey's work reveals a substantial and subtle mind. Rather than quoting him ritualistically—for the lines I have cited regularly appear without comment or interpretation in our literature—we would be better advised to untangle this underlying complexity for the light it might cast upon contemporary studies. I think this complexity derives from Dewey's use of communication in two quite different senses. Better than most of us, he understood that communication has had two contrasting definitions in the history of Western thought and he used the conflict between these definitions as a source of creative tension in his work. This same conflict led him, not surprisingly, into some of his characteristic errors. Rather than blissfully repeating his insights or unconsciously duplicating his errors, we might extend his thought by seizing upon the same contradiction he perceived in our use of the term 'communication' and use it in turn as a device for vivifying our studies.

There have been two alternative conceptions of communication alive in American culture since this term entered common discourse in the 19th century. Both definitions derive, as with much in secular culture, from religious origins, though they refer back

First published in *Communication*, 2, 1975: 1–22, Gordon & Breach Publishers (1975) as 'A Cultural Approach to Communication', pp. 1–10, 17–21.

to somewhat different regions of religious experience. We might label these descriptions, if only to provide handy pegs upon which to hang our thought, a transmission view of communication and a ritual view of communication.

The transmission view of communication is the commonest in our culture, perhaps in all industrial cultures, and dominates contemporary dictionary entries under the term. It is defined by terms such as imparting, sending, transmitting, or giving information to others. It is formed off a metaphor of geography or transportation. In the 19th century, though to a lesser extent today, the movement of goods or people and the movement of information were seen as essentially identical processes and both were described by the common noun 'communication.' The center of this idea of communication is the transmission of signals or messages over distance for the purpose of control. It is a view of communication that derives from one of the most ancient of human dreams: the desire to increase the speed and effect of messages as they travel in space. From the time upper and lower Egypt were unified under the First Dynasty, down through the invention of the telegraph, transportation and communication were inseparably linked. While messages might be centrally produced and controlled, through monopolization of writing or the rapid production of print, these messages, carried in the hands of a messenger or between the bindings of a book, still had to be distributed, if they were to have their desired effect, by rapid transportation. Telegraph ended the identity but it did not destroy the metaphor. Our basic orientation to communication remains grounded, at the deepest roots of our thinking, in the idea of transmission: communication is a process whereby messages are transmitted and distributed in space for the control of distance and people.

I said this view originated in religion, though the above sentences seem more indebted to politics, economics and technology. Nonetheless, the roots of the transmission view of communication, in our culture at least, lie in essentially religious attitudes. I can illustrate this by a devious and, in terms of historical detail, inadequate path.

In its modern dress the transmission view of communication arises, as the *Oxford English Dictionary* will attest, at the onset of the age of exploration and discovery. We have been reminded rather too often that the motives behind this vast movement in space were political and mercantile. Certainly those motives were present, but their importance should not obscure the equally compelling fact that a major motive behind this movement in space, particularly as evidenced by the Dutch Reformed Church in South Africa or the Puritans in New England, was religious. The desire to escape the boundaries of Europe, to create a New Life, to found new communities, to carve a New Jerusalem out of the woods of Massachusetts, these were primary motives behind the unprecedented movement of white, European civilization over virtually the entire globe. The vast and, for the first time, democratic migration in space was above all an attempt to trade an old world for a new, and represented the profound belief that movement in space could be in itself a redemptive act. It is a belief Americans have never quite escaped.

Transportation, particularly when it brought the Christian community of Europe into contact with the heathen community of the Americas, was seen as a form of communication with profoundly religious implication. This movement in space was an attempt to establish and extend the kingdom of God, to create the conditions under which Godly understanding might be realized, to produce a heavenly though still terrestrial city.

[···]

Soon, as the forces of science and secularization gain ground, the obvious religious metaphors fall away and the technology of communication itself moves to the center of thought. Moreover, the superiority of communication to transportation was assured by the observation of one 19th century commentator that the telegraph was important because it involved not the mere 'modification of matter but the transmission of thought.' Communication was viewed as a process and as a technology that would, sometimes for religious purposes, spread, transmit, and disseminate knowledge, ideas, information further and faster with the end of controlling space and people.

There were dissenters, of course, but they were few, and the transmission view of communication, albeit in increasingly secularized and scientific form, has dominated out thought and culture since that time. Moreover, as can be seen in contemporary popular commentary and even in technical discussions of new communications technology, the historic religious undercurrent has never been eliminated from our thought. From the telegraph to the computer the same sense of profound possibility for moral improvement is present whenever these machines are invoked. And we need not be reminded of the regularity with which improved communication is invoked by an army of teachers, preachers and columnists as the talisman of all our troubles. More controversially, the same root attitudes, as I here can but assert rather than demonstrate, are at work in most of our scientifically sophisticated views of communication.

The ritual view of communication, while a minor thread in our national thought, is by far the older of those views, old enough in fact for dictionaries to list it under 'Archaic.' In a ritual definition, communication is linked to terms such as sharing, participation, association, fellowship, and the possession of a common faith. This definition exploits the ancient identity and common roots of the terms commonness, communion, community, and communication. A ritual view of communication is not directed toward the extension of messages in space but the maintenance of society in time; not the act of imparting information but the representation of shared beliefs.

If the archetypal case of communication under a transmission view is the extension of messages across geography for the purpose of control, the archetypal case under a ritual view is the sacred ceremony which draws persons together in fellowship and commonality.

The indebtedness of the ritual view of communication to religion is apparent in the name chosen to label it. Moreover, it derives from a view of religion that downplays the role of the sermon, the instruction and admonishment, in order to highlight the role of the prayer, the chant, and the ceremony. It does not see the original or highest manifestation of communication in the transmission of intelligent information but in the construction and maintenance of an ordered, meaningful cultural world which can serve as a control and container for human action.

While this view has also been shorn of its explicitly religious origins, it also has never completely escaped its metaphoric root. Writers in this tradition often trace their heritage, in part, to Durkheim's *Elementary Forms of Religious Life* and to the argument stated elsewhere that 'society substitutes for the world revealed to our senses a different world that is a projection of the ideals created by the community.' This projection of community ideals and their embodiment in material form—dance, plays, architecture, news stories, strings of speech—creates an artificial though nonetheless real symbolic order which operates not to provide information but confirmation, not to alter attitudes or change minds but to represent an underlying order of things, not to perform functions but to manifest an ongoing and fragile social process.

The ritual view of communication has not been a dominant motif in American scholarship. Our thought and work has been glued to a transmission view of communication because this view is congenial with the underlying well-springs of American culture, sources which feed into our scientific life as well as our common, public understandings. There is an irony in this. We have not explored the ritual view of communication because the concept of culture is such a weak and evanescent notion in American social thought. We understand that other people have culture in the anthropological sense and we regularly record it—often mischievously and patronizingly. But when we turn critical attention to American culture the concept dissolves into a residual category useful only when psychological and sociological data are exhausted. We realize that the underprivileged live in a culture of poverty, use the notion of middle-class culture as an epithet, and occasionally applaud our high and generally scientific culture. But the notion of culture is not a hard edged term of intellectual discourse for domestic purposes. This intellectual aversion to the idea of culture derives in part from our obsessive individualism which makes psychological life the paramount reality, from our Puritanism which leads to a disdain for the significance of human activity that is not practical and work oriented, and from our isolation of science from culture: science provides culture-free truth where culture provides ethnocentric error.

Consequently, when looking for scholarship that emphasizes the central role of culture and a ritual view of communication, one must heavily rely on European sources or upon Americans deeply influenced by European scholarship. As a result the opportunities for misunderstanding are great. Perhaps then some of the difference between a transmission and ritual view of communication can be grasped by briefly looking at alternative conceptions of the role of the newspaper in social life.

If one examines a newspaper under a transmission view of communication, one sees the medium as an instrument for disseminating news and knowledge, sometimes divertissement, in larger and larger packages over greater distances. Questions arise as to the effects of this on audiences: news as enlightening or obscuring reality, as changing or hardening attitudes, as breeding credibility or doubt. Questions are also raised concerning the functions of news and the newspaper: Does it maintain the integration of society or its maladaption? Does it function or misfunction to maintain stability or promote the instability of personalities? Some such mechanical analysis normally accompanies a 'transmission' argument.

A ritual view of communication will focus on a different range of problems in examining a newspaper. It will, for example, view reading a newspaper less as sending or gaining information and more like attending a mass: a situation in which nothing new is learned but in which a particular view of the world is portrayed and confirmed. News reading, and writing, is a ritual act and moreover a dramatic one.

What is arrayed before the reader is not pure information but a portrayal of the contending forces in the world. Moreover, as the reader makes his way through the paper, he engages in a continual shift of roles or of dramatic focus. A story on the monetary crisis salutes him as American patriots fighting those ancient enemies Germany and Japan; a story on the meeting of the women's political caucus casts him into the liberation movement as supporter or opponent; a tale of violence on the campus evokes his class antagonisms and resentments. The model here is not that of information acquisition, though such acquisition occurs, but of dramatic action in which the reader joins a world of contending forces as an observer at a play. We do not encounter questions about the effect or functions of messages as such, but the role of presentation and involvement in the structuring of the reader's life and time. We recognize, as with religious rituals, news changes little and yet is intrinsically satisfying; it performs few functions yet is habitually consumed. Newspapers do not operate as a source of effects or functions but as dramatically satisfying, which is not to say pleasing, presentations of what the world at root is. And it is in this role, that of a text, that a newspaper is seen; like a Balinese cockfight, a Dickens novel, an Elizabethan drama, a student rally, it is a presentation of reality that gives to life an overall form, order, and tone.

Moreover, news is a historic reality. It is a form of culture invented by a particular class at a particular point of history—in this case by the middle class largely in the 18th century. Like any invented cultural form, news both forms and reflects a particular 'hunger for experience'—a desire to do away with the epic, heroic, and traditional in favor of the unique, original, novel, new—news. This 'hunger' itself has a history grounded in the changing style and fortunes of the middle class and, as such, does not represent a universal taste or necessarily legitimate form of knowledge, but an invention in historical time that like most other human inventions will dissolve when the class that sponsors it and its possibility of having significance for us evaporates.

Under a ritual view, then, news is not information but drama; it does not describe the world but portrays an arena of dramatic forces and action; it exists solely in historical time; and it invites our participation on the basis of our assuming, often vicariously, social roles within it.

Now neither of these counterposed views of communication necessarily denies what the other affirms. A ritual view does not exclude the processes of information transmission or attitude change. It merely contends that one cannot understand these processes aright except insofar as they are cast within an essentially ritualistic view of communication and social order. Similarly, even writers indisolvably wedded to the transmission view of communication must include some notion such as Malinowski's phatic communion to attest however tardily to the place of ritual action in social life. Nonetheless, in intellectual matters origins determine endings, and the exact point at which one attempts to unhinge the problem of communication largely determines the path his analysis can follow.

The power of Dewey's work derives from his working over these counterpoised views of communication. Communication is 'the most wonderful' because it is the basis of human fellowship; it produces the social bonds which tie men together and make associated life possible. Society is possible because of the binding forces of shared information circulating in an organic system. The following quotation reveals this tension and Dewey's final emphasis on a ritual view of communication:

There is more than a verbal tie between the words common, community, and communication. Men live in a community in virtue of the things which they have in common; and communication is the way in which they come to possess things in common. What they must have in common ... are aims, beliefs, aspirations, knowledge—a common understanding— likemindedness as sociologists say. Such things cannot be passed physically from one to another like bricks; they cannot be shared as persons would share a pie by dividing it into physical pieces. ... Consensus demands communication.[2]

Dewey was, like the rest of us, often untrue to his own thought. His hopes for the future often overwhelmed the impact of his analysis. Ah! 'the wish is father to the thought.' He came to overvalue scientific information and communication technology as a solvent to social problems and a source of social bonds. Nonetheless, the tension between these views can still open up a range of significant problems in communication, for they represent not merely different conceptions of communication but correspond to particular historical periods, technologies, and forms of social order.

The transmission view of communication has dominated American thought since the 1920s. When I first came into this field I felt that this view of communication, expressed in behavioral and functional terms, was exhausted. It had become academic: a repetition of past achievement, a demonstration of the indubitable. While it led to solid achievement, it could no longer go forward without disastrous intellectual and social consequences. I felt it was necessary to reopen the analysis, to reinvigorate it with the tension found in Dewey's work and, above all, to go elsewhere into biology, theology, anthropology, and literature for some intellectual material with which we might escape the treadmill we were running.

[...]

To study communication is to examine the actual social process wherein significant symbolic forms are created, apprehended, and used. Described this way some scholars would dismiss it as insufficiently empirical. My own view is the opposite, for I see it as an attempt to sweep away our existing notions concerning communication which serve only to devitalize our data. Our attempts to construct, maintain, repair, and transform reality are publicly observable activities which occur in historical time. We create, express, and convey our knowledge of and attitudes toward reality through the construction of a variety of symbol systems: art, science, journalism, religion, common sense, mythology. How do we do this? What are the differences between these forms? What are the historical and comparative variations in them? How do changes in communication technology influence what we can concretely create and apprehend? How do groups in society struggle over the definition of what is real? These are some of the questions, rather too simply put, that communication studies must answer.

Finally, let me emphasize an ironic aspect to the study of communication, a way in which our subject matter doubles back on itself and presents us with a host of ethical problems. One of the activities in which we characteristically engage, as in this essay, is communication about communication itself. However. communication is not some pure phenomenon we can discover; there is no such thing as communication to be revealed in nature through some objective method free from the corruption of culture. We understand communication insofar as we are able to build models or representations of this process. But our models of communication—like all models—have this dual aspect—an 'of' aspect and a 'for' aspect. In one mode communication models tell us what the process is; in their second mode they produce the behavior they have described. Communication can be modeled in several empirically adequate ways, but these several models have quite different ethical implications for they produce quite different forms of social relations.

Let us face this dilemma directly. There is nothing in our genes that tells us how to create and execute those activities we summarize under the term communication. If we are to engage in this activity—writing an essay, making a film, entertaining an audience, imparting information and advice—we must discover models in our culture that tell us how this particular miracle is achieved. Such models are found in common sense, law, religious traditions, increasingly in scientific theories themselves. Traditionally, models of communication were found in religious thought. For example, in describing the roots of the transmission view of communication in 19th century American religious thought, I meant to imply the following: religious thought not only described communication; it also presented a model for the appropriate uses of language, the forms of human contact permissible, the ends communication should serve, the motives it should manifest. It taught what it meant to display.

Today models of communication are found less in religion than in science, but their implications are the same. For example, American social science has generally represented communication, within an overarching transmission view, in terms of either a power or an anxiety model. These correspond roughly to what is found in information theory, learning theory, and influence theory (power), and dissonance, balance theory, and functionalism or uses and gratifications analysis (anxiety). I cannot here adequately explicate these views but they reduce the extraordinary phenomenological diversity of communication into an arena where men alternatively pursue power or flee anxiety. And one need only monitor the behavior of modern institutions to see the degree to which these models create through policy and program the abstract motives and relations they portray.

Models of communication are, then, not only representations of communication but representations for communication: templates which guide, unavailing or no, concrete processes of human interaction, mass and interpersonal. Therefore, to study communication involves examining the construction, apprehension, and use of models of communication themselves. Their construction in common sense, art, and science, their historically specific creation and use: in encounters between parent and child, advertisers and consumer, welfare worker and supplicant, teacher and student. Behind and within these encounters lie models of human contact and interaction.

Our models of communication, consequently, create what we disengenuously pretend they merely describe. As a result our science is, to use a term of Alvin Gouldner's, a reflexive one. We not only describe behavior; we create a particular corner of culture: culture that determines, in part, the kind of communicative world we inhabit.

Raymond Williams, whose analysis I shall follow in conclusion, speaks to the point:

> Communication begins in the struggle to learn and to describe. To start this process in our minds and to pass on its results to others, we depend on certain communication models, certain rules or conventions through which we can make contact. We can change these

models when they become inadequate or we can modify and extend them. Our efforts to do so, and to use the existing models successfully, take up a large part of our living energy. ... Moreover, many of our communication models become, in themselves, social institutions. Certain attitudes to others, certain forms of address, certain tones and styles become embodied in institutions which are then very powerful in social effect ... arguable assumptions are often embodied in solid, practical institutions which then teach the models from which they start.[3]

This relation between science and society described by Williams has not been altogether missed by the public and accounts for some of the widespread interest in communication. I am not speaking merely of the contemporary habit of reducing all human problems to problems or failures in communication. Let us recognize the habit for what it is: an attempt to coat reality with clichés, to provide a semantic crucifix to ward off modern vampires. But our appropriate cynicism should not deflect us from discovering the kernel of truth in such phrases.

If we follow Dewey it will occur to us that problems of communication are linked to problems of community, to problems surrounding the kinds of communities we create and in which we live. For the ordinary person, communication consists merely of a set of daily activities: having conversations, conveying instructions, being entertained, sustaining debate and discussion, acquiring information. The felt quality of our lives is bound up with these activities and how they are carried on within communities.

Our minds and lives are shaped by our total experience, or better, by representations of experience and, as Raymond Williams has argued, a name for this experience is communication. If one tries to examine society as a form of communication, he sees it as a process whereby reality is created, shared, modified, and preserved. When this process goes opaque, when we lack models of and for reality that make the world apprehensible, when we are unable to describe it and share it, when because of a failure in our models of communication we are unable to connect with others, one encounters problems of communication in their most potent form.

The widespread social interest in communication derives from a derangement in our models of communication and community. And this derangement derives, in turn, from an obsessive commitment to a transmission view of communication and the derivative representation of communication in complementary models of power and anxiety. As a result, when we think about society, we are almost always coerced by our traditions into seeing it as a network of power, administration, decision, and control— as a political order. Alternatively, we have seen society essentially as relations of property, production, and trade—an economic order. But social life is more than power and trade (and it is more than therapy as well). As Raymond Williams has argued, it also includes the sharing of aesthetic experience, religious ideas, personal values and sentiments, and intellectual notions—a ritual order.

Our existing models of communication are less an analysis than a contribution to the chaos of modern culture and we are, in important ways, paying the penalty for the long abuse of fundamental communicative processes in the service of politics, trade, and therapy. Three examples. Because we have looked at each new advance in communications technology as opportunities for politics and economics, we have devoted them, almost exclusively, to matters of government and trade. We have rarely seen them as opportunities to expand man's powers to learn and exchange ideas and experience. Because we have looked at education principally in terms of its potential for economics and politics, we have turned it into a form of citizenship, profession-alism and consumerism, and increasingly therapy. Because we have seen our cities as the domain of politics and economics, they have become the residence of technology and bureaucracy. Our streets are designed to accommodate the automobile, our side-walks to facilitate trade, our land and houses to satisfy the economy and the real estate speculator.

The object, then, of recasting our studies of communication in terms of a ritual model is not only to more firmly grasp the essence of this 'wonderful' process, but to give us a way in which to rebuild a model of and for communication of some restorative value in reshaping our common culture.

NOTES

1   John Dewey, *Democracy and Education* (New York: Macmillan, 1916), p. 5.
2   Ibid., pp. 5–6.
3   Raymond Williams, *Communications* (London: Chatto and Windus, rev. edn, 1966), pp. 19–20.

3

a 'new' paradigm?

LIESBET VAN ZOONEN

Feminist research assumes a rather straightforward 'sender–message–receiver' sequence in which media are conceived as transmitting particular messages about gender (stereotypes, pornography, ideology) to the wider public. The social control function of the media is central to all three themes, although there are some differences as to how social control is achieved. As far as the 'senders' are concerned, it is sometimes said that 'since those who control the media are almost all (rich) men, there is every incentive for them to present the capitalist, patriarchal scheme of things as the most attractive system available – and to convince the less privileged that the oppression and limitations of their lives are inevitable' (Davies et al., 1987: 2). Other authors point to the immediate producers of media content such as journalists and TV producers and claim that their traditional world views are reflected in media output. Ross Muir (1987: 8), for instance, wonders: 'If a film or television company is a mini sexist society, with women congregated in the lower paid service and support jobs, how can we expect the image of women that they produce to be anything but sexist?' According to such views, an increase in the number of female media producers would be instrumental in creating a more balanced media product (for example, Beasly, 1989).

At the 'receiving' end of the model, in research on stereotypes it is thought that children and adults learn their appropriate gender roles by a process of symbolic reinforcement and correction. For anti-pornography campaigners it is not so much learning that is at stake but imitation; men are feared to imitate the violent sexual behaviour presented to them in pornography. In research on ideology a process of familiarization with dominant ideology is assumed, leading finally to its internalization and transformation into common sense.

The differences then between functionalist theories of the media refer primarily to the specific elements of the communication process, but not to how communication works, as Table 3.1 shows.

Several elements of these feminist transmission models have become subject to criticism. Media production, for instance, is neither a straightforward derivative of the malicious intents of capitalist male owners, nor is it merely the product of the sexist inclinations of media professionals. It cannot be seen as a simple black box transmitting the patriarchal, sexist or capitalist values of its producers. It is better characterized by tensions and contradictions between individuals with different professional values and personal opinions, and between conflicting organizational demands such as creativity and innovation on the one hand and the commercial need to be popular among a variety of social groups on the other hand.

Two other elements of the model have been fundamentally reconceptualized, namely 'distortion' and 'socialization'.

DISTORTION

'Distortion' is a key concept in many feminist approaches to the media. It is often said that women are underrepresented in media content when compared to the 50 percent of

First published in *Feminist Media Studies*, L. van Zoonen, Sage Publications (1994) as 'A New Paradigm?', pp. 29–42.

TABLE 3.1 Models of communication in feminist media theory

	Sender	Process	Message	Process	Effect
Stereotypes	Men	Distortion	Stereotype	Socialization	Sexism
Pornography	Patriarchy	Distortion	Pornography	Imitation	Oppression
Ideology	Capitalism	Distortion	Hegemony	Familiarization	Common sense

the population that they constitute. Alternatively, it is argued that in reality many more women work than we get to see or read about in media content. Another argument deals with the definition of femininity presented to us in media content: submission, availability and compliance are characteristics held up as ideals, and consumption is presented as the road to self-fulfilment. Muriel Cantor (1978: 88) complains that public broadcasting in America presents images of women 'that are not representative of women's position in our highly differentiated and complex society'. Likewise, Linda Lazier-Smith accuses the advertising industry of not keeping up with changes in society: 'Although the demographies (the math) has changed dramatically, the attitude (mentality) has not... . We seem to be suffering from a cultural lag – our culture's beliefs and attitudes and opinions on women are lagging behind the reality about women' (1989: 258).

It seems indisputable that many aspects of women's lives and experiences are not properly reflected by the media. Many more women work than the media suggest, very few women resemble the *'femmes fatales'* of movies and TV series, and women's desires extend far beyond the hearth and home of traditional women's magazines. The feminist calls for more realistic images of women and definitions of femininity may therefore seem entirely legitimate. In fact, they are problematic. To begin with, stereotypes are not images in themselves but radicalized expressions of a common social practice of identifying and categorizing events, experiences, objects or persons. Stereotypes often have social counterparts that appear to support and legitimize the stereotype. A common response to the feminist claim that media distort reality by showing women in stereotypical roles of housewives and mothers, is that in reality many women are mothers and housewives too, 'and what is so problematic about showing that?'

Feminist alternatives to gender stereotypes are not as univocal as the claim for more realistic representations suggests. Feminists are divided among themselves over what is the reality of women's social position and nature. Thus before the media could transmit more realistic images of women, it would be necessary to define uncontroversially what the reality about women is, obviously an impossible project. As Brunsdon aptly argues:

> For feminists to call for more realistic images of women is to engage in the struggle to define what is meant by 'realistic', rather than to offer easily available 'alternative' images. Arguing for more realistic images is always an argument for the representation of 'your' version of reality. (1988: 149)

At the heart of the matter is the understanding of the 'reality' of gender, which in these theories is sometimes defined as social position, as in cases of calling for a more realistic reflection of women's social roles, and at other times is defined as a particular subjectivity, as in the claims for a more varied representation of women's psychological features. Apparently, in transmission models of communication, gender is conceived as a more or less stable and easily identifiable distinction between women and men which ought to be represented correctly. Such a conceptualization of gender is utterly problematic for it denies the dynamic nature of gender, its historical and cultural specificity and its contradictory meanings. What to make, for instance, of transgressions of the male/female dichotomy, manifested in the ambiguous appearances of Grace Jones, Prince or Michael Jackson; in lesbian and homosexual subcultures; in the phenomenon of transsexuality; and in daily lives and experiences of women and men whose identities belie the thought of an easily identifiable distinction between women and men?

An acknowledgement of the historical specificity of current dominant beliefs about women and men opens up new ways of thinking about gender as constructed. In such approaches 'distortion' would be an empty concept, since there is no reference point as to what the true human, male or female identity consists of, and hence there is no criterion as to what exactly the media should represent. Human identity and gender are thought to be socially constructed, in other words products of circumstances, opportunities and limitations.

Some Views on the Meaning of Gender

Psychoanalysis is one approach to theorizing the construction of gender. According to Lacanian varieties gender difference is constructed through the acquisition of language in the Oedipal phase, the submission of the self to the phallocentric symbolic order in which the feminine is undefined and cannot be spoken. The Chodorowian approach emphasizes the gender-specific symbiosis between mother and children in the pre-Oedipal phase to account for gender difference. Such arguments tend to attribute almost exclusive explanatory power to the constitution of the self in early childhood and ignore the social forces that bear on the subjectivity of human beings. In its conceptualization of gender as a property that human beings acquire early in life prior to their entry into social relations, psychoanalysis borders on the essentialistic:

> For if, as some psychoanalytic theories appear to suggest, social subjects are determined, through family relations and language acquisition, prior to the introduction of other considerations, including race, class, personal background or historical moment, the social construct thus described is a closed system unamenable to other subject formations. (Pribram, 1988: 6)

Other interpretations of gender as construction, for instance those inspired by Gail Rubin's influential theory of the 'sex-gender system', give priority to social relations and consider gender to be shaped within ideological frameworks, as socially constructed by cultural and historical processes and acquired by individuals by socialization through family, education, church, media and other agencies. Although in such an appreciation of gender, its particular meaning might vary according to history and culture, the basic 'sex-gender system', ascribing 'femininity' to biological women and 'masculinity' to biological men, is thought to be universal and all-pervasive (Rubin, 1975). Such notions of gender also perceive the concept as a relatively constant and consistent feature of human identity. 'Ungendered' or multiple and divided subjectivities are hard to envisage, and as in the psychoanalytic view the binary and oppositional character of gender remains, constraining 'feminist critical thought within the conceptual frame of a universal sex opposition ... which makes it very difficult, if not impossible, to articulate the differences ... among women or, perhaps more exactly the differences *within women*' (de Lauretis, 1987: 2; italics in original).

The notion of gender I want to advance here concerns gender as a discursive construct and is inspired by poststructuralist thought as expressed, among others, in the work of the French philosopher Michel Foucault and the feminist film theory of Theresa de Lauretis. In order to explain this notion properly we need to return to the Lacanian idea that we become subjects through the acquisition of language. In other words, as we are born and raised into this world we learn to think, feel and express ourselves with the linguistic means socially available. Of course we can invent our own words and symbols, but nobody would understand us. Thus language and its historically and culturally specific semantic and thematic combinations in discourses set limits to our experience of ourselves, others and our surroundings: 'language speaks us'. People who have travelled or migrated to foreign countries and have learned to speak foreign languages will recognize this from experience: sometimes words and concepts common to one language do not have an equivalent in another language. As a result the particular experience connected to that concept is hard to express.

Since we are born into societies that have labelled a particular difference between human beings as woman vs man, and a related difference as feminine vs masculine, we come to think of ourselves in these terms: as being and feeling a man, or being and feeling a woman. Gender, however defined, becomes a seemingly 'natural' or inevitable part of our identity and for that matter often a problematic one. According to Lacan, language not only stipulates sexual difference but also male power. In Lacan's univocal phallocentric discourse women have no means of expressing themselves; without language they cannot speak their own authentic experience, unless in ways defined by men. Thus, in Lacanian terms, feminine experience can only be defined negatively and women can only think of themselves as being 'not-men'.

In poststructuralist theory discourse is never univocal or total, but ambiguous and contradictory; a site of conflict and contestation (cf. Sawicki, 1991). Moreover, gender discourse is not conceived as the only dimension of human identity. Rather, human beings are constituted by the different social practices and discourses in which they are engaged. This is of course similar to the Marxist claim about human nature, although in Marxist theory class is the primary social condition defining a binary human identity of capitalist or worker, whereas poststructuralists speak of multiple discourses that are contradictory between and within themselves. Gender can thus be thought of as a particular discourse, that is, a set of overlapping and often contradictory cultural descriptions and prescriptions referring to sexual difference, which arises from and regulates particular economic, social, political, technological and other non-discursive contexts. Gender is inscribed in the subject along with other discourses, such as those of ethnicity, class, and sexuality. Following Foucault, de Lauretis claims that:

> the subject [is] constituted in language, to be sure, though not by sexual difference alone, but rather across languages and cultural representations; a subject engendered in the experience of race and class, as well as sexual relations; a subject therefore not unified but rather multiple, and not so much divided as contradicted. (1987: 2)

Gender should thus be conceived, not as a fixed property of individuals, but as part of an ongoing process by which subjects are constituted, often in paradoxical ways. The identity that emerges is therefore fragmented and dynamic; gender does not determine or exhaust identity. In theory, although hard to imagine in current society, it is even conceivable to be outside gender or to engage in a social practice in which gender discourse is relatively unimportant. Defined as such, gender is an intrinsic part of culture – loosely defined as the production of meaning – and is subject to continuous discursive struggle and negotiation. This struggle over meaning is not a mere pluralistic 'debate' between equal but contending frames of reference. It is traversed by existing power relations, and by the fact that 'in virtually all cultures whatever is defined as manly, is more highly valued than whatever is thought of as womanly' (Harding, 1987: 18). However, a poststructuralist notion of discourse as a site of contestation implies that the disciplinary power of discourse, prescribing and restricting identities and experiences, can always be resisted and subverted. Dominant male discourse can therefore never be completely overpowering, since by definition there will be resistance and struggle.

To view the role of the media in the construction of gender as a process of distorting the 'true' meaning of gender, as occurs in feminist transmission models of communication, thus ignores the contradictory and contested nature of gender. Before presenting an alternative perspective, first a discussion of another key problem of transmission models is necessary.

SOCIALIZATION

'Socialization' can refer to the various ways in which individuals become social subjects, although in functionalist theories of the media it usually applies to cognitive and behavioural processes. McQuail (1987: 280), for instance, defines socialization as the 'teaching of established norms and values by ways of symbolic rewards and punishment for different kinds of behaviour', and as 'the learning process whereby we all learn how to behave in certain situations and learn the expectations which go with a given role or status in society'. Defined as such it would appear that socialization takes place mainly in childhood, but socialization can be seen as an ongoing long-term process affecting adults as well.

Socialization has been studied in various ways. A common way of attempting to establish socialization effects is the experimental social psychological approach, where children or adults are exposed to a particular type of media output and subjected to some kind of measurement procedure, such as questionnaires or physical monitoring. The kind of questions posed are whether children's exposure to sexist media content is related to their perception of appropriate gender behaviour, or whether men's exposure to violent pornography leads to hostile fantasies and real aggression against women. The results of these studies are contradictory but show among other things that media effects are mediated by other variables such as age, gender or education. More fundamentally, the causal relation between media exposure and sexist attitudes is unclear since it appears that even at a very early age children have considerable knowledge of 'appropriate' gender behaviour. The direction of the causal relationship between pornography and sexual violence cannot be easily established either (cf. McCormack, 1978; Steeves, 1987).

Experimental research examines short-term cognitive or behavioural effects and does not reveal much about the influence of mass media in the long term. There has been very little research carried out in relation to feminist concerns, but some studies of long-term media effects have produced relevant results, especially in the area of cultivation theory. This theory proposes that media and television in particular present a 'pseudoreality' that is different from the social reality most people experience. People who watch television for hours on end will tend to replace their own social experience with that of television reality, resulting in a 'television view' of the world. Steeves (1987) discusses some cultivation studies which do seem to indicate that heavy viewing correlates with sexist attitudes in children. In studies focused especially on the cultivation effect of soap operas it is reported that 'exposure to soap operas correlates with the belief by viewers that men and women have affairs, get divorced, have illegitimate children, and undergo serious operations and that women are housewives, have abortions and do not work at all' (Steeves, 1987: 104). Cultivation research suffers from similar problems as experimental research: the media 'effect' turns out to be mediated by intervening variables such as education, gender and class and the direction of the effect is problematic. Perhaps a particular world view causes heavy viewing, instead of being caused by it. Moreover, cultivation theory seems primarily relevant to the United States where daily viewing times of over six hours are very common. In many areas of the world this is materially impossible since national or local television stations only broadcast a few hours a day.

Both experimental and cultivation research conceptualize the audience as a relatively passive aggregate of individuals affected differently by mass media as exposure and background variables diverge. Many feminist analyses of the media phrase the issue as 'what do media do with women', ignoring the cognitive and emotional activities of audiences in making sense of mass media. Audience reaction is conceptualized as a dichotomous activity of accepting sexist messages or rejecting them. Either audiences can accept media output as true to reality, in which case they are successfully socialized, brainwashed by patriarchy or lured into the idea that what they see and read is 'common sense', or they see through the tricks the mass media play on them and reject the sexist, patriarchal, capitalist representation of the world. Obviously, many feminists consider themselves among the latter 'enlightened' women raising themselves 'to the lofty pedestal of having seen the light' (Winship, 1987: 140). A deep gap is constructed between the feminist media critic and the ordinary female audience. Soap operas, romance novels and women's magazines are found particularly objectionable: they are said to create 'a cult of femininity and heterosexual romance' that – since these media are predominantly consumed by women – set the agenda for the female world (cf. Ferguson, 1983).

Such a strong conviction about the value (or rather lack of it) of these media for women's lives, is remarkably similar to patriarchal attitudes of men who claim to know what is best for women. Dismissing women's genres for their supposedly questionable content carries an implicit rejection of the women who enjoy them. Moreover, it does not allow 'true' feminists to enjoy these genres and condemns them to being 'closet readers', obviously at odds with the feminist mission to acknowledge and gain respect for women's experiences and viewpoints.

More recently, some feminist inquiries have turned the question around and asked 'what do women do with media', allowing for a variety of audience reactions. These studies seem to suggest that women actively and consciously seek particular types of gratification from mass media use. Soap operas, for instance, are said to satisfy the need for emotional release, identification, escape, companionship, information and relaxation (Cantor and Pingree, 1983). Similar gratifications have been found among the readers of women's magazines who derive a feeling of friendship from reading and who are informed, entertained and advised by women's magazines (Wassenaar, 1975). Such a 'uses and gratifications' perspective on media use has advantages over the earlier 'effect models' by raising the question of differential uses and interpretations of media output and in its perception of the audience as active. It is still a somewhat mechanistic functional model, presuming that an individual will recognize her own needs and will seek a rational way to satisfy them. Why it is, for example, that one turns to media instead of other means to satisfy the need for entertainment, information or relaxation remains unclear. More fundamentally, the 'uses and gratifications' approach tends to focus on individual differences, attributing them to differences of personality and psychology and neglecting the social and cultural contexts in which media use takes place (cf. Morley, 1989).

COMMUNICATION AS RITUAL

Out of the criticism of the feminist transmission model of communication, the contours of an alternative approach emerge. We need first to take a closer look at the epistemological groundwork of the transmission model before we can arrive at a comprehensive understanding of the alternative. As we said, 'reality' is a key term, but the concept itself is given little serious thought. The idea that mass media 'distort' the reality of women's lives gives a clue as to how in these models 'reality' is understood. Apparently, a real world of objects, events, situations and processes is assumed to exist independent of and prior to human perception. This real world is waiting to be measured validly and reliably, as scientists try to do; to be represented accurately and truthfully, as media should do; and to be understood and experienced correctly or mistakenly as ordinary people do. 'There is reality and then after the fact, our account of it' (Carey, 1989: 25). Almost inevitably, media performance will thus only be evaluated in terms of the quality of its representation of reality. There are two problems with this account, the first having to do with the role of the media in contemporary society, the second with the concept of reality itself.

The 'Bardic' Function

In the first place mass media accomplish much more varied activities than only those of representing reality. Film, television, (popular) literature etc. construct an imaginary world that builds on and appeals to individual and social fantasies. Mass media produce and reproduce collective memories, desires, hopes and fears, and thus perform a similar function as myths in earlier centuries. 'The search for the mythical in contemporary society is grounded not only in the plausible expectation that we too perforce must find ways of expressing basic concerns, core values, deep anxieties; and equally we must find ways of expressing publicly and collectively our attempts at resolving them' (Silverstone, 1988: 24). In their presentation of major social events like coronations, sports games or disasters media present the content of myth, and in their familiar and formulaic narratives they resemble mythical story-telling. Whereas myths connect mundane everyday life with the sacred and unreachable words of gods and ancestors, modern mass media mark the boundary between ordinary daily life and the inaccessible worlds of show business and top sports (cf. Silverstone, 1988). Carey (1989) has labelled such an approach to communication as a ritual view characterized by terms like 'sharing', 'participation', 'fellowship' and 'the possession of a common faith'.

The ritual view of communication borrows its concepts from anthropology and the sociology of religion, and is directed at the way in which a society reproduces its cohesiveness and its shared beliefs. In other words the ritual approach to communication focuses on the construction of a community through rituals, shared histories, beliefs and values. In such a view, media create 'an artificial though none the less real symbolic order that operates to provide not information but confirmation, not to alter attitudes or change minds but to represent an underlying order of things, not to perform functions but to manifest an ongoing and fragile social process' (Carey, 1989: 19). Two concrete examples will clarify the difference between the transmission and ritual models of communication. When investigating church attendance in a particular community, employing a transmission perspective one might inquire about the messages and instructions present in the sermon and the understanding and recollection of the church-goers. From a ritual viewpoint the joint prayer and chant, and of course the ceremony would be more important. Similarly, television news can be construed as a daily presentation of new information that enables people to learn and process new knowledge, while one could also stress its ritual character as a device to structure the evening and as 'the presentation ... of the familiar and the strange, the reassuring and the threatening' (Silverstone, 1988: 26).

Ritual models may fail to incorporate notions like dominance and oppression – essential to the feminist and any other critical project – suggesting a more or less pluriform and unproblematic construction of social togetherness. Fiske and Hartley's (1978) proposal to think of the mass media as contemporary bards provides a useful integration of a conception of power with the ritual view of communication. The authors claim that the media perform a social role which is similar to that of the bards in medieval societies. These poets were licensed and paid by the rulers of their time to mediate between them and the society at large by writing and performing songs and stories. They did not simply reflect the views of the courts nor those of ordinary people, but they reworked 'raw materials' into meaningful narratives, much as television does today: 'So bardic television cannot by definition simply "reflect" any supposed social or cultural reality that already exists elsewhere, since its main business is to make its own particular kind of sense of the fragmented and conflicting raw materials available to it' (O'Sullivan et al., 1989). That particular sense, however, is firmly connected to the dominant social order, for the bards' task is primarily to render the unfamiliar into the already known, or into 'common sense'. Therefore, the bardic function has inherently reactionary tendencies since it needs to rely on familiar meanings and interpretations. What falls outside an already existing consensus is hard to make sense of, except as 'otherness' or 'deviance'.

The Social Construction of Reality

The second fundamental problem of the reflection thesis in feminist transmission models of communication has to do with its limited interpretation of reality, conceptualizing it as an independent world of objects, relations and processes only, and ignoring the social processes of defining reality. In their classic treatise *The Social Construction of Reality* Berger and Luckman (1966) claim that society exists as both objective and subjective reality. While we perceive the world we live in as 'real', as something that exists beyond our own perceptions and beliefs and that will continue to exist when we are not there, we acknowledge at the same time that not everyone perceives reality in the same way. Still, it is not merely that people perceive reality in a particular way, their perception has consequences for their sense of self, relations with others, their mode of conduct and a whole range of other social practices. In these social interactions people produce, reproduce and adjust definitions of reality: 'If men define situations as real, they are real in their consequences' (Thomas, 1928: 584). Reality is not merely something that exists 'out there', but it is also (re)constructed by the social and sense-making activities of human beings. According to Berger and Luckman (1966), the most important vehicle in that process is conversation. Not that all conversation pertains to matters of meanings and definition. On the contrary, it is precisely in the ordinary, taken-for-granted exchanges that reality is reconstructed since everyday conversation requires shared definitions of the situation in order to make sense at all. Language of course is the key element in this process, as a means of both apprehending and reproducing the world. The biblical dictum 'In the beginning was the word' summarizes aptly that language constitutes the world and ourselves (Carey, 1989: 25).

[Earlier], the prerequisite of language for the development of individual subjectivity and sanity was discussed, taking its inspiration from Foucault and Lacan. We can now expand this notion and appreciate that language constitutes society and reality as well. Thus language is not a means of reflecting reality, but the source of reality itself. 'Reality is brought into existence, is produced, by communication – by, in short, the construction, apprehension, and utilization of symbolic forms' (Carey, 1989: 25). This is not to say that there is nothing out there except the images in our head, as a collision with a moving car will prove, but that we can only define the meaning and make sense of that experience through language.

'Language' should not be conceived in the limited sense of grammar and lexicons. The articulation of language in 'discourse', in specific combinations of themes and symbols is at stake here. It is not language itself that constructs reality and subjectivity, but its expression in particular cultural and individual histories, beliefs and value systems, institutional and official jargon, subcultural expressions etc. Moreover, several non-linguistic symbolic forms contribute to the sense-making process as well. Foucault (1976), for instance, has identified the dormitory lay-out of eighteenth century boarding schools as a sign of a discourse of sexuality: the presence of partitions and curtains, control of sleeping hours etc., all refer to the need to control children's sexuality. Likewise, Edelman (1964) has pointed to the use of symbols in American politics, with the American flag and the White House for instance referring to discourses of nationalism and presidential power. Through these symbolic forms societies construct their definitions of reality. It is not something an individual does by her or himself; she or he is participating in a profoundly social process, in the sense that social relations are reflected in definitions of reality as well as definitions of reality influencing social relations. The former is easily explained by referring to the processes of interaction between individuals, groups, institutions etc. that shape reality. It is important to realize, however, that these processes are not equally accessible to everyone. The power to define is intricately linked to other power relations in society, such as economic, ethnic, gender and international relations.

As emphasized earlier, dominant discourse is not monolithic and impervious, but produces its own opposition and is open to negotiation. On the other hand, discourse itself is a form of power, since both the process of discourse (the symbolic interactions) and the product of discourse (a particular set of meanings and narratives) limit the possibilities of interpretation and privilege certain meanings above others. To give an example: before the advent of the second wave of the women's movement, sexual harassment and sexual violence within heterosexual relationships were considered to be excesses of personal idiosyncrasies, and were not seen as criminal acts. The occurrence of sexual violence in the domestic sphere was made invisible by defining it as a problem which some individual women just had to cope with, an unpleasant fact of life. As a result of that definition, there was no possibility for retaliation, nor were there many support facilities. The definition of the issue as a matter of the private sphere prevented its recognition as a social problem and left the women affected without means to talk about and fight against it.

The power of discourse lies not only in its capacity to define what is a social problem, but also in its prescriptions of how an issue should be understood, the legitimate views on it, the legitimacy and deviance of the actors involved, the appropriateness of certain acts etc. This holds not only for dominant discourse, as can be easily appreciated, but also for alternative, insurgent discourse. For instance, Leong (1991) analyses how the moral discourse of radical feminists opposing pornography imposes a 'proper' standard of correct non-violent sexuality on women, and construes women as victims in need of protection.

Given that the whole idea of society, or any other collectivity for that matter, requires discourse (the mapping, description and articulation of situations and processes), which by definition has the effect of excluding, annihilating and delegitimizing certain views and positions, while including others, Foucault's seemingly extreme and hollow dictum that power is everywhere begins to make sense.

CULTURAL STUDIES

So far, I have argued that feminist transmission views of communication are unsatisfactory because of their limited conceptualization of gender and communication. With regard to gender, the problem lies mainly in the observation that media distort the 'true' nature of gender, assuming a stable and easily identifiable distinction between women and men. Alternatively, I proposed to construe gender as discourse, a set of overlapping and sometimes contradictory cultural descriptions and prescriptions referring to sexual difference. Such a conceptualization of gender does not deny the possibility of fragmented and multiple subjectivities in and among women (or men for that matter), and allows for difference and variety. The difficulties with the conceptualization of communication primarily concern the 'reflection' and 'socialization' hypothesis. The idea of a reality that media pass on more or less truthfully and successfully fails at several points: media production is not simply a matter of reflection but entails a complex process of negotiation, processing and reconstruction; media audiences do not simply take in or reject media messages, but use and interpret them according to the logic of their own social, cultural and individual circumstances; media are not only assigned to 'reflect' reality, but represent our collective hopes, fears and fantasies and perform a mythical and ritual function as well; finally, reality itself is not only an objective collection of things and processes, but is socially constructed in discourses that reflect and produce power.

How can these elements be combined into a relatively coherent approach to gender and communication? Defining gender as discourse leads to the question of what 'role' the media play in gender discourse and how that role is realized. De Lauretis (1987: 2) proposes that gender should be thought of as 'the product of various social technologies, such as cinema, and of institutionalized discourses, epistemologies and critical practices, as well as practices of daily life'. Media can thus be seen as (social) technologies of gender, accommodating, modifying, reconstructing and producing disciplining and contradictory cultural outlooks of sexual difference. The relation between gender and communication is therefore primarily a cultural one, a negotiation over meanings and values that inform whole ways of life. This is not to deny the various material aspects of the subject, for instance the underpayment of female broadcasters and the restricted access to mass media of poor and third world women. However, at the heart of the matter is the struggle over the meaning of gender.

How do these technologies of gender operate, or to put it differently, what part do the media play in the ongoing construction of gender discourse? Much depends on their location in economic structures (for example, commercial vs public media), on their specific characteristics (for example, print vs broadcast), on the particular genres (for example, news vs soap opera), on the audiences they appeal to etc. But obviously all media are central sites at which discursive negotiation over gender takes place. The concept of discursive negotiation applies to all instances of (mass) communication and is visualized in Hall's encoding/decoding model. Separately, the elements of production, texts and reception of media make no sense; they are intricately linked in the process of meaning production. At all levels discursive negotiation takes place: the production of media texts is replete with tensions and contradictions resulting from conflicting organizational and professional discourses. For instance, creative personnel such as script writers and directors will be guided mainly by aesthetic aims and personal preferences, while managing directors may have economic and public relations interests predominantly in mind. Through the fragmented production structure meaning is constructed and expressed in the variety of media texts. As a result of the tensions in the 'encoding' process, as Hall calls it, media texts do not constitute a closed ideological system, but 'reflect' the contradictions of production. Media texts thus carry multiple meanings and are open to a range of interpretations; in other words they are inherently 'polysemic'. The thus encoded structures of meaning are brought back into the practices of audiences by their similarly contradictory, but reverse 'decoding' process.

While the concept of polysemy thus assumes audiences to be producers of meaning as well – as opposed to being confronted with meaning only, as in a transmission model – the range of meanings a text offers is not infinite, despite its essential ambiguity. 'Encoding will have the effect of constructing some of the limits and parameters within which decodings will operate' (Hall et al., 1980: 135). Thus most texts do offer a 'preferred reading or meaning' which, given the economic and ideological location of most media, will tend to reconstruct dominant values.

A cultural studies perspective suggests to the feminist media critic and researcher the following questions:

How are discourses of gender encoded in media texts?

Which preferred and alternative meanings of gender are available in media texts and from which discourses do they draw?

How do audiences use and interpret gendered media texts?

How does audience reception contribute to the construction of gender at the individual level of identity and subjectivity and at the social level of discourse?

How can these processes be examined and analysed?

REFERENCES

Ang, I. (1983) 'Mannen op zicht. Marges van het vrouwelijke voyeurisme', *Tijdschrift voor Vrouwenstudies* [*Journal of Women's Studies*], 4 (3): 418–35.

Beasly, M. (1989) 'Newspapers: is there a new majority defining the news?', in P. Creedon (ed.), *Women in Mass Communication: Challenging Gender Values*. London: Sage. pp. 180–94.

Berger, P. and Luckman, T. (1966) *The Social Construction of Reality: A Treatise in the Sociology of Knowledge*. Harmondsworth: Penguin.

Brunsdon, C. (1988) 'Feminism and soap opera', in K. Davies, J. Dickey and T. Stratford (eds), *Out of Focus: Writing on Women and the Media*. London: The Women's Press.

Cantor, M. (1978) 'Where are the women in public broadcasting?', in G. Tuchman (ed.), *Hearth and Home: Images of Women in the Mass Media*. New York: Oxford University Press. pp. 78–90.

Cantor, M. and Pingree, S. (1983) *The Soap Opera*. Beverly Hills, CA: Sage.

Carey, J. (1989) *Communication as Culture: Essays on Media and Society*. Boston, MA: Unwin Hyman.

de Lauretis, T. (1987) *Technologies of Gender: Essays on Theory, Film and Fiction*. London: Macmillan.

Davies, K., Dickey, J. and Stratford, T. (eds) (1987) *Out of Focus: Writing on Women and the Media*. London: The Women's Press.

Edelman, M. (1964) *The Symbolic Uses of Politics*. Urbana: University of Illinois Press.

Ferguson, M. (1983) *Forever Feminine: Women's Magazines and the Cult of Femininity*. London: Heinemann.

Fiske, J. and Hartley, J. (1978) *Reading Television*. London: Methuen.

Foucault, M. (1976) *La Volonté de savoir*. Paris: Gallimard.

Hall, S., Hobson, D., Lowe, A. and Willis, P. (eds) (1980) *Culture, Media, Language*. London: Hutchinson.

Harding, S. (1987) *The Science Question in Feminism*. London: Cornell University Press.

Lazier-Smith, L. (1989) 'A new generation of images of women', in P. Creedon (ed.), *Women in Mass Communication: Challenging Gender Values*. London: Sage. pp. 247–60.

Leong, W.T. (1991) 'The pornography "problem": disciplining women and young girls', *Media, Culture and Society*, 13 (1): 91–118.

McCormack, T. (1978) 'Machismo in media research: a critical review of research on violence and pornography', *Social Problems*, 25 (5): 544–55.

McQuail, D. (1987) *Introduction to Mass Communication Theory*, 2nd edn. London: Sage.

Morley, D. (1989) 'Changing paradigms in audience studies', in E. Seiter, H. Borchers, G. Kreutzner and E. Warth (eds), *Remote Control: Television, Audiences and Cultural Power*. London: Routledge.

Muir, A.R. (1987) *A Woman's Guide to Jobs in Film and Television*. London: Pandora Books.

O'Sullivan, T., Hartley, J., Saunders, D. and Fiske, J. (eds) (1989) *Key Concepts in Communication*. London: Routledge.

Pribram, E. (ed.) (1988) *Female Spectators: Looking at Film and Television*. London: Verso.

Rubin, G. (1975) 'The traffic in women: notes on the "political economy" of sex', in R. Reiter (ed.), *Towards an Anthology of Women*. New York: Monthly Review Press.

Sawicki, J. (1991) *Disciplining Foucault: Feminism, Power and the Body*. London: Routledge.

Silverstone, R. (1988) 'Television, myth and culture', in J. Carey (ed.), *Media, Myths and Narratives: Television and the Press*. London: Sage. pp. 20–47.

Steeves, L. (1987) 'Feminist theories and media studies', *Critical Studies in Mass Communication*, 4 (2): 95–135.

Thomas, W.I. (1928) *The Child in America*. New York: Knopf.

Wassenaar, I. (1975) *Vrouwenbladen: Spiegels van een Mannenmaatschappij* [*Women's Magazines: Mirrors of Male Society*]. Amsterdam: Wetenschappelijke Uitgeverij.

Winship, J. (1987) *Inside Women's Magazines*. London: Pandora Press.

4

the propaganda model: a retrospective

EDWARD S. HERMAN

In *Manufacturing Consent: The Political Economy of the Mass Media*, Noam Chomsky and I put forward a 'propaganda model' as a framework for analysing and understanding how the mainstream US media work and why they perform as they do (Herman and Chomsky, 1988). We had long been impressed by the regularity with which the media operate on the basis of a set of ideological premises, depend heavily and uncritically on elite information sources and participate in propaganda compaigns helpful to elite interests. In trying to explain why media perform in this way we looked to structural factors as the only possible root of the systematic patterns of media behavior and performance.

Because the propaganda model challenges basic premises and suggests that the media serve antidemocratic ends, it is commonly excluded from mainstream debates on media bias. Such debates typically include conservatives, who criticize the media for excessive liberalism and an adversarial stance toward government and business, and centrists and liberals, who deny the charge of adversarialism and contend that the media behave fairly and responsibly. The exclusion of the propaganda model perspective is noteworthy for one reason, because that perspective is consistent with long-standing and widely held elite views that 'the masses are notoriously short-sighted' (Bailey, 1948: 13) and are 'often poor judges of their own interests' (Lasswell, 1933: 527), so that 'our statesmen must deceive them' (Bailey, 1948: 13); and they 'can be managed only by a specialized class whose personal interests reach beyond the locality' (Lippmann, 1921: 310). In Lippmann's view, the 'manufacture of consent' by an elite class had already become 'a self-conscious art and a regular organ of popular government' by the 1920s (Lippmann, 1921: 248).

Clearly, the manufacture of consent by a 'specialized class' that can override the short-sighted perspectives of the masses must entail media control by that class. Political scientist Thomas Ferguson contends that the major media, 'controlled by large profit-maximizing investors do not encourage the dissemination of news and analyses that are likely to lead to popular indignation and, perhaps, government action hostile to the interests of all large investors, themselves included' (Ferguson, 1995: 400). Political scientist Ben Page provides evidence that there are common 'elite-mass gaps', with 'ordinary citizens ... considerably less enthusiastic than foreign policy elites about the use of force abroad, about economic or (especially) military aid or arms sales, and about free-trade agreements. The average American is much more concerned than foreign policy elites about jobs and income at home' (Page, 1996: 118). Page notes that 'the problem for public deliberation is most severe when officials of both parties and most mainstream media take positions that are similar to each other and opposed to the public' (Page, 1996: 119). The propaganda model explains the 'elite-mass gaps', as well as elite and mainstream media hostility to this mode of analysis: refusal to allow it entry into the debate is understandable given that the gaps are embarrassing and suggest that the media do serve narrow elite interests.

This chapter briefly describes the propaganda model, addresses some of the criticisms that have been leveled against it and discusses how the model holds up a decade or so after its publication. Examples are provided to illustrate the ways in which the propaganda model helps explain the nature of media coverage of important political topics at the turn of the century.

First published in *Journalism Studies 1, 1*, Taylor and Francis Ltd. (2000) as 'The Propaganda Model: a retrospective', pp. 101–111.

THE PROPAGANDA MODEL

What is the propaganda model and how does it work? Its crucial structural factors derive from the fact that the dominant media are firmly embedded in the market system. They are profit-seeking businesses, owned by very wealthy people (or other companies); and they are funded largely by advertisers who are also profit-seeking entities, and who want their advertisements to appear in a supportive selling environment. The media also lean heavily on government and major business firms as information sources, and both efficiency and political considerations and, frequently, overlapping interests, cause a certain degree of solidarity to prevail among the government, major media and other corporate businesses. Government and large non-media business firms are also best positioned (and sufficiently wealthy) to be able to pressure the media with threats of withdrawal of advertising or TV licenses, libel suits and other direct and indirect modes of attack. The media are also constrained by the dominant ideology, which heavily featured anti-communism before and during the Cold War era, and was often mobilized to induce the media to support (or refrain from criticizing) US attacks on small states that were labeled communist.

These factors are linked together, reflecting the multi-leveled capability of government and powerful business entities and collectives (e.g. the Business Roundtable; the US Chamber of Commerce; the vast number of well-heeled industry lobbies and front groups) to exert power over the flow of information. We noted that the five factors involved—ownership, advertising, sourcing, flak and anti-communist ideology—work as 'filters' through which information must pass, and that individually and often in cumulative fashion they greatly influence media choices. We stressed that the filters work mainly by the independent action of many individuals and organizations; and these frequently, but not always, have a common view of issues as well as similar interests. In short, the propaganda model describes a decentralized and non-conspiratorial market system of control and processing, although at times the government or one or more private actors may take initiatives and mobilize co-ordinated elite handling of an issue.

Propaganda campaigns can occur only when they are consistent with the interests of those controlling and managing the filters. For example, these managers all accepted the view that the Polish government's crackdown on the Solidarity Union in 1980 and 1981 was extremely newsworthy and deserved severe condemnation; whereas the same interests did not find the Turkish military government's equally brutal crackdown on trade unions in Turkey at about the same time to be newsworthy or reprehensible. In the latter case the US government and business community liked the military government's anti-communist stance and open-door economic policy; the crackdown on Turkish unions had the merit of weakening the left and keeping wages down. In the Polish case, propaganda points could be scored against a Soviet-supported government, and concern could be expressed for workers whose wages were not paid by Free World employers. The fit of this dichotomization to corporate interests and anti-communist ideology is obvious.

We used the concepts of 'worthy' and 'unworthy' victims to describe this dichotomization, with a trace of irony as the varying treatment was clearly related to political and economic advantage rather than anything like actual worth. In fact, the Polish trade unionists quickly ceased to be worthy when communism was overthrown and the workers were struggling against a western-oriented neoliberal regime. The travails of today's Polish workers, like those of Turkish workers, do not pass through the propaganda model filters. *Both* groups are unworthy victims at this point.

We never claimed that the propaganda model explained everything or that it illustrated media omnipotence and complete effectiveness in manufacturing consent. It is a model of media *behavior and performance*, not of media effects. We explicitly pointed to the existence of alternative media, grassroots information sources and public scepticism about media truthfulness as important limits on media effectiveness in propaganda service, and we urged the support and more vigorous use of the existing alternatives. Both Chomsky and I have often pointed to the general public's persistent refusal to fall into line with the media and elite over the morality of the Vietnam War, the desirability of the assault on Nicaragua in the 1980s and the merits of the North American Free Trade Agreement in the 1990s, among other matters. The power of the US propaganda system lies in its ability to mobilize an elite consensus, to give the appearance of democratic consent, and to create enough confusion, misunderstanding and apathy in the general population to allow elite programs to go forward. We also emphasized the fact that there are often differences within the elite that open up space for some debate and even occasional (but very rare) attacks on the *intent* as well as the tactical means of achieving elite ends.

Although the propaganda model was generally well received on the left, some complained of an allegedly pessimistic thrust and implication of hopeless odds to be overcome. A closely related objection concerned its applicability to local conflicts where the possibility of effective resistance was often greater than in the case of national issues; but the propaganda model does not suggest that local and even larger victories are impossible, especially where the elites are divided or have limited interest in an issue. For example, coverage of issues such as gun control, school prayer and abortion rights may well receive more varied treatment than, for instance, global trade, taxation and economic policy. Moreover, well-organized compaigns by labor, human rights or environmental organizations that are fighting against abusive local businesses can sometimes elicit positive media coverage. In fact, we would like to think that the propaganda model can help activists understand where they might best deploy their efforts to influence mainstream media coverage of issues.

The model does suggest that the mainstream media, as elite institutions, commonly frame news and allow debate only within the parameters of elite perspectives; and that when the elite is really concerned and unified and/or when ordinary citizens are not aware of their own stake in an issue or are immobilized by effective propaganda, the media will serve elite interests uncompromisingly.

MAINSTREAM LIBERAL AND ACADEMIC 'LEFT' CRITIQUES

Many liberals and some academic media analysts of the left did not like the propaganda model. Some asked rhetorically where we got the information used to condemn the mainstream media if not from the media themselves (a tired apologetic point that we answered at length in our preface). Many of these critics found repugnant a wholesale condemnation of a system they believed to be basically sound, its inequalities of access regrettable but tolerable, its pluralism and competition effectively responding to consumer demands. In the postmodernist mode, global analyses and global solutions are rejected and derided and individual struggles and small victories are stressed, even by nominally left thinkers.

Many of the critiques displayed a barely concealed anger, and in most of them the propaganda model was dismissed with a few superficial clichés (conspiratorial, simplistic, etc.), without fair presentation or subjecting it to the test of evidence. Let me discuss briefly some of the main criticisms.

Conspiracy Theory

We explained in *Manufacturing Consent* that critical analyses such as ours would inevitably elicit cries of conspiracy theory, and in a futile effort to prevent this we devoted several pages of the preface to an explicit rejection of conspiracy and an attempt to show that the propaganda model is best described as a 'guided market system'. Mainstream critics still made the charge, partly because they are too lazy to read a complex work, partly because they know that falsely accusing a radical critique of conspiracy theory will not cost them anything, and partly because of their superficial assumption that, since the media comprise thousands of 'independent' journalists and companies, any finding that they follow a 'party line' that serves the state must rest on an assumed conspiracy. (In fact, it can result from a widespread gullible acceptance of official handouts, common internalized beliefs, common policies established from above within the organizations based on ideology and/or interests, and fear of reprisal for critical analyses from within the organization or from the outside.) The apologists cannot abide the notion that institutional factors can cause a 'free' media to act like lemmings in jointly disseminating false and even silly propaganda; such a charge must assume a conspiracy.

Sometimes the critics latched on to a word or phrase that suggests a collective purpose or function, occasionally ironically, to make their case. Communications professor Robert Entman, for example, stated that we damaged our case by alleging that media coverage of the 1973 Paris accord on Vietnam 'was consciously "designed by the loyal media to serve the needs of state power" ... which comes close to endorsing a conspiracy theory, which the authors explicitly disavow early on' (Entman, 1990: 126). The word 'consciously' was Entman's, and he neglected numerous statements about the media's treatment of the Paris accord that did not fit his effort to bring us 'close to' a conspiracy theory. To say that we 'disavow' a conspiracy theory is also misleading: we went to great pains to show that our view is closer to a free market model; we argued that the media comprise numerous independent entities that operate on the basis of common outlooks, incentives and pressures from the market, government and internal organizational forces.

The propaganda model explains media behavior and performance in structural terms, and intent is an unmeasurable red herring. All we know is that the media and journalists often mislead in tandem—some no doubt internalize a propaganda line as true, some may know it is false, but the point is unknowable and unimportant.

ENHANCED RELEVANCE OF THE PROPAGANDA MODEL

The dramatic changes in the economy, the communications industries and politics over the past dozen years have tended on balance to enhance the applicability of the propaganda model. The first two filters—ownership and advertising—have become ever more important. The decline of public broadcasting, the increase in corporate power and global reach and the mergers and centralization of the media have made bottom-line considerations more influential in the US, in Europe and many other countries. The competition for advertisers has become more intense and the boundaries between editorial and advertising departments have weakened further. Newsrooms have been more thoroughly incorporated into transnational corporate empires, with budget cuts and even less management enthusiasm for investigative journalism that would challenge the structure of power (Herman and McChesney, 1997). In short, the professional autonomy of journalists has been reduced.

Some argue that the Internet and the new communication technologies are breaking the corporate stranglehold on journalism and opening an unprecedented era of inter-active democratic media. There is no evidence to support this view with regard to journalism and mass communication. In fact, one could argue that the new technologies are exacerbating the problem. They permit media firms to shrink staff even as they achieve greater outputs, and they make possible global distribution systems that reduce the number of media entities. Although the new technologies have great potential for democratic communication, there is little reason to expect the Internet to serve democratic ends if it is left to the market (Herman and McChesney, 1997: 117–35).

The third and fourth filters—sourcing and flak—have also strengthened as mechanisms of elite influence. A reduction in the resources devoted to journalism means that those who subsidize the media by providing sources for copy gain greater leverage. Moreover, work by people such as Alex Carey, John Stauber and Sheldon Rampton has helped us see how the public relations industry has been able to manipulate press coverage of issues on behalf of corporate America (Carey, 1995; Stauber and Rampton, 1995). This industry understands how to utilize journalistic conventions to serve its own ends. Studies of news sources reveal that a significant proportion of news originates in public relations releases. There are, by one count, 20,000 more public relations agents working to doctor the news today than there are journalists writing it (Dowie, 1995: 3–4).

The fifth filter—anti-communist ideology—is possibly weakened by the collapse of the Soviet Union and global socialism, but this is easily offset by the greater ideological force of the belief in the 'miracle of the market' (Reagan). There is now an almost religious faith in the market, at least among the elite, so that regardless of evidence markets are assumed to be benevolent and non-market mechanisms are suspect. When the Soviet economy stagnated in the 1980s, it was attributed to the absence of markets;

the disintegration of capitalist Russia in the 1990s is blamed on politicians and workers failing to let markets work their magic. Journalism has internalized this ideology. Adding it to the fifth filter in a world where the global power of market institutions makes non-market options seem utopian gives us an ideological package of immense strength.

FINAL NOTE

In retrospect, perhaps we should have made it clearer that the propaganda model was about media behavior and performance, with uncertain and variable effects. Perhaps we should have spelled out in more detail the contesting forces both within and outside the media and the conditions under which these are likely to be influential. However, we made these points, and it is quite possible that nothing we could have done would have prevented our being labeled conspiracy theorists, rigid determinists and deniers of the possibility that people can resist (even as we called for resistance).

The propaganda model remains a very workable framework for analyzing and understanding the mainstream media—perhaps even more so than in 1988. As noted earlier in reference to Central America, the media's performance often surpassed expectations of media subservience to government propaganda. It did so, also, in their reporting on the Persian Gulf and Yugoslav wars of 1990 and 1999, respectively (Chomsky, 1999; Herman, 1999: 161–6; Kellner, 1992; Mowlana et al., 1992). We are still waiting for our critics to provide a better model.

REFERENCES

Bailey, Thomas (1948) *The Man in the Street: The Impact of American Public Opinion on Foreign Policy*. New York: Macmillan.

Carey, Alex (1995) *Taking the Risk Out of Democracy*. Sydney: University of New South Wales Press.

Chomsky, Noam (1999) *The New Military Humanism: Lessons from Kosovo*. Monroe, ME: Common Courage Press.

Dowie, M. (1995) *Torches of Liberty*. Introduction to J. Stauber and S. Rampton, *Toxic Sludge is Good for You*. Monroe, ME: Common Courage Press.

Entman, Robert (1990) 'News as propaganda', *Journal of Communication*, 40: 124–7.

Ferguson, Thomas (1995) *Golden Rule*. Chicago, IL: University of Chicago Press.

Herman, Edward (1999) *The Myth of the Liberal Media*. New York: Peter Lang Publishing.

Herman, Edward and Chomsky, Noam (1988) *Manufacturing Consent*. New York: Pantheon Books.

Herman, Edward and McChesney, Robert (1997) *The Global Media*. London: Cassell.

Kellner, Douglas (1992) *The Persian Gulf TV War*. Boulder, CO: Westview Press.

Lasswell, H.D. (1933) 'Propaganda', *Encyclopedia of the Social Sciences*. New York: Macmillan. pp. 521–8.

Lippmann, Walter (1921) *Public Opinion*. London: Allen and Unwin.

Mowlana, Hamid, Gerbner, George and Schiller, Herbert (eds) (1992) *Triumph of the Image*. Boulder, CO: Westview Press.

Page, Ben (1996) *Who Deliberates*? Chicago, IL: University of Chicago Press.

Stauber, John and Rampton, Sheldon (1995) *Toxic Sludge is Good for You*. Monroe, ME: Common Courage Press.

III

MASS MEDIA AND SOCIETY

This section illustrates some of the different ways in which the media institution has been thought to influence the experience of life in a 'modern' society (even in 'post-industrial' conditions). The excerpt from C. Wright Mills' (Chapter 5) seminal study of the discontents of modern life draws on a long radical critique of industrialism and capitalism and is a reminder of the deep roots of current notions concerning the 'public sphere' and its enemies. Mills eloquently exposes our extreme dependence on a view of reality mediated through the cultural industries of news and advertising. It would be difficult to claim that contemporary conditions of media and communication offer any more solace now than in his day. On the other hand, the assumptions made about the controlling power of media over minds and hearts have been called into question. Mills' pessimism is not only about media but also about human resourcefulness. Gouldner's (Chapter 6) reflections on the interaction between the newspaper press and the rise of democracy are not inconsistent with Mills' vision but also suggest that particular forms of public communication can have their own distinct effects on the structure and exercise of political power. This opens up prospects for change.

The nearest to a 'communication technology determinist' view in this collection is offered by Meyrowitz (Chapter 8), although it is very much nuanced and specifies certain conditions and reasons for communication influence. Inspired by McLuhan (1962, 1964) and the 'Toronto school' generally, Meyrowitz views the medium of television as it has developed as opening up to universal gaze those corners and 'backstage' areas that previously kept everyday experience very much segregated according to age, gender and, to some degree, class and status. This generally supports the line of argument that mass media are a force for social cohesion and cultural homogeneity, as well as for more openness in society. At the same time the reduced segregation of experience runs counter to some traditional notions of family life and morality. Dayan and Katz (Chapter 7) also emphasize the socially unifying character of mass media, and of television in particular, despite counter-trends of individualization and privatization. It is mass media that make possible the periodic 'coming together' (albeit in 'virtual form') of the dispersed public by way of common audience behaviour and shared emotions, in response to large-scale events with symbolic potency, often extending far beyond national frontiers. By implication, the 'demassification' of media that is alleged to be happening as a result of channel and media multiplication could undo the social benefit of these unifying experiences. The authors generally imply that the 'media event' phenomenon is beneficial, especially in respect of creating some sense of global solidarity on issues such as peace and the environment. However, there is some potential for manipulation on the part of 'creators' of media events and a growing category of 'pseudo-events' (such as *Big Brother*) that casts doubt on the value of the shared experience that mass media can engineer.

The choice of excerpts in this section is consistent with the view that communication technologies do not themselves determine the direction of social change or the predominant conditions of society. They are applied and institutionalized in particular ways (for instance, the newspaper press or 'mass television') that reflect more fundamental forces, although the particular form of institutionalization tends to acquire a life of its own and it reinforces or suppresses social and cultural trends in accordance with its particular logic.

REFERENCES

McLuhan, M. (1962) *The Gutenberg Galaxy*. Toronto: Toronto University Press.
McLuhan, M. (1964) *Understanding Media*. Toronto: University of Toronto Press.

5

the mass society

C. WRIGHT MILLS

T
he transformation of public into mass is of particular concern to us, for it provides an important clue to the meaning of the power elite. If that elite is truly responsible to, or even exists in connection with, a community of publics, it carries a very different meaning than if such a public is being transformed into a society of masses.

The United States today is not altogether a mass society, and it has never been altogether a community of publics. These phrases are names for extreme types; they point to certain features of reality, but they are themselves constructions; social reality is always some sort of mixture of the two. Yet we cannot readily understand just how much of which is mixed into our situation if we do not first understand, in terms of explicit dimensions, the clear-cut and extreme types:

At least four dimensions must be attended to if we are to grasp the differences between public and mass.

I. There is, first, the ratio of the givers of opinion to the receivers, which is the simplest way to state the social meaning of the formal media of mass communication. More than anything else, it is the shift in this ratio which is central to the problems of the public and of public opinion in latter-day phases of democracy. At one extreme on the scale of communication, two people talk personally with each other; at the opposite extreme, one spokesman talks impersonally through a network of communications to millions of listeners and viewers. In between these extremes there are assemblages and political rallies, parliamentary sessions, lawcourt debates, small discussion circles dominated by one man, open discussion circles with talk moving freely back and forth among fifty people, and so on.

II. The second dimension to which we must pay attention is the possibility of answering back an opinion without internal or external reprisals being taken. Technical conditions of the means of communication, in imposing a lower ratio of speakers to listeners, may obviate the possibility of freely answering back. Informal rules, resting upon conventional sanction and upon the informal structure of opinion leadership, may govern who can speak, when, and for how long. Such rules may or may not be in congruence with formal rules and with institutional sanctions which govern the process of communication. In the extreme case, we may conceive of an absolute monopoly of communication to pacified media groups whose members cannot answer back even 'in private.' At the opposite extreme, the conditions may allow and the rules may uphold the wide and symmetrical formation of opinion.

III. We must also consider the relation of the formation of opinion to its realization in social action, the ease with which opinion is effective in the shaping of decisions of powerful consequence. This opportunity for people to act out their opinions collectively is of course limited by their position in the structure of power. This structure may be such as to limit decisively this capacity, or it may allow or even invite such action. It may confine social action to local areas or it may enlarge the area of opportunity; it may make action intermittent or more or less continuous.

IV. There is, finally, the degree to which institutional authority, with its sanctions and controls, penetrates the public. Here the problem is the degree to which the public

First published in *The Power Elite*, C.W. Mills, Oxford University Press (1959) as 'The Mass Society', pp. 302–316.

has genuine autonomy from instituted authority. At one extreme, no agent of formal authority moves among the autonomous public. At the opposite extreme, the public is terrorized into uniformity by the infiltration of informers and the universalization of suspicion. One thinks of the late Nazi street-and-block-system, the eighteenth-century Japanese kumi, the Soviet cell structure. In the extreme, the formal structure of power coincides, as it were, with the informal ebb and flow of influence by discussion, which is thus killed off.

By combining these several points, we can construct little models or diagrams of several types of societies. Since 'the problem of public opinion' as we know it is set by the eclipse of the classic bourgeois public, we are here concerned with only two types: public and mass.

In a *public*, as we may understand the term, (1) virtually as many people express opinions as receive them. (2) Public communications are so organized that there is a chance immediately and effectively to answer back any opinion expressed in public. Opinion formed by such discussion (3) readily finds an outlet in effective action, even against – if necessary – the prevailing system of authority. And (4) authoritative institutions do not penetrate the public, which is thus more or less autonomous in its operations. When these conditions prevail, we have the working model of a community of publics, and this model fits closely the several assumptions of classic democratic theory.

At the opposite extreme, in a *mass*, (1) far fewer people express opinions than receive them; for the community of publics becomes an abstract collection of individuals who receive impressions from the mass media. (2) The communications that prevail are so organized that it is difficult or impossible for the individual to answer back immediately or with any effect. (3) The realization of opinion in action is controlled by authorities who organize and control the channels of such action. (4) The mass has no autonomy from institutions; on the contrary, agents of authorized institutions penetrate this mass, reducing any autonomy it may have in the formation of opinion by discussion.

The public and the mass may be most readily distinguished by their dominant modes of communication: in a community of publics, discussion is the ascendant means of communication, and the mass media, if they exist, simply enlarge and animate discussion, linking one *primary public* with the discussions of another. In a mass society, the dominant type of communication is the formal media, and the publics become mere *media markets*: all those exposed to the contents of given mass media.

[…]

The institutional trends that make for a society of masses are to a considerable extent a matter of impersonal drift, but the remnants of the public are also exposed to more 'personal' and intentional forces. With the broadening of the base of politics within the context of a folk-lore of democratic decision-making, and with the increased means of mass persuasion that are available, the public of public opinion has become the object of intensive efforts to control, manage, manipulate, and increasingly intimidate.

In political, military, economic realms, power becomes, in varying degrees, uneasy before the suspected opinions of masses, and, accordingly, opinion-making becomes an accepted technique of power-holding and power-getting. The minority electorate of the propertied and the educated is replaced by the total suffrage – and intensive campaigns for the vote. The small eighteenth-century professional army is replaced by the mass army of conscripts – and by the problems of nationalist morale. The small shop is replaced by the mass-production industry – and the national advertisement.

As the scale of institutions has become larger and more centralized, so has the range and intensity of the opinion-makers' efforts. The means of opinion-making, in fact, have paralleled in range and efficiency the other institutions of greater scale that cradle the modern society of masses. Accordingly, in addition to their enlarged and centralized means of administration, exploitation, and violence, the modern elite have had placed within their grasp historically unique instruments of psychic management and manipulation, which include universal compulsory education as well as the media of mass communication.

Early observers believed that the increase in the range and volume of the formal means of communication would enlarge and animate the primary public. In such opti-mistic views – written before radio and television and movies – the formal media are understood as simply multiplying the scope and pace of personal discussion. Modern conditions, Charles Cooley wrote, 'enlarge indefinitely the competition of ideas, and whatever has owed its persistence merely to lack of comparison is likely to go, for that which is really congenial to the choosing mind will be all the more cherished and increased.'[1] Still excited by the break-up of the conventional consensus of the local com-munity, he saw the new means of communication as furthering the conversational dynamic of classic democracy, and with it the growth of rational and free individuality.

No one really knows all the functions of the mass media, for in their entirety these functions are probably so pervasive and so subtle that they cannot be caught by the means of social research now available. But we do now have reason to believe that these media have helped less to enlarge and animate the discussions of primary publics than to transform them into a set of media markets in mass-like society. I do not refer merely to the higher ratio of deliverers of opinion to receivers and to the decreased chance to answer back; nor do I refer merely to the violent banalization and stereo-typing of our very sense organs in terms of which these media now compete for 'atten-tion.' I have in mind a sort of psychological illiteracy that is facilitated by the media, and that is expressed in several ways:

I. Very little of what we think we know of the social realities of the world have we found out first-hand. Most of 'the pictures in our heads' we have gained from these media – even to the point where we often do not really believe what we see before us until we read about it in the paper or hear about it on the radio. The media not only give us information; they guide our very experiences. Our standards of credulity, our standards of reality, tend to be set by these media rather than by our own fragmentary experience.

Accordingly, even if the individual has direct, personal experience of events, it is not really direct and primary; it is organized in stereotypes. It takes long and skillful training to so uproot such stereotypes that an individual sees things freshly, in an unstereotyped manner. One might suppose, for example, that if all the people went through a depression they would all 'experience it,' and in terms of this experience, that they would all debunk or reject or at least refract what the media say about it. But experience of such a *structural* shift has to be organized and interpreted if it is to count in the making of opinion.

The kind of experience, in short, that might serve as a basis for resistance to mass media is not an experience of raw events, but the experience of meanings. The fleck of interpretation must be there in the experience if we are to use the word experience seriously. And the capacity for such experience is socially implanted. The individual does not trust his own experience, as I have said, until it is confirmed by others or by the media. Usually such direct exposure is not accepted if it disturbs loyalties and beliefs that the individual already holds. To be accepted, it must relieve or justify the feelings that often lie in the back of his mind as key features of his ideological loyalties.

[···]

II. So long as the media are not entirely monopolized, the individual can play one medium off against another; he can compare them, and hence resist what any one of them puts out. The more genuine competition there is among the media, the more resistance the individual might be able to command. But how much is this now the case? *Do* people compare reports on public events or policies, playing one medium's content off against another's?

The answer is: generally no, very few do: (1) We know that people tend strongly to select those media that carry contents with which they already agree. There is a kind of selection of new opinions on the basis of prior opinions. No one seems to search out such counter-statements as may be found in alternative media offerings. Given radio programs and magazines and newspapers often get a rather consistent public, and thus reinforce their messages in the minds of that public. (2) This idea of playing one medium off against another assumes that the media really have varying contents. It assumes genuine competition, which is not widely true. The media display an apparent variety and competition, but on closer view they seem to compete more in terms of variations on a few standardized themes than of clashing issues. The freedom to raise issues effectively seems more and more to be confined to those few interests that have ready and continual access to these media.

III. The media have not only filtered into our experience of external realities, they have also entered into our very experience of our own selves. They have provided us with new identities and new aspirations of what we should like to be, and what we should like to appear to be. They have provided in the models of conduct they hold out to us a new and larger and more flexible set of appraisals of our very selves. In terms of the modern theory of the self, we may say that the media bring the reader, listener, viewer into the sight of larger, higher reference groups – groups, real or imagined, up close or vicarious, personally known or distractedly glimpsed – which are looking glasses for his self-image. They have multiplied the groups to which we look for confirmation of our self-image.

More than that: (1) the media tell the man in the mass who he is – they give him identity; (2) they tell him what he wants to be – they give him aspirations; (3) they tell him how to get that way – they give him technique; and (4) they tell him how to feel that he is that way even when he is not – they give him escape. The gaps between the identity and aspiration lead to technique and/or to escape. That is probably the basic psychological formula of the mass media today. But, as a formula, it is not attuned to the development of the human being. It is the formula of a pseudoworld which the media invent and sustain.

IV. As they now generally prevail, the mass media, especially television, often encroach upon the small-scale discussion, and destroy the chance for the reasonable and leisurely and human interchange of opinion. They are an important cause of the destruction of privacy in its full human meaning. That is an important reason why they not only fail as an educational force, but are a malign force: they do not articulate for the viewer or listener the broader sources of his private tensions and anxieties, his inarticulate resentments and half-formed hopes. They neither enable the individual to transcend his narrow milieu nor clarify its private meaning.

The media provide much information and news about what is happening in the world, but they do not often enable the listener or the viewer truly to connect his daily life with these larger realities. They do not connect the information they provide on public issues with the troubles felt by the individual. They do not increase rational insight into tensions, either those in the individual or those of the society which are reflected in the individual. On the contrary, they distract him and obscure his chance to understand himself or his world, by fastening his attention upon artificial frenzies that are resolved within the program framework, usually by violent action or by what is called humor. In short, for the viewer they are not really resolved at all. The chief distracting tension of the media is between the wanting and the not having of commodities or of women held to be good looking. There is almost always the general tone of animated distraction, of suspended agitation, but it is going nowhere and it has nowhere to go.

But the media, as now organized and operated, are even more than a major cause of the transformation of America into a mass society. They are also among the most important of those increased means of power now at the disposal of elites of wealth and power; moreover, some of the higher agents of these media are themselves either among the elites or very important among their servants.

Alongside or just below the elite, there is the propagandist, the publicity expert, the public-relations man, who would control the very formation of public opinion in order to be able to include it as one more pacified item in calculations of effective power, increased prestige, more secure wealth. Over the last quarter of a century, the attitudes of these manipulators toward their task have gone through a sort of dialectic:

In the beginning, there is great faith in what the mass media can do. Words win wars or sell soap; they move people, they restrain people. 'Only cost,' the advertising man of the Twenties proclaims, 'limits the delivery of public opinion in any direction on any topic.' The opinion-maker's belief in the media as mass persuaders almost amounts to magic – but he can believe mass communications omnipotent only so long as the public is trustful. It does not remain trustful. The mass media say so very many and such competitively exaggerated things; they banalize their message and they cancel one another out. The 'propaganda phobia,' in reaction to wartime lies and postwar disenchantment, does not help matters, even though memory is both short and subject to official distortion. This distrust of the magic of media is translated into a slogan among the opinion managers. Across their banners they write: 'Mass Persuasion Is Not Enough.'

Frustrated, they reason; and reasoning, they come to accept the principle of social context. To change opinion and activity, they say to one another, we must pay close attention to the full context and lives of the people to be managed. Along with mass persuasion, we must somehow use personal influence; we must reach people in their life context and *through* other people, their daily associates, those whom they trust: we must get at them by some kind of 'personal' persuasion. We must not show our hand directly; rather than merely advise or command, we must manipulate.

Now this live and immediate social context in which people live and which exerts a steady expectation upon them is of course what we have called the primary public. Anyone who has seen the inside of an advertising agency or public-relations office knows that the primary public is still the great unsolved problem of the opinion-makers. Negatively, their recognition of the influence of social context upon opinion and public activity implies that the articulate public resists and refracts the communications of the mass media. Positively, this recognition implies that the public is not composed of isolated individuals, but rather of persons who not only have prior opinions that must be reckoned with, but who continually influence each other in complex and intimate, in direct and continual ways.

NOTE

1   Charles Horton Cooley, *Social Organization* (New York: Scribner's, 1909).

6

the communications revolution:
news, public, and ideology

ALVIN W. GOULDNER

1

There is a profound interconnection between the new Age of Ideology—the eighteenth and nineteenth centuries' proliferation of ideologies—and the 'communications revolution' grounded in the development of printing, printing technologies, and the growing production of printed products. The fuller ramifications of these developments, of their reach both forward and backward in time, and across social subsystems, are exhibited with exceptional clarity by Morse Peckham, whom I quote at length below.

[···]

It is no surprise to learn, therefore, that in the first decade of the nineteenth century, England perfected a paper-making machine, named after the men whose fortunes went to develop it, the Fourdrinier brothers. ... It was as important as the invention of the printing press. ... This invention involved a whole chain of reactions.

[···]

By 1830, publishing had been revolutionized. Printed matter was now cheap—for the first time in human history literacy could be massively extended through all levels of the population. In England the population grew by a ratio of one to four; but the literate population grew by a ratio of one to thirty-two. Not merely book manufacture was affected, but every type of communications and record keeping involving paper—magazines, newspapers, letters; business, government and military correspondence and orders. ... The nineteenth century experienced a communications revolution which, though a part of the industrial revolution, may very well have been the most important of its results.[1]

1.1

Peckham notes one exceedingly important consequence for the writing of history, the hitherto dominant, intellectually serious, and secular effort to account for and describe the social world:

The historian's technique was developed centuries before the communications revolution. It was a product of the fact that documents were limited in number. A single human mind could master them. All the surviving documents of ancient Greece can be intimately studied within a few years. ... Consequently, we have a clear picture of the history of ancient Greece. That clarity is a consequence, not of our understanding, but solely of the fact that there is so little to understand. When the historian attempts to grapple with any period after the communications revolution had begun, he is lost in a chaos of documents. His technique no longer serves him. ... He is forced to recognize that history is a construct; he can no longer delude himself into thinking that what happened was identical with what was recorded in a very small number of surviving documents; he cannot escape the conclusions that his construct is an instrument which he uses to organize the documents.[2]

First published in *The Dialectic of Ideology and Technology*, A.W. Gouldner, Macmillan (1976) as 'The Communications Revolution: news, public and ideology', pp. 91–102.

There was, then, a tremendous increase in information due to the accelerating availability of printed materials, newspapers, or official documents. This sheer increase in the information intensified the problem of information *processing* and, above all, of clarifying the meaning of the information. Acquiring *meaning*, not information, became increasingly problematic.

It became clearer that meaning did not simply spring forth from information itself, that meaning was not dictated by the number of documents, by the facts or bits of information, but depended, at least in *part*, on prior commitments to conceptual schemes, theories, and perspectives. Differences in intra- or inter*national* news accounts, for example, became evident to traveling readers who could compare diverse accounts of the 'same' event. Meaning could thus be seen to depend on the *interests*—national, political, religious, and emphatically, economic—of both publishers and readers. The sheer increase in information, and in the diversity of the reports concerning 'one' event, generated a new public problematic: the need for publicly shareable *meaning*. The proliferation of ideologies, the Age of Ideology, was one fundamental response to the new communications revolution; it was, in part, an effort to supply meaning where the overall supply of public information was greater than ever.

1.2

The Age of Ideology, then, may be looked upon as that proliferating production of symbol systems that responded to the increased market for meaning; and, in particular, for *secularized* meanings, due partly to the attenuation of older value systems and religions that were tied to the dying old regime; due partly to the new social structures and revolutionary events that needed to be synthesized; and due greatly (as I have stressed above) to the sheer increase in *bits* of information that the communications revolution spread in every direction.

More than that, there was also the fragmented image of the world that was inherent in 'news' itself. As Robert Park commented: News deals '... with isolated events and does not seek to relate them to one another in the form of causal or teleological sequences. ... News comes to us ... not in the form of a continued story but as a series of independent incidents ... small, independent communications.' Focused on the *newness* of news, each news story tends to constrict attention to the present, and thus generates a loss of those connections with the past that is 'history.' It decontextualizes 'events.'

It is thus consistent that the Age of Ideology is not only to be seen as responsive to the fragmentation of news, but also corresponds with the modern development of history, with the development of *modern* history, that connects distant with recent events over time, and, what is newer, soon presses on to interconnect the seemingly isolated subsystems of society—for example, to write about the relationship between economics and politics. The interconnectedness of economics and politics can now be told as a kind of revelation, and history is no longer an isolated chronicle of crowns and courts. The new history is *recontextualizing* as are the new ideologies; they both seek new meaning-bestowing *contexts*.

2

With the diffusion of literacy, the technology of printing, and the development of the modern newspaper, there was, then, the development of the modern notion of 'news' itself. Indeed, between, say, about 1780 and 1830, the growth of journals, newsletters, and newspapers was so great in Europe that a fundamentally new social phenomenon comes into being—the 'news'-reading public.

In Germany, newspapers began to be issued with some regularity in the very early seventeenth century. The first French paper, *Gazette de France* appeared in 1631. Between 1700 and 1789, some 85 journals were started in France. The *London Gazette* appeared in 1665, containing articles by Jonathan Swift and Daniel Defoe, among others, and by 1774 there were seven London dailies. As early as the mid-eighteenth century, about 7½ million newspaper stamps were sold in Britain and by about 1830 these had almost reached 25,000,000. Robert E. Park notes that 'the first newspaper in America, at least, the first newspaper that lasted beyond its first issue, was *The Boston News Letter* ... published by the postmaster.'

At first, such publications were more likely to combine commentary on literature with 'news.' But by 1830 the news predominated, as parliaments and political centers became of wider interest, and as the spread of markets into national and international systems meant that distant events could affect local prices and supplies. The new media, then, appealed to a variety of audiences, including one in Leipzig (1725–26) written for women, while about 1830 working-class newspapers began appearing in London and Paris (e.g. *Le Populaire* and *L'Atelier*). Even in 1620, Ben Jonson had described subscribers to his newsletter as 'of all ranks and religion.' Subsequently, and with the development of different departments and features within one newspaper, the paper spreads itself across different 'publics' who become amalgamated and connected with one another through the newspaper's 'layout.' Typography and layout become visual ways of organizing meanings and audiences.

2.1

The emergence of the mass media and of the 'public' are mutually constructive developments. A 'public' emerges when there is an attenuation between culture, on the one side, and patterns of social interaction, on the other. Traditional 'groups' are characterized by the association and mutual support of both elements; by the fact that their members have patterned social interactions with one another which, in turn, fosters among them common understandings and shared interests which, again in turn, facilitates their mutual interaction, and so on. A 'public,' 'refers to a number of people exposed to the same social stimuli,' and having something in common even without being in persisting interaction with one another. 'Publics' are persons who need not be 'co-present,' in the 'sight and hearing of one another.'

In most traditional societies, however, markets and holidays constituted the basic specialized structures periodically spreading information to the larger community, among strangers or members of different families; and this, of course, was transmitted by word of mouth, in a context-sustained, face-to-face conversation that allowed clarifying feedback and questioning. With the growth of the mass media, exemplified at first by printing, numerous persons were now exposed to a continuous flow of information, at more or less the same time. Information becomes *de*contextualized, for it must be made intelligible, interesting and convincing even to persons of diverse backgrounds and interests, persons who do not know one another and do not meet and interact.

With the growth of the mass media, social interaction was less requisite for cultural communality. People might now share information and orientations, facts and values, without mutual access and interaction. The problem now arises as to how persons can evaluate information. The shared beliefs people defined as true and worthy could now be controlled from a remote distance, apart from and outside of the persons sharing the beliefs. Insofar as the control of media comes to be centralized and its reach becomes extended, competing values and definitions of reality no longer check one another; rational persuasion is then less necessary, and manipulation from a central source can substitute for voluntary persuasion.

Historically speaking, then, a 'public' consists of persons who habitually acquire their news and orientations from impersonal mass media where they have available to them diverse information and orientations diffused by competing individual entrepreneurs or corporate organizations, and where this diversity increases *talk* among those sharing news but seeking consensus concerning its meaning. That is a *bourgeois* public.

A *'socialist'* public differs in that talk is generated by the commonly understood lacunae of the news, by the distrust of the univocality of the news, and by the immensely greater difficulty in voicing interpretations divergent from those sanctioned officially, because of the lack of *open* support for (deviant or) dissenting views. A bourgeois public clearly has its limits in property interests, class-shaped cultural assumptions and educational backgrounds; but it also supports diversity, eccentricity and dissent among persons by allowing deviants the supportive consensual validation of a public organ, however small and poorly supported.

2.2

Newspapers strengthen enhanced public rationality in certain obvious ways. First, they provide a larger supply of information. This transcends local conditions, going beyond it to bring information concerning distant events. News thus has a cosmopolitanizing influence, allowing persons to escape provincializing assumptions, and thereby enabling them to *compare* their own conditions with others. News allows alternatives to be defined as 'realistic' by showing different conditions to exist already, thereby fostering more ready transcendence of the immediate and the local. News also enables men to see what might be coming, partly as a 'weather report' permits adjustments based on crude extrapolation, thus limiting possible costs or reaping greater gains. News itself, then, enhances rationality in these several ways.

Increasing news and information was also rationality-enhancing in the early bourgeois period by the way news came to be structured, by the separation of news and editorials, as well as because competing papers might present different reports of the same event. Both of these circumstances were fostered by bourgeois profit-seeking and competitive enterprise.

News was separated from editorial policy in part because an 'imprudent' pursuit of the paper's policy might offend and limit its market. This became enormously more important as advertising spread, intensifying concern with the size of the readership, and clearly linking income from advertising to sheer size of readership. This, then, controls the editor's single-minded pursuit of policy, splitting the presentation of news from the editorial. Indeed, it may make both news and editorial opinion subordinate to entertainment: to feature writers, 'human interest' stories, romance stories for the 'ladies,' sports for the 'gentlemen.' As entertainment develops, the newspaper as a source of rationality is profoundly undermined. But, until then, and so long as newspapers present information that requires interpretation, it fosters discussion and rational dialogue.

2.3

It was central to the pioneering analysis of the public, and of the news made by the 'Chicago school,' that news *constructed* a public by stimulating face-to-face conversation. Talk was intensified to resolve uncertainties about the *meaning* of the news, whether uncertainty was fostered by lacunae or by conflicting accounts.

But such talk premises motives for clarification. These, in turn, premise an *interest* in integrating the often fragmented bits of information that characterize news; the varied, ambiguous, or conflicting reports of news. The system at bottom premised: the publisher's dependency on the successful marketing of his product, which meant *interesting* his audience and generating a larger market; it implied a socioeconomic-political system that allowed for a multiplicity of semiautonomous producers of printing, publishers, outlets, and distributors, free to purchase writing and writers, whose work they thought would sell for a profit. It also premises writers who could sell their writing on a labor market, and who might therefore by-pass the censorship of one publisher by using another, competing publisher; or who might even be published by a publisher who disliked their views simply because they sold newspapers.

Bourgeois rationality transcended the rationality of classical antiquity primarily because it was grounded in the new technology. The class systems of classical slave society, and of capitalist society, both premised the exclusion of great parts of the society from participation in rational public dialogue. The limits of rationality in both class systems were, in part, the class and property interests of the dominant classes— slave owners and bourgeoisie.

The Greeks, however, give little or no *evidence* of ever having made slavery a problematic institution open to public discussion, except insofar as it was implicated in the politics of Greek solidarity against the Persians. While some resisted the Greek enslavement of Greeks, their own enslavement of 'barbarians,' however, seems never to have been questioned publicly in classical antiquity, nor was the institution of slavery as such. Bourgeois society, however, very swiftly generated a public critique of its most fundamental property assumptions. Quite unlike classical antiquity, it moved with breathtaking speed to plant 'the seeds of its own destruction.' Scarcely had the French

Revolution been completed when the liberating mission of the proletariat was announced. Indeed, this had been partly anticipated and heralded by the Babeuvian 'conspiracy of the equals,' in the very midst of the Revolution itself.

Publics imply a development of rational discourse because they imply the existence of a cleared and safe space in the community available for *face-to-face* discourse, concerning a commonly shared body of news-disbursed information, that is motivated by a quest for the interpretation of that shared news. Such discourse is 'rational' precisely in the sense that it is *critical*; meaning that what has been said may be questioned, *negated* and *contradicted*. This, in turn, is possible if and only if people may speak 'openly' without fear of sanctions, other than those imposed by the deficient logic and factuality of their speech, and only insofar as such sanctions are inflicted by co-speakers in their *private* capacity. The rationality of 'public' discourse thus depends on the prior possibility of separating speakers from their normal powers and privileges in the larger society, especially in the class system, and on successfully defining these powers and privileges as irrelevant to the quality of their discourse. Publics thus require men to be treated as 'private' persons.

2.4

News-grounded conversation, as a vehicle of public rationality, thus depends importantly on the *absence* of state-sponsored spies, informants, censors, and a secret police governmentally mandated to search out heresy, dissidence, or immorality.

The class system and the state, then, must *both* be excluded from the dialogue if the public is to actualize its potential for critical rationality. Any social transformation of the class system alone will, therefore, *fail* to enhance public rationality if it does not, at the same time, prevent the *state* from the surveillance and punishment of dissident talk, or at least forbid surveillance as a routine activity that does not require extraordinary justification. It is in that sense that it is not only class power but *any* source of societal domination that inhibits dialogue and undermines rationality.

The development of a public in bourgeois society clearly entailed the interaction of growing news, printing media and technologies, and a cleared, safe space within which *face-to-face talk* about news and its meaning could occur. This development begins within the confines of liberal aristocratic society, well before the bourgeois revolution. It begins in the aristocratic salons and is only later 'democratized' by the development of public cafés in bourgeois society—places where a limited group could gather and talk without fear of either class snobbery or police spies. In the case of the salon, of course, conversation concerning public matters is within the space of a *private* home, and is a form of common entertainment. One had to be invited, otherwise one could not participate. This meant that conversation was limited by the tacit requirement that it not impair conviviality and 'good taste,' as defined by a presiding hostess. This, in turn, meant that rationality was tacitly limited by a *class*-shared cultivation and tact.

With the development of the public café open to all with the price of admission, there remained only one fundamental limit on participation, and that was the limit on rationality that had persisted since antiquity: leisure. To spend time in a café talking with others implied, if it was during the *day*time, that one was not accountable to others for his time. It implied that 'he' was his own 'master' because 'he' was a reputable, independent professional or entrepreneur, or a dubiously reputable 'bohemian' who had rejected a routine occupation, and/or a student supported by others. It is important to add that even a wealthy entrepreneur who employed others might be excluded from such participation by reason of his need (or wish) actively to superintend those whom he employed.

2.5

To spend time in a café talking with others also implied, especially if it was a *night-time* activity, that it was a male-dominated group. Presence at the café premised a family system having men-dominated households from which they could depart or return at their own pleasure, without time-consuming participation in child care or housekeeping. The bourgeois public then was not just class-grounded; it was also grounded in a *patriarchical family system*. It was open primarily to those who were economically *and* sexually privileged.

In both bourgeois society and in classical antiquity, public rationality was grounded in class privilege and in unchallenged male domination of the family. Both provided that indispensable requisite for rational discourse: leisure, free from time-consuming work in the household and in the work-place, and the freedom to allocate one's own 'free time' without the control or permission of another. Patriarchical subjugation of women and private property, then, were the unmistakable conditions and limits of the post-Enlightenment development of public rationality in bourgeois society.

The existence of owning-publishers also generated a set of limits within which the distinction between editorials and news could not be altogether real; for the publisher, after all, hired both the editorialist and the head of the news department. But the sheer problem of profitability imposed its own constraints. It meant that the publisher could neither hire nor publish only in terms of his own ideological preferences. Precisely because the publisher was a capitalist and subject to the imperatives of profitability and of competition, he had to *limit* his own impulse to infuse the news with his own ideological views. For there was the compelling consideration of printing what would not offend others and could sell and turn a profit.

2.6

Ideologies serve to mobilize 'social movements' within publics through the mediation of newspapers and other media. Movements are sectors of the public committed to a common public project and to a common social identity. Movements are those sectors of the public responsive to the mobilizing efforts of ideologies; they share an ideology that, on the one side, interprets the news and, on the other, provides an awareness of their own social identity from reports in the news media. News generates ideology-centered social identities which, in turn, are now media-constructed and defined. Thus social movements in the modern world are both ideology- and news-constructed.

Indeed, between the later spread of a social movement, and an earlier formulation of an ideology, there is often the intervening organization and production of a newspaper. In the period of the consolidation of the bourgeoisie, newspapers were often instruments of parties; and parties were often mobilized and organized through the newspapers. The modern political party, which is the enduring cadre *organization* and elite of a movement, is fostered by the newspaper and its commitments and interests; in many cases, newspapers are essentially 'in-house,' party organs.

Newspaper editors sometimes doubled as editors and party chiefs. One way that the party cadre could secure livings, leaving them time for party involvement, was as party journalists or editors. No one understood this better than V.I. Lenin who deliberately undertook to mobilize a Marxist cadre in Russia by the specific tactic of launching a newspaper that was appropriately called *Iskra, The Spark*, highlighting its mediating significance. Correspondingly, one of the reasons that Marx and Engels never became the active *leaders* (but only remained the 'senior consultants') of mass socialist parties was that they *refused* to be the editors of party newspapers, even of socialist papers.[3]

2.7

The meaning of a 'public' develops along with the socially emergent idea of the 'private.' The relations between the two, however, are not always the same in all countries. In typical form, in eighteenth- and nineteenth-century France, the relation is one in which the 'private' constituted the complement and grounding of a 'public.' In Germany, the private was often a *substitute* for the public, a place of the 'mind' where one could be free, even if not openly free in public discourse. Here, the private is compensatory; a consolation prize for the stunting of a public. And even that is more complicated than it might seem, for the private here is not simply the *absence* of all dialogue but is *intense dialogue* limited to close friends and intimates. The German dwelling on *innerlichkeit* (inwardness) in the nineteenth century, in effect, made the mind (consciousness) and the close friendship a site of sanctified retreat from the repressions and dangers of a truly public discourse. In the French case, the effort was to insulate private life from the stresses of the public; above all, to prevent one's public involvements from intruding on the nuclear family.

In England, of course, the 'public' school is not one open freely to all, but a school that is conducted away from the family home and hence away from direct parental supervision. Here 'public' is that which is outside the family and is thus congruent with the French understanding. Indeed, it is not so much that the German situation differs in its *understanding* of the public as in its ability to *enact* it. There is the sociological stunting of the public in much of nineteenth-century German life. In one part, the present focus of the Critical school on the 'communicative competence' of ego-and-alter seems continuous with that tradition and, overemphasizing the early bourgeois public, depresses the value of the present public and strives to conceive of 'freedom' *apart* from the *public*. The freedom of the 'ideal speech situation' with its 'communicative competence' is not a consciousness *in* the mind, but is in the intimate communion of some abstract, timeless, and technologically innocent dyad.

Public and private thus develop together. To make matters 'public' means to open them even to those who are not known personally, to those who do not ordinarily come into one's sight and hearing. On the paradigmatic level, to make things public is to take them (or allow them to go) beyond the *family*, where all is in the sight and hearing of others, and which constructs a context for communication that may, in consequence, be cryptic, allusive, seemingly vague. The simultaneous growth of the public and private meant the development of a limit on the power of the public, the drawing of a firm boundary beyond which the public could not intrude. One could be a public being, with all the exhaustion and tension that generates, only because there was a place—the private sphere—to which one could retreat for repairs; a place in which one could find support for efforts that had failed to find public support. The private was a place where one could speak the silences of the public to a sympathetic and validating hearer.

Structurally speaking, this meant either (1) a patriarchical family system within which (sometimes) loved but commonly subjugated women and children helped the husband-father redefine his defeats, producing favorable private reassessment of unfavorable public verdicts; or, (2) it might also imply a system of well-informed and cultivated *hetaerae*, such as the ancient Greeks had perfected—the *hetaerae* were a force that helped maintain rational public discourse in ancient Greece—but which a puritanical bourgeoisie could not countenance; and (3) the development of close male friendships, as a framework of intimate intellectual expressivity, but which, also, premises (as it did both in ancient Greece and modern bourgeois society) a male-dominated family system. Thus the very strengthening of the sphere of the private is, in these conditions, necessary (not antithetical) to the strengthening of the public.

NOTES

1   M. Peckham, *Beyond the Tragic Vision* (New York: George Braziller, 1962), pp. 25–7.
2   Ibid., pp. 27–8.
3   Thus Engels remarks in a letter of 18 November 1892, written to August Bebel: 'Marx and I always agreed that we would never accept such a position [as editor of a party journal] and could only work for a journal financed independently of the party itself.' They regarded this as a 'barren position', inhibitive of their freedom of discussion.

7

defining media events

DANIEL DAYAN AND ELIHU KATZ

TELEVISION WITH A HALO

Even if it is true that most of television melds into some seamless 'supertext' (Browne, 1984), there are certain types of programs that demand and receive focussed attention (Liebes and Katz, 1990). Media events are one such genre. Unique to television, they differ markedly from the genres of the everynight.

Readers will have no trouble identifying the kinds of broadcasts we have in mind. Every nation has them. Our sample of a dozen of these events, internationally, includes the funerals of President Kennedy and Lord Louis Mountbatten, the royal wedding of Charles and Diana, the journeys of Pope John Paul II and Anwar el-Sadat, the debates of 1960 between John Kennedy and Richard Nixon, the Watergate hearings, the revolutionary changes of 1989 in Eastern Europe, the Olympics, and others. We have studied accounts and video recordings of these events, and have ourselves conducted empirical research into five of them.

The most obvious difference between media events and other formulas or genres of broadcasting is that they are, by definition, not routine. In fact, they are *interruptions* of routine; they intervene in the normal flow of broadcasting and our lives. Like the holidays that halt everyday routines, television events propose exceptional things to think about, to witness, and to do. Regular broadcasting is suspended and preempted as we are guided by a series of special announcements and preludes that transform daily life into something special and, upon the conclusion of the event, are guided back again. In the most chara-cteristic events, the interruption is *monopolistic*, in that all channels switch away from their regularly scheduled programming in order to turn to the great event, perhaps leaving a handful of independent stations outside the consensus. Broadcasting can hardly make a more dramatic announcement of the importance of what is about to happen.

Moreover, the happening is *live*. The events are transmitted as they occur, in real time; the French call this *en direct*. They are therefore unpredictable, at least in the sense that something can go wrong. Even the live broadcast of a symphony orches-tra contains this element of tension. Typically, these events are *organized outside the media*, and the media serve them in what Jakobson (1960) would call a phatic role in that, at least theoretically, the media only provide a channel for their transmis-sion. By 'outside' we mean both that the events take place outside the studio in what broadcasters call 'remote locations' and that the event is not usually initiated by the broadcasting organizations. This kind of connection, in real time, to a remote place—one having major importance to some central value of society, as we shall see—is credited with an exceptional value, by both broadcasters and their audiences (Vianello, 1986). Indeed, the complexity of mounting these broadcasts is such, or is thought to be such, that they are hailed as 'miracles' by the broadcasters, as much for their technological as for their ceremonial triumphs (Sorohan, 1979).

The organizers, typically, are public bodies with whom the media cooperate, such as governments, parliaments (congressional committees, for example), political parties (national conventions), international bodies (the Olympics committee), and the like. These organizers are well within the establishment. They are part of what Shils (1975)

First published in *Media Events*, D. Dayan & E. Katz, Harvard University Press (1992) as 'Defining Media Events', pp. 4–23.

calls the center. They stand for consensual values and they have the authority to command our attention. It is no surprise that the Woodstock festival—the landmark celebration of protesting youth in the Sixties—was distributed as a film rather than as a live television event.

[...]

These events are *preplanned*, announced and advertised in advance. Viewers—and, indeed, broadcasters—had only a few days' notice of the exact time of Sadat's arrival in Jerusalem; Irish television advertised the Pope's visit to Ireland a few weeks in advance (Sorohan, 1979); the 1984 Los Angeles Olympics were heralded for more than four years. Important for our purpose is that advance notice gives time for anticipation and preparation on the part of both broadcasters and audiences. There is an active period of looking forward, abetted by the promotional activity of the broadcasters.

The conjunction of *live* and *remote*, on the one hand, and *interrupted* but *preplanned*, on the other, takes us a considerable distance toward our definition of the genre. Note that live-and-remote excludes routine studio broadcasts that may originate live, as well as feature programs such as 'Roots' or 'Holocaust.' The addition of interruption excludes the evening news, while preplanned excludes major news events—such as the attempted assassination of a pope or a president, the nuclear accident at Three Mile Island, and, at first glance (but we shall reconsider this), the so-called television revolutions in Romania and Czechoslovakia. In other words, our corpus is limited to ceremonial occasions.

Returning to the elements of definition, we find that these broadcast events are presented with *reverence* and *ceremony*. The journalists who preside over them suspend their normally critical stance and treat their subject with respect, even awe. Garry Wills (1980) called media coverage of the Pope, including that of the written press, 'falling in love with love' and 'The Greatest Story Ever Told.' He was referring to the almost priestly role played by journalists on the occasion, and we find a reverential attitude characteristic of the genre as a whole. We have already noted that the broadcast transports us to some aspect of the sacred center of the society (Shils, 1975).

Of course, the very flow of ceremonial events is courtly and invites awe. There is the playing of the national anthem, the funereal beat of the drum corps, the diplomatic ceremony of being escorted from the plane, the rules of decorum in church and at Senate hearings. The point is that in media events television rarely intrudes: it interrupts only to identify the music being played or the name of the chief of protocol. It upholds the definition of the event by its organizers, explains the meaning of the symbols of the occasion, only rarely intervenes with analysis and almost never with criticism. Often advertising is suspended. There are variations: the live broadcast of Sadat's arrival in Jerusalem was treated differently by Israeli television than by the American networks, which had more explaining to do (Zelizer, 1981). While we shall have occasion to point out these differences, they are outweighed by the similarities.

Even when these programs address conflict—as they do—they celebrate not conflict but *reconciliation*. This is where they differ from the daily news events, where conflict is the inevitable subject. Often they are ceremonial efforts to redress conflict or to restore order or, more rarely, to institute change. They call for a cessation of hostilities, at least for a moment, as when the royal wedding halted the street fighting in Brixton and the terror in Northern Ireland. A more permanent truce followed the journeys of Sadat to Jerusalem and the Pope to Argentina. These events applaud the *voluntary* actions of great personalities. They celebrate what, on the whole, are establishment initiatives that are therefore unquestionably *hegemonic*. They are proclaimed *historic*.

These ceremonials *electrify very large audiences*—a nation, several nations, or the world. They are gripping, enthralling. They are characterized by a *norm of viewing* in which people tell each other that it is mandatory to view, that they must put all else aside. The unanimity of the networks in presenting the same event underlines the worth, even the obligation, of viewing. They cause viewers to *celebrate* the event by gathering before the television set in groups, rather than alone. Often the audience is given an active role in the celebration. Figuratively, at least, these events induce people to dress up, rather than dress down, to view television. These broadcasts *integrate* societies in a collective heartbeat and evoke a *renewal of loyalty* to the society and its legitimate authority.

[···]

WHY STUDY MEDIA EVENTS?

Implicit in this definition of the genre are answers to the question, Why study media events? The student of modern society—not just of television—will find a dozen or more powerful reasons for doing so. Let us spell them out.

1. The live broadcasting of these television events attracts the *largest audiences in the history of the world*. Lest we be misunderstood, we are talking about audiences as large as 500 million people attending to the same stimulus at the same time, at the moment of its emission. It is conceivable that there were cumulative audiences of this size prior to the electronic age—for the Bible, for example. Perhaps one might have been able to say that there were several hundred million people alive on earth who had read, or heard tell of, the same Book. But it was not until radio broadcasting—and home radio receivers— that simultaneity of exposure became possible. The enormity of this audience, together with the awareness by all of its enormity, is awesome. It is all the more awesome when one realizes that the subject of these broadcasts is ceremony, the sort which anthropologists would find familiar if it were not for the scale. Some of these ceremonies are so all-encompassing that there is nobody left to serve as out-group. 'We Are the World' is certainly the appropriate theme song for media events. To enthrall such a multitude is no mean feat; to enlist their assent defies all of the caveats of media-effects research.

2. The power of these events lies, first of all, in the rare *realization of the full potential of electronic media technology*. Students of media effects know that at most times and places this potential of radio and television is restricted by society. In principle, radio and television are capable of reaching everybody simultaneously and directly; their message, in other words, can be total, immediate, and unmediated. But this condition hardly ever obtains. Messages are multiple; audiences are selective; social networks intervene; diffusion takes time. On the occasion of media events, however, these intervening

mechanisms are suspended. Interpersonal networks and diffusion processes are active before and after the event, mobilizing attention to the event and fostering intense hermeneutic activity over its interpretation. But during the liminal moments, totality and simultaneity are unbound; organizers and broadcasters resonate together; competing channels merge into one; viewers present themselves at the same time and in every place. All eyes are fixed on the ceremonial center, through which each nuclear cell is connected to all the rest. Social integration of the highest order is thus achieved via mass communication. During these rare moments of intermission, society is both as atomized and as integrated as a mass-society theorist might ever imagine (Kornhauser, 1959).

3. Thus, the media have power not only to insert messages into social networks but to create the networks themselves—to atomize, to integrate, or otherwise to design social structure—at least momentarily. We have seen that *media events may create their own constituencies*. Egypt and Israel were united for Sadat's visit not only by images of the arrival of the leader of a theretofore hostile Arab nation, but by means of an ad hoc microwave link between the broadcasting systems of the two countries. Similarly, the royal wedding reunited the British Empire, and Third World nations joined the first two worlds for the Olympics. That media events can talk over and around conventional political geography reminds us that media technology is too often overlooked by students of media effects in their distrust of hypotheses of technological determinism. Papyrus and ancient empire, print and the Protestant Reformation, the newspaper and European nationalism, the telegraph and the economic integration of American markets, are links between attributes of communication technologies and social structures. They connect portability, reproducibility, linearity, simultaneity, on the one hand, to empire, church, nation, market, on the other.

By extension, it can be seen that the 'center' of these media-engendered social structures is not bound by geography either. In the case of media events, the center—on which all eyes are focussed—is the place where the organizer of a 'historic' ceremony joins with a skilled broadcaster to produce an event. In this sense, Britain is often the center of the world; one has only to compare the broadcast funeral of the assassinated Mountbatten with the broadcast funeral of the assassinated Sadat or India's Indira Gandhi to understand why.

4. Conquering not only space but time, media events have the power to declare a holiday, thus to play a part in the *civil religion*. Like religious holidays, major media events mean an interruption of routine, days off from work, norms of participation in ceremony and ritual, concentration on some central value, the experience of communitas and equality in one's immediate environment and of integration with a cultural center. The reverent tones of the ceremony, the dress and demeanor of those gathered in front of the set, the sense of communion with the mass of viewers, are all reminiscent of holy days. The ceremonial roles assumed by viewers—mourner, citizen, juror, sports fan—differentiate holiday viewing from everyday viewing and transform the nature of involvement with the medium. The secret of the effectiveness of these televised events, we believe, is in the roles which viewers bring with them from other institutions, and by means of which passive spectatorship gives way to ceremonial participation. The depth of this involvement, in turn, has relevance for the formation of public opinion and for institutions such as politics, religion, and leisure. In a further step, they enter the collective memory.

5. *Reality is uprooted* by media events. If an event originates in a particular location, that location is turned into a Hollywood set. The 'original' is only a studio. Thus conquering space in an even more fundamental way, television causes events to move off the ground and 'into the air.' The era of television events, therefore, may not only be one in which the reproduction is as important as the original, as Benjamin (1968) proposed, but also one in which the reproduction is more important than the original.

[...]

6. The process of producing these events and telling their story relates to the arts of television, journalism, and narration. Study of the rhetorical devices for communicating festivity, enlisting participation, and mobilizing consensus demands answers to the questions of how television manages to project ritual and ceremony in the two-dimensional space of spectacle. Essential to an understanding of these events—in addition to the readiness of the audience to assume ceremonial roles—is an analysis of how the story is framed, how interest is sustained, how the event aggregates endorsements, how the broadcasting staff is deployed to give depth to the event, how viewers interact with the screen, what tasks are assigned to the viewers. Media events give insight into the *aesthetics of television production*, together with an awareness of the nature of the contract that obtains between organizers and broadcasters.

The audience is aware of the genre of media events. We (and certain fellow researchers) recognize the constituent features of this rare but recurrent narrative form, and so do producers and viewers. The professional networks of producers buzz with information on the extraordinary mobilization of manpower, technology, aesthetics, and security arrangements required to mount a media event. At the same time, the networks of viewers carry word of the attitudes, rehearsals, and roles appropriate to their celebration. The expectation that certain events in the real world will be given media-events treatment is proof of public awareness of the genre. Israelis appealed to the High Court of Justice demanding that the war-crimes trial of John Demjanjuk be broadcast live.

7. Shades of *political spectacle*. Are media events, then, electronic incarnations of the staged events of revolutionary regimes and latter-day versions of the mass rallies of fascism? We think not, even if they might seem to be. It is true that media events find society in a vulnerable state as far as indoctrination is concerned: divided into nuclear cells of family and friends, disconnected from the institutions of work and voluntary association, eyes and ears focussed on the monopolistic message of the center, hearts prepared with room. This is reminiscent, mutatis mutandis, of the social structure of a disaster that strikes at night, or of a brainwashing regimen. The threshold of suggestibility is at its lowest the more isolated the individual is from others, the more accessible he or she is to the media, the more dependent the person is, the more the power to reward conformity or punish deviation is in the hands of the communicator.

Nevertheless, media events are not simply political manipulations. Broadcasters—in Western societies—are independent of, or at least legally differentiated from, government. They can, and sometimes do, say no to an establishment proposal to mount an event. Journalists need convincing before suspending professional disbelief, and even commercial interest sometimes acts as a buffer. Second, public approval is required for an event to succeed; official events cannot be imposed on the unwilling or unbelieving.

Third, individuals are not alone, not even alone with family, but in the company of others whom they invite to join in the thrill of an event and then to sit in judgment of it. Some societies provide public space for such discussion and interpretation; others provide only living rooms and telephones. Family friends, home, and living-room furniture are not a likely context for translating aroused emotion into collective political action. Fourth, the audience, too, has veto power. Oppositional readings are possible and hegemonic messages may be read upside down by some. These checks and balances filter the manipulative potential of media events and limit the vulnerability of mass audiences.

Still, the question of hegemonic abuse must be asked continually. Almost all of these events are establishment initiated, and only rarely, one suspects, do the broadcasters say no. Instead, journalists—sometimes reluctantly—put critical distance aside in favor of the reverent tones of presenters. Broadcasters thus share the consensual occasion with the organizers and satisfy the public—so we have hypothesized—that they are patriots after all.

8. When media events are seen as a *response to prior events* or to social crisis, the link to public opinion is evident. Thus, certain media events have a commemorative function, reminding us—as on anniversaries—of what deserves to be remembered. Others have a restorative function following social trauma. The most memorable of them have a transformative function inasmuch as they illustrate or enact possible solutions to social problems, sometimes engendering yet further events which actually 'change the world.' In the restorative domain, media events address social conflict—through emphasizing the rules (as in Contests), through praising the deeds of the great in whom charisma is invested (Conquests), and through celebrating consensual values (as do Coronations).

9. At the same time, certain events have an *intrinsically liberating* function, ideologically speaking; they serve a transformative function. However hegemonically sponsored, and however affirmatively read, they invite reexamination of the status quo and are a reminder that reality falls short of society's norm. Taking place in a liminal context, evoking that climate of intense reflexivity which Victor Turner characterized as the 'subjunctive mode of culture,' their publics exit the everyday world and experience a shattering of perceptions and certainties (Turner and Turner, 1978). Even if the situations in which they are immersed are short-lived and do not institutionalize new norms, at least they provoke critical awareness of the taken-for-granted and mental appraisal of alternative possibilities. They possess a normative dimension in the sense of displaying desirable alternatives, situations which 'ought to' exist but do not. These are previews, foretastes of the perhaps possible, fragments of a future in which the members of society are invited to spend a few hours or a few days. Activating latent aspirations, they offer a peek into utopia.

10. One wonders whether the media-events genre is not an expression of a *neo-romantic desire for heroic action* by great men followed by the spontaneity of mass action. In this sense, media events go beyond journalism in highlighting charisma and collective action, in defiance of established authority. The dissatisfaction with official inaction and bureaucratic ritualism, the belief in the power of the people to do it themselves, the yearning for leadership of stature—all characterize media events. We can join Sadat or the Pope and change the world; the people can unite to save Africans from starvation by supporting 'Live Aid.' The celebration of voluntarism—the willful resolve to take direct, simple, spontaneous, ostensibly nonideological action—underlies

media events, and may indeed constitute part of their attraction. The desire for spontaneous action, of course, recalls the erratic rhythm of arousal and repose predicted by the theory of mass society (Kornhauser, 1959). In the telling of media events, establishment heroes are made to appear more defiant then they actually were. But media events and collective action may be more than a dream. The escalation of interaction among public opinion, new or old leadership, and the mass media fanned the revolutions of Eastern Europe in the fall of 1989.

11. The *rhetoric of media events* is instructive, too, for what it reveals not only about the difference between democratic and totalitarian ceremonies, but also about the difference between journalism and social science, and between popular and academic history. The media events of democracies—the kind we consider here—are persuasive occasions, attempting to enlist mass support; they take the form of political contests or of the live broadcasting of heroic missions—those that invite the public to embrace heroes who have put their lives and reputations on the line in the cause of a proposed change. The ceremonies of totalitarian societies (Lane, 1981) are more commemorative. They also seek to enlist support, but for present and past; the First of May parade was a more characteristic media event in postwar Eastern Europe than a space shot. Terrorist events contrast with both of these in their display not of persuasion but of force, not of majesty but of disruption and provocation.

The rhetoric of media events contrasts—as does journalism, generally—with academic rhetoric in its emphasis on great individuals and apocalyptic events. Where social science sees long-run deterministic processes, journalism prefers heroes or villains who get up one morning resolved to change the world. Where academic historians see events as projective of underlying trends, journalists prefer a stroboscopic history which flashes dramatic events on and off the screen.

12. Media events *privilege the home*. This is where the 'historic' version of the event is on view, the one that will be entered into collective memory. Normally the home represents a retreat from the space of public deliberation, and television is blamed, perhaps rightly, for celebrating family and keeping people home (Newcomb, 1974). When it is argued that television presents society with the issues it has to face, the retort, 'narcotizing dysfunction'—that is, the false consciousness of involvement and participation—is quick to follow (Lazarsfeld and Merton, 1948). Yet the home may become a public space on the occasion of media events, a place where friends and family meet to share in both the ceremony and the deliberation that follows. Observational research needs to be done on the workings of these political 'salons.' Ironically, critical theorists, newly alert to the feminist movement, now see in the soap opera and other family programs an important 'site of gender struggle,' and their derision of the apolitical home is undergoing revision.

But there is more to politics than feminism, and we need empirical answers to the question of whether the home is transformed into a political space during and after a media event. In fact, we need basic research on who is home and when (in light of the growing number of one- and two-person households), who views with whom, who talks with whom, how opinion is formed, and how it is fed back to decision-makers. These everyday occasions of opinion formation should then be compared with media events. It is hard to believe, but nevertheless true, that the study of public opinion has become disconnected from the study of mass communication.

REFERENCES

Benjamin, W. (1968) 'The work of art in the age of mechanical reproduction', in Hannah Arendt (ed.), *Illuminations*. Trans. Harry Zohn. New York: Harcourt Brace Jovanovitch.

Browne, N. (1984) 'The political economy of television's supertext', *Quarterly Review of Film Studies*, 9 (3): 174–83.

Jakobson, R. (1960) 'Linguistics and poetics', in T. Sebeok (ed.), *Style in Language*. New York: Wiley.

Kornhauser, W. (1959) *The Politics of Mass Society*. New York: Free Press of Glencoe.

Lane, C. (1981) *The Rites of Ruler: Ritual in Industrial Society – the Soviet Case*. New York: Cambridge University Press.

Lazarsfeld, P.F. and Merton, R.K. (1948) 'Mass communication, popular taste and organized social action', in L. Bryson (ed.), *The Communication of Ideas*. New York: Harper and Row. pp. 95–118.

Liebes, T. and Katz, E. (1990) *The Export of Meaning: Cross-Cultural Readings of Dallas*. New York: Oxford University Press.

Newcomb, H. (1974) *TV: The Most Popular Art*. Garden City, NY: Anchor.

Shils, E. (1975) *Center and Periphery: Essays in Macrosociology*. Chicago, IL: Chicago University Press.

Sorohan, J. (1979) 'Pulling off a broadcasting miracle with nine weeks notice', *Irish Broadcasting Review*: 46–7.

Turner, V. and Turner, E. (1978) *Image and Pilgrimage in Christian Culture: Anthropological Perspectives*. New York: Columbia University Press.

Vianello, R. (1986) 'The power politics of live television', *Journal of Film and Video*, 37 (3): 26–40.

Wills, G. (1980) 'The greatest story ever told', *Columbia Journalism Review*, 18: 25–33.

Zelizer, B. (1981) 'The parameters of broadcast of Sadat's arrival in Jerusalem'. Master's thesis, Communications Institute, Hebrew University.

8

media and behavior – a missing link

JOSHUA MEYROWITZ

Almost everyone who has commented on electronic media, whether as casual observer or as scholar, whether in praise or in condemnation, has noted the ability of electronic media to bypass former limitations to communication. Electronic media have changed the significance of space, time, and physical barriers as communication variables. We can now speak to someone in Alaska while we are sunning in Florida, we can experience distant news events as they are happening or *reexperience* images, actions, and voices of those long dead, and we can sit in any room in any house in the country and get a close-up view of a football huddle.

Yet neither the pervasiveness of electronic media nor the common awareness of their seemingly miraculous capabilities has spawned widespread analysis of the impact of such new patterns of information flow on social behavior. The overwhelming majority of television studies conducted in the United States, for example, has followed the dominant tradition in research on earlier mass media and has focussed primarily on *message content*. The potentially different effects of different types of media are largely ignored.

The focus on media messages grew out of early concerns that propaganda transmitted through the mass press or over radio could have a nearly universal effect on different people and could lead to a mass or mob reaction. The general failure of researchers to demonstrate clear and direct effects of media content on social behavior, however, has led to many modifications in theory and approach over the last sixty years. The old 'hypodermic needle' theory (popular in the 1920s), which postulated a direct and universal response to a message stimulus, has been abandoned by almost all researchers. The tendency, instead, has been to put additional variables in between the stimulus and the behavioral response. Individual differences, group differences, the role of influential peers, stages of cognitive development, and other social and psychological variables are now seen as muting, changing, or negating the effects of the messages. But ultimately, the new models are still based on the concept of a response to a stimulus—the message.

No matter how many intervening factors are taken into account, the vast majority of media studies do not stray very far from the original assumptions that media 'inject' something into people and that the study of media effects, therefore, must begin with an analysis of *what* is injected. With a focus on media content, studies of television have examined what people watch, how much they watch, how they perceive and understand what they watch, and how what they watch affects what they later think and do. The concern is with media messages, not with the different patterns of information flow fostered by different media.

Even some studies that look beyond specific messages and claim to be studying the 'environment of television' often turn out to maintain the traditional content focus. George Gerbner's 'cultivation analysis,' for example, examines television as a symbolic environment in which we live, an environment that cultivates a specific world view.[1] But the aspect of the environment that most concerns Gerbner and his associates is the image of reality as portrayed in television messages. Cultivation analysis focusses on the ways in which the totality of media content creates a mythology about women, minorities, crime, and so forth, a mythology that subsequently shapes viewers' perceptions of and responses to their real environments.

First published in *No Sense of Place*, J. Meyrowitz, Oxford University Press (1985) as 'Missing Behavior: a missing link', pp. 13–23.

Disenchantment with the limited knowledge that has been generated by the various 'effects models' has led a number of researchers over the last two decades to embrace a different perspective: the 'uses and gratifications' approach. In this model, people, even young children, are not passive recipients of or reactors to media stimuli; rather they are purposive and conscious selectors of messages that fulfill personal needs (such as 'keeping in touch with important events' or 'escape from boredom'). This approach turns the old stimulus-response model on its head. It suggests that it is not so much that the media affect people, as it is that people selectively use, and thereby affect, the media. This model suggests, for example, that in order to survive, media such as newspapers or radio stations, or genres such as soap operas or situation comedies, must adapt to people's needs. While this approach rejects many of the old assumptions, it is very similar to the traditional studies in one key respect: its focus is still on message content. It asks why people choose the messages they choose and it examines the functions that various types of media messages fulfill. Even when these studies look at which medium people use in order to gratify a particular need, the concern is rarely focussed on the particular characteristics of different media of communication.

A number of political and economic critiques of media institutions (and of mainstream media research) appear to ask very different questions: Who controls the conduits of information in a society? And how are media institutions structured to further ideological, economic, and political ends? But even these critiques often return to a content focus by asking how control over media institutions determines what gets on television and what does not. These are legitimate and extremely important questions, but they, too, often overlook the particular natures of various media. There is little discussion of how the same political and economic system might be affected differently by different media, or of the difference between attempts to control the content of newspapers and attempts to control the content of television.

While all these examinations of media content have much social significance, it is surprising that other types of questions about media are so rarely asked. Indeed, most studies of the impact of media ignore the study of the media themselves. The content and control of television are studied the same way the content and control of newspapers, comics, movies, or novels have been studied. The medium itself is viewed as a neutral delivery system.

Scholars who study the effects of other types of technology have rarely taken such an exclusively narrow perspective. Few who have studied the effects of the Industrial Revolution, for example, would claim that the only important things to study are the specific goods that the new machines produced. Instead, historians, sociologists, and others have long noted that the important things to look at in the industrialization of society are the effects of the new means of production themselves on such variables as the balance of rural and urban life, division of labor, degree of social cohesion, structure of the family, value systems, perceptions of time and space, class structure, and rate of social change.

The research on television has been severely limited to the extent that it views electronic media merely as new links among pre-existing environments. That is, such research ignores the possibility that, once widely used, electronic media may create new social environments that reshape behavior in ways that go beyond the specific products delivered. While much concern with television, for example, has focussed on the effects of violent or sexist content on the behavior of children, there has been almost no attention paid to the possibility that different *ways* of communicating cultural content may lead to different social conceptions of 'childhood' and 'adulthood' or of 'masculinity' and 'femininity.' Like the person perusing the television listings in a newspaper, those who focus only on media content are more concerned with what media bring into the home than with the possibility that new media transform the home and other social spheres into new social environments with new patterns of social action, feeling, and belief.

To explore such a possibility further, we need to know at least two things: (1) how changes in media may change social environments, and (2) what effects a change in social environments may have on people's behavior. To come to a new understanding of the effects of electronic media on social behavior, [we need to fuse] together two theoretical perspectives that have dealt with these issues: (1) 'medium theory'—the historical and cross-cultural study of the different cultural environments created by different media of communication, and (2) 'situationism'—the exploration of the ways in which social behavior is shaped by and in 'social situations.' These two fields have developed independently of each other and the questions explored in them have traditionally been far removed from the main concerns of most mass communication researchers. Yet each of these areas of inquiry offers partial clues to a detailed theory of the effects of electronic media on social behavior. The remainder of this chapter summarizes these two perspectives, reviews their strengths and weaknesses, and describes the gap between them that needs to be filled before we can begin to see how changes in media may affect everyday social behavior.

MEDIA AS CULTURAL ENVIRONMENTS

While social scientists have focussed on the study of media messages, a few scholars in fields outside of communication, sociology, and psychology have taken a more historical and cross-cultural approach to communication technologies and have tried to call attention to the potential effects of media apart from the content they convey. I use the singular, '*medium* theory,' to describe this research because what makes it different from other 'media theory' is its focus on the particular characteristics of each individual medium.

The observations of the medium theorists are often incomplete and difficult to analyze and apply, yet they are of significance to this study because they suggest that media are not simply channels for conveying information between two or more environments, but rather environments in and of themselves. The best known and most controversial of these scholars are Harold Adams Innis and Herbert Marshall McLuhan.

A political economist by training, Harold Adams Innis extends the principles of economic monopolies to the study of information monopolies.[2] He sees control over communication media (such as a complex writing system controlled by a special class of priests) as a means through which social and political power is wielded. New media, however, can break old monopolies. The Medieval Church's monopoly over religious information (and thereby over salvation), argues Innis, was broken by the printing press. The printing press bypassed the Church's scribes and made the Bible and other religious materials widely available. The same content, the Bible, therefore, had different effects in different media.

Innis argues that different media have different potentialities for control. A medium that is in short supply or that requires a very special encoding or decoding skill is more likely to be exploited by an elite class that has the time and the resources to gain access to it. Conversely, a medium that is very accessible to the common person tends to democratize a culture.

Innis also claims that every medium of communication has a 'bias' either toward lasting a long time or toward traveling easily across great distances. He suggests that the bias of a culture's dominant medium affects the degree of the culture's stability and conservatism as well as the culture's ability to take over and govern large amounts of territory. 'Time biased' media such as stone hieroglyphics, he argues, lead to relatively small, stable societies. Stone carvings, after all, are difficult to revise frequently, and their limited mobility makes them poor means of keeping in touch with distant places. In contrast, messages on 'space biased' papyrus allowed the Romans to maintain a large empire with a centralized government that delegated authority to distant provinces. But papyrus also led to more social change and greater instability.

In *Empire and Communications* and *The Bias of Communication*, Innis rewrites the history of civilization as the history of communication media. He begins with the cradle of civilization in Mesopotamia and Egypt and ends with the British Empire and the Nazis.

Among the people Innis influenced before his death in 1952 was a scholar of medieval literature, Herbert Marshall McLuhan. To Innis's concepts of information monopolies and media 'biases,' McLuhan adds the notion of 'sensory balance.' He analyzes media as extensions of the human senses or processes, and he suggests that the use of different technologies affects the organization of the human senses.[3] McLuhan divides history into three major periods: oral, writing/printing, and electronic. Each period, according to McLuhan, is characterized by its own interplay of the senses and therefore by its own forms of thinking and communicating.

Oral societies, McLuhan argues, live in an 'ear culture' of simultaneity and circularity. The oral 'tribal' world of the ear is a 'closed society' of high interdependence and lack of individuality. People in oral cultures, according to McLuhan, have a mythic 'in-depth experience' where all the senses live in harmony. McLuhan claims that writing and, to a greater degree, print, break through the tribal balance, give oral people an 'eye for an ear,' make the sense of sight dominant, and distance people from sound, touch, and direct response. The break from total reliance on oral communication allows people to become more introspective, rational, and individualistic. Abstract thought develops. From the circular world of sound with its round huts and round villages, people move, over time, toward linear, cause-and-effect thinking, grid-like cities, and a one-thing-at-a-time and one-thing-after-another world that mimics the linear lines of writing and type. Allegiance to those one lives with and can hear, see, and touch shifts to allegiance to an abstract 'nation' or to a 'brotherhood' of a particular religion. To McLuhan, many of the characteristics of Western rationality and civilized behavior can be attributed to the influence of the printing press.

According to McLuhan, electronic media are like extensions of our nervous systems that embrace the planet. Electronic sensors return us to village-like encounters, but on a global scale. As a result of the widespread use of electronic media, everyone is involved in everyone else's business, and there is a decline in print-supported notions of delegated authority, nationalism, and linear thinking.

Innis and McLuhan are unique in terms of the breadth of history and culture they attempt to include within their frameworks. Other medium theorists, however, have looked at specific segments of the spectrum of media effects. J.C. Carothers, Jack Goody and Ian Watt, Eric Havelock, A.R. Luria, and Walter Ong have studied various aspects of the shift from orality to literacy.[4] They have argued convincingly (indeed, much more convincingly than Innis and McLuhan) that literacy and orality involve completely different modes of consciousness. They describe how the introduction of literacy affects social organization, the social definition of knowledge, the conception of the individual, and even types of mental illness.

H.J. Chaytor and Elizabeth Eisenstein have examined the significance of the shift from script to print.[5] Print is often thought of merely as the 'mechanization' of writing, yet Chaytor argues that the shift altered conceptions of literary style, created a new sense of 'authorship' and intellectual property, fostered the growth of nationalistic feelings, and modified the psychological interaction of words and thought. Eisenstein echoes many of these themes and presents an enormous amount of evidence and many cogent analyses to support the argument that the printing press revolutionized Western Europe by fostering the Reformation and the growth of modern science.

Walter Ong, Edmund Carpenter, Tony Schwartz, and Daniel Boorstin have looked at the effects of electronic media on thinking patterns and social organization.[6] Schwartz and Carpenter are generally McLuhanesque in content, method, and style. Ong and Boorstin, however, present more traditional scholarly analyses that support McLuhan's basic arguments but also go beyond them. Ong describes the similarities and differences between the 'primary orality' of preliterate societies and the 'secondary orality' that results from the introduction of electronic media into literate societies. He looks at the spiritual and psychological significance of the return of 'the word' in an electronic form. Boorstin describes how new media 'mass-produce the moment,' make experience 'repeatable,' and join many other recent technological inventions in 'leveling times and places.' Boorstin also compares and contrasts political revolutions with technological revolutions and discusses the impact of new technologies, including electronic media, on our conceptions of nationality, history, and progress.

The medium theorists do not suggest that the means of communication *wholly* shape culture and personality, but they argue that changes in communication patterns are one very important contributant to social change and one that has generally been over-looked. Their analyses of media and social change also suggest that the transformations are not sudden or complete. There is always a 'cultural lag,' in William Ogburn's words,[7] in which parts of the culture are ahead of the rest. Homer's successors, for example, had the benefit of a writing system to help them compose and organize poems, but they continued to write for an audience that listened to, rather than read, their poems, and they still saw widespread memorization of their works as their chance for immortality.

Further, although new media are seen within these theories as transforming culture and modes of consciousness, they do so by *adding* to the spectrum of communication forms, rather than by destroying old means of communicating. Thus, writing did not destroy oral discourse, but it changed the function of speech and of individual memory. Similarly, television has not eliminated reading and writing, nor has the telephone eliminated letter writing. Yet, at the same time, the addition of a new medium to a culture alters the functions, significance, and effects of earlier media. The telephone, for example, has surely affected the function and frequency of letter writing. Indeed, historians and biographers are now bemoaning the decline in personal correspondence and the resulting loss of a significant personal and social record. There is a clear analogy here to the industrialization of society, which had a great impact on social organization and labor, and ended 'agricultural' forms of society, but without destroying our fundamental dependence on the production of food. The important underlying principle is firmly rooted in systems theory and ecology: when a new factor is added to an old environment, we do not get the old environment plus the new factor, we get a new environment. The extent of the 'newness' depends, of course, on how much the new factor alters significant forces in the old system, but the new environment is always more than the sum of its parts.

Put simply, the medium theorists are arguing that the form in which people communicate has an impact beyond the choice of specific messages. They do not deny the significance of message choice *within* a cultural milieu. (McLuhan himself, for example, expressed a clear preference for certain programs, including '60 Minutes,' saying, 'There are certain things I just don't like to miss that's all'; as for other programs, such as 'Star Trek,' he added, 'I don't give a damn.') But these theorists are primarily interested in a higher level analysis—a cross-cultural and historical perspective.

This type of analysis in other fields is rarely controversial. If a political historian were to argue that it often matters less what the leader of a country says in his or her speeches than it matters whether the leader is an elected official in a democracy or a monarch who has inherited a throne, few would blink an eye. And while a barefoot peasant might prefer to get a pair of shoes rather than a hammer—regardless of whether the shoes and hammer are hand-made or mass-produced—an economic historian will note the ways in which a shift from manual to mechanical production of all goods affects many aspects of the society, including the proportion of the population that is barefoot.

Yet for a number of reasons, the medium theory perspective has failed to penetrate deeply into scholarly activity or the popular consciousness. For one thing, much of the funding for media research is generated from sources interested in the administration of existing media institutions or in the formation of public policy concerning media regulation and control. Further, the search—especially in the United States—for 'scientific' evidence of media effects has led most researchers to focus on collecting data that can be quantified and analyzed statistically. Since the medium theorists' comparisons and contrasts of different media environments do not have much to say about how to run or regulate media *within* a specific technological environment, and since it is difficult, if not impossible, to 'test' the medium theorists' broad historical and cultural theories through surveys, direct observation, or experiments, most media research has focussed on much narrower questions. Similarly, one of the reasons the medium theorists have not attracted much long-term popular enthusiasm is that their attempts to avoid saying that one form of communication is 'better' or 'worse' than another sharply contrasts with many popular views such as the belief that reading books is inherently good and watching television is inherently bad.

Furthermore, there is a general tendency for people, including many scholars and researchers, to ignore or even deny the effects of the invisible environments of media simply because they are invisible. It is ironic that we often distinguish ourselves from the beasts in terms of our ability to communicate, yet many of us are very resistant to considering the impact of significant shifts in the means through which we communicate. Most people are much more willing to accept the widespread social and psychological effects of physical and material causes (such as industrialization, new means of transportation, drought, war, and economic depression) than they are willing to consider informational contributants to social change. It is generally simpler, for example, for people to consider the impact of a ten percent rise in gasoline prices than it is for them to consider the impact of a tenfold increase in the capacity of computer memory chips. Material changes are concrete and imaginable; informational changes seem very abstract and mystical. And even within informational changes, people are more likely to grasp onto those aspects of the information environment that are most visible: particular messages. Yet by concentrating popular and scholarly attention primarily on message content, our approach is often not that different from a hypothetical attempt to grasp the impact of the automobile by ignoring the issue of new patterns of travel and by focussing instead on a detailed examination of the names and faces of passengers.

Although many people are resistant to the types of claims made by the medium theorists, a number of the problems with the acceptance and further study of medium effects grow out of the limitations of the medium theory works themselves. Innis and McLuhan, for example, make broad claims concerning the impact of various media, but these claims lack the development of clear, linear arguments and evidence. Their books seem to be written in the midst of revelations, with both the excitement and the impatience caused by blinding flashes of insight. They run past details and skip over logical arguments as if they are certain that their widely spaced footsteps will lead the reader to the same conclusions.

[...]

But perhaps the greatest problem with the medium theory works is that ultimately they provide more of a *perspective* for studying the effects of media on behavior than they present a detailed *theory*. The insights, observations, and evidence they collect point to the need to study media environments in addition to studying media messages, but they do not form a clear set of propositions to explain the means through which media reshape specific behaviors. McLuhan's discussion of sensory balance is rich in insights and intuitions that ring true; Ong adds stong evidence concerning the ideas of a shifting sensorium and changing modes of consciousness. But discussions of 'media biases,' 'sensory balance,' and 'new modes of consciousness' are very abstract. They identify important processes, but in the end, they mystify the effects of media even as they seem to clarify them. How, exactly, does a new sensorium or a new mode of consciousness affect one's behavior? Eisenstein offers a concrete analysis of the effects of the new diffusion of information caused by the printing press. Yet her detailed discussion of the Reformation and the Scientific Revolution does not offer us much information about the ways in which media, *in general*, affect culture, nor even about the specific effects of the printing press on the behavior of individuals.

Finally, perhaps because environments are most visible when one is outside of them, the studies on the effects of writing and print have tended to be much more detailed and scholarly than the studies of electronic media. McLuhan's difficult mosaics remain the richest source of hypotheses that relate specifically to the telephone, radio, and television. Ultimately, the medium theory literature offers little competition for the mainstream television content studies in terms of concrete, comprehensible effects of electronic media on *everyday social behavior*.

Part of what is missing from the medium theory studies is any real attempt to link an analysis of media characteristics with an analysis of the structure and dynamics of everyday social interaction. Most people would acknowledge that new media lead to new links among people and places, new ways of storing and retrieving social information. But a question that remains unanswered is: Why and how do technologies that merely create new *connections* among people and places lead to any fundamental shift in the structure of society or in social behavior? One potential answer to this question rests in the ways in which *disconnectedness*—the separation of social situations and interactions—shapes social reality.

NOTES

1   G. Gerbner and L. Gross, 'Living with television: the violence profile', *Journal of Communication*, 26 (2) (1976), pp. 173–99.

2   H.A. Innis, *The Bias of Communications* (Toronto: University of Toronto Press, 1951); *Empire and Communications* (Oxford: Clarendon Press, 1950).

3   M. McLuhan, *The Gutenberg Galaxy* (Toronto: University of Toronto Press, 1962); *Understanding Media: The Extensions of Man* (Toronto: Toronto University Press, 1964).

4   J.C. Carothers, 'Culture, psychiatry and the written word', *Psychiatry*, 22 (1959), pp. 307–20; A. Luria, *Cognitive Development: Its Cultural and Social Foundations* (Cambridge, MA: Harvard University Press, 1976); J. Goody and I. Watt, 'The consequences of literacy', *Comparative Studies in Society and History*, 5 (1963), pp. 304–45; E. Havelock, *A Preface to Plato* (Cambridge, MA: Harvard University Press, 1973); W. Ong, *Orality and Literacy: The Technology of the Word* (New York: Methuen, 1982).

5   H.J. Chaytor, *From Script to Print* (London: Sidgwick and Jackson, 1945/1966); E. Eisenstein, *The Printing Press as an Agent of Change*, 2 vols (New York: Cambridge University Press, 1979).

6   D.J. Boorstin, *The Image* (New York: Atheneum, 1962); E. Carpenter, *Oh What a Blow that Phantom Gave Me* (New York: Ballantine, 1973); T. Schwartz, *The Responsive Chord* (Garden City, NY: Anchor, 1974).

7   W.F. Ogburn, *On Culture and Social Change: Selected Papers*. Ed. O.D. Duncan (Chicago, IL: University of Chicago Press, 1964).

IV

FROM OLD TO NEW MEDIA

The issue of interaction between media and society raised in the Introduction to Part III also arises when considering the consequences of the latest forms of communication technology, based on computers, satellites and telecommunications. There are two main reasons why this topic should be dealt with in a reader on mass communication theory, given that new media are usually distinguished by their 'non-mass' character. One is the need to face up to the growing potential obsolescence of a body of media theory based on the fundamental assumption of a 'mass character', as outlined in Part I.

Secondly, there is an increasing acceptance of the view that we are gradually moving into a form of society that can be described as an 'information society', in which activities and relationships are increasingly mediated through communication networks, and power is based on control of these networks and the information and cultural products that flow through them. New thinking edges somewhat more in the direction of giving some primacy of social effect to communication technology, but the basic premise of an interaction between communication technology and social forms and trends remains unaffected. New conditions, however, call for a joint analysis of 'new media' at the level of structure (systems and ownership) and individual use.

At the time of writing (and it will remain the case for some time to come), it is still unclear how much and what kind of change will be brought about by the take-up of new media potential. The staying power of existing media institutions is already being demonstrated by the growing success of media industries in absorbing the new media and incorporating them into multi-media strategies with global extension. Mass communication still seems to flourish (see the excerpt from Neuman, Chapter 34 in Part IX), and many of the innovative uses of new technology for multiple and unbounded intercommunication and opportunities to 'publish' appear, as time goes on, to be frequently marginalized or simply marginal.

The items chosen for this section mainly focus on conceptual issues and on early (thus contemporary) formulations of the significance of new media for individuals and society. The earliest piece, by Bordewijk and van Kaam (Chapter 9) offers a conceptual analysis of basic communication patterns, with telecommunications supporting a decisive shift from older 'centre-peripheral' flows (the essence of mass communication) to interactive and consultative patterns in which control shifts from centre to periphery (individual users). Morris and Ogan (Chapter 11) explore what this might mean for the experience of the Internet user conceived as an 'audience member'. The extent to which and the manner in which 'new media' are *new*, as so widely assumed, are explored by Rice (Chapter 10), and Slevin (Chapter 12) considers the implication for society of interactive communication in the light of Thompson's (1995) and Giddens's sociological theories of media and society.

This section has been compiled in the belief that there are important changes underway in society in which communications are deeply implicated, and that there is something intrinsically new about technologies that undermine monopolies of property and skills in publication and extend opportunities for communicative contact and experience. It also recognizes that innovative potential is often suppressed or controlled (Winston, 1986). It would also be unwise to forget the apparent lesson of communication history that new technologies rarely, if ever, replace existing forms or destroy institutions, but instead bring about adaptation of systems and behaviour with outcomes of increasing complexity for the blueprint of social communication, in line with ideas of an 'information' or 'network' society.

REFERENCES

Thompson, J.B. (1995) *The Media and Modernity*. Cambridge: Polity Press.
Winston, B. (1986) *Misunderstanding Media*. Cambridge, MA: Harvard University Press.

9

towards a new classification of tele-information services

JAN L. BORDEWIJK AND BEN VAN KAAM

Tele-information systems, based on an alliance of digital telecommunication and computer technology, will play an increasingly important role in inter-human communications. They are in fact ready to enter almost every area of human communication activity.

As a consequence the spread of knowledge, the cornerstone of democracy, seems to be headed towards a time of flourishing, but this optimistic expectation reflects only one side of the coin. The reverse side tells us that the penetration of technology in human information paths, on such a large scale as we witness today, can only succeed thanks to a huge information services industry. Such an industry, providing information-oriented products as well as technical facilities and employing many, many people, saddles us with a new concern: its own power. In order to avoid the risk of an Orwellian scenario, society should at least have at its disposal a clear and simple picture of what the power positions and relations are on the vulnerable terrain of human communication. We need some sort of classification of tele-information services with respect to their social role. The often intuitively applied classification by reference to their technical properties is untrustworthy and will cause more and more confusion as multifunction networks and terminal equipment replace the present dedicated systems.

This classification should be replaced by one based on social power relations. A classification in terms of idealized information traffic patterns provides a logical and unambiguous alternative. It provides a solution that harks back to the time when no technical devices were available, so that there was no danger of mistaking incidental technical designs for guidelines as to the character of the communication. It can moreover be defined independently both of the form of presentation and of the information content.

We start with a detailed description of the four definable information traffic patterns.

First published in *Intermedia 14, 1*, International Institute of Communications (1986) as 'Towards a New Classification of Tele-Information Services', pp. 16–21.

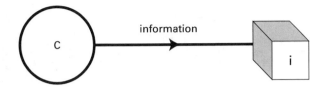

FIGURE 9.1   Allocution: information flow from service centre (C) to individual consumer (i)

ALLOCUTION

Let us first look at the situation that occurs when a single human being, called C (centre), addresses another person called i (individual) (Figure 9.1).

When the information flow is always in the same direction, we have to assume that C has at his or her disposal an unlimited amount of information, possibly of a specialist nature. We will call C the 'information services provider' and i an 'information services consumer'. This formulation has the twofold advantage of including technical facilities and leaving open the direction of the information flow.

This situation resembles that of a master–slave relationship, or general–soldier, teacher–pupil etc. If we assume that the master owns more than one slave, the general commands more than one soldier and so on, we obtain a pattern in which C is the central leader and i. i_1, i_2 etc. are the individual followers (Figure 9.2).

In practical situations the followers will often be able to provide a certain amount of feedback, be it only the shuffling of feet, depending on the harshness of the regime. The figures show idealized situations without any sign of feedback. We will say that they follow an 'idealized information traffic pattern'.

This pattern will be labelled: 'allocution', from the Latin word 'allocutio' (the address of a Roman general to his troops, and afterwards a special address of the pope to his cardinals). 'Allocution' is more appropriate than the term formerly used, 'distribution', because, inter alia, information cannot be 'cut into pieces' distributed among a number of consumers. In fact every participating consumer receives the same information and the information store at the centre never becomes empty!

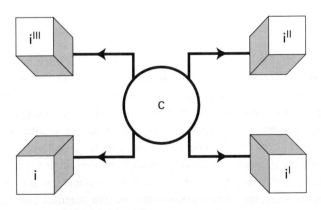

FIGURE 9.2   Allocution: general pattern

If we refrain from a particular presentation form or a particular information content, the second figure can be used as a stylized representation of many other situations. For example, C might represent a broadcasting organization and the i's the listeners and viewers. C can also represent a stage performance and the i's the public. In an extreme case C could even represent a drowning person and the i's the passers by.

Characteriztic of the 'social status' of allocution is that C is the owner of the information and alone decides what part of the information stock will be 'handed over' and when. The 'destinations' receive the information simultaneously at a normal human perception rate. The simultaneous-perception effect often plays an important role.

All the 'power' is clearly concentrated in C. The i's have none at all. The term 'power' in this connection should not be taken too literally. It should be understood as 'being entitled to some kind of remuneration'. This can be of a financial nature, but can also take the form of obedience, respect, care, help etc. In many cases C will also provide technical facilities as part of the total information service.

A preliminary definition of allocution that covers both the situations described above could run: *the issue of information by an information service centre under programmatic control of the centre itself.*

CONVERSATION

If two terminals, both representing an average human information services consumer, exchange information, we obtain a different picture. We assume that the ownership of the information as well as the information handling capacities are divided equally between the two terminals. We will name the pattern obtained, independent of the form of presentation and the information content, 'conversation' (Figure 9.3). Instead of speech, the information exchanged could just as well be text, written or printed on a sheet of paper or any other carrier, or moving pictures, and could deal with any subject.

The idealized conversation pattern shows a balance of power. In many practical situations, however, the 'information levels' of two partners will not be equal. We shall encounter applications that are completely asymmetric. The number of partners in a conversation need not be restricted to two, but above about six the need for a chairman

FIGURE 9.3   Conversation: information flow between individual consumers

is felt. The chairman has to coordinate and allocate speaking time. One arrives more or less at a situation of sequential allocation. In a conversation situation people do not normally pay one another for the information supplied. They only pay for the use of the means of transport (telephone bill, postage etc.).

One might wonder whether conversation by telephone, which allows almost instantaneous reaction, and conversation by telex or mail should be covered by the same pattern. Our view is that they belong together because the principal social and legal desiderata connected with conversation in a democracy hold equally for telephone and mail services. No state interference and protection of privacy are the two conditions that consumers will demand for both services. The close connection between the two can further be illustrated by observing that modern hybrid services such as voicegram and voicemail are being introduced, combining the presentation form of telephone and the response times of mail.

The conversation pattern is characterized by the property that the ownership of the information as well as the choice of subject and time of information exchange rest in the hands of information service consumers i. This includes a kind of 'self-conversation', in which one could include meditation, but also 'communication' with a personal (electronic) file, i.e. all the information stored for personal use.

If such personal utterances are meant to be made public in some way or another the person (a speaker, an author or a composer) has changed role, is acting as a C-terminal involved in 'allocution' or in a pattern dealt with later under the title of 'consultation'.

In a more general picture of the conversation pattern, the connection between i and i_1 passes an information service centre C (Figure 9.4).

In a classic telephone connection C represents a technical facility: a telephone exchange or a cascade of telephone exchanges needed for the routing of the telephone call, and does not participate as an information terminal. In a direct conversation between two people of different tongues, C could be an interpreter, providing content-oriented services also. In a future world telephone system C could be an (automatic) translation or correction centre. For purposes of data transmission nowadays C could be a packet-switching transmission system in which the data to be transported from different origins and with different destinations are arranged so that transport cost is minimized. These last examples belong to the classes of value-added services or networks.

Generally C can handle more than one conversation-connection, leading to a more general configuration (Figure 9.5).

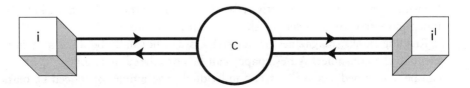

FIGURE 9.4   Conversation via centre C

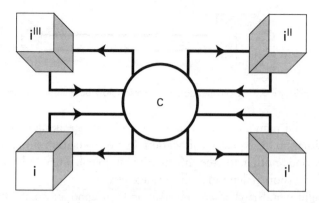

FIGURE 9.5   Conversation: general pattern

A preliminary definition of conversation could run: *the issue of information by information services consumer(s) under programmatic control of the consumer(s) themselves.*

CONSULTATION

If an information service centre C (Figure 9.6) only delivers information upon the request (dotted line) of an information service consumer i, there is a markedly different power relationship from those considered above. C is the owner of a large (ideally infinite) amount of information, but the i-terminal decides at what time and on which subject information should be delivered.

In a practical approximation to this idealized situation the i-terminal could be a person who consults a human memory when phoning a doctor or seeing a lawyer, but it could also be a person consulting an encyclopedia, a dictionary or an electronic memory. Consultation requires more activity by the consumer than allocution, but also grants much more freedom in selecting the information required.

Reading books, magazines or newspapers can normally be done at a time convenient to the consumer. A newspaper can be considered as a collection of items that can be 'consumed' according to an individual programme, or indeed be marked as a databank refreshed daily (rather than a dynamic one). Reading is not always consultative.

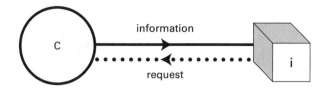

FIGURE 9.6   Consultation

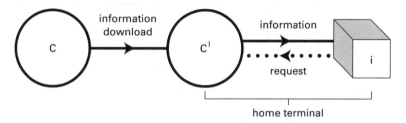

FIGURE 9.7   Virtual consultation centre C^1 (e.g. teletext terminal)

A good example of 'allocutive reading' can be found in television news magazines for the deaf, with pages broadcast at a standard speed.

Consultation is not restricted to graphic or pictorial information. Examples of voice consultation are found in the telephone enquiry systems for time, weather, traffic conditions or medical information. They are all examples of tele-consultation, like tele-text and some videotex applications.

The objection is often made that teletext is not such a good example because the (dotted) request line is missing. In fact, it is present but is very short. The trick with tele-text is that the whole information stock of C is periodically offered to the receiving equipment of the consumer. In this way the consumer i disposes of a virtual service centre C_1 within the terminal (Figure 9.7). (In some configurations C_1 is housed in the head-end of a cable television system.)

In case the storage capacity of C_1 is the same as that of C, a realiztic proposition nowadays, the waiting time will be reduced practically to zero. A consultation centre

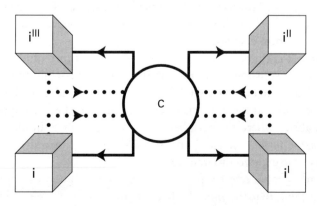

FIGURE 9.8   Consultation: general pattern

can generally be interrogated by several consumers, giving a more complex configuration (Figure 9.8).

A preliminary definition of consultation could run: *the issue of information by an information service provider under programmatic control of an information service consumer.* This definition also embraces the special case in which a consumer requests information to be delivered to another consumer or consumers.

REGISTRATION

If the information flow directions are reversed, we obtain a pattern that we shall call 'registration'. In this pattern the centre no longer has the task of issuing information, but of collecting it. Modern tele-applications such as tele-opinion polling, tele-metering, tele-alarm, earth observation from satellites and so on can be conceived, but simple well known services like civil registration centres or news agencies follow a good approximation of this pattern.

A second task of such a centre can be to process the incoming information (rearranging, translation or mathematical operation). The purpose of the processing can be to prepare a publication along either an allocutive or a consultative pattern. But then the centre is changing its role.

Registration is characterized by the fact that the information is owned by the information service consumers, located at the periphery, while the programme (opening hours for each subject!) is controlled by C, the provider of the information service. (It could be said that the centre is consulting the periphery, as opposed to the situation described above where the periphery consults the centre. In older work[1] we therefore used the same term 'consultation' for both patterns. In order to avoid confusion we now propose using two different terms.)

Sometimes people reject a fire alarm service as a good example of the registration pattern, arguing that the time the fire sets in is not determined by C. But the characterization given does not claim so: the centre C determines only at what time(s) it will

TABLE 9.1 Pattern matrix

	Information issue by centre	Information issue by consumer
Programme control by centre	Allocution	Registration
Programme control by consumer	Consultation	Conversation

be interested in which subject. A good fire alarm service will be on the alert 24 hours a day, ready for the message 'fire' as well as the message 'no fire'.

A preliminary definition of registration could run: *the issue of information by an information service consumer under the programmatic control of an information service centre.*

We are now in a position to combine the preliminary definitions of the four idealized information traffic patterns: allocution, conversation, consultation and registration, into a single matrix definition (Table 9.1). In order to obtain this general matrix definition, we only have to bear in mind that the four preliminary definitions represent exactly the four different combinations of answers to the following two questions:

- is the owner of the information issued an information service providing centre, or an individual information service consumer?
- is the programme of information issue controlled by an information service providing centre C, or by an individual information service consumer?

Each element of the matrix can comprise a group of different interconnection modes. The members of such a group of interconnection modes all follow the same idealized information traffic pattern. This is more than a flow diagram. It informs us not only about the routes and directions of an information flow, but also about the responsibilities of the information terminals involved. That is why we have a slight preference for the expression 'traffic pattern' over 'flow pattern'.

The pattern matrix can serve as a basis in drawing up a legal framework. It does not of course solve the problem of whether, how or to what extent the interests of operators and clients of tele-information systems should be protected by law. That is a matter for political discussion and decision. But it must be expected that for all services which follow one and the same information traffic pattern, similar action will be considered relevant because the four patterns refer to four mutually exclusive social power relations that differ from one another in principle.

It should not be inferred that certain patterns may not have some regulatory aspects in common. As Jens Arnbak[2] has pointed out, we may even expect that possible laws adopted for one pattern will overlap with those for 'neighbouring' patterns:

- copyright issues are generally confined to the lefthand column of the matrix
- the protection of privacy is relevant to the righthand column
- formal public access and control procedures will usually be needed or appropriate in the upper row
- the free flow of information is generally served by minimizing state interference in services belonging in the lower row.

In this way each element of the matrix lies at the crossing of two lines of desiderata. The systematic approach thus obtained immediately clarifies the social and legal position of old and new information services, which follow sufficiently closely one of the four idealized information traffic patterns.

Many practical information services, however, do not follow a single pattern to the total exclusion of the others. Moreover, in daily life many centres will operate simultaneously, functioning and competing within a complex communication structure with lots of cross-connections, in which the idealized information traffic patterns will only play the role of building blocks. Therefore, in application of the foregoing theory, we shall deal with some multi-pattern services, the development of multi-pattern networks and the relation between the two phenomena.

From these examples it will, we hope, become clear how important it is to classify information services as correctly as possible according to their social and, from that standpoint, their legal position, and not according to the incident technology that they employ, their form of presentation or their information content.

MULTI-PATTERN SERVICES

The matrix definition offers a sharp demarcation between the four areas of 'idealized information services'. The borderlines between actual (tele-) information services will not always be so clear cut. Some information services are typical of a multi-pattern type, i.e. that several patterns occur almost simultaneously. Sometimes a number of patterns will occur in alternation. In other situations the presence of more than one provider centre plays a role.

Broadcasting presents a good approximation to an idealized allocution pattern. But for the viewer it makes all the difference whether there is a large group of TV channels from different centres with a broad range of programmes, or whether choice is restricted to one or two channels of similar quality.

If, moreover, in the first case some of the channels carry programmes that are frequently repeated, so that the consumer has a certain influence on the time of 'consumption', we can say that the service shows consultative features.

Another example of a diffuse pattern is encountered when a talented (political) orator in a direct address transforms his 'allocution' more or less into 'registration' by only forwarding rhetorical questions and after each sentence waiting for applause.

Conversely, a consultation service may possess strong allocutive features. A newspaper, for example, can be considered as a kind of databank that is consulted by each reader according to a personal programme. But the fact that so many people are confronted with centrally selected headlines reduces the influence of the consumer considerably.

Another instructive example can be found in the telephone service. Although it offers an almost ideal example of the conversation pattern, we have to admit that two other patterns also play a role. A telephone call is initiated by dialling a number. That number has to be found by 'consultation', be it from a directory, a voice-based enquiry service or an electronic directory. At the end of the call, the distance and duration have to be 'registered' in order to enable the telephone service provider to recover charges.

As a consequence, a telephone service provider also has to pay heed to copyright issues and registration regulations. If a connection with a mobile station has to be built up, the service provider is involved in a further privacy problem: the approximate position of the mobile station has to be known to him.

In this case it is clear that conversation is the main or primary pattern and that consultation and registration play a secondary role. But telephone systems lend themselves to other patterns than conversation alone. The technical properties are not very pattern-selective.

Finally, we might refer to an age-old information service that is typically multi-pattern in character: education. A teacher lecturing is clearly operating in allocution mode. But pupils putting questions to their teacher or studying books are working in consultation mode. A teacher trying to measure the progress of pupils by subjecting them to examination applies a registration mode. And pupils discussing the subject matter among themselves follow a conversation mode. The four modes are roughly of the same weight. This implies that for a complete tele-education system a multi-pattern network is inevitable, and contains a warning for those broadcasters who believe that tele-education is their exclusive domain.

MULTI-PATTERN NETWORKS

As long as the recognized specialists in certain kinds of tele-information services operate their own strongly differing technical systems, there exists no great need for a new classification of tele-information services. And that has been the situation up to the present day: telephone and broadcasting use their own service-dedicated technical solutions.

But today a strong trend towards the setting up of multifunctional, or perhaps better, multi-pattern networks is also making itself felt. European telephone administrations are working hand in hand in order to unite telephone, telex and data networks into one so-called integrated services digital network (ISDN), to be implemented in the coming decade. Several studies have been started on the possible coupling of local wideband networks (cable TV, local area networks) with the ISDN. Even satellite communication will play a role in this context.

This means that it will become increasingly difficult to characterize a tele-information service on the basis of the technical appearance of the network or terminal equipment used. We may expect more and more multi-pattern terminal equipment to appear on the market. Already existing networks originally designed for only one of the patterns are provisionally used for others. The same applies to terminal equipment. Teletext and videotex are two well known examples of an alternative use of video equipment, which leads to misunderstanding and disputes between broadcasting and PTT monopolies.

Here we touch upon the very reason to review our classification system. With teletext as well as with videotex we run the risk that technology plays the role of the Trojan horse.

Neither consultation nor registration services need technical transport systems and terminal equipment of a completely new character. They differ strongly from the classic telephone and broadcasting services but largely in a non-technical sense. Consultation, for example, is the 'bread and butter line' for press and other publishers who disclose information stored on paper or other 'artificial memories'. It seems not illogical that the legislation in existence for these publishing activities will also be applicable to tele-consultation services. To subject these services to telephone or broadcasting regulation on the grounds that they make use of similar networks and terminal equipment would be a grave mistake.

The analysis presented in this paper rests on social power relations but is in fact politically neutral. No political programme of action can be derived from the pattern theory. It improves insight and facilitates a more systematic approach to legislation. It contains no prescriptions for specific laws.

It should be realized, however, that the fact that the classification in traffic patterns does not depend on technological properties does not imply that technical developments and technical management may not exercise a certain influence on the relative balance of the four different patterns. The history of the art of printing proves that such influences can even be very marked. Governments can greatly influence specific activities by promoting or retarding certain technical developments, as with cable television and the restrictions often placed on alternative use of these networks.

The pattern theory provides the yardstick by which to check whether governments follow a pattern-neutral course or not. It is obvious that under a dictatorial regime such a neutral course will not be found. Adolf Hitler, for example, had a notorious dislike for books, in fact, for consultation. He even made apologies for writing *Mein Kampf*. And of course he loved allocution, be it by personal address, by radio or by means of the cinema.

But we should not conclude this reflection on a downbeat. For each example of abuse of the power position inevitably connected with a centre of allocution we can find numerous cases in which allocution is put forth as a means of reaching the masses with messages of understanding and tolerance.

International broadcasting in particular bears a great responsibility in this respect and should be constantly on the look-out for positive opportunities. Yet the main ambition of broadcasters should perhaps be to resist any temptation to acquire some kind of hegemony over the other patterns.

NOTES

1 J.L. Bordewijk, 'The combined use of CATV and telephone networks for pur-
    poses of education and consultation', in *Two-Way Cable Television*, Ed.
    W. Kaiser et al. (Heidelberg: Springer, 1997).
2 J.C. Arnbak, 'Potential impacts of modern communication technology on data
    protection', Document CJ-PD(85)4 (Council of Europe, Strasbourg, 17 April
    1985).

10

artifacts and paradoxes in new media

RONALD E. RICE

W hat are some of the ways that new media differ from traditional media (including face-to-face) in their configurations of constraints and processes available to those who wish to communicate? And what are some conceptual challenges associated with those configurations?

New media are (currently) new to the extent that they combine (1) computing (which allows processing of content, such as retrieval through associations of words or other indices, and structuring of communication, such as conversational threads in newsgroups), (2) telecommunication networks (which allow access and connectibility to diverse and otherwise distant other people and content), and (3) digitization of content (which allows transference across distribution networks, reprocessibility of the content as data, and integration and presentation of multiple modes such as text, audio and video). These components alter the possible combinations of four basic dimensions of attributes associated with any medium, including face-to-face and traditional media: constraints, bandwidth, interactivity, and network architectures (Rice, 1987). My general argument here consists of two primary propositions:

(1) Although all media are to some extent social constructions, many of the comparisons involving new media implicitly refer to artifactual or idealized notions of interpersonal communication. By 'artifact' I mean the second definition of the word in Webster's dictionary, a product of artificial character due to extraneous (as human) agency – here, a particular form of social construction.

(2) We would do far better by studying attributes of media in general, and paradoxes raised by new and familiar media, than by confounding each medium with different sets of specific attributes, and therefore with unidirectionally positive or negative uses and outcomes, ignoring potential paradoxes. By 'confounding' I mean it as used in traditional research design: not controlling for two or more distinct influences, so that any analysis will misleadingly attribute all differences to one or the other influence, instead of separating out their unique influences.

ARTIFACTS

Media are of course imbued with the social conventions, expectations, practices, constraints and other influences of their technological, historic, economic, social, political and cultural times (Rice, 1987; Rice and Gattiker, 1999). This is most obvious during the initial development and diffusion of new media, when people try to fit new media into old conventions, or develop new ones. So, for instance, discussions of electronic mail are still often concerned with the development of norms for address, style, debate, and intimacy.

This lesson is much harder to learn and apply when we refer to the more traditional media, where such issues are typically taken-for-granted and thus deeply embedded in daily practice, if not invisible. For example, there is a remarkably small body of social science (as opposed to technical or economic) research on the telephone. One reason,

First published in *New Media and Society, 1, 1*, Sage Publications (1999) as 'Artifacts and Paradoxes in New Media, pp. 24–32.

I would argue, is largely because it was already firmly in place in social meanings, behavior and contexts before communication research came along: there was nothing obvious to study.

I would extend this point to include media that appear somehow less vulnerable to critics of communication technologies – for example, the book. Consider our notions of how books are displayed and accessed, both by themselves and in libraries. Because the content (words, numbers, pictures) is conveyed on the physical marker (paper pages), both reading a book and finding it in library stacks are sequential access procedures (Chang and Rice, 1993). In the days of the card catalog, this sequential nature of the book was replicated by the card (in a few different sequences, such as author or subject). There are, in fact, very few retrieval/access points to both books and their content, until they are managed in electronic form. Further, books are, after all, also technologies.

Thus, much of what we feel is natural about traditional media (such as face-to-face interaction, or a book) is in fact an artifact of a wide variety of components, such as material production, access mechanisms, social conventions, etc., available and developed at the time. Over time, and with continued use and structuration, this artifact becomes idealized, so that primarily positive social aspects are associated with familiar media, especially interpersonal communication. This idealization becomes fairly impervious to evidence especially in contrast to alternate conceptualizations and forms of media. This is not to say that there is no critique of prior media forms; just that the traditional, especially personal, media, tend to be invoked in their artifactual, idealized form when new media are critiqued. Jensen (1990) makes a related argument, showing that as media develop, they are often analyzed on the basis of a few idealized metaphors (art, information, education), instead of on their full range of uses and possibilities.

For example, extend this notion to unmediated communication. Face-to-face communication has been largely immune from the kinds of critiques applied to new media. Perhaps it is because the social practices of interpersonal communication are so much more firmly embedded in our socialization and culture, but some writers still project onto face-to-face communication a sort of romantic, mythic, idealized notion. Thus, interpersonal communication is still privileged and much of its artifactual nature has yet to be uncovered.

Now, I am *not* saying that social practices, etc., of interpersonal communication are not widely studied or debated, etc. What I am saying is that new media are often compared to, or critiqued from, a privileged, artifactual, idealized notion of interpersonal communication.

For another example, when we confront debates about the technological intrusions and ways of negotiating new services provided through the intelligent network such as caller ID or desktop video conferencing systems, we forget that the social calling card was a medium that represented a major social convention that solved similar problems in pre-telephone days. As Marvin (1988) points out, this is one of the reasons that initial telephone subscribers (well-to-do members of dense social circles with a critical mass of people wanting to talk with each other) opposed public telephones, aghast at letting the rabble join the network and perhaps invade the privacy of their homes without prior screening. Why new media services, such as call screening, or ways of managing computer-based visual glances into your office are any more or less ethical, or irritating, than the pre-electronic media practice of sending one's card into a house one wanted to visit has not, to my knowledge, been explored.

So, certainly one important agenda for research on new media and society is to identify and better understand the artifactual nature of familiar communication so that we do not prejudice our understandings of new media. There are, of course, examples of such an approach. Griffith and Northcraft (1994) explicitly separated out media features from media in a controlled experiment comparing conditions of anonymity/ identification across paper and pencil/email. Their study emphasized implications of differences in the same feature both between and across media. More generally, Nass and Mason (1990) develop a very general typology of media variables that constitute the 'black box' usually used to conceptualize a particular medium. Meyrowitz carefully develops a typology of three media literacies (content, media grammar, and medium literacies). My argument here would be considered one of 'medium literacy': media as environments of relatively fixed characteristics, both shared and unique, for communication and social processes. I have reviewed other approaches to this issue of conceptually distinguishing media from features (Rice, 1987, 1992). Indeed, this understanding will uncover a variety of paradoxes in the uses, evaluations, and critiques of both traditional and new media.

PARADOXES

New technologies, as well as traditional media, have 'dual lives' of positive and negative consequences (de Sola Pool, 1983), are implicated in the 'duality of technology and structure' (Orlikowski, 1992; Rice and Gattiker, 1999), may be adapted in use up to material limits (DeSanctis and Poole, 1994) and have multiple levels and time horizons of effects (Sproull and Kiesler, 1991). What are some of the paradoxes associated with the new configurations of attributes made possible by new media, and what do they reveal about the artifactual nature of our social constructions of traditional media?

Artifact as Confound or Guide?

We may be approaching some freedom from the blinder of the artifactual conceptualization of each traditional medium as a unique channel wholly distinct from other channels. That is, treating each attribute as binary (a medium 'has it' or doesn't), allocating attributes uniquely to different media, and then confounding those attributes with a specific medium. As the same content, once in digital form, may now be provided through a wide variety of media, the social conventions associated with and thereby privileged by, specific media, may become more issues of fashion and taste and less confounded with specific communication processes. An example is the oft-heard critique of new media that they aren't 'interactive' or 'personal' like face-to-face – as though these attributes are simply dichotomous, and face-to-face communication is distinct because only it provides them. As audiences become joint producers, the argument goes, there will be more choice in how to achieve appropriate levels of interactivity or personalness, perhaps more local content and discussion, more personalized or demassified communication One paradox here is that we may have less to rely on in novel

social settings, compared to familiar forms of communication, to guide us as to how
to use, evaluate or interpret communication through new media: which of the possible
media in a particular situation provides more contextualization or socially constructed
meaning? While we may debate choices of coverage and editorial positions in newspapers, we can still generally rely on some criteria for the veracity of the content, either
because of professional standards, or because of the ease with which readers can identify
content with producer. In World Wide Web pages, or in anonymous discussion lists or
chat rooms populated with fabricated identities, accountability and credibility may be
difficult to establish, at best.

Meta-information

Individuals, groups, and organizations, both for-profit and non-profit, transnational
and community, may be freed from dependence on media distributors on the one hand,
and individual members of their organizations on the other, for information about the
communicative processes involved in reaching their audiences. That is, new media can
be used to provide meta-information – information about the distribution, content and
use of information and users within and across providers. For example, optical scanners
do help grocery stores maintain better inventories, reduce errors at checkout, and
improve the internal accounting process. But they can also be used to analyze food consumption patterns over time and within markets, and to integrate this purchasing
information with other data sources. This of course raises issues of privacy, identity,
incorrect records, consumer redlining, hiring and insuring practices, and 'social triage'
whereby uneconomic consumer groups are excluded from targeted marketing efforts
(Gandy, 1993).

Conceptually, there is no reason this meta-information might not also be used as one
of many measures of the effects of community health campaigns, or used in critically
analyzing industry strategies and linkages. Practically, of course, there are many obstacles
to such innovative use of meta-information for non-commercial social purposes.

Choice

The boundaries between publisher, producer, distributor, consumer, and reviewer of
content are blurring. Mass media now incorporate many interpersonal and interactive
aspects (such as call-in radio and TV shows, home shopping through televisions with
viewer conversations and telephone or online ordering, online commentaries and
information accompanying television programs, 900-number hotlines or newsgroup
discussions about weekly soap opera plot lines and characters, etc.). Thus new media
provide many more ways to choose content, which increases the influence of structural
and cultural [factors] on people's notion of choice. Providing multiple forms of access
to content which is freed from its linkage to particular physical distribution forms
(consider, for example, full-text articles online) frees us from constraints on allocation

and transformation. Many people can use the same content at the same time. Selected aspects of content may be used in the sequence and timing preferred by the individual.

One paradox of this increased accessibility, and decreased dependence on specific distribution media, is that now individuals must make more choices, must have more prior knowledge, and must put forth more effort to integrate and make sense of the communication. Interactivity and choice are not universal benefits; many people do not have the energy, desire, need or training to engage in such processes. It is partially due to the idealization of the interactive nature of face-to-face communication that we expect everyone will desire such capabilities. Some people really do love ATMs (automatic telling machines) and answering machines. Being forced to wait in line to interact with people we have no connection with, while taking time away from interacting with others with whom we really do want to share a bond, is not as attractive as proponents of interpersonal community dialogue imply.

Many prefer the one-way aspect of some mass media and the ability to experience simulated or vicarious choice. Alternatively, the loss of programmed scripts and producer-developed plot lines in hypertext novels or interactive programs may in fact lead to more uncertainty and confusion by users, and a lost sense of shared meaning.

These changes also imply alterations in asymmetries of choice: that is, traditional media tended to locate the choice of initiating the communication in one place. The common example is of the broadcast station distributing the programming, but a more complex example is of traditional telephone calling: a person initiates a call to another without the other having any choice in the initiation. With the traditional telephone, one could choose not to answer it, but, even with answering machines, that is not a widely acceptable social choice. Because we have not, until recently (due to the proliferation of new telephone services), assessed the social aspects of telephone choice, we remain somewhat ambivalent about the telephone because of this asymmetry of choice. The meta-information about consumers, noted earlier, enables telemarketers to target potential consumers much more precisely and aggressively, increasing our discomfort with this asymmetry. Thus new media, such as answering services, caller ID, and private cellular phone networks, are sometimes used primarily to offset the asymmetry of choice inherent in this familiar 'old' medium.

Diversity or Division?

Interconnectivity – of content, medium, and form, through computers, networks, and digitization – allows open dialogue, connectivity, interrelatedness. The book, telegraph, railroads, telephone, highways (and now telecommunication networks) all overcame geographic and temporal (and now associational and retrieval) obstacles, and thus brought wider diversity of ideas, people, experiences. From certain philosophical, developmental, medical and moral perspectives, such changes are an unalloyed good.

Yet, this interconnectivity of new media (and infrastructure) also fills in space, time, location, and reduces the existence and relevance of uniqueness by imposing commonality. Note that such language implies an unalloyed bad. However, interconnectedness and uniqueness are inherently intertwined. Becoming more exposed to other, divergent perspectives also increases our own understanding and potential for respecting difference. Encouraging xenophobia and tribalism by avoiding interaction with other groups does not seem the way to foster beneficial communities. But asserting a causal and negative effect of systems on interconnectedness, while proclaiming a moral preference for uniqueness, is paradoxical.

Time

One of the most familiar refrains is that new media help to overcome temporal constraints. A novel example of this is when voice mail users send messages to themselves to be delivered at a future date, an audio 'tickler file'. Yet the idealized notion of interpersonal communication presumes a socially constructed aura of immediate interaction.

It is true that negotiating time through new media generates new problems: people in the same organization may have a hard time defining what is a 'quick' response to a voice message. Paradoxically, however, decreasing the time delays in making communication possible might in some cases actually harm communication. Some people leave messages or use asynchronous media (such as the familiar letter) because they want to leave a message that can be well considered and dealt with later on, to avoid confrontation, or to escape one's own (or someone else's) poor social skills. Note that such media can also be used to overcome constraints of temporal synchronization, in order to increase overall interactivity and personalization; having voice mail means never having to say you were sorry you missed the call, while removing acceptable excuses for not responding eventually.

Social Goods versus Individual Use

With traditional mass media, the individual audience member was the locus of evaluating the value of the medium and content. However, as new media foster subaudiences who communicate among themselves, the evaluations, benefits and disadvantages may also accrue at the group level. In complementary fashion, many information services are seen as valuable only when they provide a critical mass of diverse sources and kinds of information.

Yet some policies and research continue to emphasize the individual in these interdependent contexts of new media. One particularly noticeable instance is the growing emphasis in telephone regulations from access-pricing to usage-sensitive pricing. Many communities maintain their cohesion through social uses of the telephone that cannot be evaluated on strict cost-benefit analyses of individual telephone calls. Yet, usage-sensitive pricing presumes just this sort of analysis. This leads to losses by individuals, who can no longer afford their telephone bills, but there are losses to the collective benefit too. The larger social good is being reduced as fewer members of communities can engage in telephone connections. Similar issues arise with proposals for usage-sensitive charging for local loop connectivity to the Internet.

Use

'Using' a new medium involves many possible sources, distribution channels, interfaces, configurations of content, and creators, including the users themselves. Usage itself becomes less constrained as the computer, telecommunications and digital components can process and display content at various locations, format, multi-media mode, or time for us, depending on personal profiles, prior activities, system capabilities, activity context, or others' requests.

But this of course generates confusion as to what component is under our control, or is the source of problems. For example, when considering how individuals use online journals, of the many aspects being used, which is most salient: the type of computer, the operating system, the display interface, the application, the organization of the content, the content, the graphics, or the pricing approach? Thus, both in our daily use, as well as in research analyses, increased possibilities of use may foster increased confusion or confounding as to what the actual nature of 'use' is, and where problems, control, solutions, and interpretation reside.

CONCLUSION

Thus, I argue that we need to focus more on the underlying dimensions of attributes available, to different extents and combinations, in all communication forms instead of focussing on the particular medium. We are less likely then to fall prey to identifying the medium with its artifactual nature, as the 'medium' becomes so familiar to us that it becomes 'natural', 'idealized', 'human'. Indeed, much communication research – whether mass media, interpersonal, or organizational, positivist or qualitative, radical or functional – ignores the paradoxes noted earlier (and others) associated with new media. This is because confounding the values one holds about new, and traditional, media with the dimensions and attributes of communication processes ignores inherent paradoxes. Note that the underlying argument here is that all communication forms – from face-to-face through new media – due to their varying combinations of attributes, present opportunities for positive and negative uses, meanings, control, and consequences. The argument is not solely that 'new media' are unfairly critiqued from a perspective of 'idealized' notions of familiar media that take on the nature of artifacts – though this is true – but also that to better understand new media, we must also better understand traditional communication forms, by unconfounding their attributes (whether socially constructed or material) from their artifactual and idealized forms.

REFERENCES

Chang, S.-J. and Rice, R.E. (1993) 'Browsing: a multidimensional framework', in M. Williams (ed.), *Annual Review of Information Science and Technology*, Vol. 28. Medford, NJ: Learned Information. pp. 231–71.

DeSanctis, G. and Poole, M.S. (1994) 'Capturing the complexity in advanced technology use: adaptive structuration theory', *Organization Science*, 5: 121–47.

de Sola Pool, I. (1983) *Technologies of Freedom*. Cambridge, MA: Harvard University Press.

Gandy, O., Jr (1993) 'Transaction-generated information (TGI): signaling, sorting and the communication of self', in J. Schement and B. Ruben (eds), *Between Communication and Information: Information and Behavior*, Vol. 4. New Brunswick, NJ: Transaction Publishers. pp. 421–33.

Griffith, T. and Northcraft, G. (1994) 'Distinguishing between the forest and the trees: media, features, and methodology in electronic communication research', *Organization Science*, 5 (2): 272–85.

Jensen, J. (1990) *Redeeming Modernity: Contradictions in Media Criticism*. Newbury Park, CA: Sage.

Marvin, C. (1988) *When Old Technologies Were New*. New York: Oxford University Press.

Nass, C. and Mason, L. (1990) 'On the study of technology and task: a variable-based approach', in J. Fulk and C. Steinfield (eds), *Organizations and Communication Technology*. Newbury Park, CA: Sage. pp. 46–67.

Orlikowski, W. (1992) 'The duality of technology: rethinking the concept of technology in organizations', *Organization Science*, 3 (3): 397–427.

Rice, R.E. (1987) 'Computer-mediated communication and organizational innovation', *Journal of Communication*, 37 (4): 65–94.

Rice, R.E. (1992) 'Contexts of research on organizational computer-mediated communication: a recursive review', in M. Lea (ed.), *Contexts of Computer-Mediated Communication*. Hemel Hempstead: Harvester-Wheatsheaf. pp. 113–44.

Rice, R.E. and Gattiker, U. (1999) 'New media and organizational structuring of meanings and relations', in F. Jablin and L. Putnam (eds), *New Handbook of Organizational Communication*. Newbury Park, CA: Sage.

Sproull, L. and Kiesler, S. (1991) *Connections: New Ways of Working in the Networked Organization*. Cambridge, MA: MIT Press.

the Internet as mass medium

MERRILL MORRIS AND CHRISTINE OGAN

T he Internet has become impossible to ignore in the past two years. Even people who do not own a computer and have no opportunity to 'surf the net' could not have missed the news stories about the Internet, many of which speculate about its effects on the ever-increasing number of people who are on line. Why, then, have communications researchers, historically concerned with exploring the effects of mass media, nearly ignored the Internet? With 25 million people estimated to be communicating on the Internet, should communication researchers now consider this network of networks a mass medium? Until recently, mass communications researchers have overlooked not only the Internet but the entire field of computer-mediated communication, staying instead with the traditional forms of broadcast and print media that fit much more conveniently into models for appropriate research topics and theories of mass communication.

However, this paper argues that if mass communications researchers continue to largely disregard the research potential of the Internet, their theories about communication will become less useful. Not only will the discipline be left behind, it will also miss an opportunity to explore and rethink answers to some of the central questions of mass communications research, questions that go to the heart of the model of source–message–receiver with which the field has struggled. This paper proposes a conceptualization of the Internet as a mass medium, based on revised ideas of what constitutes a mass audience and a mediating technology. The computer as a new communication technology opens a space for scholars to rethink assumptions and categories, and perhaps even to find new insights into traditional communication technologies.

This paper looks at the Internet, rather than computer-mediated communication as a whole, in order to place the new medium within the context of other mass media. Mass media researchers have traditionally organized themselves around a specific communications medium. The newspaper, for instance, is a more precisely defined area of interest than printing-press-mediated communication, which embraces more specialized areas, such as company brochures or wedding invitations. Of course, there is far more than a semantic difference between conceptualizing a new communication technology by its communicative form than by the technology itself. The tradition of mass communication research has accepted newspapers, radio, and television as its objects of study for social, political, and economic reasons. As technology changes and media converge, those research categories must become flexible.

CONSTRAINTS ON INTERNET RESEARCH

Mass communications researchers have overlooked the potential of the Internet for several reasons. The Internet was developed in bits and pieces by hobbyists, students, and academics (Rheingold, 1994). It didn't fit researchers' ideas about mass media, locked, as they have been, into models of print and broadcast media. Computer-mediated communication (CMC) at first resembled interpersonal communication and was relegated to the domain of other fields, such as education, management information science, and

First published in *Journal of Communication 46, 1*, Oxford University Press (1996) as 'The Internet as Mass Medium, pp. 39–50.

library science. These fields, in fact, have been doing research into CMC for nearly 20 years (Dennis and Gallupe, 1993; O'Shea and Self, 1983), and many of their ideas about CMC have proven useful in looking at the phenomenon as a mass medium. Both education and business researchers have seen the computer as a technology through which communication was mediated, and both lines of research have been concerned with the effects of this new medium.

Disciplinary lines have long kept researchers from seeing the whole picture of the communication process. Cathcart and Gumpert (1983) recognized this problem when they noted how speech communication definitions 'have minimized the role of media and channel in the communication process' (p. 267), even as mass communication definitions disregarded the ways media function in interpersonal communication: 'We are quite convinced that the traditional division of communication study into interpersonal, group and public, and mass communication is inadequate because it ignores the pervasiveness of media' (p. 268).

The major constraint on doing mass communication research into the Internet, however, has been theoretical. In searching for theories to apply to group software systems, researchers in MIS have recognized that communication studies needed new theoretical models: 'The emergence of new technologies such as GSS (Group Support Systems, software that allows group decision-making), which combine aspects of both inter-personal interaction and mass media, presents something of a challenge to communi-cation theory. With new technologies, the line between the various contexts begins to blur, and it is unclear that models based on mass media or face-to-face contexts are adequate' (Poole and Jackson, 1993: 282).

Not only have theoretical models constrained research, but the most basic assumptions behind researchers' theories of mass media effects have kept them from being able to see the Internet as a new mass medium. DeFleur and Ball-Rokeach's attitude toward computers in the fifth edition of their *Theories of Mass Communication* (1989) is typical. They compare computers to telephones, dismissing the idea of computer communication as mass communication: 'Even if computer literacy were to become universal, and even if every household had a personal computer equipped with a modem, it is difficult to see how a new system of mass communication could develop from this base alone' (pp. 335–6). The fact that DeFleur and Ball-Rokeach find it difficult to envision this development may well be a result of their own constrained perspective. Taking the telephone analogy a step further, Lana Rakow (1992) points out that the lack of research on the telephone was due in part to researchers' inability to see it as a mass medium. The telephone also became linked to women, who embraced the medium as a way to overcome social isolation.

RETHINKING DEFINITIONS

However, a new communication technology can throw the facades of the old into sharp relief. Marshall McLuhan (1960) recognized this when, speaking of the computer, he wrote, 'The advent of a new medium often reveals the lineaments and assumptions, as it were, of an old medium' (p. 567). In effect, a new communication technology may perform an almost postmodern function of making the unpresentable perceptible, as Lyotard (1983) might put it. In creating new configurations of sources, messages, and receivers, new communication technologies force researchers to examine their old definitions. What is a mass audience? What is a communication medium? How are messages mediated?

Daniel Bell (1960) recognized the slippery nature of the term *mass society* and how its many definitions lacked a sense of reality: 'What strikes one about these varied uses of the concept of mass society is how little they reflect or relate to the complex, richly striated social relations of the real world' (p. 25). Similarly, the term *mass media*, with its roots in ideas of mass society, has always been difficult to define. There is much at stake in hanging on to traditional definitions of mass media, as shown in the considerable anxiety in recent years over the loss of the mass audience and its implications for the liberal pluralist state. The convergence of communication technologies, as represented by the computer, has set off this fear of demassification, as audiences become more and more fragmented. The political and social implications of mass audiences and mass media go beyond the scope of this paper, but the current uneasiness and discussion over the terms themselves seem to indicate that the old idea of the mass media has reached its limit (Schudson, 1992; Warner, 1992).

Critical researchers have long questioned the assumptions implicit in traditional media effects definitions, looking instead to the social, economic, and historical contexts that gave rise to institutional conceptions of media. Such analysis, Fejes (1984) notes, can lead to another unquestioning set of assumptions about the media's ability to affect audiences. As Ang (1991) has pointed out, abandoning the idea of the mass media and their audiences impedes an investigation of media institutions' power to create messages that are consumed by real people. If the category of mass medium becomes too fuzzy to define, traditional effects researchers will be left without dependent variables, and critical scholars will have no means of discussing issues of social and political power.

A new communication technology such as the Internet allows scholars to rethink, rather than abandon, definitions and categories. When the Internet is conceptualized as a mass medium, what becomes clear is that neither *mass* nor *medium* can he precisely defined for all situations, but instead must be continually rearticulated depending on the situation. The Internet is a multifaceted mass medium, that is, it contains many different configurations of communication. Its varied forms show the connection between interpersonal and mass communication, which has been an object of study since the two-step flow associated the two (Lazarsfeld et al., 1944). Chaffee and Mutz (1988) have called for an exploration of this relationship that begins 'with a theory that spells out what effects are of interest, and what aspects of communication might produce them' (p. 39). The Internet offers a chance to develop and to refine that theory.

How does it do this? Through its very nature. The Internet plays with the source–message–receiver features of the traditional mass communication model, sometimes putting them into traditional patterns, sometimes putting them into entirely new configurations. Internet communication takes many forms, from World Wide Web pages operated by major news organizations to Usenet groups discussing folk music to E-mail messages among colleagues and friends. The Internet's communication forms can be understood as a continuum. Each point in the traditional model of the communication process can, in fact, vary from one to a few to many on the Internet. Sources of the messages can range from one person in E-mail communication, to a social group in a Listserver or Usenet group, to a group of professional journalists in a World Wide Web page. The messages themselves can be traditional journalistic news stories created by a reporter and editor, stories created over a long period of time by many people, or simply conversations, such as in an Internet Relay Chat group. The receivers, or audiences, of these messages can also number from one to potentially millions, and may or may not move fluidly from their role as audience members to producers of messages.

VIEWING THE INTERNET AS MASS MEDIUM

Producers and audiences on the Internet can be grouped generally into four categories: (a) one-to-one asynchronous communication, such as E-mail; (b) many-to-many asynchronous communication, such as Usenet, electronic bulletin boards, and Listservers that require the receiver to sign up for a service or log on to a program to access messages around a particular topic or topics; (c) synchronous communication that can be one-to-one, one-to-few, or one-to-many and can be organized around a topic, the construction of an object, or role playing, such as MUDs (Multi-User Dungeons and their various transformations as MOOs, MUCKs and MUSHs), Internet Relay Chat and chat rooms on commercial services; and (d) asynchronous communication generally characterized by the receiver's need to seek out the site in order to access information, which may involve many-to-one, one-to-one, or one-to-many source–receiver relationships (e.g., Web sites, gophers, and FTP sites).

Reconceptualizing the audience for the communication that takes place on the Internet is a major problem, one that becomes increasingly important as commercial information providers enter the Internet in greater numbers. To date, thousands of commercial sources have created home pages or gopher sites for people to access their services or information about those services. As of September 1995, search tools on the Internet turned up as many as 123 different US newspaper services and more than 1300 magazine services with distinct web sites. Some newspapers seem to be creating home pages to mark their place in cyberspace until their managers determine how to make them commercially viable. Others may be moving to the Internet out of fear of the electronic competition. Thus, it remains difficult to envision the future of traditional mass media on the Internet—who will be the audience, how will that audience access the information and entertainment services, and what profit might be made from the services?

A parallel question investigates the impact of Internet communication on the audience. Mass communications researchers will want to examine information-seeking and knowledge gaps as well as a range of uses-and-gratifications-based questions concerning the audience. Since the Internet is also being used for entertainment as well as information, effects researchers will want to know whether the Internet is a functional equivalent of other entertainment media and whether there are negative effects in the distribution of pornography and verbal attacks (e.g., flaming and virtual rapes) on members of the audience. There are also questions of audience addiction to certain types of Internet communication and entertainment.

When the uses of the Internet as a mass medium are explored, questions arise about the nature of its communicative content. As commercial providers increase on the Internet, and more political information is provided, the problem of who sets the agenda for the new medium also becomes a concern.

Credibility is another issue with mass media. Traditional mass media make certain claims about the veracity of their information. The Internet makes few such claims at the moment, and it is possible that the concept of credibility will also change as a result. Recently, on a feminist newsnet group, an individual began to post what appeared to be off-base comments to a serious discussion of feminist issues. Several days later it was determined that 'Mike' was a computer-generated personage and not a real contributor to the discussion at all. At present there is no way to know when the Mikes on the Internet are even real, let alone credible (Ogan, 1993). Consequently, we wish to underscore the fundamental importance of this issue.

Traditional mass media have addressed the issue within their organizations, hiring editors and fact checkers to determine what information is accurate. Source credibility will vary on the Internet, with commercial media sites carrying relatively more credibility and unknown sources carrying less. A much greater burden will be placed on the user to determine how much faith to place in any given source.

Another question relates to the interchangeability of producers and receivers of content. One of the Internet's most widely touted advantages is that an audience member may also be a message producer. To what extent is that really the case? We may discover a fair amount about the producers of messages from the content of their electronic messages, but what about the lurkers? Who are they and how big is this group? To what extent do lurkers resemble the more passive audience of television sitcoms? And why do they remain lurkers and not also become information providers? Is there something about the nature of the medium that prevents their participation?

Other questions concern production of culture, social control, and political communication. Will the Internet ultimately be accessible to all? How are groups excluded from participation? Computers were originally created to wage war and have been developed in an extremely specific, exclusive culture. Can we trace those cultural influences in the way messages are produced on the Internet?

APPLYING THEORIES TO CMC

In an overview of research on computers in education, O'Shea and Self (1983) note that the learner-as-bucket theory had dominated. In this view, knowledge is like a liquid that is poured into the student, a metaphor similar to mass communication's magic-bullet theory. This brings up another aspect to consider in looking at mass communication research into CMC—the applicability of established theories and methodologies to the new medium. As new communication technologies are developed, researchers seem to use the patterns of research established for existing technologies to explain the uses and effects of the new media. Research in group communication, for example, has been used to examine the group uses of E-mail networks (Sproull and Kiesler, 1991). Researchers have studied concepts of status, decision-making quality, social presence, social control, and group norms as they have been affected by a technology that permitted certain changes in group communication.

This kind of transfer of research patterns from one communication technology to another is not unusual. Wartella and Reeves (1985) studied the history of American mass communication research in the area of children and the media. With each new medium, the effects of content on children were discussed as a social problem in public debate. As Wartella and Reeves note, researchers responded to the public controversy over the adoption of a new media technology in American life.

In approaching the study of the Internet as a mass medium, the following established concepts seem to be useful starting points. Some of these have originated in the study of interpersonal or small group communication; others have been used to examine mass media. Some relate to the nature of the medium, while others focus on the audience for the medium.

Critical Mass

This conceptual framework has been adopted from economists, physicists, and sociologists by organizational communication and diffusion of innovation scholars to better understand the size of the audience needed for a new technology to be considered successful and the nature of collective action as applied to electronic media use (Markus, 1991; Oliver et al., 1985). For any medium to be considered a mass medium, and therefore economically viable to advertisers, a critical mass of adopters must be achieved. Interactive media only become useful as more and more people adopt, or as Rogers (1986) states, 'the usefulness of a new communication system increases for all adopters with each additional adopter' (p. 120). Initially, the critical mass notion works against adoption, since it takes a number of other users to be seen as advantageous to adopt. For example, the telephone or an E-mail system was not particularly useful to the first adopters because most people were unable to receive their messages or converse with them. Valente (1995) notes that the critical mass is achieved when about 10 to 20 percent of the population has adopted the innovation. When this level has been reached, the innovation can be spread to the rest of the social system. Adoption of computers in US households has well surpassed this figure, but the modem connections needed for Internet connection lag somewhat behind.

Because a collection of communication services—electronic bulletin boards, Usenet groups, E-mail, Internet Relay Chats, home pages, gophers, and so forth—comprise the Internet, the concept of critical mass on the Internet could be looked upon as a variable, rather than a fixed percentage of adopters. Fewer people are required for sustaining an Internet Relay Chat conference or a Multi-User Dungeon than may be required for an electronic bulletin board or another type of discussion group. As already pointed out, a relatively large number of E-mail users are required for any two people to engage in conversation, yet only those two people constitute the critical mass for any given conversation. For a bulletin board to be viable, its content must have depth and variety. If the audience who also serve as the source of information for the BBS is too small, the bulletin board cannot survive for lack of content. A much larger *critical mass* will be needed for such a group to maintain itself—perhaps as many as 100 or more. The discretionary data base, as defined by Connolly and Thorn (1991), is a 'shared pool of data to which several participants may, if they choose, separately contribute information' (p. 221). If no one contributes, the data base cannot exist. It requires a critical mass of participants to carry the free riders in the system, thus supplying this public good to all members, participants, or free riders. Though applied to organizations, this refinement of the critical mass theory is a useful way of thinking about Listservers, electronic bulletin boards, Usenet groups, and other Internet services, where participants must hold up their end of the process through written contributions.

Each of these specific Internet services can be viewed as we do specific television stations, small town newspapers, or special interest magazines. None of these may reach a strictly mass audience, but in conjunction with all the other stations, newspapers, and magazines distributed in the country, they constitute mass media categories. So the Internet itself would be considered the mass medium, while the individual sites and services are the components of which this medium is comprised.

Interactivity

This concept has been assumed to be a natural attribute of interpersonal communication, but, as explicated by Rafaeli (1988), it is more recently applied to all new media, from two-way cable to the Internet. From Rafaeli's perspective, the most useful basis of inquiry for interactivity would be one grounded in responsiveness. Rafaeli's definition of interactivity 'recognizes three pertinent levels: two-way (non-interactive) communication, reactive (or quasi-interactive) communication, and fully interactive communication' (1988: 119). Anyone working to conceptualize Internet communication would do well to draw on this variable and follow Rafaeli's lead when he notes that the value of a focus on interactivity is that the concept cuts across the mass versus interpersonal distinctions usually made in the fields of inquiry. It is also helpful to consider interactivity to be variable in nature, increasing or decreasing with the particular Internet service in question.

Uses and Gratifications

Though research of mass media use from a uses-and-gratifications perspective has not been prevalent in the communication literature in recent years, it may help provide a useful framework from which to begin the work on Internet communication. Both Walther (1992b) and Rafaeli (1986) concur in this conclusion. The logic of the uses-and-gratifications approach, based in functional analysis, is derived from '(1) the social and psychological origins of (2) needs, which generate (3) expectations of (4) the mass media and other sources, which lead to (5) differential patterns of media exposure (or engagement in other activities), resulting in (7) other consequences, perhaps mostly unintended ones' (Blumler and Katz, 1974).

Rosengren (1974) modified the original approach in one way by noting that the 'needs' in the original model had to be perceived as problems and some potential solution to those problems needed to be perceived by the audience. Rafaeli (1986) regards the move away from effects research to a uses-and-gratifications approach as essential to the study of electronic bulletin boards (one aspect of the Internet medium). He is predisposed to examine electronic bulletin boards in the context of play or Ludenic theory, an extension of the uses-and-gratifications approach, which is clearly a purpose that drives much of Internet use by a wide spectrum of the population. Rafaeli summarizes the importance of this paradigm for electronic communication by noting uses-and-gratifications' comprehensive nature in a media environment where computers have not only home and business applications, but also work and play functions.

Additionally, the uses-and-gratifications approach presupposes a degree of audience activity, whether instrumental or ritualized. The concept of audience activity should be included in the study of Internet communication, and it already has been incorporated in one examination of the Cleveland Freenet (Swift, 1989).

Social Presence and Media Richness Theory

These approaches have been applied to CMC use by organizational communication researchers to account for interpersonal effects. But social presence theory stems from an attempt to determine the differential properties of various communication media, including mass media, in the degree of social cues inherent in the technology. In general, CMC, with its lack of visual and other nonverbal cues, is said to be extremely low in social presence in comparison to face-to-face communication (Walther, 1992a).

Media richness theory differentiates between *lean* and *rich* media by the bandwidth or number of cue systems within each medium. This approach (Walther, 1992a) suggests that because CMC is a lean channel, it is useful for simple or unequivocal messages, and also that it is more efficient 'because shadow functions and coordinated interaction efforts are unnecessary. For receivers to understand clearly more equivocal information, information that is ambiguous, emphatic, or emotional, however, a richer medium should be used' (p. 57).

Unfortunately, much of the research on media richness and social presence has been one-shot experiments or field studies. Given the ambiguous results of such studies in business and education (Dennis and Gallupe, 1993), it can be expected that over a longer time period, people will communicate on Usenets, and bulletin boards will restore some of those social cues and thus make the medium richer than its techno-logical parameters would lead us to expect. As Walther (1992a) argues: 'It appears that the conclusion that CMC is less socioemotional or personal than face-to-face communi-cation is based on incomplete measurement of the latter form, and it may not be true whatsoever, even in restricted laboratory settings' (p. 63). Further, he notes that though researchers recognize that nonverbal social context cues convey formality and status inequality, 'they have reached their conclusion about CMC/face-to-face differences without actually observing the very non-verbal cues through which these effects are most likely to be performed' (p. 63).

Clearly, there is room for more work on the social presence and media richness of Internet communication. It could turn out that the Internet contains a very high degree of media richness relative to other mass media, to which it has insufficiently been compared and studied. Ideas about social presence also tend to disguise the subtle kinds of social control that go on on the net through language, such as flaming.

Network Approaches

Grant (1993) has suggested that researchers approach new communication technologies through network analysis, to better address the issues of social influence and critical mass. Conceptualizing Internet communities as networks might be a very useful approach. As discussed earlier, old concepts of senders and receivers are inappropriate to the study of the Internet. Studying the network of users of any given Internet service can incorporate the concept of interactivity and the interchangeability of message producers and receivers. The computer allows a more efficient analysis of network communication, but researchers will need to address the ethical issues related to studying people's communication without their permission.

These are just a few of the core concepts and theoretical frameworks that should be applied to a mass communication perspective on Internet communication. Reconceptualizing the Internet from this perspective will allow researchers both to continue to use the structures of traditional media studies and to develop new ways of thinking about those structures. It is, finally, a question of taxonomy. Thomas Kuhn (1974) has noted the ways in which similarity and resemblance are important in creating scientific paradigms. As Kuhn points out, scientists facing something new 'can often agree on the particular symbolic expression appropriate to it, even though none of them has seen that particular expression before' (p. 466). The problem becomes a taxonomic one: how to categorize, or, more importantly, how to avoid categorizing in a rigid, structured way so that researchers may see the slippery nature of ideas such as mass media, audiences, and communication itself.

REFERENCES

Ang, I. (1991) *Desperately Seeking the Audience*. London: Routledge.
Bell, D. (1960) *The End of Ideology*. Glencoe, IL: Free Press.
Boyd-Barrett, O. and Scanlon, E. (eds) (1991) *Computers and Learning*. Workingham: Addison-Wesley.
Blumler, J. and Katz, E. (eds) (1974) *The Uses of Mass Communications*. Beverly Hills, CA: Sage.

Cathcart, R. and Gumpert, G. (1983) 'Mediated interpersonal communication: toward a new typology', *Quarterly Journal of Speech*: 267–8.

Chaffee, S.H. and Mutz, D.C. (1988) 'Comparing mediated and interpersonal communication data', in R.P. Hawkins et al. (eds), *Advancing Communication Science: Merging Mass and Interpersonal Processes*. Newbury Park, CA: Sage. pp. 19–43.

Connolly, T. and Thorn, B.K. (1991) 'Discretionary data bases: theory, data, and implications', in J. Fulk and C. Steinfield (eds), *Organizations and Communication Technology*. Newbury Park, CA: Sage. pp. 219–33.

DeFleur, M. and Ball-Rokeach, S. (1989) *Theories of Mass Communication*, 5th edn. New York: Longman.

Dennis, A. and Gallupe, R. (1993) 'A history of group support systems empirical research: lessons learned and future directions', in L.M. Jessup and J.S. Valacich (eds), *Group Support Systems: New Perspectives*. New York: Macmillan. pp. 59–77.

Fejes, F. (1984) 'Critical mass communications research and media effects: the problem of the disappearing audience', *Media, Culture and Society*, 6: 219–32.

Krol, E. (1994) *The Whole Internet: User's Guide and Catalog*, 2nd edn. Sebastopol, CA: Reilly.

Kuhn, T. (1974) 'Second thoughts on paradigms', in F. Suppe (ed.), *The Structure of Scientific Theories*. Urbana: University of Illinois Press. pp. 459–82.

Lazarsfeld, P., Berelson, B. and Gaudet, H. (1944) *The People's Choice*. New York: Duell, Sloan & Pearce.

Lyotard, J.-F. (1983) 'Answering the question: what is postmodernism?', in I. Hassan and S. Hassan (eds), *Innovation/Renovation*. Madison: University of Wisconsin Press. pp. 71–82.

McLuhan, M. (1960) 'Effects of the improvements of communication media', *Journal of Economic History*, 20: 566–75.

McQuail, D. (1987) *Mass Communication Theory: An Introduction*, 2nd edn. London: Sage.

McQuail, D. and Windahl, S. (1993) *Communication Models for the Study of Mass Communication*, 2nd edn. New York: Longman.

Markus, M. (1991) 'Toward a "critical mass" theory of interactive media', in J. Fulk and C. Steinfield (eds), *Organizations and Communication Technology*. Newbury Park, CA: Sage. pp. 194–218.

Marvin, C. (1988) *When Old Technologies Were New*. New York: Oxford University Press.

Oates, W. (1982) 'Effects of computer-assisted instruction in writing skills on journalism students in beginning newswriting classes'. Unpublished doctoral dissertation, Indiana University, Bloomington, IL.

Ogan, C. (1993) 'Listserver communication during the Gulf War: what kind of medium is the electronic bulletin board?', *Journal of Broadcasting and Electronic Media*, 37 (2): 177–96.

Oliver, P., Marwell, G. and Teixeira, R. (1985) 'A theory of the critical mass: interdependence, group heterogeneity, and the production of collective action', *American Journal of Sociology*, 91 (3): 522–56.

O'Shea, T. and Self, J. (1983) *Learning and Teaching with Computers: Artificial Intelligence in Education*. Englewood Cliffs, NJ: Prentice-Hall.

Poole, M. and Jackson, M. (1993) 'Communciation theory and group support systems', in L.M. Jessup and J.S. Valacich (eds), *Group Support Systems: New Perspectives*. New York: Macmillan. pp. 281–93.

Rafaeli, S. (1986) 'The electronic bulletin board: a computer-driven mass medium', *Computers and the Social Sciences*, 2: 123–36.

Rafaeli, S. (1988) 'Interactivity: from new media to communication', in R. Hawkins et al. (eds), *Advancing Communication Science: Merging Mass and Interpersonal Processes*. Newbury Park, CA: Sage. pp. 110–34.

Rakow, L. (1992) *Gender on the Line: Women, the Telephone and Community Life*. Urbana: University of Illinois Press.

Reardon, K. and Rogers, E. (1988) 'Interpersonal versus mass media communication: a false dichotomy', *Human Communication Research*, 15 (2): 284–303.

Rheingold, H. (1994) *The Virtual Community: Finding Connection in a Computerized World*. London: Secker & Warburg.

Rogers, E. (1983) 'Communication as an academic discipline: a dialogue', *Journal of Communication*, 33 (3): 18–30.

Rogers, E. (1986) *Communication Technology: The New Media in Society*. New York: Free Press.

Rosengren, K. (1974) 'Uses and gratifications: a paradigm outlined', in J. Blumler and E. Katz (eds), *The Uses of Mass Communications*. Beverly Hills, CA: Sage. pp. 269–86.

Schudson, M. (1992) 'Was there ever a public sphere? If so, when? Reflections on the American case', in C. Calhoun (ed.), *Habermas and the Public Sphere*. Cambridge, MA: MIT Press. pp. 143–63.

Sproull, L. and Kiesler, S. (1991) *Connections: New Ways of Working in the Networked Organization*. Cambridge, MA: MIT Press.

Swift, C.R. (1989) 'Audience activity in computer-mediated communication'. Unpublished doctoral dissertation, Indiana University, Bloomington, IL.

Walther, J.B. (1992a) 'Interpersonal effects in computer-mediated interaction: a relational perspective', *Communication Research*, 19 (1): 52–90.

Walther, J.B. (1992b) 'When mediated dyadic communication is not interpersonal'. Paper presented at the International Communication Association annual meeting, Miami, FL.

Warner, M. (1992) 'The mass public and the mass subject', in C. Calhoun (ed.), *Habermas and the Public Sphere*. Cambridge, MA: MIT Press. pp. 359–76.

Wartella, E. and Reeves, B. (1985) 'Historical trends in research on children and the media', *Journal of Communication*, 35 (2): 118–33.

12

the Internet and forms of human association

JAMES SLEVIN

The internet is enabling the emergence of new mechanisms of human association which are shaped by – yet also shape – the development of this new medium of communication. My starting point in this chapter is the view that, in late modernity, we are increasingly engaged in forms of social interaction which are becoming intensely reflexive and open-ended. In this respect, technologies such as the internet are serving to increase the capacity for both reciprocal and non-reciprocal communication. These new conditions challenge individuals and organizations to seek out new possibilities for reciprocal bonding and collaboration, and to create opportunities that were previously only associated with the sharing of a common locale. Taking up these challenges, however, raises issues of a complicated kind which are part and parcel of our attempts to generate active trust and integrity in social relationships in which knowledge is increasingly uncertain, and in which clear-cut answers to problems are increasingly absent. A proper understanding of these processes will afford us an essential grounding in our attempts at developing new ways of coping with risk and uncertainty.

Although I shall be arguing in favour of a very different interpretation of the issue, the use of the internet to facilitate gatherings in virtual meeting places has already generated a considerable amount of interest. Howard Rheingold's work, for example, is often mentioned in this context. He argues that when 'enough people' carry on these relationships in virtual reality with 'sufficient feeling', and for a 'long enough' period of time, 'virtual communities' emerge which are only accessible via a computer screen.[1] He describes these communities, in a somewhat traditional fashion, as self-defined networks of interactive communication organized around particular interests or purposes.

> People in virtual communities use words on screens to exchange pleasantries and argue, engage in intellectual discourse, conduct commerce, exchange knowledge, share emotional support, make plans, brainstorm, gossip, feud, fall in love, find friends and lose them, play games, flirt, create a little high art and a lot of idle talk.

People in virtual communities, Rheingold writes, 'do just about everything people do in real life'.[2]

Available studies of online community often have lofty goals and a sense of urgency about them. Rheingold, for example, hopes to 'inform a wider population about the potential importance of cyberspace to political liberties and the ways virtual communities are likely to change our experience of the real world as individuals and communities'.[3] The problem, however, with most of these studies is that they elaborate the impact of the internet on forms of human association and conduct within strictly limited terms. They do not develop a critical approach to the concept of community' in late modernity. As such, they fail to grasp the broader implications of the internet for human association and conduct, beyond that of narrowly conceived online interaction. They often think of participants in these online communities as 'leaving their bodies behind' and 'migrating to virtual communities' where they are deemed to spin 'webs of personal relationships in cyberspace'.[4]

By contrast, we need to start working out the implications of Mark Poster's claim that:

First published in *The Internet and Society*, J. Slevin, Polity (2000) as 'The Internet and Forms of Human Association, pp. 90–100.

the internet and virtual reality open the possibility of new kinds of interactivity such that the idea of an opposition of real and unreal community is not adequate to specify the differences between modes of bonding, serving instead to obscure the manner of the historical construction of forms of community.[5]

In this respect, Rheingold's own observations concerning his personal experiences of virtual communities are very much at odds with the way he himself approaches them. He explains, for example, that his 'invisible friends sometimes show up in the flesh, materializing from the next block or other side of the planet'.[6] From this vantage point, he cannot get close enough to the significance of such face-to-face confrontations and the situated character of everyday life. He writes:

> I remember the first time I walked into a room full of people IRL ('in real life') who knew many intimate details of my history and whose stories I knew very well. ... I looked around the room full of strangers when I walked in. It was one of the strangest sensations of my life. ... There wasn't a recognizable face in the house. I had never seen them before.[7]

We must resist any temptation to follow Rheingold in laughing off such situations as merely involving the clumsiness of a first acquaintance. We must instead take a more positive approach and examine how the internet is contributing to the construction of forms of solidarity and association in which the most intimate and the most distant have become directly connected. We must ask why we are increasingly prepared to subject ourselves to these mixed feelings of intimacy and estrangement in our day-to-day lives. What is it about our modern condition that motivates so many millions of individuals and organizations to participate in forming new forms of social relationship via the internet or intranets? Will the rise of 'virtual' communities mean that 'real' communities are on their way out, or will 'real' communities be transformed and endowed with a new lease of life? How can we relate the reported mediated experiences within online communities to the practical contexts of our day-to-day lives? If we do not begin to sort out issues like these, then we cannot hope to understand how nation-states might, for example, use the internet to tackle problems of governability by fostering new forms of solidarity and identity. Nor will we be able to understand how organizations might use intranets or extranets to promote team work, intrafirm networking and knowledge sharing. Nor will we be in a position to properly comprehend the ways in which individuals might use the internet or intranets in their day-to-day communication to forge new kinds of commitment and mutuality. Moreover, we may not be fully aware of the dangers these new situations might hold and the unintended consequences that might flow from them.

TOWARDS A NEW SENSE OF COMMUNITY?

The concept of 'community' is a particularly elusive one. It might be used to refer to the communal life of a sixteenth-century village – or to a team of individuals within a modern organization who rarely meet face to face, but who are successfully engaged in online collaborative work. In this section, I shall start by examining two usages of the concept of 'community' in the light of the complexity of both the reality and the idea. Both usages still occupy a central place in social and political thought today. Second, I shall discuss in what sense these usages are being eclipsed by new forms of human association, and consider critically the appropriateness of the concept of 'community' as a way of describing them. I shall end this section by highlighting some of the key difficulties that those wishing to establish new forms of communal solidarity might encounter.

Real and Imagined Communities

The importance of the idea of community in modern social life is often demonstrated by referring to the idea of 'nation-ness'. It is often perceived as a phenomenon that has achieved the most profound emotional legitimacy in our time.[8] The nation, Mark Poster explains, is 'generally regarded as the strongest group identification in the modern period and thus perhaps the most "real" community of this era'.[9] Consequently, the modern nightmare, in Manning Nash's words, 'is to be deracinated, to be without papers, alone, alienated, and adrift in a world of organized others'.[10] Yet although a nation may be a 'real' community, territorially or by way of its symbols – and most certainly so for those who are excluded from it – it differs greatly from the *Gemeinschaft* of Ferdinand Tönnies. Tönnies formulated this ideal-type to describe cosy realities, where social relationships are based on locality and neighbourliness, fellowship, a sharing of responsibilities, and a furtherance of mutual good through understanding and the exercise of natural sentiment.[11] Viewed from this end of the continuum of social organizations, nations are best defined as what Benedict Anderson calls 'imagined communities'.[12]

Now, we might argue that there is a fundamental sense in which all communities are imagined, given that their very production and reproduction always presumes the employment of a range of symbolic devices. But in modernity, for nation-states and other forms of modern organization, this is brought to a more intense pitch by the mobilization of power through the storage and control of information and other symbolic content. Tönnies-type communities linger 'effortlessly, as if merely by dint of physical proximity and absence of movement'. As for communities that are imagined, 'belief in their presence is their only brick and mortar'.[13] Anderson sets out four senses in which modern communities can be described as being 'imagined'. First, members of an imagined community will never know most of their fellow members and will never meet, 'yet in the minds of each lives the image of their communion'. Second, they are imagined as limited in that even the largest of communities is finite and has boundaries beyond which lie other communities. Third, these communities are imagined to be sovereign and their members dream of being free from the interference of outsiders. Finally, these communities are imagined because, regardless of the inequality and exploitation that might prevail among their members, they are always conceived of as exhibiting 'a deep, horizontal comradeship'.[14]

Communication media facilitate the representation of this constructed 'reality' by making possible the transmission of shared histories of common 'hows' and shared landscapes of common 'essences'. But also by the sequestration and symbolic expulsion from the imagined community of anything which might intrude.[15] This whole process has, of course, important ideological implications, as Jean-Luc Nancy argues: 'The thinking of community as essence … is in effect the closure of the political.'[16] In this respect, there are a number of strategies that have gone a long way towards pacifying conflict over the outcome of political and economic decisions. These have greatly contributed to stability in the production and reproduction of imagined communities over time–space. One way in which modern communities have generated a cloak of permanence is by reflexively organizing the horizons of possible activity, for example by inventing a variety of traditions and modern rituals, or by drawing up rules of conduct. A second way involves the defining of issues that may count as being political and, therefore, open to intervention and critique. A third way involves the process of defining generally accepted standards and practices which, if pursued, will make the community better off as a whole.[17] Mostly these strategies went undiscussed, or were pushed through by ritual assertion, or by the enactment of centralized control. They result in forms of human association constituted by *modes of relationship* which Michael Oakeshott characterizes as 'organic, evolutionary, teleological, functional or syndromic'.[18] Under such circumstances, when individuals are confronted with forms of association with two or more discrepant purposes, they have a limited range of options open to them. Either discrepant purposes have to be suppressed, or they have to be 'related to one another systematically or in terms of means to end'.[19] Although these kinds of association do not exist in these strict terms, they are what Oakeshott refers to as 'compulsory associations … 'because the relationships they constitute are those recognized by the authority of common purposes and in terms of the authority of managerial decisions which specify how the common purpose should contingently be pursued'.[20]

These pacifying strategies are quite successful where, as Giddens writes, 'people have relatively stable preferences and where their level of reflexive involvement with wider social and economic processes is relatively low'.[21] Today, however, the success of these strategies is severely hampered by the conditions of late modernity. In culturally cosmopolitan societies, for example, the representations of 'nation-ness' are no longer taken as given and acted upon as a matter of course. We only need to think of the various crises that have confronted the Balkan states. But in modern commercial enterprises as well, such conditions are both demanding, and leading to, greater autonomy of action. This is a process which increasingly involves companies having to reinvent themselves in an attempt to gain competitive advantage by allowing their employees to team up non-hierarchically as 'clever people', empowered to take decisions themselves on the basis of their knowledge and skills.[22] Organic, evolutionary, teleological, functional modes of relationship would stifle much of the cutting-edge creativity needed for such a process.

The Revival of Community in Late Modernity

In late modernity, the fear of social disintegration as an unintended consequence of the levelling of hierarchies and the demise of 'official approving agencies' is resulting in a renewed interest in community. It is in this context that Habermas draws our attention to the resurgence of communities which he sees as 'the revaluation of the particular, the natural, the provincial, of social spaces that are small enough to be familiar'.[23] Bauman also writes that 'community is now expected to bring the succour previously sought in ... the legislative acts of the national state'.[24] He points to the new kind of togetherness brought about by so-called 'neo-tribes' that are 'conjured up with the intention of giving those choices that solidity the choosers sorely miss'.[25]

There is, however, a good deal of scepticism concerning the possibility of restoring the certainties traditionally associated with community in present-day social conditions. Giddens, for example, describes it as being an 'impractical dream',[26] and Bauman argues that the modern-day tribes 'share in the *inconsequentiality* of choices, and change little in the episodicity of the chooser's life'.[27] The communities of late modernity are, therefore, anything but cosy and natural. They are

> hard work and uphill struggle, a constantly receding horizon of the never ending road. ... The foremost paradox of the frantic search for communal grounds of consensus is that it results in more dissipation and fragmentation, more heterogeneity. ... The only consensus likely to stand a chance of success is the acceptance of heterogeneity of dissensions.[28]

Community today, Bauman asserts, is

> thought of as the uncanny (and in the end incongruous and unviable) mixture of difference and company: as uniqueness that is not paid for with loneliness, as contingency with roots, as freedom with certainty; its image, its allurement are as incongruous as that world of universal ambivalence from which – one hopes – it would provide a shelter.[29]

This process of 'uncertainization' is one which is only bound to continue and intensify in late modernity.[30]

Given these observations we might begin to doubt the appropriateness of the concept of 'community' to describe the rise of new forms of human association in late modernity. There is an obvious tension arising from a general longing for community together with a gradual realization that we cannot go back to the certainties of social arrangements which no longer exist. Let us dwell on this problem for a while, for it would seem that there is a need to seek to understand the opportunities for new forms of association in somewhat different terms, and to rethink what we should expect from them.

At a first glance, it is not difficult to see why, as Castells sometimes suggests, new forms of human association seem to resemble the kind of fragmented 'tribal' societies of days gone by.[31] Yet such a similarity is more apparent than real. Premodern tribal culture may well have been highly fragmented and segmented, but it also displayed a high level of presence availability and it was confined in respect of its configuration across time and space.[32] Modern developments in communication media are creating new networks of information diffusion which are profoundly altering the way in which we can construct shared 'realities'. Any comparison between tribalism of the past and the practices of groups of individuals in the late modern age is at best only superficial and not really very useful.

Neither should we equate new forms of communal life like those described by Claude Fischer in our modern cities with those available in premodern settings.[33] Fischer demonstrates that the infrastructure of modern cities and modern communications provides the means for generating new forms of human association which were unavailable to individuals in premodern settings.[34]

Applying the concept of community to the creation of new forms of human association tends to narrow down the spatial and temporal coordinates of their creation in a way that is mostly irrelevant to modern social life. Instead, we ought to emphasize and examine the ubiquitous nature of the thrust towards new kinds of human association, occurring as it does at all levels of our organizational culture: from national and paranational communities to regional and local ones, from communities in economic organizations engaged in collaborative work to communities created by social movements and other groups. No matter how fragmented human experience has become, under reflexive modernization most of us live in the same 'discursive space'. Giddens writes that 'there has never been a time when information about current events and problems has been more publicly debated, in a chronic fashion, than in the present day'.[35] In this respect, the idea of a twenty-four-hour economy refers to the fact that those who can afford to participate in it now also live in the same 'discursive time'.

What we are coming to terms with today is that modern communication technologies such as the internet are opening up opportunities for new forms of human association. Today, the production and reproduction of social reality are becoming re-embedded in local communal life in ways that were largely unavailable in previous modern settings. The possibilities of virtual reality are boosting to the extreme the dynamism of modern everyday life by heightening the process which Giddens describes as tearing 'space away from place by fostering relations between "absent" others'; 'the severing of time from space', he continues, 'provides a basis for their recombination in relation to social activity. ... This phenomenon serves to open up manifold possibilities of change by breaking free from the restraints of local habits and practices.'[36] In late modernity, the settings for human association come and go at an unprecedented rate, and more often than not individuals participate in a multitude of them.

Such a view radically opposes Rheingold's interpretation of 'community', which he still regards as necessarily deeply sedimented in time. These new forms of human association demand the spontaneous coordination constituted by modes of relationship characterized by Oakeshott not as the 'organic, evolutionary, teleological, functional or syndromic relationship' associated with traditional communities, but as 'an understood relationship of intelligent agents'.[37] Being in an *intelligent relationship*, Giddens writes, 'means living along with others in a way that respects their autonomy'.[38] Consequently, individuals who are thus associated 'are not partners or colleagues in an enterprise with a common purpose to pursue or a common interest to promote or protect. ... They are related in terms of a practice.'[39] The efficiency of these new ways of teaming up can no longer be measured in terms of goals alone, but needs to be evaluated in terms of 'their capacity to share in a give and take experience'.[40]

Unlike traditional communities, these new forms of association embrace in Giddens's view 'cosmopolitanism, as an attitude of mind and as an institutionalized phenomenon'.[41] The cosmopolitan, Giddens argues, often misunderstood as an individualist and as an enemy of old-style communities, is 'someone who is able to articulate the nature of those commitments, and assess their implications for those whose values are different'. As such, a cosmopolitan attitude is not one in which anything goes, and thus is not a threat to communality and commitment. Nor is it an attitude that insists that all values are equivalent. It is an attitude which, according to Giddens, emphasizes 'the responsibility that individuals and groups have for the ideas they hold and the practices in which they engage'.[42]

There are those who claim that the beginnings of the new kinds of human association we are witnessing today signal our entry into a new age which they label as 'post-modernity'. However, as Thompson writes,

> if the debates sparked off by postmodernism have taught us anything, it is not that the developmental processes characteristic of modern societies have propelled us beyond modernity to some new and as yet undefined age, but rather that our traditional theoretical frameworks for understanding these processes are, in many respects, woefully inadequate.[43]

As we shall see later in this chapter, the discussion concerning 'virtual communities' is deeply steeped in postmodern rhetoric, thus making this a matter to which we shall need to return.

The Problems of Solidarity in Late Modernity

Group identity, Fredrik Barth writes, is always exclusionary in that the way forms of human association are perceived depends on the way their participants view outsiders.[44] Any attempt to create new forms of human association on more spontaneous and 'inclusive' grounds is therefore beset by a range of problems. Bauman rightly observes that 'in the world of imagined communities, the struggle for survival is a struggle for access to the human imagination'.[45] Besides a great many practical problems, mobilizing the opportunities offered by new technologies of communication will always involve interests that may be contested by others. Let us therefore look at some of the problems which Giddens claims might be encountered in a quest for establishing new forms of human conduct and solidarity in late modernity.[46]

First, the idea and reality of community has long been bound up with forms of centralized authority and claims to universal truths defended within hierarchically organized social settings. Now, in an era of intensified detraditionalization, neither states nor economic organizations have clear-cut ideas about how dynamic, high-paced, ephemeral forms of human association ought to be run, or about how the direction of their progress ought to be judged. For Jean-François Lyotard,

> the community required as a support for the validity of such judgement must always be in the process of doing and undoing itself. The kind of consensus implied by such a process, if there is any consensus at all, is in no way argumentative but is rather allusive and elusive, endowed with a spiral way of being alive, combining both life and death, always remaining *in statu nascendi* or *moriendi*, always keeping open the issue of whether or not it actually exists. This kind of consensus is definitely nothing but a cloud of community.[47]

Thus in an age of detraditionalization we urgently need to address the renewal of tradition guided by tolerance and dialogue.

A second problem to be encountered in establishing new forms of human conduct, Giddens claims, is that the levelling up of hierarchies and of 'official approving agencies' could quite easily prove dangerous and result in 'tyranny' rather than in new forms of solidarity.[48] The prospects hailed by Rheingold and other writers of the anarchic characteristics of the internet might not turn out to be so exciting after all.[49] In most industrialized societies, the nation-state has achieved a very high level of consolidation and internal pacification, and hierarchical organizations have equally achieved high levels of administrative unity and control.[50] The opening up of all forms of authority to critical questioning results in yet more conflict and struggle. Giddens, in this respect, warns of the possible upsurge of fundamentalism.[51] We might also fear the return of oppressive parochiality and other communal pressures as organizations increasingly involve the work of autonomous teams, empowered by new information technologies, striving to deliver projects and benefits at the expense of those preferred by others. Frustrations may run high as we begin to realize, as Bauman explains, that

> even with absolute truth defunct and universality dead and buried – some people at least can still have what their past (legislatively predisposed) benefactors, now decried as deceitful, promised to give: the joy of being 'in the right' – though now perhaps not at all times, not in all places at the same time, and only for certain people.[52]

The third problem in establishing new forms of human conduct, Giddens argues, is that the idea of democratization, and thereby the revitalization of community, is a problematic one.[53] Guaranteeing the rights of members of a community to free speech and free association, for example, has never led to the successful creation of community. Without some kind of balance between individual freedoms on the one hand and responsibilities for issues that go beyond individual needs on the other, any sense of community may soon evaporate, like Lyotard's cloud, in the heat of the moment.

The fourth problem recognized by Giddens is that while new technologies of communication may provide the means for creating new forms of action and interaction, they do not automatically result in understood relationships of intelligent agents.[54] We need, I think, to be strongly reminded of Thompson's critique of the notion of *participatory opinion formation*, a possibility that he believes to be far removed from the political reality and possibility of our time. He writes that 'at the level of national and international politics, and at the upper levels in which power is exercised in large-scale civil and commercial organizations, it is difficult to see how the idea of participatory opinion formation could be implemented in any significant way'.[55]

Despite these problems, new forms of human association remain of central importance because they constitute the spaces in which the processes of meaning generation and truth validation are set. As Bauman writes:

> Privatized existence has its many joys: freedom of choice, the opportunity to try many ways of life, the chance to make oneself to the measure of one's self-image. But it also has its sorrows as well: loneliness and incurable uncertainty as to the choices made and still to be made. ... This is why we all feel time and again an overwhelming 'need of belonging' – a need to identify ourselves not just as individual human beings, but as members of a larger entity.[56]

However sceptical we might be about the nature of and need for new forms of human association in late modernity, we need to develop an understanding of the kinds of threats and chances they may bring.

NOTES

1 H. Rheingold, *The Virtual Community: Homesteading on the Electronic Frontier* (Reading, MA: Addison-Wesley, 1993).
2 Ibid., p. 3.
3 Ibid., p. 4.
4 Ibid., pp. 1–16.
5 M. Poster, *The Second Media Age* (Cambridge: Polity Press, 1995), p. 35.
6 Rheingold, *The Virtual Community*, p. 1.
7 Ibid., p. 2.
8 B. Anderson, *Imagined Communities: Reflections on the Origin and Spread of Nationalism* (London: Verso, 1983), pp. 13–14.
9 Poster, *The Second Media Age*, p. 34.
10 M. Nash, *The Cauldron of Ethnicity in the Modern World* (Chicago, IL: University of Chicago Press, 1989), pp. 128–9.
11 F. Tönnies, *Community and Association* [*Gemeinschaft and Gesellschaft*]. Trans. C.P. Loomis (London: Routledge and Kegan Paul, 1887/1955).
12 Anderson, *Imagined Communities*.
13 Z. Bauman, *Intimations of Postmodernity* (London: Routledge, 1992), p. xix.
14 Anderson, *Imagined Communities*, pp. 15–16.
15 A. Giddens, *The Nation-State and Violence*, Vol. 2 of *A Contemporary Critique of Historical Marxism* (Cambridge: Polity Press, 1985), pp. 192–7.
16 J.-L. Nancy, *The Inoperative Community* (Minneapolis: University of Minnesota Press, 1991), p. xxxviii.
17 R. Dworkin, *A Matter of Principle* (Oxford: Clarendon Press, 1986), p. 2.
18 M. Oakeshott, *On Human Conduct* (Oxford: Clarendon Press, 1975), p. 112.
19 Ibid., pp. 315–16.
20 Ibid., p. 316.
21 A. Giddens, *Beyond Left and Right: The Future of Radical Politics* (Cambridge: Polity Press, 1994), p. 67.
22 H.C. Lucas, *The T-Form Organization: Using Technology to Design Organizations for the Twenty-First Century* (San Francisco, CA: Jossey-Bass, 1996).
23 J. Habermas, *The Theory of Communicative Action*, Vol. 2, *The Lifeworld and System: A Critique of Functionalist Reason* (Cambridge: Polity Press, 1987), p. 395.
24 Bauman, *Intimations of Postmodernity*, pp. xvii–xix.
25 Z. Bauman, *Postmodernity and its Discontents* (Cambridge: Polity Press, 1997), p. 196.
26 Giddens, *Beyond Left and Right*, p. 124.
27 Bauman, *Postmodernity and its Discontents*, p. 196.
28 Bauman, *Intimations of Postmodernity*, pp. 138–9.
29 Ibid., pp. 134–5.
30 Bauman, *Postmodernity and its Discontents*, p. 203.
31 M. Castells, *The Information Age: Economy, Society and Culture*, Vol. 3, *End of Millennium* (Oxford: Blackwell, 1998), p. 352.
32 A. Giddens, *The Constitution of Society: Outline of the Theory of Structuration* (Cambridge: Polity Press, 1984), pp. 184–95.
33 C. Fischer, *To Dwell among Friends: Personal Networks in Town and City* (Chicago, IL: University of Chicago Press, 1982).
34 A. Giddens, *The Consequences of Modernity* (Cambridge: Polity Press, 1990), p. 116.
35 Giddens, *Beyond Left and Right*, p. 94.
36 Giddens, *The Consequences of Modernity,* pp. 18–20.

37 Oakeshott, *On Human Conduct*, p. 112.
38 Giddens, *Beyond Left and Right*, p. 130.
39 Oakeshott, *On Human Conduct*, p. 122.
40 J. Dewey, *Democracy and Education* (New York: Macmillan, 1917), p. 120.
41 Giddens, *Beyond Left and Right*, p. 131.
42 Ibid., p. 130.
43 J.B. Thompson, *The Media and Modernity: A Social Theory of the Media* (Cambridge: Polity Press, 1995), pp. 8–9.
44 F. Barth (ed.), *Ethnic Groups and Boundaries: The Social Organization of Culture Difference*, the results of a symposium held at the University of Bergen, 23–26 February 1967 (London: Allen and Unwin, 1969).
45 Bauman, *Intimations of Postmodernity*, p. xx.
46 Giddens, *Beyond Left and Right*, pp. 124–5.
47 J.-F. Lyotard, *Peregrinations: Law, Form, Event* (New York: Columbia University Press, 1988), p. 38.
48 Giddens, *Beyond Left and Right*, pp. 124–5.
49 Rheingold, *The Virtual Community*, p. 14.
50 Giddens, *The Nation-State and Violence*, pp. 181–92.
51 Giddens, *Beyond Left and Right*, p. 125.
52 Bauman, *Intimations of Postmodernity*, p. 135.
53 Giddens, *Beyond Left and Right*, pp. 124–5.
54 Ibid.
55 J.B. Thompson, *Ideology and Modern Culture: Critical Theory in the Era of Mass Communication* (Cambridge: Polity Press, 1990), p. 120.
56 Z. Bauman, *Life in Fragments: Essays in Postmodern Morality* (Oxford: Blackwell, 1995), p. 275.

V

NORMATIVE THEORY

Much theorizing in the social sciences about mass media has been driven less by intellectual curiousity or practical concerns to increase communications efficiency than by value commitments and ideas of potential benefit or harm to individuals or society. These concerns embrace issues of public enlightenment and progress, morality and good order, justice and equality, social identity and cohesion, cultural 'quality', the working of democratic political institutions and much more. There can be no unified body of 'normative theory' because of the diversity of values and aspirations of theorists and their followers, but they all share the view that the operations of every means of *publication* is never a purely neutral matter, but has implications for society as a whole as well as component individual members and groupings. Ideas about what is a 'good society' inevitably lead to some consideration of forms of public communication. The transition from mass to more specialized and individualized flows of communication made possible by 'new media' opens a potentially new perspective. In theory, responsibility shifts from centralized provision and controllers of mass communication channels to the individual or organized 'users'. In practice, the old media have not withered away and 'new media' are being considered according to long-established normative principles.

The unbreakable link that been established in modern Western society between freedom to communicate and to publish, on the one hand, and human rights and principles of democracy, on the other hand, is the firmest rock on which normative theories are based. But not far behind is the belief that communications are a resource for social betterment or a potential source of social harm, and on both grounds they fall within the legitimate jurisdiction of action on behalf of the 'public good'. Between them, these considerations ensure that normative theory is not only diverse and very much alive, but also replete with contradictions and tensions. The selections for the most part relate to different perspectives on the role of media in democracy (especially Dahlgren, Chapter 16, and Lichtenberg, Chapter 14), but they also deal with wider claims to direct, apply and limit media according to ideas of the 'public interest', itself a very contested concept, despite its wide currency (Dennis, Chapter 13).

What media that exist specifically to serve the public interest might be like, in the sense of meeting certain expectations of information and cultural performance, is examined in respect of an established public broadcasting model (Blumler and Hoffmann-Reim, Chapter 17). The excerpt from Nerone (Chapter 15) examines the main principles on which self-regulation of the press has been based, primarily, that is, under the banner of 'social responsibility theory'. Although 'public service broadcasting' as a media structural arrangement is not widely diffused and is in relative decline even in its own European heartlands, it has acquired the status of a model of what is possible in applying communications media to the ends of public enlightenment in a democracy and service to other social institutions, thus without the primary motive of profit. Its theoretical virtues and potential have gained more recognition under conditions of marginalization and external threat. There may be lessons for securing the much vaunted public benefits of 'new media', in the face of the realities of commercialization.

13

the press and the public interest:
a definitional dilemma

EVERETTE E. DENNIS

Whether the interest of the press as the issuer of information is necessarily the same as that of the consumer of the information is central to many critiques of the mass media. This conflict of interests between the individual and the mass media is often resolved by invoking the public interest as a mediating principle. While the truism that the press should serve the public interest is accepted by nearly everyone, the satisfactory definition of that concept has proven much more difficult. '[T]here are two distinct interests,' wrote philosopher William Ernest Hocking, 'only one of them needs ... protection; to protect the issuer is to protect the consumer.'[1] Freedom of the press, Hocking suggested, 'has always been a matter of public as well as individual importance. Inseparable from the right of the press to be free has been the right of the people to have a free press.'[2]

Examining the public interest concept in terms of the motivation for legislative attacks on executive secrecy, Professor Francis E. Rourke noted that the strongest efforts in this area had come initially from the press and the scientific community. This, he said, 'reflects the wide variety of interests [but] each ... can also point to a clear public interest in the success of its special efforts.'[3] Professor Rourke continued:

[T]he public has an obvious stake in the effective performance of the legislative task, as it does in the availability of information in the hands of executive officials to the media of communications upon which the people depend for knowledge concerning the affairs of government. And the public has no less an interest in keeping open the channels of communications upon which the economic progress of society may be said to depend.[4]

Rourke's rationale that the public has a deep interest in the free flow of information, and thereby a free press, is frequently echoed by students of government, the press, newsmen and judges. That was what Mr Justice Brennan has in mind in *New York Times Co. v. Sullivan* when he enunciated a profound national commitment to the principle of debate on public issues which he said should be 'uninhibited, robust and wide open.'[5] This principle brought an exasperated response from Jerome A. Barron, law professor and authority on access to the news media. Fumed Barron: 'newspaper publishers' interests and the public interest are held to be identical,' and the result of the *Times* decision was 'romantic and lopsidedly pro publisher.'[6]

Clearly, Barron and others believe that the consumer of communication should also have a right to determine what shall constitute freedom of the press. The exercise of this prerogative, in Barron's view, would serve the public interest. Such a position is sharply at odds with the 1947 Commission on Freedom of the Press which observed '[that] the work of the press always involves the interest of the consumer; but as long as the consumer is free his interest is protected in the protection of the freedom of the issuer.'[7]

First published in *Enduring Issues in Mass Communication*, E.E. Dennis, A.H. Ismach and D.M. Gillmor, St. Paul, MN: West Publishing Company (1978) as 'The Press and the Public Interest: a definitional dilemma, pp. 327–340.

THE SEARCH FOR DEFINITION

Few concepts have attracted as much scholarly probing as the public interest. 'It is probable that as much mischief has been perpetrated upon the human race in the name of "the public interest" as in the name of anything else,' wrote Daniel Bell and Irving Kristol as they introduced a new journal titled *The Public Interest* in 1965.[8] Although the concept traces its origins to the writings of Plato and Aristotle and has provided the substance for many books, papers and scholarly presentations, the public interest is little more than 'a conceptual muddle,' as suggested by political scientist Frank Sorauf, who wrote: 'Clearly, no scholarly consensus exists on the public interest, nor does agreement appear to be in the offing.'[9]

In part the disillusionment with the concept springs from the vague and confusing meanings that have been attached to it. The rubric of public interest seems to belong to that genre of euphemisms that includes the public welfare, the common good, and the national interest. In part, the problem with the concept is its idealistic and pristine nature as demonstrated in Walter Lippmann's comment that 'the public interest may be presumed to be what men would choose if they saw clearly, thought rationally, acted disinterestedly and benevolently.'[10] The British writer Robert Skidelsky, however, sees the term as a dying metaphor because one man's metaphor is always another man's reality.[11]

The despair of the critics notwithstanding, the term is not to be escaped. It is pervasive in the literature of the first amendment and serves as a guiding principle for the courts and the public philosophers. The public interest 'is the central concept of a civilized polity [and] its genius lies not in its clarity but in its perverse and persistent moral intrusion upon the internal and external discourse of rulers and ruled alike....'[12]

Even though a political scientist's 1960 observation that 'there is no public interest theory worthy of the name'[13] remains valid in 1973, there have been some notable attempts in recent years to explicate the concept more fully. One of the best efforts is a brilliant treatise by political scientist Virginia Held, *The Public Interest and Individual Interests*.[14] Before defining the concept in her own terms, she synthesizes the literature of the public interest and proposes three classifications: (1) preponderance theories, (2) the public interest as common interest, and (3) unitary conceptions.

The preponderance theories are based on the assumption that if the public interest has any meaning at all it 'cannot be in conflict with a preponderance or sum of individual interests, although this preponderance may be thought to be constituted and to be calculable in very different ways.'[15]

The preponderance theories are traced to the writings of Hobbes, who believed in a preponderance of force; Hume, an exponent of preponderance of opinion; and Bentham, who advanced the idea of superior sum of individual interests. A contemporary application of preponderance theory is the relationship between the Federal Communications Commission and the networks' programming on television, a kind of lowest common denominator guided by ratings designed to give the public what it says it wants.

In examining the public interest as a common interest, Ms Held says, 'the equation of the public interest with those interests which all members of a polity have in *common*,' forms the core of this idea.[16] This concept agrees with preponderance theories in not ruling out the possibility of justifiable conflicts of individual interest, but it defines the public interest in terms of unanimity and compatibility. Common interest theory finds support in the writings of Rousseau who spoke of the common good and the general will. A modern application of this common interest theory would be shared interest and mutual trust. The unitary formulation is based on universal moral precepts and hence,

> individual interests cannot justifiably conflict with the public interest or with each other. Only a universal moral order can confer validity, or justifiability, and the same universal order which renders a judgment that a given action or state is right or good cannot also render a judgment that the same action or state is wrong or evil.[17]

The formulation advanced by Ms Held is an attempt to outline a norm for public interest that would function within the political and legal systems and would be governed by authoritative rules of conduct. She asserts that

> the policy may be understood as a system which validates public interest claims ... [and] ... that only the political system provides an effective decision method which could be associated with the term *public* for claims of what is or is not in the public interest. Any such decision method or network of methods for a given society is constitutive of a political system.[18]

This system suggests that 'no judgment concerning the public interest can be valid outside the political system whose decision procedures validate claims about it, although judgments concerning ... the public interest, and the political system can itself be judged in moral terms.'[19]

How would Ms Held's construct be applied? In the instance of the regulation of television programming, for example, there would be at least two levels for consideration. First, the question of the *preferences* of a majority of the population would be determined empirically. Similarly, the *interests* of the majority could also be determined empirically, but

> [b]oth of these questions would be distinct from that of whether existing programming practices are in the *public interest*. It might or it might not be considered in the interest of the polity to satisfy majority interest in this field. The question of majority interest might well be the one with which we were concerned, in a particular discussion, but if so, we would do well to use this term, not the public interest. We might conceivably decide, for instance, that it is not in the public interest for government to interfere with television programming, no matter what is produced, and that this decision has priority over any evaluation of program content. Discussion of the latter,

then, might be in terms of majority interests, of the responsibilities of the networks to minority interests, or of aesthetic considerations, and perhaps not in terms of the public interest at all.[20]

The Held system depends, of course, on statutory regulations and the courts as a mechanism for adjudicating public interest disputes.

Perhaps the most useful distinction in this conceptual definition is the clear dividing line between preference and interest. What interests the public, in terms of its wants, desires and tastes may necessarily be in the public interest. For example, in a developing nation, the immediate desires of pre-literate people for a certain content in television programming might not comport with the government's desire to use television as a channel for education and culture. Thus, even in a democracy, majority rule might be in conflict with the public interest. In American society, for example, freedom of speech is a fundamental tenet of constitutional law and of societal values. However, in a single instance the majority of the community might favor censorship. Under Ms Held's system, public interest doctrine would dictate adherence to societal rules, overturning the immediate will of the majority. In many instances such an approach is essential to the preservation of minority rights, aesthetic values and other public interest concerns.

The public interest definitional dilemma indicated in this section illustrates the still turbulent nature of the debate over this most complex of concepts. ...

[...]

MEDIA INTEREST AND PUBLIC INTEREST

In a variety of polemic treatises over the years, spokesmen for the communications industry in America have maintained that they operate *in* the public interest. This is a traditional view of the first amendment and is solidly grounded in the cases previously cited. It is, most commentators agree, a negative interpretation of the first amendment, focussing on the phrase, 'Congress shall make no law,' a command that has been interpreted as a shield against interference with the free flow of information. Clearly this interpretation favors the issuer of communication. It is an ultimate triumph for the 'trickle-down' theory of mass communication and press freedom. By allowing the purveyors of communication maximum freedom, the means for the free flow of information to the public is determined.

Arguing for a positive interpretation of the first amendment, law professor and authority on mass media Jerome Barron takes sharp issue with the 'trickle-down' theory. He sees this traditional interpretation of the first amendment as abrogating individual rights of communications access to a small number of vital voices in the marketplace of ideas. Barron's model, however, may be likened to a pinball machine. He would add more voices to the marketplace and while they would shoot their messages on different vectors, the ultimate result would be pinballs moving in the same direction and within a fixed range which may be designated as 'press freedom.' According to this view, the diversity of many voices rather than the stable force of a few, best serves freedom and the public interest.

While the argument centering on the question of whether the press interest and public interest are synonymous rages, the work of the public philosophers and the jurists has helped to clarify its components. They do not, however, offer any objective criterion for deciding what is *in* the public interest. Since one ultimate controlling mechanism for adjudicating the public interest and sorting it out among a range of individual and private interests is the courts, one would hope to find guidance in the opinions of the judiciary. But any expectation for definition from this sector is quickly cooled since the courts have consistently blended public interest into an ambiguous rhetorical concept. As most of the decisions previously reviewed indicate, the courts have said that what is *of* public interest is *in* the public interest. Such a position suggests that the public interest is a larger superstructure than the preferential information demands of individuals, although their needs and wants fall under the concept's general rubric.

In American society the Constitution is the ultimate statement of the public interest. Operation of the society under the provisions of the Constitution, which imply and specifically state general goals, *is* in the public interest. Thus, a free press is a means by which the public interest is transmitted and eventually achieved. It is the visible barometer, the expression of performance. If one accepts this general precept, the public's interest is much more than giving the public what it wants. Preferential choice needs to be consistent with constitutional rules. Inherent in our constitutional government is the assumption that the process of democracy is delegated—as a public trust—to public servants and officials. In delegating this trust, society takes an important step in the view of audience researcher Robert Silvey, who wrote:

> It is as though society says in effect to the public servant: 'It is up to you to look after our interests. You must immerse yourself in your subject, because we haven't time to do so. There may come times when we shall demand that you take a certain course which you, having weighed it in the light of your knowledge and experience, will tell us is not in fact in our interest. Though you are our servant you must, in such a case, refuse to obey us. You will be right to do so, for though at the time you will be refusing to give us what we want, you will, paradoxically, be doing what in the long run we want you to do.'[21]

So it is that the courts find themselves adjudicating press freedom cases. In this process they must be concerned not only with the aggregate preferences of society, but also with larger constructs of freedom for the social order—as well as for the individual. It has been in such a spirit that the courts have decided that:

a.   The free flow of information is in the public interest.
b.   Information about public affairs is of public interest and in the public interest.

c. The publication of newsworthy information is in the public interest.
d. Communications diversity is in the public interest.
e. Government regulation of certain communications activities 'affected with a public interest' is in the public interest.
f. Matters *of* public interest or matters *in* the public interest are usually immune from libel and privacy recovery.

Although these statements provide the foundation for defining the public interest in regard to media behavior, it is first necessary to dispense with the suggestion that the public interest is a mere myth. The reasoning of Professor Hans Morgenthau is useful in performing this task:

> I happen to believe that there is a possibility by rational political analysis to arrive at certain objective conclusions which define in negative terms what it is not. So, you see, if you assume that the national interest is a mere fiction, a mere ideological justification and rationalization of particular parochial interests, you have nothing to go on except the rivalry of different and frequently incompatable [*sic*] powerful interests, each claiming to be the national interest.[22]

Thus by the very act of being free, the press operates in the public interest. However, as Barron points out, because freedom of the press belongs to all of the people, the press, as an issuer of communication, has no right to prevent the communication of others. Activities by the press that drive out competition, encourage censorship, or prevent free discussion and debate on matters of public concern are at odds with the notion of positive freedom of the press. They are, therefore, not in the public interest. Thus the public interest and the media interest are congruent only when there is a viable relationship between issuer and consumer of communication that is operating to the satisfaction of both. This does not mean simply giving the public what it wants; rather, it entails acquainting the public with the broad range of possibilities and then allowing it to make a free choice within that extensive panoply. When immediate whims and curiosity-seeking by the issuer or the consumer conflict with other social rights, the government, through the court system, should act as the regulator. For example, the interest in a celebrated trial may be quite high and the media may want to cover it in all aspects. However, such coverage might conflict with an individual's right to a fair trial. In such an instance it is up to the courts to sort out the conflicting interests and values.

If communication law cases were decided in a public interest framework, a quite precise, measurable definition of the public interest would no doubt emerge. That definition would be dynamic, flexible and accommodating, while at the same time it would provide a standard and a rationale for media behavior.

Government, however, is not the only check and balance between purely private interests and the public interest. In examining other entities that also advance and protect the public interest, the public health model of disease prevention is useful. The public health model suggests three levels of prevention—primary, secondary and tertiary. When applied to the public interest problem at hand it can be expressed schematically as it is in Figure 13.1.

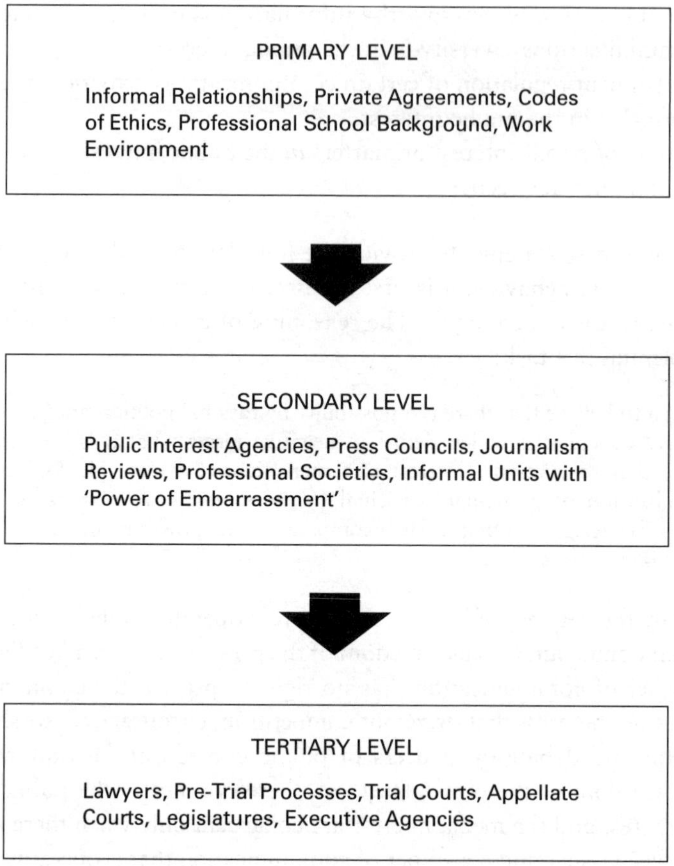

PRIMARY LEVEL

Informal Relationships, Private Agreements, Codes of Ethics, Professional School Background, Work Environment

---

SECONDARY LEVEL

Public Interest Agencies, Press Councils, Journalism Reviews, Professional Societies, Informal Units with 'Power of Embarrassment'

TERTIARY LEVEL

Lawyers, Pre-Trial Processes, Trial Courts, Appellate Courts, Legislatures, Executive Agencies

---

FIGURE 13.1 Adjudicatory means for public interest conflicts

At the primary level, prevention of public interest violations could be accomplished through informal educational processes in which the various parties in society would interact and settle their differences privately. In this arena, the universities, especially schools of journalism, have a broad mandate to teach ethics and responsible performance. Ideally, all disputes could be settled in this free and informal forum.

At the secondary level of prevention, watchdog agencies would monitor press behavior and attempt to curb abuses and point out public interest violations. These agencies would include such public interest bodies as Ralph Nader's Center for the Study of Responsive Law and John Gardiner's Common Cause. Further, the press could be more directly influenced through press councils, communications task forces and foundations, journalism reviews and professional groups.

Finally, and only after the other two levels had failed, would the prevention measures of the tertiary level be employed. This would include the courts, the legislature and the executive branch of government.

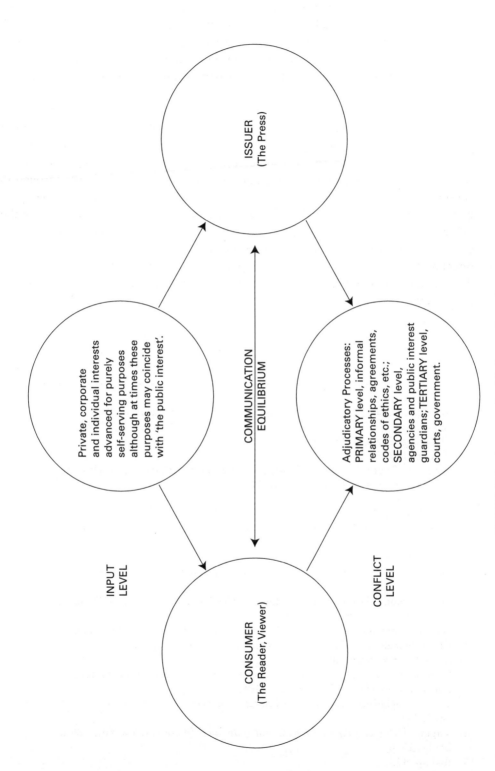

FIGURE 13.2 A system of public interest/press interest

As previously discussed, the public interest and the press interest would be contiguous when maximum freedom and minimal interference exist in both. Operationally, the press interest/public interest would be measured in terms of the degree to which the press fostered the free flow of information and satisfied the justifiable information needs of its consumers. Only when such a balanced ratio is achieved will the interest of the press and the interest of the public be one and the same.

Figure 13.2 illustrates such a scheme in which the public interest would begin to define itself. It would be the reaction of the press to higher-order interests expressed in the Constitution, blended with the interests of individuals and groups in society. The input for this information pool would be the expressions of public and private interests related directly to the issuer of communication or indirectly to the issuer through the consumer. This interplay between issuer and consumer would determine the appropriate messages to be communicated to society and hopefully would solidify the public interest content of those messages. All conflicts would be adjudicated through the primary, secondary and tertiary processes indicated above. Monitoring such an operational system would yield a system of public interest/press interest with attendant doctrine and methodologies. Only then could the public interest be determined with any validity and certainty.

NOTES

1   William Ernest Hocking, *Freedom of the Press: A Framework of Principle*, a report from the Commission on Freedom of the Press (Chicago, IL: University of Chicago Press, 1947), p. 164.
2   Ibid., p. 169.
3   Francis E. Rourke, *Secrecy and Publicity: Dilemmas of Democracy* (Baltimore, MD: Johns Hopkins Press, 1966), p. 31.
4   Ibid., p. 31.
5   *New York Times Co. v. Sullivan*, 376 U.S. 254, 270 (1964).
6   Jerome A. Barron, *Freedom of the Press for Whom? The Right of Access to the Mass Media* (Bloomington: University of Indiana Press, 1973), p. 12.
7   Hocking, *Freedom of the Press*, p. 224.
8   Daniel Bell and Irving Kristol, 'What is the public interest?', *The Public Interest* (Fall 1965), p. 4.
9   Frank Sorauf, 'The conceptual muddle', in *The Public Interest*, Carl J. Friedrich (ed.) (New York: Atherton, 1962).
10 Walter Lippmann, *The Public Philosophy* (New York: Mentor, 1955), p. 40.
11 Robert Skidelsky, 'Politics is not enough: on the dying metaphor of the national interest', *Encounter* (January 1969), p. 47.
12 Stephen K. Bailey, 'The public interest: some operational dilemmas', in Friedrich (ed.) *The Public Interest*, p. 106.
13 Glendon Schubert, *The Public Interest* (Glencoe, IL: Free Press, 1960), pp. 223–4.
14 Virginia Held, *The Public Interest and Individual Interests* (New York: Basic Books, 1970).
15 Ibid., p. 43.
16 Ibid., p. 44; emphasis in original.

17 Ibid., p. 136.
18 Ibid., pp. 176–7; emphasis in original.
19 Ibid., p. 183.
20 Ibid., p. 192; emphasis in original.
21 Robert Silvey, 'Giving the public what it wants', *Contemporary Review* (May 1961), p. 261.
22 Noam Chomsky and Hans Morgenthau, 'National interest and the Pentagon Papers', *Partisan Review* (Summer 1972), pp. 336–75.

14

foundations and limits of freedom of the press

JUDITH LICHTENBERG

I confess that I do not entertain that firm and complete attachment to the liberty of the press which is wont to be excited by things that are supremely good in their very nature.

Alexis de Tocqueville, *Democracy in America*[1]

Freedom of the press is guaranteed only to those who own one.

A.J. Liebling, *The Press*[2]

Tocqueville and Liebling notwithstanding, freedom of the press in democratic societies is a nearly unchallengeable dogma – essential, it is thought, to individual autonomy and self-expression, and an indispensable element in democracy and the attainment of truth. Both its eloquent theoreticians and its contemporary popular advocates defend freedom of speech and freedom of the press in the same stroke, with the implication that they are inseparable, probably equivalent, and equally fundamental.

At the same time, we know that the press in its most characteristic modern incarnation – mass media in mass society – works not only to enhance the flow of ideas and information but also to inhibit it. Nothing guarantees that all valuable information, ideas, theories, explanations, proposals, and points of view will find expression in the public forum. Indeed, many factors lead us to expect that they will not. The most obvious is that 'mass media space-time' is a scarce commodity: Only so much news, analysis, and editorial opinion can be aired in the major channels of mass communication. Which views get covered, and in what way, depends mainly on the economic and political structure and context of press institutions, and on the characteristics of the media themselves.

These are some of the most important factors: (1) More often than not, contemporary news organizations belong to large corporations whose interests influence what gets covered (and, what is probably more central, what does not) and how. (2) News organizations are driven economically to capture the largest possible audience, and thus not to turn it off with whatever does turn it off – coverage that is too contro- versial, too demanding, too disturbing. (3) The media are easily manipulated by government officials (and others), for whom the press, by simply reporting press releases and official statements, can be a virtually unfiltered mouthpiece. (4) Characteristics of the media themselves constrain or influence coverage; thus, for example, television lends itself to an action-oriented, unanalytical treatment of events that can distort their meaning or importance.

It is not surprising, therefore, that a great range of opinion and analysis outside the narrow mainstream rarely sees the light of the mass media. This lack of diversity manifests itself in two ways. One is simply lack of adequate exposure to information and ideas that are true or interesting or useful, that help us to understand the world better or make life more satisfactory in one way or another. The range of views considered respectable enough to appear regularly in the American mass media is extraordinarily narrow. As a result, we are more ignorant and more provincial than we could be, and we may be worse off in other ways as well.

First published in *Democracy and the Mass Media*, J. Lichtenberg, Cambridge University Press (1990), as 'Foundations and Limits of Freedom of the Press', pp. 102–115.

The other consequence more directly concerns justice. The press, once thought of as an antidote to established power, is more likely to reinforce it, because access to the press – that is, the mass media – is distributed as unequally as are other forms of power. It is not, of course, that the less powerful never speak in the mass media or that their doings are never reported, or never sympathetically. But the deck is stacked against them because the press is itself a formidable power in our society, allied intimately (although not simply) with other formidable powers. Displacing the attention of the media from the usual sources of news – the words and deeds of public officials and public figures – often demands nothing less than the politics of theater, for which those using such tactics may also be blamed.

There are regulations meant to remedy these defects, to counteract the tendencies inhibiting diversity in the press. Until recently, when the Federal Communications Commission under Ronald Reagan rescinded it, the fairness doctrine required broadcasters to devote a 'reasonable percentage' of broadcast time to public issues in a way that presents contrasting viewpoints. Ownership of multiple media properties is limited (although rules limiting ownership were relaxed under Reagan's FCC). Cable television systems must dedicate some channels to public access. Nothing like the fairness doctrine ever applied to the print media, which, it is commonly thought, are rendered immune to such regulations in the United States by the First Amendment. In any case, regulations mandating coverage of any kind, or enacting even limited rights of access to the press (whether print or electronic), are much in dispute today. In part the dispute centers on the utility of such regulations – whether they produce or can be made to produce the intended effects. But at least as important in the current controversies is a central question of principle. Critics of regulation argue that freedom of the press, like freedom of speech, is at the core of what our society is about, and that commitment to it prohibits the policies in question: regulation of the press is incompatible with freedom of the press.

I believe that we have misunderstood what a modern democratic society's commitment to freedom of the press means and should be. Unlike freedom of speech, to certain aspects of which our commitment must be virtually unconditional, freedom of the press should be contingent on the degree to which it promotes certain values at the core of our interest in freedom of expression generally. Freedom of the press, in other words, is an instrumental good: It is good if it does certain things and not especially good (not good enough to justify special protections, anyway) otherwise. If, for example, the mass media tend to suppress diversity and impoverish public debate, the arguments meant to support freedom of the press turn against it, and we may rightly consider regulating the media to achieve the ultimate purposes of freedom of the press.

I

The press is often described as having a special 'watchdog function' or as being a kind of 'fourth branch of government.' Some writers, noting the First Amendment's mention of freedom of the press in addition to freedom of speech (the only reference in the Constitution, they emphasize, to a specific commercial enterprise), argue that the press is entitled to special protections, beyond those accorded speech in general. Yet when we examine the most famous arguments for freedom of the press, we find nothing to distinguish them from those for freedom of speech or expression generally. Mill's discussion in *On Liberty* begins by asserting the need for 'liberty of the press' and proceeds to enumerate arguments for freedom of expression in general. Similarly, in 'What Is Enlightenment?' Kant defends freedom of the press with general arguments for the benefits of freedom of thought and discussion.[3] It is much the same with the other standard sources in the literature of freedom of the press: The press is treated as a voice, albeit a more powerful one, on a par with individual voices, and defending press freedom is then tantamount to a general defense of free speech.

In one way there is nothing wrong with this. The arguments for freedom of the press *are* arguments for a more general freedom of expression. But it does not follow that whatever supports freedom of speech also supports freedom of the press, for at least two related reasons, which are discussed in the sections that follow. First, considerations internal to the theory of free speech itself may provide reasons for limiting freedom of the press. That is what is at issue in the claim that the contemporary mass media may suppress information and stifle ideas rather than promote them. Second, the modern press consists largely of vast and complex institutions that differ in essential respects both from individuals and from the early press, around which the concept of freedom of the press grew. Arguments that support freedom of expression for individuals or for small publications do not necessarily support similar freedoms for the mass media. But contemporary defenders of freedom of the press commonly assimilate the new forms to the old.

It remains to be seen, then, to what extent the arguments for free speech support freedom of the press.

II

We want free speech for many reasons. Some involve essentially individual interests; others, the public interest or the common good. Some have to do with politics, or democratic politics in particular; others concern intellectual values like truth. Still others have to do with promoting certain virtues of character, such as tolerance. Some involve the interests of speakers; others, the interests of listeners or society at large. Some arguments emphasize the disadvantages of suppressing speech rather than the advantages of allowing it. These considerations vary in strength and persuasive power, and not all support free speech in the same way. But one thing is clear: Any 'monistic' theory of free speech, emphasizing only one of these values, will fail to do justice to the variety and richness of our interests in free speech.

But plurality is not miscellany. It is striking that these considerations do not stand to one another accidentally as distinct arguments for a single conclusion but are bound together in various ways. Each of the main arguments I shall consider shares assumptions with some of the others. (Together they stand as a fine example of Wittgensteinian family resemblances.) In some cases, this is not surprising; in others, the connections are less apparent. In the following pages, I hope to make some of these connections clear and so go some way toward explaining why the existence of a variety of arguments for free speech is not simply fortuitous.

Let us begin by imposing some order on these arguments, first, by asking what we want when we want free speech. I believe we have two main goals: (1) that people be able to communicate without interference and (2) that there be many people communicating, or at least many different ideas and points of view being communicated. These commitments can be described in terms of two basic principles. The first we may call the *noninterference* or *no censorship principle*: One should not be prevented from thinking, speaking, reading, writing, or listening as one sees fit. The other I call the *multiplicity of voices principle*: The purposes of freedom of speech are realized when expression and diversity of expression flourish. Although, as we shall see, the arguments for free speech demonstrate the importance of both principles, they seem capable of conflict. Indeed, their conjunction partly explains our dilemma about freedom of the press: Government intervention seems to intrude on the first principle, but it may advance the second.

In theory, and often in practice, the principles are compatible: My being free to speak without interference in no way inhibits others from expressing themselves. I can write in my diary and you can write in yours; I can distribute my propaganda in the airport and you can distribute yours. (Even here we can see the beginnings of strain: The airport will support only so many.) To the extent that the principles peacefully coexist – and assuming that communication is a natural human urge – we satisfy the multiplicity of voices principle, a 'positive' principle requiring that something (talk, conversation, debate) happen, when we satisfy the 'negative' noninterference principle, which requires that something (interference) not happen. Yet, in fact, the freedom of editors and publishers from outside control can inhibit the multiplication of voices in the public forum. A newspaper may not interfere with a person's right to speak or write, but it may very well prevent her from expressing her views in that newspaper, even if it is the only one in town, and even if she has a legitimate and significant grievance or point of view and no comparable opportunity to publicize it. Such decisions are simply exercises of the newspaper's editorial autonomy, which appears to fall neatly under the noninterference principle. It may seem just as obvious that when this principle clashes with the multiplicity of voices, it is the latter that must give way.

But things are not so simple; what seems obvious may be false. Our interests in free speech make it plausible to speak of a fundamental right or freedom to think and speak and write and listen and read without interference; but there is no 'right to publish' or right to editorial autonomy in the same sense. No one – not even network presidents or newspaper publishers – possesses a fundamental right to editorial autonomy that is violated by regulation designed to enhance the multiplicity of voices.

To see why this is so, we must first examine the main arguments for free speech.

III

Among our deepest interests in free speech is a concern about individual autonomy and self-expression that cuts across any particular social or political ideal that is likely to divide us. Most basically, we take it to be of overriding importance that a person be able to think for himself, that whatever his 'outer' condition he not be intellectually or psychologically subjugated to another's will. Autonomy so understood requires freedom of speech because of the close connection between thought and language. A person cannot think freely if he cannot speak; and he cannot think freely if others cannot speak, for it is in hearing the thoughts of others and being able to communicate with them that we develop our thoughts. Thus, autonomy requires freedom to speak as well as freedom to hear. And it implies freedom of speech for others as well as for oneself – not simply on grounds of fairness but in order to attain one's own interests in freedom of speech.

To value autonomy is to value a certain intellectual or psychological condition, distinct from 'outer' freedom – the ability to govern our actions. We want the latter as well, of course, but outer freedom is subject to all the limits that the rights and like freedom of others impose. An appeal to freedom-in-general will not, then, carve out special protections for speech. But autonomy, conceived as the ability to think for oneself, differs from this much broader freedom of action. And it is precisely because one person's autonomy does not limit another's that we can value autonomy in an unqualified, nearly absolute way.

Yet the focus on autonomy might seem to signal an exaggerated preoccupation with the inner life. Surely, it will be objected, our interest in freedom of speech does not derive only from our concern with freedom of thought; surely we want also to be able to express our thoughts 'in the world.' Our fundamental interest in freedom of expression is an interest not only in freedom to think for ourselves but also in communicating our thoughts to others, leaving a mark on the world, making outer what is inner.

[···]

IV

Very different from the arguments from autonomy and self-expression is the argument from democracy, usually credited to Alexander Meiklejohn.[4] Because democracy means popular sovereignty, Meiklejohn argues, the citizens in a democracy, as the ultimate decision makers, need full (or at least a lot of) information to make intelligent political choices. Meiklejohn's argument stresses two functions of freedom of speech and press in a democracy. One is the informative function: Free speech permits the flow of information necessary for citizens to make informed decisions and for leaders (public servants) to stay abreast of the interests of their constituents (the sovereign electorate). Second, and not easily separated from the first, is the critical function: The press, in particular, serves as the people's watchdog, ensuring independent criticism and evaluation of the established power of government and other institutions that may usurp democratic power.

But Meiklejohn's account ignores an essential feature of democracy and an important function of free speech. Democracy means not only that 'the people' are collectively self-governing, but also that they are equal in an important sense. The democratic equality of persons bears on free speech in two ways. First, democracy functions as it should only when each person's interests are represented in the political forum; freedom of speech and press enhances opportunities for representation. Second, we show the sort of respect for persons associated with democracy both by acknowledging that anyone (regardless of race or class or lack of company) may have a view worth expressing, and by assuming that people can be open-minded or intelligent enough to judge alien views on their merits. Only under these conditions can majority rule become morally respectable and not merely the best of a bad lot of decision procedures.

The second point connects the democratic argument for free speech with the argument that freedom of speech is an indispensable means to the attainment of truth. The belief that anyone might make a valuable contribution to the search for truth or for better ways to do things does not mean that we think 'anyone' is likely to. It means: (1) There is no way of telling in advance where a good idea will come from. (2) Valuable contributions to arriving at truth come in many forms, speaking the truth being only one of them. We arrive at truth or the best policy largely by indirection. (3) Thus, much of the value of a person's contribution to the 'marketplace of ideas' is its role in stimulating others to defend or reformulate or refute, and that value may be quite independent of the merits of the original view. Even fallacy has its place in the search for truth. These are essentially Mill's points in Chapter 2 of *On Liberty*.

As I suggested earlier, the connection between the arguments from democracy and truth is not simply serendipitous. Most of us are democrats not only because we believe in an ultimate moral equality but in part because we believe that *things turn out better* in democracies. If this is not simply crude relativism (truth or goodness is whatever the majority thinks it is), then it must be rooted in the belief that the public exchange of ideas transforms popular decision making into something morally and epistemologically respectable. Moreover, egalitarianism, a linchpin of democracy, and fallibilism, a central assumption in the argument from truth, are mutually supportive: The first bids us attend to the views of the 'lowly' and the second bids us question those of the expert and the elite.

V

The interconnections among the various grounds for free speech help us understand another of its standard defenses. Both Kant and Mill stressed the role of freedom of expression in human self-realization or self-development. Although commentators usually cite Chapter 2 of *On Liberty* for the argument from truth, the whole work is an extended defense of the connection between freedom of expression and self-realization. Quoting Wilhelm von Humboldt, Mill proclaims that 'the end of man … is the highest and most harmonious development of his powers to a complete and consistent whole,' and that for this two conditions are requisite: 'freedom, and variety of situations.'[5] A variety of ideas is obviously both a precondition of and an essential ingredient in the latter. Kant argues that the 'public use of man's reason,' by which he means a person's ability to communicate ideas to the public at large, is essential to human enlightenment. On its face the argument from self-realization is vulnerable to the same kind of objection made against the argument from self-expression: All sorts of things (education and travel, for example) may enhance self-development, and nothing in the argument distinguishes speech. Self-development – making the most out of oneself, or making oneself as wise as possible – is surely an admirable goal, but one so broad and open-ended that it fails to mark out speech.

[···]

All our interests in free speech have an important social and even a public component. To satisfy them, a certain quantity and diversity of speech must exist and be heard – a multiplicity of voices. That there must be a multiplicity of voices if free speech is to advance the causes of democracy and truth is obvious. But the same goes for autonomy and self-development, values that can seem purely private and isolated from the public world, and that may at first sight seem to support only the non-interference principle. This is not simply because all thinking involves language, which is public, but because thinking for oneself is a matter not of coming up with wholly original ideas but rather of subjecting one's ideas, which come largely from others, to certain tests. Autonomy is not a matter of believing what you feel like believing, as freedom, on some accounts, is a matter of doing what you feel like doing and therefore tantamount to noninterference. Autonomy and self-development in an intellectual vacuum are impossible. Thus, a multiplicity of voices is central to achieving individual autonomy and not only to the more obviously social goods, democracy and truth. And, on the other hand, noninterference – the opportunity to express oneself and to hear others express themselves – is as essential to the attainment of the social values underlying free speech as to the individual.

VI

Taken together, these arguments support a strong free speech principle, one that enables individuals and groups to think, speak, write, listen, read, and publish freely.

Even under a strong free speech principle, however, all such activities take place under constraints. I may read what I like, but not without your permission if the only copy of my favorite book happens to be in your private library. I may orate on the evils of fluoridation, but not (unless she permits) in the dentist's waiting room. I may write what I think is a groundbreaking tract, but nothing guarantees its publication in the journal of my choice (or any, for that matter).

How do we account for these constraints? One way is to say that our commitment to free speech amounts only to prohibitions against restriction by *government*, leaving open restriction by private parties. But this is unsatisfactory because insofar as we value free speech we will want to remove obstacles to it from whatever source, public or private. That we are morally barred from taking remedies when the obstacle is private must be demonstrated; it cannot simply be assumed.

A related account of the constraints on free speech asserts that a person's freedom of speech is limited by the property rights of others. But this is inadequate because it suggests both that property rights are ultimate, simple, and straightforward, marking a natural line between mine and thine, and that they always take priority, setting a rigid framework within which free speech (and other important moral and political principles) must maneuver a narrow course.

But the system of property relations, and its connection with other interests, is much more complicated than this account allows. Ownership rights over things (including everything from your toothbrush to the corner drugstore to General Motors) evolve in response to a variety of factors. Some are moral values, like privacy and equality. Some are pragmatic considerations: convenience, efficiency, and utility. Property rights are complex sets of relationships: With different kinds of property one can do different things; hardly ever can one do with one's property exactly what one pleases. Zoning laws; eminent domain; regulations concerning environmental protection, public utilities, health and safety – all attest to the qualified nature of property rights even in a system such as ours that accords great respect to private property.

If property relations did not have this character, the idea of a free speech principle (or anything rightly called a principle) would be very frail. However one thinks any specific free speech issue should be settled, a commitment to free speech of the kind embodied in the First Amendment means that when free speech clashes with other interests, the former has a pressing claim not automatically defeated by competing claims of property rights.

[…]

VII

The case of publishing, central to our discussion of freedom of the press, raises further complications. What is obvious is that no one has a right to publish, if that means a right to succeed in publishing where one chooses. I may send off my writings to any number of book or journal publishers – that is to say, I have the right to *try* to publish – but whether I succeed typically depends on choices that they are entitled to make.

This is just to acknowledge that the ability to publish is embedded in a system of property relations. But this is the beginning, not the end, of inquiry. For, as I have argued, property rights are not the simple and ultimate given from which all policy choices must begin; they themselves result from the interplay of a variety of considerations moral and pragmatic. And exactly what rights and duties follow upon property ownership in a particular kind of case depends on the interests at stake there.

It does not suffice, then, simply to assert the property rights of publishers and editors against all claims to regulate the press. The publisher may say, 'It's my newspaper and I can print what I want,' but the question remains why we should accept the absolutist conception of property rights lurking in that statement as defining the publisher's role. The appeal to property rights may explain why it is the publisher – rather than the reporter or the printer or the janitor – in whom editorial authority is invested, but it does not explain why newspapers and other media organizations should be immune from regulation when other businesses are not.

The answer cannot be that editorial autonomy is implicit in the commitment to free speech, for, as we have seen, the free speech principle does not imply a right to publish where one chooses. And that is as true for newspaper owners and network presidents as for anyone else. This point undercuts a great deal of the moral suasion that is supposed to attach to the assertion of editorial autonomy: Editorial autonomy – unlike the kind of individual autonomy discussed earlier – is not a fundamental human right, and defending it requires more than the appeal to the nobility of free speech values.

We can now see that the typical claim of editorial autonomy by publishers and editors is really a disguised property claim – it is the assertion of a property right in the guise of a free speech right. Because, as we have seen, property claims are not always decisive, and because the 'right' to free speech does not equal the right to editorial autonomy; the defense of editorial autonomy requires something more. If, even where there are serious costs to diversity and public debate, we grant publishers or editors the right of editorial autonomy, that is because on the whole doing so is the best way to advance free speech values. The question is whether a policy of nonregulation of the press is good for the values underlying free speech.

Let me put these conclusions in terms of the two basic principles described earlier as characterizing our interests in free speech: *noninterference* and the *multiplicity of voices*. Obviously, our worry about editorial autonomy is that it can inhibit the multiplicity of voices. But does the noninterference principle not support editorial autonomy? And how do we arrive at the judgment (which may seem to conflict with a standard liberal presumption in favor of noninterference as definitive of liberty) that multiplicity of voices takes priority over noninterference?

The answer has two parts. First, while the term 'noninterference' covers some crucial free speech values, it is made to carry more weight than it can bear. Its essential core is autonomy: What we fear most when we fear interference with freedom of expression is mind control, Big Brother style, being thrown into prison for opposing the government, and generally the extreme suppression we find in totalitarian regimes. Everyone can agree that these form the core of our concern with free speech – it is the freedoms at stake here that must be protected first and foremost. As soon as we get beyond these fundamental freedoms, however – as soon as the question is not whether one may speak, but where and in what form – the ability to express oneself becomes entangled with questions of property. It is not that at that point noninterference ceases to matter, but that its value is spread so thin as to make it a useless guide to action: The question is whether to interfere with my freedom to orate in the dentist's office or with her freedom to exclude trespassers from her property. The fact that here the dentist's claim wins hands down shows that noninterference-in-matters-of-speech is not the knockdown argument it sometimes seems. 'Time, place, and manner' restrictions – often added as if they were minor qualifications – lie at the heart of the matter.

While the first part of the answer shrinks the scope and power of the noninterference principle, the second enhances the multiplicity of voices. All the arguments for freedom of expression, with the possible exception of the argument from self-expression, demonstrate the centrality not of speech simply but of discussion, debate, diversity of ideas and sources of information. They point to the multiplicity of voices as their central and unifying theme. Noninterference is sovereign in its place – but its place is much smaller.

NOTES

1 A. de Tocqueville, *Democracy in America*, Vol. 1 (New York: Random House, Vintage, 1945), Chap. 11.
2 A.J. Liebling, *The Press* (New York: Ballantine Books, 1964), pp. 30–1.

3 H. Reiss (ed.), *Kant's Political Writings* (Cambridge: Cambridge University Press, 1970).
4 A. Meiklejohn, *Political Freedom: The Constitutional Powers of the People* (New York: Harper, 1960), pp. 8–28.
5 J.S. Mill, *On Liberty* (Indianapolis, IN: Bobbs-Merrill, 1956), pp. 69–70.

15

social responsibility theory

JOHN C. NERONE

S ocial responsibility theory is one response to the perceived impasse of classical liberalism in the twentieth century. Coalescing in the report of the Hutchins Commission in 1947, social responsibility theory takes seriously many of the accusations of critics (from both left and right) of a laissez-faire media system. These critics contend that there are tendencies toward monopolization in the media, that the people or the public are inattentive and not concerned with the rights or interests of those unlike themselves, and that commercialization produces a debased culture and a dangerously selfish politics. In response, social responsibility theory proposes that the media take it upon themselves to elevate their standards, providing citizens with the sort of raw material and disinterested guidance they need to govern themselves. It is urgent that the media do this, social responsibility theorists warn, or an enraged public will allow, if not force, the government to take steps to regulate the media.

The media have both repudiated and embraced social responsibility theory. When *A Free and Responsible Press*, the report of the Commission on Freedom of the Press (the official name of the Hutchins Commission [1947]), appeared, its elaborate rethinkings of liberal theory were denounced by industry organizations such as the American Newspaper Publishers Association (ANPA) and others as an entering wedge for government control of the media. At the same time, the notion of 'responsibility' appealed to the media on a common-sense level, and in the intervening half century, most of the specific recommendations of the Commission have become mainstays of the workplace culture of journalists, who after all have long had an interest in upgrading their public image and professional status.

This chapter presents a series of arguments about the origins, merits, and shortcomings of social responsibility theory. One argument is that this theory has been adopted in practice (if not in theory) because developments in society, politics, and the media all made it appropriate. This implies that there is really no novelty in the situation—no new idea under the sun, so to speak. Social responsibility theory amounts to a sterile intellectual exercise, on the one hand, and an apparently spontaneous ideological development, on the other.

But we might argue that there is a serious intellectual battle being fought around the concept of responsibility. In this view, the adoption of social responsibility theory means a radical reconstruction of the relationship between individuals and communities, with a new emphasis on the latter. Social responsibility theory thus represents the triumph of community over the lone individual.

This begs the argument from the liberal perspective that responsibility is just a nice name for authoritarian regulation. In terms of the paradigm of *Four Theories*, social responsibility theory should be seen as aligned with the authoritarian and Soviet communist theories as permutations of collectivism, all quite inimical to liberal thought.[1]

This argument in turn begs a rebuttal from the left. Rather than being a true communitarianism, and rather than posing a serious threat to class and corporate control of the media, social responsibility theory actually endorses the status quo by erecting standards of performance that can make monopoly media seem like the voice of the people, even as the media keep the people silent and stupid.

First published in *Last Rites: revisiting four theories of the press*, J.C. Nerone, University of Illinois Press (1995), as On Social Responsibility Theory, pp. 77–100.

Of course, all of these arguments presuppose a media system with bottlenecks everywhere. Responsibility, after all, can be exercised only by those with some kind of power. We expect the publishers of newspapers with circulations in the hundreds of thousands and the producers of television shows with audiences in the tens of millions to be responsible in a way that we do not require of soapbox orators. But suppose the future is the soapbox? Many claim that that will be the likely outcome of innovations in telecommunications technology—the information superhighway will have no bottleneck. Will responsibility be a thing of the past?

[...]

RESPONSIBILITY, YES; THEORY, NO?

Social responsibility theory was formulated at a time when the United States was coming to terms with what commentators have called 'late capitalism' and, in retrospect, it may have been only a reaction to changing public expectations. Prior to World War II, many of the most prestigious news organizations in the United States had come under the dominance of wealthy media tycoons, such as William Randolph Hearst, Robert R. McCormick, and Henry Luce. These powerful and successful media owners controlled large newspapers, wire services, radio stations, movie studios, and magazines. They were politically active and used their positions to support candidates and influence elections and legislative action. At the same time, the federal government's power was increasing drastically. President Franklin D. Roosevelt's New Deal dealt with the crises of depression and world war by instituting new programs that both expanded the influence of federal government and altered public attitudes toward government's relationship with the private sector. Roosevelt's liberal spending policies also earned him the animosity of most wealthy media figures, who abhorred big government. Roosevelt, in turn, used their virulent opposition to stir public sympathy for his presidency.

Social responsibility theory was developed just after Roosevelt's death, when influential publishers were unpopular with the public. The public remained suspicious of the press, even though new industry leaders were replacing the older, more politically active ones, the press had been formulating 'codes of ethics' for decades (the American Society of Newspaper Editors [ASNE] adopted its 'Canons of Journalism' in 1923), and television was becoming the most popular medium in the country.

The story of the Hutchins Commission is a familiar one (Blanchard, 1977; McIntyre, 1987). It was formed in the midst of World War II when Henry Luce, publisher of *Time* and *Life* magazines, asked his old Yale classmate, Robert Maynard Hutchins, then president of the University of Chicago, to recruit a commission to inquire into the proper function of the media in modern democracies. This issue had become urgent for a number of reasons, including the vigorous atmosphere of press criticism of the past few decades, the outbreak of the war, widespread fears of propaganda and totalitarianism, and the expected rise of a generation of new media technologies in the postwar world. The Commission, which consisted mostly of academics with a connection either to Yale or the University of Chicago, deliberated for four years and interviewed dozens of important figures from the media, government, and the academy before issuing its landmark report in 1947.

The Hutchins Commission worked in the context of national and global social change. The Commission's suggestions, while mirroring the public's distaste for powerful media owners, also seemed to reflect a growing expectation for social change. In fact, this call for change actually took a firmer hold in the years to come. Civil rights demonstrations spread throughout the South in the next decade, and legislative and judicial successes followed. Changes in public attitudes affected African Americans but also touched the lives of many disenchanted groups. In the late 1960s and early 1970s, a spontaneous women's rights movement took aim at male-dominated societal values and norms. American Indians, gays, Hispanics, and other groups, who were oppressed or denied equal opportunities by mainstream society, also sought general public acceptance of their cultures, ideas, and status as equal partners in society and the workplace.

By the 1960s, within a decade after the publication of *Four Theories*, media began to reflect new societal standards, not only by opening channels and pages to alternate ideas but by supplementing all-male, white staffs with women and minorities. By their very backgrounds, many of these new journalists seemed to offer fresh perspectives. Since early in the nineteenth century, minority publications had served as voices for their respective communities, but now it was expected that integrated news staffs would bring the minority agenda into the white community, keeping minority issues in front of community leaders and decision makers.

Media were also alert to the movements of government. The federal government had already exercised some control over broadcast content; later, local governments similarly asserted their rights in bargaining with new cable companies. The fear of censorship repeatedly led Hollywood to display its 'responsibility,' most recently through the ratings system.

While not responding necessarily to government mandates, newspapers and magazines realized that a new, younger, better educated, post-World War II audience wanted less politically biased news coverage and more interpretive writing. Audiences also looked for publications that reflected a wide spectrum of ideas in the community and the nation. This audience demand could not be ignored.

[...]

In general, major newspapers and magazines became more audience-oriented. News was more interpretive; consumer, business, and lifestyle news competed with political news for space in newspapers and magazines. In the 1970s, many newspapers experimented with consumer advice columns and help hotlines. Newspaper managers not only allowed publication of a variety of letters to the editor and opinion or commentary columns, but also instituted daily corrections to set straight published, factual errors. Publishers appointed ombudsmen to hear complaints from readers. By the last decade of the twentieth century, few newspapers or magazines arrogantly devoted their energies to hyping certain political parties or candidates favored by wealthy media owners and, instead, turned to reader surveys to learn more about what the community or nation wanted to read. Conservatives argued that a new, liberal bias dominated the nation's most prestigious media during this new era of news coverage, but in fact newspapers and magazines were far more stringent in seeking news and editorial balance than they had been fifty years earlier.

It would seem on the surface, then, that the social responsibility theory not only existed but that the formulation of such a concept appeared ever more prescient as each decade passed. But the question remains: Is this social responsibility theory so radically different from liberal theory, does it really embody new concepts, or is it merely an evolutionary descendant of classical liberal doctrines, not really so new in its purposes and goals?

From the moment the US Constitution was ratified, newspapers never really developed into the public-spirited vehicles envisioned by men like Thomas Jefferson. They were often mean-spirited and consumed by political bias but they evolved over the next two centuries to concentrate on news and advertising. The definition and presentation of news also evolved. Fairness and balance coupled with a more objective writing style came to be accepted as the rule, instead of fiery opinion and rhetoric; it is this style that we usually recognize as 'responsible journalism.' When, then, did the social responsibility theory overtake the libertarian theory? With the era of the mass circulation press? When the rise of advertising made newspapers financially independent of political parties in the late nineteenth century? When Joseph Pulitzer turned the *New York World* into a mass appeal, working-class paper in the 1880s? With the sensational revelations of the reformist muckrakers in the early twentieth century? When radio brought news instantly into living rooms in the 1920s? When Roosevelt declared war on influential media owners?

Vestiges of social responsibility can be found all along the way, long before the Hutchins Commission. But who is to say this was social responsibility rather than just good business? Pulitzer earned a fortune by publishing a newspaper devoted to working-class men and women but treated his own working reporters and editors shamefully. While bringing the world into American living rooms, radio maintained editorial neutrality but devoted almost all its airtime to entertainment, thus avoiding controversy and slighting serious presentation of the news. Media came to seem responsible without embracing the totality of social responsibility theory.

THE RADICAL NATURE OF RESPONSIBILITY

We might, then, understand social responsibility theory as a limited adjustment in liberalism brought about by perceived business demands. But such a reading neglects any analysis of the ideas and justifications behind this adjustment. In order to assess social responsibility theory's importance, we must take a closer look at the fundamental concepts that intellectually shaped it.

In a seminal essay in 1958, Sir Isaiah Berlin differentiated negative and positive liberty as two streams in democratic political philosophy—two models distinguishing John Locke from Jean-Jacques Rousseau. Berlin observed that liberal politics avoids schizophrenia by a compromise in everyday affairs, placing positive freedom in the service of its negative counterpart: 'Perhaps the chief value for liberals of political—positive—rights, of participating in the government, is as a means of protecting what they hold to be an ultimate value, namely individual—negative—liberty' (Berlin, 1958/1969: 165).

Positive freedom is the conceptual axis around which social responsibility revolves. The legal implications of positive freedom were developed by Zechariah Chafee in his two-volume *Government and Mass Communications* (1947). In his emphasis on rights and in his suspicions of government action, Chafee's connections to the liberal tradition are clear. His influence on the Hutchins Commission was balanced by William Ernest Hocking (McIntyre, 1987), a philosopher whose reformulations of the concepts of freedom and rights as moral (rather than natural or utilitarian) constituted the philosophical core of the Commission's final report. Chafee's work had more practical impact than Hocking's, especially in First Amendment law, and Chafee prevailed over Hocking in restricting the Commission's endorsement of government intervention to promote responsibility. But Hocking remains the most distinctive and innovative contributor to the Commission's work; he is largely responsible for any element of radical change in the final report.

The logic and rationale of positive freedom are the centerpiece of William Ernest Hocking's foundational book, *Freedom of the Press: A Framework of Principle* (1947). Hocking developed in this volume a definition of freedom distinctive from classical liberalism where (negative) liberty means the absence of arbitrary restraint. In the political theory underlying classical liberalism, individuals possess an inner citadel that is inviolate and, therefore, they must be left alone to pursue those ends each considers right or sacred. To contravene these natural rights, from this perspective, is to violate the self's autonomy.

Liberalism's notion of individualistic, negative liberty has typically been contrasted with social responsibility theory in terms of jurisprudence and governmental policy. These debates over policy, shield laws, Freedom of Information probes, and Supreme Court rulings, however, obscure social responsibility's more critical challenge to defend its view of freedom philosophically. The question is whether positive freedom can be reconstructed in terms of the nature of human being. Hocking developed an intellectually rich notion of positive freedom, though it has been largely ignored. Endless fussing about functional matters such as government intrusion prevents a more fundamental analysis of liberty's character. The vitality of social responsibility at this juncture depends more on conceptually recovering positive freedom than on winning debates over journalistic strategy.

[···]

'POSITIVE FREEDOM' AS THE 'ENTERING WEDGE'

While communitarians welcome 'responsibility' and 'positive freedom' as an expansion of the realm of liberty, libertarians are wary. In terms of libertarian *thought*, the philosophical underpinnings of social responsibility theory are indeed radical. But their import in *practice* is really very familiar: 'responsibility' must mean accountability; accountability requires state intervention; and state intervention, history shows, comes at the expense of liberty as defined by libertarians. Their argument follows.

Social responsibility theory, in one sense, is difficult to criticize. Taken at its most benign, who could oppose the goal of an honest, industrious, conscientious press committed to the free flow of all information necessary to self-government? The goal is admirable—but it is also consistent with classical liberal or libertarian theory.

This leads to the first criticism of social responsibility theory: its name. Its authors leave the negative inference that any other theory is socially irresponsible. Libertarian theory did not condone abuse of liberty and it, too, sought to further the public interest. The distinction, though, is one of procedure and presumptions. According to James Madison who crafted what libertarians hold to be their classic statement of principles, the First Amendment: 'Some degree of abuse is inseparable from the proper use of everything, and in no instance is this more true than in that of the press. It has accordingly been decided by the practice of the States, that it is better to leave a few of its noxious branches to their luxuriant growth, than, by pruning them away, to injure the vigour of those yielding the proper fruits' (1787/1941: 570).

But where a libertarian might expect the public interest to be fulfilled in the long run by emphasizing the private, individual interest in each case (e.g., Wortman, 1800: 140–8), a neoliberal (as Jay Jensen [1957: 167] termed those espousing social responsibility theory) looks to the public interest. With its emphasis on a variable public interest and ad hoc analysis, neoliberal theory is decidedly short-term in its approach. 'Freedom for the thought that we hate' is more easily defensible if focussing on the individual speaker's freedom from government, in other words, negative liberty. But under neoliberal theory the burden is on the speaker in each case to justify freedom for such speech as in the public interest, and that can be a hard sell. Imagine a speaker trying to convince an audience that freedom for speech even though offensive by definition to it is in its best interest.

The fundamental distinction between the two theories regards their contrary attitudes toward speakers and government. According to libertarians, government is the 'chief foe of liberty,' as Theodore Peterson noted (FT, 76), and the government that governs least, governs best. But where libertarians are concerned primarily with abuses by government, neoliberals seem more concerned with abuses by corporations and other nongovernment entities. Roberto Mangabeira Unger notes that, in 'post-liberal' society, 'private organizations are increasingly recognized and treated as entities with the kind of power that traditional doctrine viewed as the prerogative of government' (1976: 193). Neoliberals do not share libertarians' skepticism toward government and, instead, concentrate on the power they see exercised by, in the present instance, the mass media and their deficiencies, indeed dangers, in exercising that power. For example, when Peterson listed the themes of twentieth-century criticism of the press, first among them was the criticism that it had 'wielded its enormous power for its own ends' (FT, 78). Peterson cited the report of the Hutchins Commission as a primary authority for developing and giving impetus to social responsibility theory (FT, 75).

The Hutchins Commission based its call for responsibility on what libertarians consider to be an exaggerated sense of the power of the media. In its report, the Commission noted often that continued misuse of press power and freedom would necessitate regulation (1947: 3, 5, II, 48–51). Regulation was thus the fault of the press, not the government, as a libertarian would contend.

Ideas do have a certain power, but the press rarely has the kind of power ascribed to it. Those critical of press power almost always are guilty of attempting to divert attention from other matters, ignoring other influences, or in essence wishing the press would use its supposed power to support their point of view—an argument about content more than power. As Walter Karp (1983) has pointed out, however, even the press fosters the concept of press power. As long as the press is dependent on advertising for its subsidy, the press is well advised to perpetuate the notion that it is inordinately persuasive. Karp added that it behooves those with real power—the politicians and others who can actually declare war, raise taxes, and imprison or execute wrongdoers—to comply with the myth of press power. Such complicity in perpetuating the myth diverts attention and accountability for their own actions.

Even assuming a considerable power of the press, though, why should regulation follow? A convincing case can be made that a powerful press is advisable as a check on government. For government to regulate the press would negate the check, not to mention place more power in the government, which clearly is already powerful.

The Commission indicated numerous times that it preferred nonregulation and that governmental involvement posed its own risks for freedom. But its reservations usually accompanied remonstrances that there was no other option if the agencies of mass communication did not live up to their potential on their own (1947: 3, 5, II, 80, 86, 91, 131). The Commission posed self-regulation as a possibility—the ideal even—but at the same time made clear what it saw as the inherent obstacles to that ideal in the nature of competitive, profit-oriented, mass-market media.

[…]

Although the Commission emphasized self-regulation, it left the door open for considerable government intrusion. The press, in the Commission's view, had the primary responsibility to define and realize standards of social responsibility but the process should also 'be systematically associated with corresponding efforts of community, consumers, and government' (1947: 127). Government, the Commission continued, may assist in 'making distribution more universal and equable, removing hindrances to the free flow of ideas, reducing confusion and promoting the reality of public debate' (1947: 127) and providing new legal remedies for 'the more patent abuses of the press' (which the Commission likened to clearing the highways of drunken drivers) (1947: 127–8). Finally, government should supplement the press's commentary and news supply. The next sentence is telling of the Commission's faith in government: 'In so doing, it may present standards for private emulation' (1947: 128). The 'new legal remedies' were to be implemented with the 'precautions' that the Commission had 'emphasized' at some unidentified other points in its report (1947: 127).

[…]

Indeed, we may wonder why the Commission was so anxious to impose its theory of social responsibility on the press when it might apply with equal if not greater force to government. Government, too, engages in speech. Its meetings, documents, and official pronouncements all constitute speech. If government held itself fully accountable to the public's right to know, we may wonder about the need to hold the press accountable. If government cannot hold itself fully accountable, what reason is there to believe it can hold the press accountable?

Applying neoliberal theory to government speech would seem to compensate largely for any shortcomings involved in applying libertarian theory to private speech. Such an approach would obviate many of the major issues in applying neoliberal theory to the press: the definition of press, whether and to what extent its rights exceed those of the public, and the different treatment accorded rights of news gathering and publication.

Indeed, such an approach might be the only way to reconcile the Commission's resort to both negative and positive freedom. Lee C. Bollinger (1991) has suggested essentially that libertarian theory can apply to the print press and neoliberal theory to the broadcast press, which is another reconciliation of the contradiction in the Commission's report. But such an approach is tied to technology, and a dichotomy in theories based on whether the speaker is or is not government seems to best serve the interests of the public in the short- and long-terms.

While *Four Theories* contemplated more than two theories, a credible argument can be made that there really are only two. They simply differ in the extent to which they arrange the balance between speakers and government. History has occasioned no era when the press has been accorded absolute freedom but there have been plenty of instances of government control. Whether the latter go by the labels of authoritarian theory, Soviet communist theory, or social responsibility theory matters little. The real question is whether and when the balance will swing back to liberty.

RESPONSIBILITY ENDORSES LIBERALISM

To many, this apprehension concerning the Hutchins Commission and the concept of responsibility generally seems altogether misplaced. From a left perspective, for instance, neither the Commission nor subsequent theorists have rejected either a liberal hostility to government, a liberal faith in reason, or a liberal belief in private property. Social responsibility is clearly a species of liberalism, as the label 'neoliberal' implies.

First and most important, social responsibility theory does not challenge existing legal rights. It makes a point of leaving the machinery of negative liberty intact, despite the radical implications of Hocking's philosophy; instead, it satisfies itself with claims that the landscape of moral rights is different from that of legal rights. It offers not a clue to the practical implementation of moral rights, other than to rule out any radical means—for instance, creating a right of access, defining the media as common carriers (on the legal side), or insisting on the break-up of monopoly daily newspapers or on subsidies for alternative media. If it is philosophically radical, it is programmatically conservative.

Social responsibility theory retains a liberal notion of healthy public discourse. Essentially, it adheres to the notion of a marketplace of ideas but acknowledges that the marketplace must be represented inside a medium. Put another way, where media previously competed in the marketplace, now the marketplace is contained within the media. Here the libertarian critique misjudges the neoliberal notion of the power of the press. The power of the press does not consist of promoting specific ideas or images; the power of the press is the ability of the major media to be the gatekeepers of the public sphere. This power is presupposed in each of the Commission's 'Requirements' (1947: chap. 2) for a responsible press.

Social responsibility theory thus seems to renege on its diagnosis of the media's structural problems. It grants that there is a 'media monopoly' (in the sense later elaborated by Ben H. Bagdikian [1990]) but aspires to little more than seeing the monopolists behave better. Ultimately it embraces professional autonomy for journalists; which seems like an infringement on the rights of media proprietors, though it also seems to be perfectly functional in terms of media profitability. Professionalism, like responsibility, is a notion so commonly accepted that it seems impossible to criticize—who wants their journalists, much less their doctors and teachers, to be less professional? But certainly professionalism is a kind of elitism. And while we hope our doctors are more learned medically than we are, we should be uncomfortable with the notion that our journalists are more learned politically than we are. After all, in democratic societies, it is the public who should govern; democratic media then should let the people talk to each other rather than just listen to experts.

There is no question that the media have adopted a stance of professionalism in the last half century. This might be looked upon as the triumph of social responsibility theory over liberalism. But can we say that this stance has really fulfilled the expectations of the Hutchins Commission?

NOTE

1   See F. Siebert, T. Peterson and W. Schramm, *Four Theories of the Press* (Urbana: University of Illinois Press, 1956). This work is referred to below in the text as FT.

REFERENCES

Bagdikian, B. (1990) *The Media Monopoly*, 3rd edn. Boston, MA: Beacon Press.

Berlin, I. (1958/1969) 'Two concepts of liberty', in *Four Essays on Liberty*. New York: Oxford University Press. pp. 118–72.

Blanchard, M. (1977) 'The Hutchins Commission, the press and the responsibility concept', *Journalism Monographs*, 49.

Bollinger, L.C. (1991) *Images of a Free Press*. Chicago, IL: Chicago University Press.

Chafee, Z., Jr (1941) *Free Speech in the United States*. Cambridge, MA: Harvard University Press.

Chafee, Z., Jr (1947) *Government and Mass Communications*. Chicago, IL: University of Chicago Press.

Commission on Freedom of the Press (Hutchins Commission) (1947) *A Free and Responsible Press*. Chicago, IL: University of Chicago Press.

Hocking, W.E. (1947) *Freedom of the Press: A Framework of Principle*. Chicago, IL: Chicago University Press.

Jensen, J. (1957) 'Liberalism, democracy and the mass media', PhD dissertation, University of Illinois at Urbana-Champaign.

Karp, W. (1983) 'The lie of TV's political power', *Channels of Communication*, 3: 37–40.

McIntyre, J.S. (1987) 'Repositioning a landmark: the Hutchinson Commission on freedom of information', *Critical Studies in Mass Communication*, 4: 130–60.

Madison, J. (1787/1941) 'Madison's report on the Virginia resolutions', in Jonathan Elliot (ed.), *The Debates in the Several State Conventions on the Adoption of the Federal Constitution*, 2nd rev. edn, 5 vols. Philadelphia, PA: J.B. Lippincott. Vol. 4, pp. 570–1.

Siebert, F., Peterson, T. and Schramm, W. (1956) *Four Theories of the Press*. Urbana: University of Illinois Press.

Unger, R.M. (1976) *Law in Modern Society*. New York: Free Press.

Wortman, T. (1800) *Treatise Concerning Political Enquiry, and the Liberty of the Press*. New York: G. Forman.

16

the public sphere as historical narrative

PETER DAHLGREN

THE PUBLIC SPHERE AS HISTORICAL NARRATIVE

Notions of what is termed the public sphere, or public space, which thematize the role of interaction among citizens in the political process, can be traced back to the ancient Greeks. Notions of what is 'public' are of course premised on conceptions of what constitutes the 'private'. The public/private polarity has several overlapping historical strands. In recent modern political thought, however, the idea of 'public' in relation to the processes of democracy has been given ambitious formulations in the work of many writers; among the most prominent are Dewey (1923/1954), Arendt (1958), and Habermas (1962/1989). The concept is by no means identical in these three authors; they work out of different traditions and their approaches vary. The functions and problematics of the mass media, for example, are explicitly central to Dewey and Habermas, but not to Arendt. There are similarities and differences in their political, sociological and historical horizons, but it is Habermas' version which is the most fruitful, despite a number of serious difficulties. Thus, my focus here will be on his concept of the public sphere and the response it has evoked. Specifically, my emphasis will be on his notion of the political public sphere, rather than the more broad cultural public sphere, where literature and the arts circulate. I will also consider some of his ideas regarding communicative rationality, which can be seen to extend and modify his earlier thinking on the public sphere. While I will focus on Habermas, the three authors can be and have been fruitfully compared; a recent effort in this regard, with an hermeneutic perspective on citizenship, is found in Alejandro (1993).

In this section I will first briefly summarize Habermas' (1962/1989) theory of the public sphere. This will only be a compressed synopsis; a comprehensive overview of this topic, containing many commentaries, is found in Calhoun (1992). From there I will review the major criticisms that have been levelled against it. Finally, I will present a scheme of four dimensions as a conceptual aid in approaching the public sphere analytically.

In ideal terms, Habermas conceptualizes the public sphere as that realm of social life where the exchange of information and views on questions of common concern can take place so that public opinion can be formed. The public sphere 'takes place' when citizens, exercising the rights of assembly and association, gather as public bodies to discuss issues of the day, specifically those of political concern. Since the scale of modern society does not allow more than relatively small numbers of citizens to be physically co-present, the mass media have become the chief institutions of the public sphere. Yet Habermas' concept of the public sphere insists on the analytic centrality of reasoned, critical discourse. The public sphere exists, in other words, in the active reasoning of the public. It is via such discourse that public opinion is generated, which in turn is to shape the policies of the state and the development of society as a whole.

Of course this is not how society today actually operates. Habermas tells a story; it is a rather melancholic historical narrative in two acts. In the first act he portrays a fledgling bourgeois public sphere emerging under liberal capitalism in the eighteenth century. This 'category' of the public sphere is historically specific to the societal arrangements of Britain, France and Germany in this period. Prior to this, in the

First published in *Television and the Public Sphere*, P. Dahlgren, Sage Publications (1995), pp. 7–12.

Middle Ages, there was no social space which could be called 'public' in contrast to 'private'; powerful feudal lords (as well as the Church) may have displayed themselves and their power to the populace, but this did not in any way constitute a public sphere in Habermas' sense. With the demise of feudalism, and the growth of national states, parliaments, commerce, the middle classes and, not least, printing, a public sphere began to take root in certain societies of Western Europe. This public sphere consisted of certain segments of the educated, propertied strata (almost exclusively male), and operated via such media as intellectual journals, pamphlets and newspapers, as well as in such settings as salons, coffee houses and clubs. This exchange of factual information, ongoing discussion and often heated debate was a new phenomenon, to which Habermas attributes much significance.

The second act traces the decline of the bourgeois public sphere in the context of advanced industrial capitalism and the social welfare state of mass democracy. With mass democracy, the public loses its exclusivity: its sociodiscursive coherence comes apart as many less educated citizens enter the scene. The state, to handle the growing contradictions of capitalism, becomes more interventionist; the boundaries between public and private, both in political economic terms and in cultural terms, begin to dissipate. Large organizations and interest groups become key political partners with the state, resulting in a 'refeudalization' of politics which greatly displaces the role of the public. The increasing prevalence of the mass media, especially where the commercial logic transforms much of public communication into PR, advertising and entertainment, erodes the critical functions of the public. The public becomes fragmented, losing its social coherence. It becomes reduced to a group of spectators whose acclaim is to be periodically mobilized, but whose intrusion in fundamental political questions is to be minimized.

The story of the decline of the public sphere is still very much with us, continuously being replayed in updated versions by researchers and commentators. On the other hand, the gloomy portrayal of the modern public sphere's demise has been rejected in more optimistic corners as overstating the case. From yet other corners, Habermas' affirmative historical picture of the rise of the bourgeois public sphere has been contested. Some may even question the utility of the notion of the public sphere itself. However, I find the concept still to be a valid and helpful one. It points to those institutional constellations of the media and other fora for information and opinion – and the social practices around them – which are relevant for political life. That these institutional constellations and practices may be anaemic does not *per se* mean they are irrelevant.

The political public sphere constitutes a space – a discursive, institutional, topographical space – where people in their roles as citizens have access to what can be metaphorically called societal dialogues, which deal with questions of common concern: in other words, with politics in the broadest sense. This space, and the conditions for communication within it, are essential for democracy. This nexus of institutions and practices is an expression of public culture – visible and accessible sets of societal meanings and practices – and at the same time presupposes a public culture. One could say that a functioning public sphere is the fulfilment of the communicational requirements of a viable democracy. And like the concept of democracy, to use the notion of the public sphere does not suggest that what we see today is its consummate embodiment. Again, we would be advised to try to position ourselves between 'dismally ideological' and 'blatantly Utopian' views.

Habermas' intellectual roots lie with the Frankfurt school, and his theses about the public sphere became inspirational for much critical media research. But as Peters (1993) points out, his basic understanding of democracy and the public sphere is not totally remote from the Anglo-American liberal tradition and its notion of the market-place of ideas. The liberal discourses (that is, the 'classic', not 'neo-liberal' ones) on media and democracy normally do not use the category 'public sphere', but they nonetheless underscore the citizens' need for useful and relevant journalism. With access to reliable information from a variety of perspectives, and a diversity of opinions on current affairs, citizens will arrive at their own views on important issues and thus prepare themselves for political participation. Both the public sphere and the market-place of ideas can be seen as normative and very idealized pictures, easily contrasted with current realities.

But there are differences as well. Habermas situates the bourgeois public sphere within the history of capitalism, the rise of the interventionist state, and the emergence of the culture industries, emphasizing not least the difficult conditions which democracy requires and how the modern media can obstruct those conditions. Thus, we should not lose sight of the fact that the public sphere retains an anchoring in critical theory, and to use the term incorporates the media within a critical perspective on democracy (see, for example, Dahlgren and Sparks, 1991). If the shortcomings of the marketplace of ideas at best tend to generate calls for reforms in the conditions and operations of journalism, the disparity between the model and reality of the public sphere goes further. It evokes wide-ranging critical reflection on social structure, the concentration of power, cultural practices, and the dynamics of the political process.

Many have written on the inspirational quality of Habermas' text, lauding the weight he gives to the modern media, the historical perspective on their evolution, and, not least, his emphatic reminder of the twin dangers of state power and corporate control over the logic of their operations. Criticisms from many angles have also been forthcoming; many have pointed to the ambiguous status of the entire concept of the public sphere in Habermas' book, arguing that it appears both as a normative ideal to be strived for and as a manifestation of actual historical circumstances in early bourgeois Europe. In other words, how are we to view those social features in the late eighteenth and early nineteenth centuries whereby a relatively small group of economically and politically privileged men communicated with each other within the context of a small, budding press and the settings of salons, coffee houses and exclusive societies? Was this a genuine public sphere or merely an exercise in bourgeois self-delusion? Should we see this only as an emancipatory space or should we also see it in terms of Foucault's per-spective, as Verstraeten (1996) suggests: he makes the point that we can also look at the public sphere's social disciplining and exclusionary functions which stand in contrast to its liberatory aspects.

However, if we allow that the public sphere was not merely an ideological mis-conception but contained at least the germ of something new and progressive (which Habermas argues for by contrasting the bourgeois public sphere with previous historical versions of what constituted publicness), it was in any case very much grounded in a notion of small-scale print media and rational, conversational interaction among a small sector of, at that time, much smaller populations. Where does that leave us in the age of massive-scale societies and electronic media? If the public sphere today is so dominated by the mass media, what does this suggest for the viability of the larger analytical category of civil society? If we do not simply equate the public sphere with the mass media, there remain many questions for democracy about the nature and extent of face-to-face communication.

Feminists have criticized not only the actual exclusion of women in the bourgeois public sphere, but also Habermas' failure to make a critical point of this in his evaluation. Such feminist encounters with Habermas' work (see especially Fraser, 1987, 1992) merge with the larger critical feminist projects illuminating the gender partiality within the public/private distinction of liberal theory and within political philosophy more generally; at bottom this project has to do with reconstructing the concept of democracy in the light of feminist analysis. Feminist as well as other writers have taken up the overly rationalistic view of human communication in Habermas' work. This rationalist quality of Habermas' understanding of discourse becomes more explicit and central in his later work, particularly in his major theoretical contribution from the early 1980s, *The Theory of Communicative Action* (1984). It is understandable that critics take into account the perspectives from this later study, and commentaries on Habermas' view of communication often connect the two phases of his work.

Habermas (1992) responded to these and many other criticisms of his *Structural Transformation of the Public Sphere* (1962/1989) in the context of a conference. He expressed appreciation for the interest and critical insights of the contributors, while reminding them that the book came out in the early 1960s. He self-critically assured his colleagues that were he to write the book today, he would make many changes, yet felt justified in asserting its continued usefulness, despite its limitations. It is hard not to agree. If the concept of the public sphere is one which hovers between philosophical and historical groundings, as one of the conference contributors (Hohendahl, 1992) suggested, we can perhaps turn this into a strength. We can take the idea – the vision of a public sphere – as inspirational, yet accept that there is no single universal model that is possible or even suitable for all historical circumstances. The task becomes to try to devise new forms and strategies. If modesty must prevail on our social and historical analyses, we should allow ourselves to be ambitious and expansive in our conceptual and normative thinking.

FOUR DIMENSIONS

As we can already see, critical encounters with Habermas' conception of the public sphere have come from a variety of directions. I cannot attend to all the issues here; for example, one question to which many have pointed has to do with his historical interpretation which ignores alternative public spheres which functioned parallel with the bourgeois one. But by synthesizing a number of key points in the commentaries – I make particular use of texts by Garnham (1992), Peters (1993), Fraser (1992), Thompson (1990) – we can conveniently sort the critical themes and questions into four areas: media institutions, media representation, social structure and sociocultural interaction. This in turn offers us a framework for conceptualizing four analytic dimensions of the public sphere. Each dimension serves as an entry port to sets of issues about the public sphere, both theoretical and conceptual questions as well as empirical and evaluative ones about its actual functioning. No one dimension stands on its own; all four interlock with each other and constitute reciprocal conditions for one another.

The dimension of media institutions, their organization, financing, regulation, and the dimension of media representation, chiefly in regard to journalistic coverage, are the two which generally receive most attention. Both figure at the centre of considerable policy debate. The dimension of social structure points to the broader horizon of factors that constitute the historical conditions and institutional milieu of the public sphere. These structural elements from the broader institutional arrangements of society include social stratification, power alignments, and, not least, the state. Economic, political and legal aspects are included here. Also, the nature and quality of the entire educational system, and its place in the social order, become relevant in this regard. This is a topic I cannot pursue here, but the role of education in shaping the analytic and communicative competencies of the citizenry is crucial for the character of the public sphere, despite the inevitable ideological dimensions of schooling. Finally, socio-cultural interaction refers to non-mediated, face-to-face encounters between citizens, to relevant aspects of subjectivity and identity processes, and also to the interface of media and citizens, that is, the processes of reception. Civil society composes the space for much of the public sphere beyond the media; without attention to this inter-actionist dimension of the public sphere, the whole conceptual foundation of democracy is undermined.

The dimension of social structural factors defines not least the 'political ecology' of the media, setting boundaries for the media's institutional and organizational profile, as well as for the nature of the information and forms of representation and expression which may circulate. Obviously the social structural dimension also impacts on the patterns of sociocultural interaction. Thus, social structure complexly constitutes a set of conditions for the public sphere which can also be charted via the three other dimensions. Social structure is no doubt the dimension that is conceptually the most difficult to deal with, since it is potentially so vast. In fact, at some point in the analysis, social structure must be put in brackets if we are not to lose our specific focus on the public sphere. However, its role must not be lost from view. That the public sphere cannot be seen as a space operating in isolation from all other social, political and economic domains, as if it were a self-contained entity, is one of Habermas' central points. To understand the public sphere under any specific historical circumstances requires taking into account the larger societal figurations that both comprise its space and constitute the preconditions for its functioning.

A society where democratic tendencies are weak and the structural features of society are highly inegalitarian is not going to give rise to healthy institutional structures for the public sphere. Such structural features translate into mechanisms whereby the basic patterns of power and social hierarchy detrimentally shape the character of the public sphere. These mechanisms operate by institutionally *delimiting* the public sphere as such; for instance, the state, together with vested interests, can pursue media policies that hinder the flow of relevant information and constrict the range of opinion. Alternatively, such mechanisms may operate *through* the public sphere to hinder democratic development, for example 'news plants', disinformation, trivialization. Further, power and social hierarchy can shape the public sphere at the level of inter-action, impacting on the sites and settings where such contact takes place.

REFERENCES

Alejandro, R. (1993) *Hermeneutics, Citizenship and the Public Sphere*. Albany, NY: State University of New York Press.

Arendt, H. (1958) *The Human Condition*. Chicago, IL: University of Chicago Press.

Calhoun, C. (ed.) (1992) *Habermas and the Public Sphere*. London: MIT Press.

Dahlgren, P. and Sparks, C. (eds) (1991) *Journalism and Popular Culture*. London: Sage.

Dewey, J. (1923/1954) *The Public and its Problems*. Chicago, IL: Swallow Press.

Fraser, N. (1987) 'What's critical about critical theory? The case of Habermas and gender', in S. Benhabib and D. Cornell (eds), *Feminism as Critique*. Cambridge: Polity Press.

Fraser, N. (1992) 'Rethinking the public sphere: a contribution to the critique of actually existing democracy', in C. Calhoun (ed.), *Habermas and the Public Sphere*. London: MIT Press. pp. 109–42.

Garnham, N. (1992) 'The media and the public sphere', in C. Calhoun (ed.), *Habermas and the Public Sphere*. London: MIT Press. pp. 359–76.

Habermas, J. (1962/1989) *Structural Transformation of the Public Sphere*. Cambridge: Polity Press.

Habermas, J. (1984) *The Theory of Communicative Action*, 2 Vols. Cambridge: Polity Press.

Habermas, J. (1992) 'Further reflections on the public sphere', in C. Calhoun (ed.), *Habermas and the Public Sphere*. London: MIT Press. pp. 421–61.

Hohendahl, P. (1992) 'The public sphere: models and boundaries', in C. Calhoun (ed.), *Habermas and the Public Sphere*. London: MIT Press. pp.

Peters, J.D. (1993) 'Distrust of representation: Habermas on the public sphere', *Media, Culture and Society*, 15 (4).

Thompson, J.P. (1990) *Ideology and Modern Culture*. Cambridge: Polity Press.

Verstraeten, H. (1996) 'The media and the transformation of the public sphere', *European Journal of Communication*, 11 (3): 347–70.

17

new roles for public service television

JAY G. BLUMLER AND WOLFGANG HOFFMANN-REIM

THE POSITION OF PUBLIC BROADCASTERS IN A COMMERCIAL SETTING

Hereafter, public broadcasters must be in both a competitive and a complementary relationship to private broadcasters. Their policies should be designed to strike a balance between these relations which subordinates neither to the other, while harnessing each to the other.

Competition arises with respect to products that companies distribute and consumers receive. In television, competitive success is predominantly measured with respect to programmes. Inevitably, one gauge of their success must be the amount and share of viewing. A public broadcaster who almost always caters only for minorities will have lost a significant part of the competitive battle. But broadcasting as a public service may not compete with private broadcasters only for high viewership. It should strive to ensure that the competition is understood, both internally and externally, in multi-dimensional terms. Politicians especially need this understanding if they are not to make crude estimates of relative success or failure. For individual programmes and for the structure of offerings as a whole, then, dimensions other than audience size should continually be stressed: quality, innovation, professionalism, standards, social relevance, serving a variety of interests, etc. That is why public broadcasters have an interest in, and should encourage the establishment of, vigorous forums of public accountability, in which both private and public broadcasters have to answer for their performance in light of multiple criteria.

The *complementary* function of public broadcasting arises, on the one hand, from the implacably narrowing imperatives of the market, and, on the other, from the significance for viewers, programme makers and society at large of preserving the values that private broadcasters tend to neglect. From an economic standpoint, complementarity is expressed in the fact that public broadcasting receives significant funding from public sources and is not directly dependent on economically calculated success. It may therefore more often do things that will not necessarily result in high viewer ratings. It may take risks with the innovative and less tried. It may distribute resources in such a way that lower-audience programmes can sparkle in production-value terms as brightly as higher-audience ones.

In other words, public broadcasters should *compete complementarily* with private broadcasters by offering a truly different mix of programming. This would combine thoughtful and involvementworthy mass appeal programmes with programmes targeted at the more defined tastes of smaller but more committed audiences; a range of programme types in which none is consistently restricted to low budgets or relegated to minority viewing hours; and a greater incursion of surprises amidst the tried and true than private channels are likely to deliver. Above all, public broadcasting should distinguish itself by offering a variety of ways of depicting social reality – that is to reflect it, to comprehend it, to deplore and attack it, to enjoy it, or to redesign the concept of it. By making such variety available, discoveries are possible and curiousity has a field of activity. Only in such a manner can current viewpoints and preferences be refreshed and developed from a potentially wealthy supply instead of standing stagnant.

First published in *Television and the Public Interest*, J.G. Blumler, Sage Publications (1992), as New Roles for Public Service Television, pp. 206–215.

Public broadcasters must not only get the competition/ complementarity relationship right, however. They must also find ways of so conveying their distinctive identities that understanding and support for their functions are generated in such terms. This underscores the trailer function of programme publicity. In it public broadcasters should emphasize the qualitative benefits of their offerings. They should seek to produce hallmark broadcasts and to publicize them as highlights, special events and outstanding features. These are productions that signal the special merits of a public service system – which may sometimes be programmes for an esoteric minority (opera or ballet or Greek drama, say) and sometimes for a majority (a Briton might think in this connection of certain *nonpareil* BBC comedies). It is also important that information and other challenging kinds of programmes should not be projected and stigmatized as uninteresting, heavy or boring. Trailers for them should instead strive to attract the attention of audience segments that might initially not expect to be interested in them.

PROGRAMMING PRIORITIES

The new role for public broadcasting must stem from a considered sense of priorities. Partly this is due to the strains imposed on limited resources by ever-rising television production costs. It is also inherent in the need to decide how best to differentiate public television from its private competitors.

Three models appear available at this level. One would prioritize by *programme type*, presuming that if commercial television concentrates on entertainment and topical news, public television should offer documentaries, plays, education, the arts and science. This, however, is a formula for decidedly boxing public television into a corner, offering almost nothing for those entertainment gratifications that are central (though not necessarily exclusive) in many viewers' expectations of television. US public television is an object lesson: having been forced into such a mould for historical and financial reasons, it is only now struggling to break out of it. More fundamentally, this model ignores the fact that in principle *all* kinds of programmes can differ from how private broadcasting tends to shape them.

Another model would prioritize *by audience target*, presuming that if commercial – and especially advertising-supported – television concentrates on mass appeal programmes, public television should serve the neglected minorities. Such a prescription is not only open to the same objections as those raised against differentiation by programme type; it also arbitrarily excludes the majority from the benefits of a public service approach. The equation between 'public' and 'universal' should not be lightly dismissed. When public broadcasting does justice to the needs it strives to meet, not selectively but as widely as possible, it enables an openness in the process through which views, insights and preferences initially shared by a few can also be found to be interesting and worthwhile by a majority. It is through such a dynamic component that public broadcasting can serve as a meaningful 'cultural forum' (Newcomb and Hirsch, 1983) and a factor in cultural development.

Only a third model would enable public broadcasting at one and the same time to be different, meet public needs and stay attuned to all viewers. It must be guided by a sense of *qualitative priorities*, differing from market-driven television not so much by the areas of programming presented as by the characteristics – of functions, gratifications, standards and quality – striven for in them, as well as by its cultivation of a reputation for accessibility to public concerns and responsiveness to public needs. Though no single policy outcome follows from this prescription, which must be applied differently in the varying cultures and conditions of diverse broadcasting systems, a number of emphases could flow from it.

Information Provision

The audience's familiarity with certain events can readily be established through the news services of a private broadcasting system. But commercial broadcasting will tend all the more to televise an event, the more it is capable of attracting attention. This means that sensational and extraordinary events tend to be accorded a special rank. There is also a certain arbitrariness with respect to the socio-geographic region from which the news comes, favouring parochialism. Moreover, when the whole world is used as a resource for the display of extraordinary images, reality becomes distorted, forced toward those characterizations that vividness, simplicity and intensity tend to generate (Cohen et al., 1990).

The public system should distinguish itself through greater roundedness and depth of treatment in five directions. First, the information it provides should take into account those areas of reality which, though not necessarily high in sensation value, are nevertheless relevant to how viewers live and especially to what is shaping the social conditions that determine how they may live.

Second, its reporting should ensure that the several dimensions of an event are recognizable. Mere revelation of an event does not satisfy needs for orientation or even simple understanding. If viewers do not wish to be reduced to slates momentarily imprinted with high-profile events that are quickly wiped away to make room for the next round of incidents; if they wish to obtain some control over what has been seen by forming their own impressions of its significance; then they need access to background, fuller information, surrounding contexts and relevant judgements of experts and others. Overall, the presentation of events should be guided by a sense of the questions to be raised about them to which answers, however problematic, are needed.

Third, viewer understanding and control also require awareness that a considerable number of events are staged, that is, intentionally arranged to foster certain impressions. It is not sufficient, however, to stress simply that this is often the case, which may do little more than breed disenchantment. Instead viewers must be in a position to read the staged scene as such – that is, to recognize the calculation and strategy behind it – and to go beyond it, helped by the affirmatively scrutinizing role of reporters, determined to draw publicists into meaningful comment on the issues of controversy concerned.

Fourth, public broadcasters should transcend the interests that the competing parties have in depicting themselves in certain ways and see to it that their contributions and standpoints join in debate, enabling the questions at issue to be substantively sifted. Such a dialogue should not always be confined to the best-equipped and ever-familiar protagonists. Also to be promoted is dialogue with non-professional interpretations and perspectives, since this can avoid a uniformly top-down formation of public agendas and facilitate the insertion of concerns that official commentators are tempted to ignore.

Fifth, opportunities to step out of the circle of immediacy and event-determined news should also be afforded, occasionally striving for a more analytical consideration of underlying trends and social processes. Here the emphasis would be more on connections and structures than on event-bound happenings.

Entertainment Provision

Bases for a similar differentiation apply to television entertainment. Among commercial programmers, much competition is waged over attention-holding, production values (attractive stars, glossy sets, glamorous locations, pace, etc.) and sustaining tension. Stories are built around figures that can be speedily and universally understood and appreciated. Actors' local and social ties tend to be treated as theatrical props. Personalities are simplified into near-unidimensional stereotypes, only momentarily enriched to generate paradox or an unexpected story twist. The imagination is piqued as external stimulus, but there is little incentive for deeper reflection. The melodramatic tension that arises from scene to scene *is* the plot, instead of its being an outcome of some deeper development. Emotions are excited without imaginative faculties being put to work.

In the face of such tendencies, public television should not primarily set out to imitate the predominant commercial style. Given the high costs of entertainment programming, such an approach would amount to a squandering of public resources on *purely* competitive (and in no way complementary) ends. Entertainment in public channels should aim to stimulate and quicken imagination and thought, not shut it off. Its characters, even when standing for something emblematic, should have those less resolved qualities of complexity, potential and uncertainty that stamp real-life individuals. Its conflicts should invite reflection on interests, temperaments, taboos and preferences that originate in the real world and pose dilemmas that viewers can absorb as belonging to life as they know it or could imagine it. Images should tell a story about real persons, not just allegories. Neither should institutions that often provide the backcloth of television fiction (police, law, medicine, education, politics) always be painted in the same drastically simplifying strokes (see Turow, 1989, for a detailed analysis of misleading depictions of medicine in US network television). Since many people will probably tend to watch more entertainment as channels increase, the occasional provision in public television's fictional output of such a 'reality-righting' corrective to the distortions and banalities of commercial programming is particularly important.

Cultural Self-determination

In Europe, commercial channels are likely to schedule a significant amount of US programming, available at relatively cheap prices with an already proven appeal. In the mixed television economy, it falls to public television to look to its society's more indigenous cultural needs. This is not to fly the flag of cultural sovereignty or to value the static preservation of some cultural *status quo*. The role envisaged is rather to enhance a society's ability to find for itself appropriate terms of adaptation and change in response to the incoming flow of international communication. In addition to coverage of national developments in sports, science, industry, the arts, etc., some priority follows for the cultivation of domestic talent – writers, dramatists, musicians, film-makers – in the programme commissioning efforts of public broadcasters. In multicultural societies (for example, Belgium, Switzerland and Spain) efforts are also called for to support linguistic diversity and to maintain the functionality of language as a bearer of cultural identity.

Innovation and the Ability to Surprise

Commercial television dances to strongly conformist and imitative tunes. Financial backers need assurances that every effort has been made in the programme-commissioning process to protect their investments and to score ratings successes. Premiums are put on stars, formats, formulae, and themes that have worked in the past. The odds are stacked against creative risk-taking, which must struggle to pierce a prior climate of scepticism. Although multichannel competition also generates pressures on commercial programmers to find ways of distinguishing themselves from the clutter of all the rival offerings, such needs are more likely to be met by infusing the standardized approaches with presentation gimmicks than by departing from them.

In contrast, public television could assume the vocation of promoting freshness, a quality that can be applied to both the invigoration of old formulae and the gene-ration of new programme ideas (Nossiter, 1986). Overall, the emphasis would be on programmes that are refreshingly different, make people sit up and take notice, awaken them to new experiences or encourage them to try out new notions. Such a philosophy would give public broadcasting the pioneering role of leading the way in new programme development, not abdicating it to the private sector.

Programme Quality

In ratings-driven commercial broadcasting systems, powerful influences subvert and dilute *distinctive* meanings of 'quality' programming. It is subtly conflated with popu-larity, equated with what has proved itself in the ratings market by achieving hit status or attracting an above average level of viewing.

For their part, public broadcasters should hold out against this tendency and adhere to other, independent criteria of quality – fostering their identification; setting out to ascertain through research what producers and viewers regard as marks of quality; discussing the achievements and deficiencies of their schedules in quality terms; and aiming for a pallet of programming that incorporates as many standards of quality as possible. Such standards might include, not only the aforementioned criterion of freshness, but also: imaginativeness; an ability to illuminate controversy; authenticity (aiming to do justice to a subject, a problem, or a situation in terms of what it is really like, instead of distorting it for the sake of drama, attention holding or viewers' comfort); social relevance; expressive richness (operating artistically with more elements, at many levels, or at greater depth); and integrity (being shaped by a vision that has not been grossly violated, diluted or compromised to satisfy the quite different ideas of others).

The ability to attain such standards will turn partly on how programme makers are recruited and treated. In some European countries the public service broadcasting corporations had a particularly good record for fostering major talents and supporting their creativity with resources and encouragement. The more this tradition can be continued, the better the chance that high-quality programmes, appreciated by audiences as among their 'favourites', will often emerge.

An International Presence

Much of the impetus behind the recent globalization of television has been commercial – and American. Nowhere has this been more strikingly evident than in the 24-hour news field, which is dominated by Ted Turner's CNN at present. Though such an operation has a global reach, its heart is in Atlanta, Georgia. Its programming tends to be stamped with a particular editorial standpoint and a certain way of exploring issues, events, and the actors involved in them. This threatens a diminution of plurality in the increasingly vital international opinion-forming arena (Hallin and Mancini, 1992). It therefore seems important for an alternative to be launched from Europe with as little delay as possible; that it be run under public direction; and that the news resources of the major public broadcasting corporations, including their extensive foreign correspondent networks, be pooled in its service. This might even be designed to pursue a non-uniform editorial policy – aiming to acquaint viewers with the many different perspectives taken in the world on major international events and conflicts.

THE SOCIAL CHARACTER OF PUBLIC BROADCASTING

Unlike private television, which is predominantly accountable to the market, public television is rooted in the social system from which it draws its existence. In charter and governance, it is thus a public institution and its primary funding sources are public.

There is also a close pragmatic tie of impact between all forms of television and the social system. Because of the amount of time that viewers spend with their sets, the level of resources devoted to programming, and its pivotal position in the calculations of would-be opinion formers, television has become an omnipresent institutional influence, touching, penetrating, even tending to bend all facets of organized social life to its rhythms and requirements. How television is organized and programmed is thus relevant to a host of societal goods: the realization of democracy through channels of discourse and choice, leadership and accountability; the vitality of culture; the quality of leisure; the interpretation of many social institutions to themselves and to each other (business, the military, education, labour, religion, science, medicine, etc.); and informal processes of acculturation, socialization and education (Blumler, 1989). But whereas commercial television can take such societal factors into account only rarely and incidentally (witness as object lesson its impoverishing role in US election campaigns), public television can build them more centrally into their programming policies.

Cultural Functions

As a cultural institution, broadcasting projects an image of society and its activities. Public broadcasting should therefore define itself as an influential factor in cultural reproduction and renewal – and act accordingly. It thus has a responsibility to provide programming in culturally significant areas, to institute forums of cultural debate, to examine critically its own cultural contributions (and those of other media) and to maintain close ties with society's creative and artistic sectors. It should manifest this not only in activities directly related to transmission but also in other policies: support for independent producers, even when their work does not bring high ratings; support for programme archives; and development of other distribution channels, such as videocassettes and rental libraries.

Political Functions

As a political institution, broadcasting provides an image of political life, its leading players, preoccupations and activities. In this sphere public broadcasting has the vocation of standing for the integrity and viewer utility of civic communication against the many (and still mounting) pressures that threaten to subvert it, including: sloganized messages and soundbites; advanced political advertising techniques; ever more sophisticated news management strategies; the downgrading of cognitive appeals; and the erosion of confidence in the information-processing capacities and interests of ordinary electors.

With the emergence of the dual broadcasting system, chances might also be sought to push back some of the political constraints under which monopoly public broadcasters have laboured in the past. With the advent of private channels and competition, public television should be able to put on programmes with more venturesome profiles without fear of the assumption that the fortunes of individual parties, groups or leaders could be seriously damaged by a single broadcast. More priority could be given to looking at and giving access to the marginal elements and lesser voices of society – not always falling back on major parties and mainstream standpoints. This could tap vital sources of social change and extend the province of broadcasting system norms of pluralism, choice and fairness more generously to groups that sometimes feel excluded from them. By the same token, in systems that sought to guarantee pluralism in the past by representing the main parties and affiliated social groups in public broadcasters' governing boards, opportunities for relaxation, more broadcaster discretion, journalistic autonomy – even structural reform – might be sought.

Social Functions

As a social institution, public broadcasting is significant for a range of functions. One – with important implications for children's programming, which private television tends grossly to commercialize and trivialize – is that of socialization, or to serve as a trustee for the maturing development, quickening curiosity and educative needs of children and growing youngsters. A second is that of normative orientation, entailing broadcaster sensitivity to notions of standards, including a respect for the boundaries within which the chase for audiences should normally be contained (for example, not following commercial broadcasting into the more exploitative depths of 'tabloid television'). A third is that of multicultural understanding, representing the diverse groups of a pluralistic society to themselves and to each other. In addition, public broadcasting is significant for processes of both social change and social integration. As to the former, it should enable social critics to voice their views, not as 'free rides' or as exceptional token gestures to an enlarged marketplace of ideas, but as points of view to be seriously tested against other opinions and sources of evidence. Through occasional 'outreach' activities, the programming of public television may also be linked with social action in the community at large. As to the integrative function, it is no longer necessary for all persons, or as many as possible, to view the same programmes and, through subsequent conversations about them, help society to unite around the same symbolic offerings. Instead, public broadcasting should aim to contribute to social integration through its openness to diversity in how society is regarded and by the way in which different perspectives are creatively related to each other in its programming.

REFERENCES

Blumler, Jay G. (1989) *The Role of Public Policy in the New Television Marketplace*. Washington, DC: The Benton Foundation.

Blumler, Jay G. and Nossiter, T.J. (1991) 'Broadcasting finance in transition: an international comparison', in Jay G. Blumler and T.J. Nossiter (eds), *Broadcasting Finance in Transition: A Comparative Handbook*. New York and Oxford: Oxford University Press. pp. 405–26.

Cohen, Akiba A., Adoni, Hanna and Bantz, Charles R. (1990) *Social Conflict and Television News*. Newbury Park, CA, London and New Delhi: Sage.

Green, Damien (1991) *A Better BBC: Public Service Broadcasting in the '90s*. London: Centre for Policy Studies.

Hallin, Daniel C. and Mancini, Paolo (1992) 'The summit as media event: the Reagan–Gorbachev meetings on U.S., Italian and Soviet television', in Jay G. Blumler, Jack M. McLeod and Karl Erik Rosengren (eds), *Comparatively Speaking* ... : *Communication and Culture across Space and Time*. Newbury Park, CA, London and New Delhi: Sage.

Minow, Newton N. (1991) *How Vast the Wasteland Now?* New York: Gannett Foundation Media Center.

Newcomb, Horace and Hirsch, Paul (1983) 'Television as a cultural forum: implications for research', *Quarterly Review of Film Studies*, 8 (1): 45–55.

Nossiter, T.J. (1986) 'British television: a mixed economy', in *Research on the Range and Quality of Broadcasting Services*. London: HMSO. pp. 1–71.

Peacock Committee (1986) *Report of the Committee on Financing the BBC*. Cmnd 9824. London: HMSO.

Smith, Anthony (1990) *Broadcasting and Society in 1990s Britain*. London: W.H. Smith.

Turow, Joseph (1989) *Playing Doctor: Television, Storytelling, and Medical Power*. New York and Oxford: Oxford University Press.

GLOBAL MASS COMMUNICATION

The degree to which mass communication should be considered as a national or an international phenomenon has always been somewhat uncertain and also the source of some controversy. The issue has theoretical as well as practical implications, since some theory has posited mass media as a strong force for national unity, while other theory views it as undermining national cultural identity and auto-nomy (see the discussion of 'media' or 'cultural imperialism', as defined by Tomlinson, Chapter 19). The ambiguity over the issue stems in part from the fact that the organization of production, the technologies of distribution and the content that is disseminated can all vary independently from each other in their degree of 'inter-nationalization'. The controversy stems not only from the alleged effects of cultural or informational dependency, but also from the fact that national autonomy in respect of production, content and distribution is related to the size and wealth of the country concerned.

The United States is the only country that is more or less self-sufficient and self-contained in media terms, although it is still not immune to the effects of globalization since its major media industries are also positioned as major exporters, and production is thereby affected. Audience reception theory and research (see Part IX) has tended to downplay the extent to which cultures are undermined by imported media content, since meanings are changed and renegotiated at the point of reception according to local circumstances.

The media, since the early days of printing, have always been to some extent inter-national in respect of content and distribution, although the intended audiences for mass media are primarily national. The rise of the mass newspaper owed a good deal to the international news agencies that for much of their history were also related to the governments of the 'great powers' and thus closely linked to the international political system (Boyd-Barrett and Rantanen, Chapter 18). Imperialism and war fed the news media amply before the Second World War, and after it the Cold War did the same for 40-plus years. The media of emerging post-colonial and developing societies provided the battleground for the media wars between West and East. Mass news media, as a result, were both national and international, and their 'global' content was mediated through the gates and perspectives of national interest, largely as seen by government or business (as well as the assumptions of media about their audiences). Critical theory sought to combat the extreme imbalance that developed between developed 'North' and developing 'South' in the flow of content and communicative power through the 'international media system'. Strictly speaking, international media that seek deli-berately to transmit across national frontiers have been and still are quite uncommon and are held back by the lack of global audience markets and the barriers of culture and language.

Underlying ideas about the potential of international communication for good or ill are certain assumptions about the *effects* of such communication. Two aspects of this are dealt with briefly by Rosengren (Chapter 20). These relate to the diffusion by way of mass media (there is not likely to be any other effective way) of news of events occur-ring in other countries and to the 'mental maps' of the world that are as likely to be shaped by media fiction as by news. The notion of global mass communication received an impetus during the 1980s and beyond (Ferguson, Chapter 21) from the application of satellite and telecommunication technology that allowed direct communication (broadcasting) over much larger distances. However, the main forces working towards 'global mass communication' have continued to be the industries that produce similar content for global media markets, especially in the form of music, film and television fiction, sport and advertising. Global mass communication is also strongly promoted by trends towards the international conglomeration of (multi-) media firms so that it is not only a familiar audience experience, but also a phenomenon of media systems.

The Internet was hailed as a 'worldwide' medium from the start but is gradually being integrated into the structure of national as well as international media business. There continues to be an underlying tension between the forces of technology and economics that work towards global systems and cultural forces that generally operate within sub-global (although not necessarily national) networks of human association.

18

theorizing the news agencies

OLIVER BOYD-BARRETT AND TERHI RANTANEN

Within the range of different media forms, news agencies are sometimes presented as among the least glamorous or interesting. They represent an extreme form of a 'journalism of information' in contrast to a more refined and creative 'journalism of opinion'. Although the Anglo-Saxon invention of 'journalism of information' has enjoyed increasing worldwide influence over the past century, in contrast to its more literary, discursive, and 'European' shadow, newspapers do still remain in many ways the media of overt partisanship, political commentary, invective, and analysis. The extent to which such characteristics invade 'news' as opposed to 'opinion' spaces within a newspaper varies, but the boundaries between these concepts are unclear even at the best of times – they have more to do with the construction of an appearance of credibility than with the actual and impossible expulsion of ideology from news texts. Specialist correspondents, including foreign correspondents, are credited with the creative task of making interpretive sense out of a range of diverse sources, which include, to varying degrees of visibility, news agencies.

News agency news is considered 'wholesale' resource material, something that has to be worked upon, smelted, reconfigured, for conversion into a news report that is suitable for consumption by ordinary readers. It has also suited the news agencies to be thus presented: they have needed to seem credible to extensive networks of 'retail' clients of many different political and cultural shades and hues. They have wanted to avoid controversy, to maintain an image of plain, almost dull, but completely dependable professionalism. This image has sat more successfully with major news agencies such as Associated Press or Reuters, than with government-owned or backed national news agencies where association with state-supported propaganda has compounded the sense of dullness, even while reducing perceptions of professionalism and dependability.

To some extent this image, nurtured by the agencies themselves over the past century and a half, has also asserted itself in the world of media history and media study, where agencies sometimes have been barely visible actors in analysis of print and broadcast news, and have often attracted the least theoretically inclined, though most historically inflected of academic analysis. Needless to say, the absence of overt theory does not signify the absence of *any* kind of theory, and in practice, we will argue, agencies have always been theorized, and the manner of their theorization corresponds to some degree, but not entirely, with more general movements in the history of communications research.

Some 19th-century references to news agencies, most famously that of the French novelist Balzac in an 1840 article in *La Revue Parisienne* (quoted in Levebre, 1992: 69–71), about Havas, indicate that they were viewed as both hidden but powerful. Balzac's observation indicated a concern that behind the apparent diversity of news channels in retail media was a much more restricted range of sources.

Early, implicit theorization of news agencies sees them as powerful, but hidden, and, because hidden, perhaps even more powerful than commonly suspected. Added to the view of agencies as powerful is the view of them as services of propaganda. This was manifest during the First World War when at least some of the resources and services of the agencies were placed at the disposal of government propaganda campaigns. The German Karl Bücher talked in 1915 of the dangers of monopoly holdings of services

First published in *The Globalization of News*, O. Boyd-Barrett and T. Rantanen, Sage Publications (1998), as 'Theorizing the News Agencies', pp. 6–12.

such as Reuters and Havas, which he considered official and thus biased sources of information, and which were partly responsible for war propaganda activities (quoted in Hardt, 1979: 21). This view was apparent throughout much of the politicking between state, national and international agencies in Europe during the second half of the 19th century, where agencies are seen as potential or actual sources of hostile propaganda, on account of the identity of their host countries, or as actual or potential channels for the transmission of such propaganda overseas. The Russian government's fear of the dominance of Wolff in the transmission of international news gathered by the cartel for distribution in Russia, is one such example (Rantanen, 1990). The propaganda value extended from the political to the economic: the mere presence or absence of the British news agency, Reuters, in certain territories during the 1930s was seen as relevant to British trade interests by both agency and state sources. Added to the view of agencies as vehicles of propaganda is the left-wing view, expressed powerfully by Villard (1930) in relation to Associated Press, that they were part of the apparatus of class oppression. His discussion directed attention away from the state itself, to a more general consideration of ideology through social class division.

Whether it is the state or social class, or both, that is identified as enemy, a polar opposition was proposed here between propaganda and truth. This did raise helpful questions and issues about the proper role of the state in news agency activities, and the advantages of alternative forms of ownership and control, including private or co-operative structures. But it was also somewhat simplistic in its model of social representation, insensitive to the subtleties of news construction and agenda-setting.

In summary, we would argue that up until the Second World War the agencies belonged to any mixture of three prevailing discourses about media: media as powerful and influential; media as vehicles of nation-state or class propaganda; media as exemplars of a modern, technologically sophisticated professionalism.

The range of such discourses was amplified with the transition from British to American world hegemony. The American agencies had resisted and eventually defeated the cartel practices of the old ring combination, of which Reuters was the cynosure. The American agencies propagated effectively the models of both co-operative and private ownership which, they claimed, would guarantee unbiased news (see, for example, Cooper, 1942). They preached the advantages of an open market in news, a line supported by the US State Department, and which contributed to the formation of the 'free flow of information' doctrine later adopted by the UN, and which informed the UN's activity in the sphere of communications (Schiller, 1976). In practice, it has been argued, the doctrine supported the rights of western media, especially those of the US, UK and France, to continue distributing their media products throughout the world, while most countries of the world lacked the means to establish any kind of reciprocity of influence. Even national agencies in the communist bloc, set up for the purpose of preventing the intrusion of western ideas, still subscribed to the services of the major western agencies.

The UN, through UNESCO, consistently endeavoured to encourage the spread and development of national news agencies, and of news-exchange arrangements between them, especially during the great wave of independence in Africa during the 1960s. Setting up a national news agency became one of the essential things, part of the 'script' of what it meant to be a 'nation'. Through a national news agency, a state could lay down information links domestically and internationally which would facilitate the generation and exchange of news. National news agencies became the natural local business partners for the western-based international agencies: they provided a conduit, albeit government controlled, through which international news could be funnelled to local media, and domestic news released to the wider world. All this was assumed to contribute to national formation and national development, although these assumptions were rarely tested.

This then was a progressive, modernist discourse that treated news agencies as though they were public service institutions, fulfilling positive functions for nation-building, including the local provision of international news and projection of national news on to a larger world stage through the international agencies. In this model, the news agencies forged closer links between communities within nations, and between nations, in a largely pluralistic world. It was a model that suited the literature of Schramm (1964), Pye (1963), Lerner (1958) and others, in which the media play a positive, even indispensable role in the process of modernization and the expansion of democracy. Little thought is given in detail to issues of media control, content or finance, or to the precise ways in which given kinds of content lead to the consequences attributed to them. It avoided some difficult questions: for example, do agencies really contribute to 'development', or might they be counter-productive to some definitions of 'development' (for example, where used to bolster the power of particular ethnic groups)? The tension between 'development' as positive news and traditional western news values was not addressed, and there was a confusion between 'western news criteria' on the one hand, and 'really useful information' on the other. This model still retained a view of media as powerful at a time when, in the western world, newer models prevailed, emphasizing the role of 'intervening variables' and the essentially limited character of media power (Klapper, 1960). The model stimulated interest in pluralism at a global level, but casually tolerated monopolies at a local level, offering little insight into the structural impediments to pluralism at either level.

The reality of news agency coverage, reflected in early content analysis of agency wires (IPI, 1953) did little to sustain the credibility of the 'free flow' model. National agencies were generated within a global news system largely controlled by the 'Big Four' western agencies (AFP, AP, Reuters, UPI), and by the two leading state agencies of the communist world, TASS (Soviet Union) and Xinhua (China), serving their allies in the eastern bloc and communist Asia. These provided international news which was dominated (at that time) by news of their own host countries and subscribed to specific sets of news values characteristic of western media and communist media. The national agencies often served as funnels for local distribution for the Big Four agencies (though AP more often contrived to remain independent). In this way the international agencies could reach a larger number of outlets, with less pressure on local foreign exchange, than probably would have been the case had they tried or been allowed to distribute directly to all local media. The national agencies, sometimes with editorial tutelage from the Big Four agencies whose services they received, provided a rudimentary service of local news dominated at least as much by urban and elite news as the services of the Big Four, because their resources for coverage of the rural majorities were slender or non-existent, and political controls too often reduced their coverage to sycophantic and superficial reports of the doings of heads of state and their ministers, and ministerial meetings with counterparts from other countries ('protocol news' – Harris et al., 1980). Together with the editorial staff of the national agency, acting as stringers for the international agencies, such a service could provide a source of cheap, local coverage, at least in non-crisis periods.

Post-independence disillusionment was best expressed in the 'dependency' theories from South America, which had experienced a comparatively longer period of constitutional independence, but extensive experience of US capitalist expansionism. The news agencies fitted dependency theory very well given the character of the world news system, and the way in which it could be seen to facilitate the integration of new states into the world capitalist economy and its values. They provided an example in the cultural arena of the tendency identified by Galbraith (1967/1977) for industries to be dominated by a few big players, closely interlinked with a second tier of national or regional players, and with a much larger number of small, local or niche-market players lagging well behind.

Dependency theory dominated the vision of countries of the second and third worlds in the NWICO movement as it spread its influence through the non-aligned movement and through UNESCO in the 1970s. For countries of the south, the role of the major news agencies was especially significant in provoking official anger at how the international news system favoured western definitions of the exceptional and significant, and seemed to obstruct the ability of new southern nation states to contribute to the representation of their national image and national interests in northern media markets, with potentially enormous implications, politically and economically. The McBride Report (UNESCO, 1980) placed all this in a much broader context, focusing on the full range of media industries. But McBride came too soon to make sense of the extraordinary sensitivity of the western (political and media) world to southern criticism, which was soon to lead to the withdrawal of the US, UK and Singapore from UNESCO (the UK returned in 1997) and which, in retrospect, serves as a lesson – which cannot be emphasized enough – demonstrating the extent to which maintenance of world political hegemony is considered to depend upon a pliable global media system.

Dependency discourse had the merit that it focused attention on the global news system and on the political economy of news agencies. It explored the factors that have made it difficult for newcomers, especially newcomers with alternative ideas as to the functions and content of news agencies, to gain entry. It went some way towards exploring the dynamics between political economy and content, although this was achieved mainly through quantitative content analysis. Sophisticated qualitative analysis of day-to-day coverage was rare, although there were strong examples, among them Vietnam war coverage (see Boyd-Barrett, 1979: chap. 13; Boyd-Barrett and Palmer, 1981: chap. 13), and agency coverage of the NWICO debate itself (Salinas, 1977). But it did not recognize the growing importance of the international video news agencies. Further on the debit side, the dependency framework as manifested in the NWICO debate still seemed to subscribe to the view that nation states were the most useful units of analysis, even though the integration of nation states into a global capitalist economy rendered it necessary to look at the relationship of national media to the local incorporation of elite social classes within the global economy.

At the level of concrete action within UNESCO, NWICO discourse about news agencies was undermined by an absence of empirical support for claims that agencies are indeed important contributors to national and economic development. The dynamics of this supposed relationship to development have never been clear. NWICO discourse could not shake itself free of the notion that the proper way to set up or to support a news agency was through governmental or intergovernmental action. Thus the Non-Aligned News Agencies Pool (NANAP) was supported by UNESCO, despite NANAP's heavy and unreasonably over-optimistic reliance on the participation of national news agencies that were themselves integral components of statist, authoritarian regimes. The pool was coordinated by a country (Yugoslavia) that was soon to collapse in on itself in an explosion of extreme bigotry. UNESCO assistance to the Pan-African News Agency (PANA) supported an under-resourced creation of another intergovernmental body, the Organization for African Unity (OAU). PANA was committed to promotion of African unity, restricted in what it could say about member African regimes, and hopelessly dependent on inadequate, partial and impecunious government-backed national news agencies (Boyd-Barrett and Thussu, 1992).

Since dependency theory, in what further ways have news agencies been 'theorized'? The collapse of the communist east in the late 1980s coincided with a period in media research in which the influence of cultural studies predominated. This involved a welcome concentration on the semiotic construction of texts, and on processes by which actual readers make and take meaning from texts. This was a period that celebrated the notion of textual 'polysemy' and audience autonomy. Significant determiners of individual meaning were found in cultural contexts impinging on the use and consumption of texts. Cultural studies ignored news agencies, whose original texts could only be accessed with difficulty, and which lacked direct 'audiences'.

Temporarily, but remarkably, all this diverted mainstream attention from the fact that the global media industries were undergoing processes of concentration, deregulation, privatization and commercialization to a wholly unprecedented degree, and that for more than 99.999 percent of the world's population access to mass audiences was an extremely remote likelihood, the proclaimed universality of the Internet notwithstanding. In the same period, ownership of the former state-owned agencies in eastern and central Europe was transformed. New private agencies were founded, and major western agencies began to penetrate their markets. During this time, the modest level of interest in news agencies which had been sparked by the NWICO debates tailed off into insignificance, with the exception of a few new organizational histories. Interest was revived in the mid-1990s by the development of interest in global television and the role within it of the major video news agencies. Two of the three leading video news players had significant affiliations with existing global print agencies (Reuters Television and AP Television) and the third (WTN, previously UPITN) had evolved from a partnership in which one of the previous Big Four had played a significant part (UPI). The speed of development of global television reinvigorated a political economy perspective, and the political economy approach has been influential in recent research by Boyd-Barrett, Palmer, Paterson and Rantanen, for example. This is a political economy moulded by a discourse of globalization – not the free-market globalization of neo-liberal apologists, but the oligopolistic hegemonic globalization of their critics. Like most political economy of media, its major weakness is in the analysis of content, although here too we have sought rectification.

Globalization theory, drawing alike on cultural studies and political economy, on processes of meaning as well as on economics of communication, posits a more complex world than political economy on its own, and may thus be able to build a bridge between the two approaches. There is a post-modern dimension here which distrusts systems and polarities. None the less, we want to argue that globalization theory should not lose sight of agency, and that there is still considerable evidence of system: this is manifest in the patterns of dependent interaction among strong and weaker players, the advantages that favour western agencies, consistent inequalities in the distribution of resources, the application of a constant set of news values, and evidence of system capacity to adjust to a changing external environment.

REFERENCES

Boyd-Barrett, O. (1979) 'Theory and practice: from Cuba to Vietnam', in O. Boyd-Barrett, *The World-Wide News Agencies: Development, Organization, Competition, Markets and Product*, PhD thesis. Milton Keynes: Open University Press. pp. 833–55.

Boyd-Barrett, O. and Palmer, M. (1981) *Le Trafic des nouvelles*. Paris: Alain Moreau.

Boyd-Barrett, O. and Thussu, K. (1992) *Contra-Flow in Global News*. London: John Libbey.

Cooper, K. (1942) *Barriers Down*. New York: Farrar & Rinehart.

Galbraith, J.K. (1967/1977) 'The technostructure and the corporation in the new industrial state', in M. Zeitlin (ed.), *American Society Inc*, 2nd edn. Chicago, IL: Rand McNally College Publishers. pp. 202–13.

Hardt, H. (1979) *Social Theories of the Press: Early German and American Perspectives*. Beverly Hills, CA and London: Sage.

Harris, P., Malczek, H. and Ozkol, E. (1980) *Flow of News in the Gulf*. New Communication Order Series no. 3, Paris: UNESCO. pp. 43–63.

IPI (International Press Institute) (1953) *The Flow of News*. Zurich: IPI.

Klapper, J. (1960) *The Effects of Television*. New York: Free Press.

Lerner, D. (1958) *The Passing of Traditional Society*. New York: Free Press.

Levebre, A. (1992) *Havas: les arcanes du pouvoir*. Paris: Bernard Grassett.

Pye, L. (1963) *Communications and Political Development*. Princeton, NJ: Princeton University Press.

Rantanen, T. (1990) *Foreign News in Imperial Russia: The Relationship between International and Russian News Agencies 1856–1914*. Helsinki: Suomalainen Tiedeakatemia.

Salinas, R. (1977) 'News agencies and the new information order', in T. Varis et al. (eds), *International News and the New Information Order*. Institute of Journalism and Mass Communication: University of Tampere, Finland.

Schiller, H. (1976) *Communication and Cultural Domination*. New York: International Arts and Sciences Press.

Schramm, W. (1964) *Mass Media and National Development*. Stanford, CA: Stanford University Press.

UNESCO (1980) *Many Voices, One World: Towards a New, More Just and More Efficient World Information and Communication Order*. McBride Report. The International Commission for the Study of Communication Problems, Paris: UNESCO. London: Kogan Page.

Villard, O. (1930) 'The Associated Press', *The Nation*, 16 April/23 April.

19

the discourse of cultural imperialism

JOHN TOMLINSON

FOUR WAYS TO TALK ABOUT CULTURAL IMPERIALISM

Actually, five, but we can dispose of the first one quite briefly. Sometimes critics of cultural imperialism refer to it as cultural domination.[1] Is there a substantive issue at stake in this distinction? I don't think so. Both the terms 'imperialism' and 'domination' have a fairly high level of generality, but any possible preference turns on one being the more precise. Thus it may be argued that 'imperialism' grasps a specific form of domination, that associated with 'empire'. So, in the case of cultural imperialism in the Third World, this term might point towards the links between present domination and a colonial past. The term is ambiguous between a set of economic and a set of political meanings; this ambiguity has significant implications for the way we think about the Third World today. To maintain the sort of specificity we might desire in choosing the term 'imperialism', we would have to engage with these ambiguities to the point of choosing one particular inflection of the term 'cultural imperialism': as a pattern of inherited colonial attitudes and practices say, or as the practices and effects of an ongoing system of economic relations within global capitalism. Going for precision in this context means closing off available meanings.

At their most usefully general, both 'imperialism' and 'domination' contain the negatively marked notions of power, dominion or control. The real problem for us is that there are various *orders* of power, dominion or control involved in claims about cultural imperialism: those exercised by nations for example, or by capitalism, or some global process of development or context of modernity. So we come to the problem of representing this diversity without referring our discussion to some implicit 'master narrative' of cultural imperialism; without, that is, blindly assuming the existence of the elephant.

The best approach I can devise for this is to think in terms of different ways in which it is *possible* to speak of cultural imperialism. What I mean by this is simply reasonably coherent ways of speaking intelligibly about the subject. I shall suggest and briefly describe four here, and in discussing these I shall, of course, refer to specific texts and authors. But it would be a mistake to identify particular texts too closely with each general way of speaking: sometimes two or more possible ways exist within the same text, occasionally, though not always, in tension.

One of the virtues of this approach is to keep our discourse reasonably open to other possibilities: there are *other* ways of speaking, voices not heard in this text, nor indeed in the 'global conversation'.

CULTURAL IMPERIALISM AS 'MEDIA IMPERIALISM'

The great majority of published discussions of cultural imperialism place the media – television, film, radio, print journalism, advertising – at the centre of things. There is, however, an argument about the actual use of the terms 'cultural imperialism'/'media

First published in *Cultural Imperialism*, J. Tomlinson, Pinter (1991), as 'The Discourse of Cultural Imperialism', pp. 19–28.

imperialism' which we ought to acknowledge at the outset. We can do this by referring briefly to the way this distinction is handled in Chin-Chuan Lee's account of media imperialism.

Lee argues that 'neo-Marxists' prefer the broader term 'cultural imperialism' because they 'adopt a more holistic view of the role of the media', seeing them as necessarily implicated in a larger totality of domination. 'Non-Marxists' on the other hand are said to 'prefer to deal with media imperialism rather than the all encompassing "cultural imperialism"', since they do not accept, a priori, the implied broader context of domination, nor media imperialism's situation within it. The non-Marxist preference is for a term that grasps 'a more specific range of phenomenon [*sic*] that lends itself more easily to a rigorous examination'.[2]

This is a fair general assessment, and the point that emerges from it is that the term 'media imperialism' is often used in a deliberately restrictive sense by 'non-Marxists' or, as we might call them, 'pluralist' theorists. Pluralist views of 'media imperialism' thus tend to be theoretically unassuming, and to locate themselves fairly close to what are seen as the empirical grounds of the debate. They tend to keep the focus on the media so as to try to establish the 'facts' without making more general theoretical assumptions about cultural imperialism. In this perspective, Lee suggests, whatever links exist between the media and other aspects of culture, or indeed the connections between 'economics, politics and culture' generally, are not assumed in terms of a grand theory at the outset. They remain to be seen – that is, empirically demonstrated. Though Lee attempts to find some sort of balance between Marxist and pluralist approaches, the general drift of his book seems at least to accept the pluralist view that 'media imperialism' is a viable term on its own (deliberately restrictive) grounds.

This approach seems to me to be mistaken for two reasons. First, though the media may be analytically separable from other aspects of culture, it is clear that they are intimately connected with these other aspects in terms of people's 'lived experience'. People's experience of television, for example, is very often within the cultural context of the family and this context has a significant mediating effect. The general principle, then, of abstraction from a cultural totality is highly problematic. Second, there is a danger with the pluralist, anti-theoreticist approach that any *critical* sense of the term 'media imperialism' will be lost. I suggested earlier that the notion of 'domination' is essential to the notion of imperialism: thus to speak of 'media imperialism' is to understand a priori a context of domination. This is a theoretical assumption underpinning the term. Now it is clear from the general context of Lee's book that he would accept at least this level of theoretical assumption; yet to minimize theoretical assumptions is to risk losing any critical edge. As Fejes has suggested, within the literature of 'media imperialism' there do, in fact, exist *non-critical* accounts:

Most importantly, without theory, there is lacking the critical standpoint and set of standards and concepts by which one can judge and evaluate the research efforts which deal with the issues raised by this approach. A good example of this last point is William Read's study *America's Mass Media Merchants* (1976). As an empirical work the subject of this study – the expansion of American media overseas – falls within the concerns of the media imperialism approach. But the study's overall purpose and conclusion – to demonstrate that 'through the market place system by which America's mass media merchants communicate with foreign consumers, both parties enjoy different, but useful benefits'

(Read, 1976: 181) – is diametrically opposed to the central thrust of the previous work done in this area.[3]

That is, Read speaks of media imperialism without the notion of domination. I would argue that the pluralist argument for theoretical modesty – which lies behind the preference for 'media imperialism' rather than 'cultural imperialism' – could ultimately license studies like Read's.

This discussion has necessarily moved towards more general theoretical issues, so let's bring it back in summary to the central question of media imperialism as a way of talking about cultural imperialism. I have argued that it is necessary to see arguments about the media as aspects of cultural imperialism and not to try to separate out a discrete range of phenomena called 'media imperialism' having no imputed connection with a broader cultural totality. Media imperialism then, as I understand it, is a particular way of discussing cultural imperialism. It is not simply a name for the study of the media in developing countries or of the international market in communications. It involves all the complex political issues – and indeed, the political *commitments* – entailed in the notion of cultural domination.

Having established our view of media imperialism as a way of talking about cultural imperialism, we can now mention some of the more interesting questions that arise from this way of talking.

The main cluster of issues arising out of the discourse of media imperialism has to do with the way in which domination is said to occur. Critics of media imperialism often concern themselves with the structural and institutional aspects of the global media. By focusing on such issues as the 'dumping' of cheap television programmes in the Third World or the market dominance of Western news agencies, they produce critiques of what are basically political-economic forms of domination. The assumption seems to be, in this sort of discourse, that this is all that 'cultural imperialism' actually is. In contrast with these approaches are those which recognize a specifically 'cultural' level of domination, but which merely *assume* that imported cultural goods like television programmes, adverts, comics and so on have a self-evident cultural effect. Both of these assumptions are problematic and represent general difficulties in the discourse of cultural imperialism. The discourse of media imperialism provides us with a first context in which to consider the general problem of what cultural dominance actually means.

But talking about cultural imperialism as media imperialism also generates another important issue: the question of the centrality of the media in claims about cultural imperialism. Sometimes writers use the two terms as synonyms and this might imply that the media have an overwhelming importance in the processes referred to as 'cultural imperialism'. We must consider quite carefully what is at stake in attributing this massive central significance to the media. On the one hand, it is clear that the mass media are constantly and rapidly expanding in terms of technical power and penetration, coverage and representation of both public and private life in the West. To this extent it is tempting to see the media as the central cultural reference point of modern Western capitalism. And if this is so, then cultural imperialism might be seen to centre on the media in two ways: either as the dominance of one culture's media (texts, practices) over another; or as the global spread of 'mass-mediated culture' as such. These two understandings have quite different dimensions of implication, the second being much the wider. But both involve the idea that the media are at the crux of modern culture.

However, as Conrad Lodziak has pointed out in a very useful corrective to the general drift of writings on media sociology, media theories often have a tendency to exaggerate the broader social significance of their subject of study.[4] People in modern societies may watch a lot of television, but they do many other things besides, and to overemphasize the representational aspects of cultural action and experience is, perhaps, to end up with a rather narrow view of culture. Indeed, as we shall see, the more radical theorists of media-as-culture seem to believe that this narrowness is the reality of the lived experience of people in modern capitalism. Though it has a certain iconoclastic attraction this idea is, I think, ultimately implausible. To understand claims about cultural imperialism we need to examine the relationship of the media to other aspects of culture without assuming its 'centrality' from the outset.

CULTURAL IMPERIALISM AS A DISCOURSE OF NATIONALITY

If the media are the most common *focus* for discussions of cultural imperialism, the idea of the invasion of an indigenous culture by a foreign one is the commonest way of articulating the *process* involved. Nearly everyone who talks about cultural imperialism talks in this way at some point.

The reason why this discourse has such common currency is that it is a highly ambiguous way of speaking and thus very accommodating. Here is one ambiguity to be going on with: 'indigenous culture'. This trips pretty easily off the sociological tongue, but what does it mean? 'Indigenous' may be taken uncontroversially as a synonym for 'native', meaning 'belonging to a geographical area'. But *how* does a culture 'belong' to an area? A subsidiary sense of 'indigenous' is that of 'belonging *naturally*',[5] and though this may offer a sort of answer to how a culture belongs, it is one fraught with theoretical problems. For if we can take anything for granted about culture, it is that it is *not* a natural phenomenon. Culture is entirely – even definitively – the work of human beings. So it is not merely implausible that a culture may belong to a region in the sense that flora and fauna are 'natural' to it; it is theoretically incoherent to juxtapose culture and nature in this way. Yet this does not prevent a lot of discourse proceeding as though 'authentic' cultures were somehow 'natural'.[6]

So we need another sense of 'belonging'. How about something like 'being accepted or established practices in an area'? This moves, rightly, from a 'natural' to an *historical* way of speaking. But how is a cultural practice 'established' through time? How long does the process take? Is it merely length of time that produces 'authenticity'? Is the process of cultural establishment ever finished? The answers we give to these questions will be heavy with implications for judgements of cultural imperialism.

Let us try substituting 'local' for 'indigenous'. This displaces (but does not conjure away) the problems of 'belonging': yet it creates its own difficulties. How local is local? Do we mean the culture of a village, a region, a nation or a supra-national region (for example, Latin America)? In fact, as we shall see, the talk is mostly of nations. Talk in UNESCO is indeed in a certain sense restricted to nations. This being so, the arguments we shall have to examine cluster around the idea of a *national cultural identity* and the threats posed to this by cultural imperialism. In dealing with this (dominant) discourse of national cultures we shall inevitably confront the other levels of 'locality' at which cultural imperialism may be said to operate.

The other main area of ambiguity in this discourse has already been mentioned: the question of how specifically *cultural* domination is said to occur. This is the question of the grounds for attributing domination (expressed in the peculiarly martial language of 'invasion', 'attack', 'assault' and so on) rather than the neutral or even positively valued notion of 'influence'. To put this another way, we will begin to examine the critical basis of the concept of cultural imperialism.

One attractive candidate for such a ground is the principle of *cultural autonomy*. We shall have to decide, first, what this could mean and, second, whether indeed it provides any stable basis for a critique of cultural imperialism. This problem of critical grounds is a major one for all discourses of cultural imperialism.

[...]

CULTURAL IMPERIALISM AS THE CRITIQUE OF GLOBAL CAPITALISM

This way of speaking is typical of neo-Marxists. In a sense it follows from the Leninist tradition of inflecting the term 'imperialism' towards the economic rather than the political.[7] It usually involves seeing the world as a political-economic *system* of global capitalism, rather than the more common view of it as a collection of political entities called nation-states. This has the consequence of casting capitalism itself, rather than particular nation-states, as the real imperialist power. So it is a way of speaking that should be quite distinct from the previous one. But critics who set out to speak in this way soon find themselves in theoretical difficulties and begin to speak of the activities either of nation-states (and particularly the United States) or of 'multinational corporations'. In both cases they implicitly recognize the common view of the world as a set of nation-states. The reasons for this compromise have to do with the difficulty of thinking through the *existence* of capitalism in global terms. Neo-Marxists rightly wish to emphasize the enormous and globally integrated and integrative power of capitalism, but they face problems in 'mapping' this system on to the 'political existence' of the world as nation-states. Such problems are major ones for general, political-economic theories of neo-imperialism, and as such stretch beyond our chosen level of specificity. Yet it is important to acknowledge them, and we can do this conveniently by referring to the way they arise in the theoretical assumptions of certain neo-Marxist writers on cultural imperialism.

'Cultural imperialism' is a rather uncomfortable discourse for Marxists. Apart from the tensions that arise in the attempt to map capitalist domination on to the relations of domination between nation-states, Marxism has difficulties with the notion of 'culture' itself. This problem usually presents itself at a surface level in what is often called the 'economic reductionism' of Marxist analysis. Crudely, this refers to the tendency for (some) Marxists to represent everything (in this context, specifically cultural processes) in terms of a supposed underlying and, in some sense, *causal*, political-economic process. But there is another sense in which specifically cultural issues may become subordinated in neo-Marxist accounts. This is where the processes of cultural imperialism are seen as having a functional role to play in the spread of capitalism as an economic system and a set of class relations. In this case the arguments become shaped by the presumption that the cultural goods on offer from the capitalist West are almost a set of trinkets offered to the Third World in exchange for their labour power. As we shall see, there is a marked tendency, particularly among some of the Latin-American accounts of cultural imperialism, to see 'culture' in this servicing relation to class domination. This misrepresents not only the nature of cultural processes, but also, perhaps, the nature of the reproduction of capitalism itself.

Lurking behind these specific difficulties is the big general problem of how we are to think about capitalism as culture. Capitalism, as Marx certainly saw,[8] is more than a 'mode of production'. It implies a cultural totality of technical-economic, political, social-relational, experiential and symbolic moments. There ought, therefore, to be a way of speaking of cultural imperialism as the global dominance of capitalist culture. The best of the Marxist accounts strive to articulate this sense. But this is a considerable task, made the more difficult by our cultural immersion in the 'totality' of capitalist culture. We will consider two main approaches.

The first is the claim, common to many critical discourses of cultural imperialism, that capitalism is an *homogenizing* cultural force. The perception here is that everywhere in the world is beginning to look and to feel the same. Cities in any part of the world display uniform features determined, for example, by the demands of automobiles; architectural styles become similar; shops display a uniform range of goods; airports – the potential gateway to cultural diversity – have an almost identical 'international' style; Western popular music issues from radios and cassette players from New York to New Delhi. In the discourse of neo-Marxists, it is the economic imperatives of multinational capitalism that are behind this cultural convergence. There are disputes about the scale and pace of this process and about the potential for cultural resistance to the Juggernaut of multinational capitalism. But I think the evidence of a general drift towards cultural convergence at certain levels is undeniable. What we shall be mainly concerned with is how this process may be seen as a form of domination. This involves another quite separate judgement about the culture of capitalism: that it is in some way inherently incapable of providing meaningful and satisfying cultural experience.

This is the second approach, focusing on the claim that the spread of capitalism is the spread of a culture of consumerism: a culture that involves the commodification of all experience. This is, again, a very common claim, both in the discourse of cultural imperialism and in the wider neo-Marxist critique of capitalist societies. But there are difficulties both with the view that a consumer culture is *imposed* on developing societies, and with the criteria used to judge 'consumerism' as a cultural ill in the wider sense. The issues here are complex, but the general conclusion here will be that the difficulties of conceiving of 'capitalist culture' derive from the way it is abstracted, in much neo-Marxist discourse, from the broader social-cultural context of *modernity*. The discourse of cultural imperialism which takes capitalism as its target needs to be connected with that which addresses the discontents of modernity itself.

CULTURAL IMPERIALISM AS THE CRITIQUE OF MODERNITY

The final way of speaking is that which stresses the effects of cultural imperialism not on individual cultures but, as it were, on the world itself. It is what we may call the critical discourse of *modernity*. This discourse is not the domain of theorists who claim to speak directly about something called cultural imperialism; rather it is a way of speaking about global historical developments which encompasses, and in certain ways reformulates, the claims of the theorists of cultural imperialism.

'Modernity', as we shall understand it, refers to the main cultural direction of global development. Thus the drift towards a sort of global cultural homogeneity is seen in this discourse to derive from the dominance of a particular – 'modern' – way of life that has multiple determinants. These include capitalism (seen as a set of productive and consumerist practices), but also urbanism, mass communications, a technical-scientific-rationalist dominant ideology, a system of (mainly secular) nation-states, a particular way of organizing social space and experience and a certain subjective-existential mode of individual self-awareness. Cultural imperialism as a critique of modernity implies a critique of the dominance of these global cultural determinants.

This critique can have more or less theoretical depth. At its most superficial it can appear as the simple complaint against homogenization and the championing of cultural diversity. Another simplification it always risks is the reduction of the idea of modernity to that of 'capitalist society'. Though we must recognize the major significance of capitalism in the making of modern societies, it is important to maintain that capitalism is a certain *inflection* of modernity and not vice versa; and not least because there are senses in which Marxism, the major critical perspective on capitalism, can itself be situated within the cultural context of modernity.

But on another theoretical level the critique of modernity becomes an argument against the dominant trends of global development. Indeed, it involves an argument about the meaning of 'development' itself. This is because the goal of development for what is considered the 'underdeveloped world' is generally conceived of as 'modernity'. 'Modernity' and 'development', though by no means necessarily linked as concepts, have become closely identified. The most interesting arguments about the dominance of modernity, then, are those which question its claims to be, in some way, the destination of all cultural development.

What is centrally at stake in this critical discourse is a way of responding to the ambiguous cultural condition of modernity. Critics of modernity within the West have tended to harp on its cultural and existential discontents, whilst taking its material benefits for granted. But this sort of anxiety will probably seem less pressing for those Third World societies that do not share the general level of material provision of the West. To put it crudely, they may think the prospect of 'modern' clean water worth the cultural risk. And if clean water, why not motorways, fast food, personal computers, hypermarkets? The problem for the critique of modernity is how to criticize its discontents whilst recognizing its comforts, thus to avoid the self-indulgence involved in romanticizing 'tradition'.

These then are the four discourses within which our discussion will be organized. This, of course, imposes our own 'discipline' on what is said. The processes of classification adopted in this text represent my attempt, in Foucault's terms, to 'gain mastery over the chance events' of the unruly discourse of cultural imperialism. This element of domination in representation is unavoidable: it is a function of academic discourse. But it is useful to bear in mind, in a text that purports to speak of domination, Foucault's claim that all discourse is 'a violence we do to things'.

NOTES

1   For example, H.E. Schiller, *Communication and Cultural Domination* (New York: M.E. Sharpe, 1976).
2   C.-C. Lee, *Media Imperialism Reconsidered* (Beverly Hills, CA: Sage, 1979), pp. 41–2.
3   F. Fejes, 'Media imperialism: an assessment', *Media, Culture and Society*, 3 (3) (1981), pp. 281–9 citing (on p. 282) W. Read, *America's Mass Media Merchants* (Baltimore, MD: Johns Hopkins University Press, 1976).
4   See C. Lodziak, *The Power of Television: A Critical Appraisal* (London: Frances Pinter, 1986).
5   I take this and all definitions, unless otherwise stated, from *The Concise Oxford Dictionary*.
6   On this, see Barthes's claim that one purpose of cultural criticism is 'to establish Nature itself as historical' – R. Barthes, *Mythologies* (London: Paladin, 1973), p. 101. Some of the most precise analysis of the confusion of nature and culture comes, of course, from the literature of feminism. See, for example, C. Delphy, *Close to Home: A Materialist Analysis of Women's Oppression* (London: Hutchinson, 1984).
7   See V.I. Lenin, *Imperialism: The Highest Stage of Capitalism* (Moscow: Progress Publishers, 1966).
8   See, for example, the discussion of the cultural experience of capitalism in the 'Manifesto of the Communist Party', in L.S. Feuer (ed.), *Marx and Engels: Basic Writings on Politics and Philosophy* (London: Fontana, 1969).

20

international communication
at the mass media level

KARL ERIK ROSENGREN

In order to communicate successfully, the parties to communication must have some basic knowledge about each other. Two very basic conditions for successful and efficient international communication, therefore, are that important news be, first, efficiently *distributed* around the globe, and second, relatively quickly *diffused* among the various populations of the globe. Let us start by discussing the diffusion of news.

The study of the diffusion of national and international news is a research tradition in its own right. Figure 20.1 offers one example of the types of result that can be gained within this tradition. It shows how, in 1986, news about the assassination of Swedish Prime Minister Olof Palme spread within a number of national populations around the globe. It will be seen that the diffusion was very rapid, but also that, quite naturally, there were considerable differences between the diffusion processes within different countries. It was shown by multivariate statistics that no less than 50 precent of this variation could be explained in terms of effects from only three basic variables:

- geographical distance from the location of the event;
- the extent of trade relations between Sweden and the other countries under study;
- the amount of already existing communicative relations between Sweden and the countries under study (mail, telephone, etc.).

The fact that a piece of international news can be diffused among the different populations of the globe as quickly as is sometimes the case is due, of course, to the relative efficiency of the international mass media system. In their capacities as collectors and distributors of 'hard news' (basic news about important events) the various components of the international mass media system are efficient, although somewhat lopsided. Most of us get most of our knowledge about the world outside our home country from the mass media – and not only by way of news programs, but also by other types of content, not least fictional programs imported from other parts of the world. We thus get a somewhat distorted picture about what human life looks like in other parts of the world – and in our own.

Indeed, we may get a lopsided and distorted picture not only about what human life looks like in other parts of the world, but also about *what the world itself looks like*. What have been called our 'mental maps' are clearly affected by our media habits, and not always positively so.

A crude but quite instructive measure of individuals' mental maps can be obtained by asking people where they would go if they had to leave their home country for one reason or another. On the basis of people's answers, one can draw maps in which the size of the different parts of the world are made proportionate to their representation in the answers obtained. Highly preferred parts of the world are thus made bigger; less preferred parts, smaller. As expected, we found that the amount of TV viewing strongly influenced the mental maps of the youngsters under study. Obviously, other variables – primarily, age and gender – also exerted an influence on the mental maps of the viewers. When combined, the effects from age, gender and TV viewing were strong indeed,

---

First published in *Communication: an introduction*, K.E. Rosengren, Sage Publications (2000), pp. 184–190.

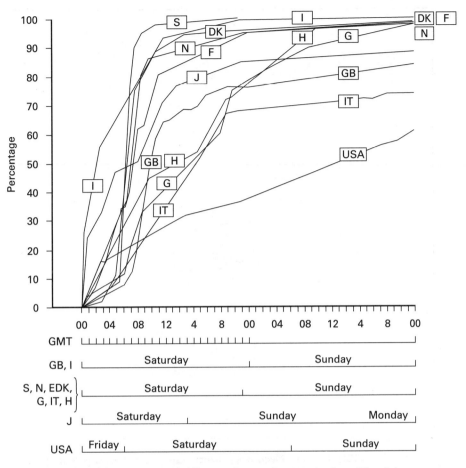

FIGURE 20.1   International diffusion of news: the assassination of Swedish
Prime Minister Olof Palme in 1986 (Rosengren, 1987)

as can be seen from Figures 20.2a and 20.2b. As a comparison, the corresponding map of the world, as reported in Swedish television news and measured in a governmental report published at about the same time (the late 1980s), is also shown (Figure 20.2c).

It will be seen that while the world at the time reported in Swedish television news (Figure 20.2c) certainly was somewhat distorted, it was not grotesquely so. The mental map of girls aged 11 and with a low TV viewing rating (Figure 20.2a) is not exactly grotesque either, but it may perhaps be called rather narrow. The mental map of Swedish boys aged 15 and with a high TV viewing rating (Figure 20.2b), however, deserves to be called grotesque. Their own part of the world, Western Europe, is not over-distorted *per se*, perhaps, but Eastern Europe is completely missing, and Asia stands out as an isolated little island. North America, on the other hand, is much larger than the rest of the world taken together. South America is as invisible as Eastern Europe. This is a fictitious world: the world created by US fiction and entertainment which dominates even a vital public service media system such as that of Sweden in the 1980s, and which is strongly favoured by young people in particular. Sadly, there is little hope that the mental maps cultivated by the television contents that are available

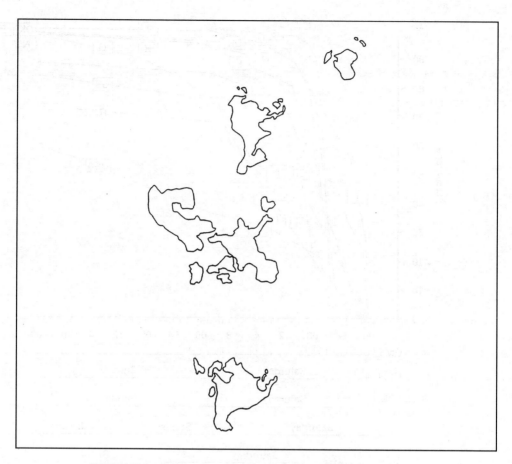

FIGURE 20.2a   Media maps, mental maps and real maps: girls aged 11,
low TV (Rosengren and Windahl, 1989: 230)

to youngsters around the globe today will be any better than they were in the late 1980s. Indeed, it is pretty safe to guess that they are not better at all but rather the reverse. Only the production of new models of mental maps will substantiate this guess, however.

Individual mental maps, then, are highly dependent on individual mass media habits. The greater the television use, the more lopsided the mental maps. The reason why this is so is obvious as we have already seen that even the 'international maps' offered by the media may be rather lopsided. Indeed, the amount of news reaching us from various parts of the world is strongly dependent on a few basic variables, the most important ones being the economic relations prevailing between countries.

In order to study such relationships systematically, we need other types of data than the ones discussed so far. That problematic will be shortly discussed in the following section.

INTERNATIONAL NEWS: INTRA AND EXTRA MEDIA DATA

National and international mass media offer all of us a never-ending flow of pictures of the world surrounding us. Some of these pictures are obviously fictitious – indeed,

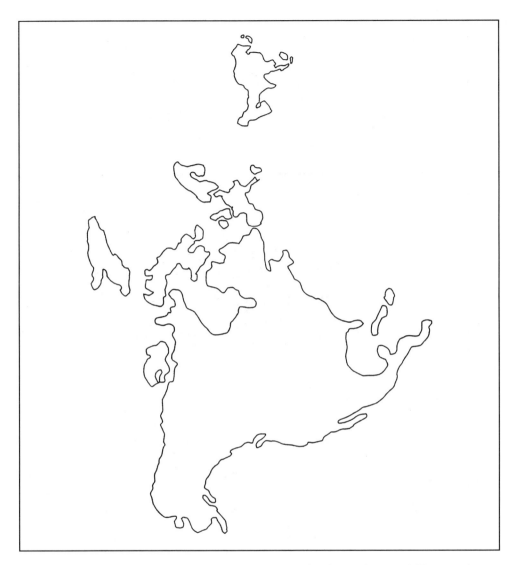

FIGURE 20.2b   Media maps, mental maps and real maps: boys aged 15,
high TV (Rosengren and Windahl, 1989: 231)

the value of those types of picture resides precisely in the fact that they *are* fictitious. Abdicating from the ambition of offering detailed truths about these or those events, processes or structures, the ambition of fictional programming is to arrive at another type of truth: a type of more general truth, perhaps, or truth grossly and obviously exaggerated and distorted, so that we may really come to know what it is all about. Other types of programming have the ambition to offer what may be considered virtually true pictures of the world or, at least, as true and trustworthy as possible. This type of picture of the world is found in news programs, of course, and also in the kinds of programs that are based on news programs: programmes offering comments to, views about, and discussions of the world as more or less truthfully mirrored in the content of news programs. How could we study these types of programs?

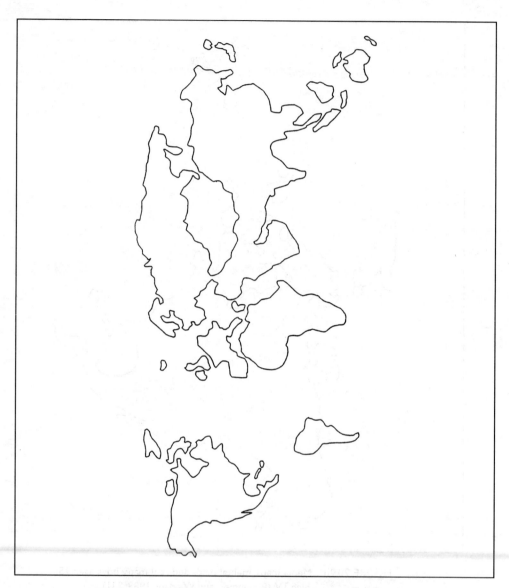

FIGURE 20.2c   Media maps, mental maps and real maps: media map of
Swedish TV (Rosengren and Windahl, 1989: 230)

In order systematically to study mass media news about the world, we need two sets of data. We need *data about news*, and we need *data about the world* (see Rosengren, 1970. The two sets of data should be as independent as possible in the sense that they should ideally stem from two different types of source. Obviously, data about media news must come from within the media; they must be what has been called *intra media data*. Data about the world, then, should stem from somewhere other than from within the media. They should be what has been called *extra media data*. By combining intra and extra media data we arrive at two types of new knowledge.

In the first place, we may use the two sets of data to *evaluate the news*: how true, reliable, representative, trustworthy, relevant, etc. are media stories about the world when compared to reality as defined in terms of extra media data? Intra media data about the world as rendered in Swedish television were graphically presented in Figure 20.2c above. The world as pictured in television news was found to be somewhat lopsided when (implicitly) compared to corresponding extra media data: the world as pictured in traditional maps of the world.

Second, we may use the two sets of data to *explain*, and thus better to *understand*, certain characteristics of the pictures of the world offered by mass media. Studies based on the intra/extra media data methodology have used extra media data regarding as different phenomena as, for instance, parliamentary elections and earthquakes in different parts of the world, with a view to examine the relative strength of the factors presumably explaining international news flow. In such studies it has been shown that considerable portions (30 percent) of existing variations in international news coverage are due to simple factors such as the size of population in the country of the event, and the geographical distance between the location of the event and the reporting mass medium.

REFERENCES

Rosengren, K.E. (1970) 'International news: intra and extra media data', *Acta Sociologica*, 13: 96–109.

Rosengren, K.E. (1987) 'News diffusion: a special issue', *European Journal of Communication*, 2 (2): 135–42.

Rosengren, K.E. and Windahl, S. (1989) *Media Matter: TV Use in Childhood and Adolescence*. Norwood, NJ: Ablex.

21

the mythology about globalization

MARJORIE FERGUSON

From sound bites to learned texts, 'globalization' reverberates through the corridors of politics, commerce, industry, scholarship, communication, environmentalism and popular culture. In moving from prophecy to assumption about the world, globalization is invoked to signify sweeping social, cultural and institutional change, the end results of which are sometimes said to define our age. If for no other reason than pervasiveness, this notion raises interesting but problematic issues.

First, there is the problem of *meaning*. It is not clear whether the different parties invoking globalization mean the same thing or even if they are addressing the same issue. Second, there is the problem of evidence. Despite its frequent attribution, neither the indices, nor the extent, of its actual occurrence are always clear. Third, there is the problem of evaluation. To whatever extent globalization (however defined) actually is occurring (and to whom), its alleged positive benefits or negative costs are difficult to assess. The deeper questions are: 'cui bono?' and 'who is being globalized (or de-globalized), to what extent and by whom?'

This chapter attempts to come to grips with this problematic notion, first in a more general way, and later, more specifically, through a collection of myths that have gathered around it. Finally, it seeks to raise for discussion a larger concern: the ideological overtones of the historical inevitability which has been asserted by globalizationists.

THE PROBLEM OF MEANING

Although proponents and critics may differ in their definitions, there is broad consensus that globalization denotes both a journey and a destination: it signifies an historical process of becoming, as well as an economic and cultural result; that is, arrival at the globalized state.

The idea is not new. Ever since Magellan's early sixteenth-century circumnavigation of the globe founded a material reality, this worldview has gathered substance and force. Current interpreters tend to focus on the key domains of economics, politics, culture and technology. Increased economic interdependence and worldwide corporate enterprise, decreased political sovereignty for nation states, common patterns of material and cultural consumption, with converging satellite, computer, cable, VCR, telephone, fax, television and radio technologies have between them been assigned a causal role in achieving interconnectivity and interaction in all four domains.

For many social scientists, structural processes of institutional change are at the heart of this reordering. Thus, the topic of globalization provides a conceptual entry point to an evolving world order and a concept for evaluating 'a particular series of developments concerning *the concrete structuration of the world as a whole*' (Robertson, 1990: 20). More holistically and in terms of process, our incorporation into a one-world, global society is contingent on changing value orientations that propel us towards 'the whole earth as the physical environment, everyone living as world citizens, consumers and producers with a common interest in collective action to solve global problems' (Albrow, 1990: 8–10).

First published in *European Journal of Communication*, 7, Sage Publications (1992), as 'The Mythology about Globalization', pp. 69–93.

Postmodernist interpretations of globality, on the other hand, focus more on the emergence of a common culture of consumption and style (see, for example, Baudrillard, 1985; Jameson, 1984). Acknowledging that transsocietal processes of cultural integration and disintegration lie outside the bounds of the nation state, the revisionist model of postmodernist globalization is both relativist and absolutist, allowing for cultural diversity in global unity (see, for example, Featherstone, 1990: 1; 1991: 144–7).

The divergences between the 'globalizationists' and their critics should not obscure the extent of agreement between the parties. All locate their concerns in the empirical reality of a more visible and powerful supranational order, a 'world system' in Wallerstein's (1990) terms, that shifts many former national concerns to the world geopolitical stage.

THE PROBLEM OF EVIDENCE

These changing contours of political and cultural economy may be located in space and, to a certain extent, in time. In the 1980s, the globalizing impetus manifested itself in science, politics and economics, in technology, deregulation and the Friedmanite free market, as new commercial imperatives oscillated between North America, Western Europe and Japan.

Typically, economic indicators are used as the yardstick of globality: multiconti-nental flows of capital, services, manufacture, goods, data, telecommunications; the large-scale privatization of publicly owned assets in countries as far flung as Britain, Australia and Mexico; the deregulation and reregulation of broadcasting systems, most notably in Europe; and the institutionalization of twenty-four-hour electronic world trading and money markets. But sociodemographic indicators also point to other forms of culture and value migration: for instance, the transborder passage of social movements, such as environmentalism; of antisocial artefacts, such as drugs and weapons; and of people, i.e. the massive movements of refugees, professionals, tourists and immigrants.

The centrality of media technology and artefacts to the globalizing process, as noted above, builds on pre-existing international production and distribution systems and markets. In the information industries, for example, Reuters Holdings plc is paradigmatic of global empire building on the back of new technologies and services. Between the 1960s and 1980s, the organization metamorphosed from being a respectably low-key, non-profit-making international news agency to high-profile market leadership. In 1990, the 'world's foremost electronic publisher' recorded revenues of £1396 million and profits of £287.9 million. Similarly, in the entertainment field, Hollywood's film and television producers have been global traders almost from their inception.

These data also indicate an exploding world audience for television news, spurred in part by the spread of a genre here called 'television vérité': that is, the live, raw video eye as recorder of instant history and shared video experiences of 'live' television news—protests in China, revolution in Eastern Europe, war in the Middle East. All serve to reinforce political, popular and scholarly perceptions of globalization as social and media-defined reality.

[...]

THE PROBLEM OF EVALUATION

Notwithstanding the repertoire of meanings and material indicators noted above, there is a significant aspect of globalization that goes relatively unremarked: its rhetoric is as much concerned about what *should be* as what *is*. Globalization conflates the normative and descriptive, and consequently carries ideological as well as temporal, spatial, historical and geopolitical implications.

Thus, if powerful nation states and corporate interests promote globalization as a self-fulfilling prophecy for political or profit ends, it is incumbent on us to examine not only what is being hawked by whom, but who stands to lose or gain materially, politically, culturally or militarily.

As a conceptual notion, then, 'globalization' offers mixed messages. It sounds like a relatively value-neutral descriptor of a supranational universe of media interconnectivity and material and symbolic goods exchange. But on closer examination it reveals extensive causal assumptions, normative intentions and value judgements.

What are important here are the overtones of historical inevitability embedded in inferences of globalization as a unidirectional process or a fait accompli. Such rhetoric, far from being value-free, implies reification and carries ideological baggage whereby globalization becomes the new dynamic, the motor of world change. What this suggests, and what this chapter argues, is that this concept has taken on a life of its own: as a sine qua non for our age, its status may be moving from that of mythology to ideology.

GLOBALIZATION AS MYTHOLOGY

Myth, in the context of globalization, is not used here in the sense of an untruth, but rather as a way of classifying certain assumptions about the modern world found in sets of ideas (myths) about world history, politics, economics, culture, communication and ecology.

Myths, then, are stories we are told, tell to others and ourselves; tales that explain, adapt and evolve as their context changes. Typically, myth has a complex relationship to social reality. It builds on what is already at work. Combining the real with the ideal, it produces something of an ideal type that stretches beyond what the evidence will show. Being both '*real* and *sacred*, the myth becomes exemplar, and consequently *repeatable*, for it serves as a model, and by the same token as a justification, for all human actions' (Eliade, 1954/1968: 23).

By guiding decisions and justifying events, myths help to structure our sense of belonging to a particular culture, to the 'our' world that is also the 'whole world'. It is the all-inclusive spatiality and explanatory aspects of myths that make them so appropriate for this study. These are not myths *of* globalization as such but myths *about* the objectives of and relationships between the disparate interests and institutions seeking to ride on the back of the globalizing momentum.

The mythology about globalization also reveals how old myths adapt and new ones arise. Some are familiar, others not. Some serve particular interests or groups. But taken together they explain and justify much about the topography of a shifting global, political and cultural economy. Nothing is finite about this structuring of social reality. Like all the best mythologies, this too is fluid, as new myths emerge to explain a changing world so old ones adapt or fade away.

At this point in the globalization mythology's life history, seven myths are identified: 'Big Is Better', 'More Is Better', 'Time and Space Have Disappeared', 'Global Cultural Homogeneity', 'Saving Planet Earth', 'Democracy for Export via American TV' and 'The New World Order'. Individually and collectively they interact with one another; some emphasize the journey of becoming, while others focus on the destination, the globalized state; and some represent both the process and the result.

SEVEN MYTHS ABOUT GLOBALIZATION

The Myth of 'Big Is Better'

As political ideology, public policy or corporate strategy, 'Big Is Better' serves the doctrine of market liberalism. Considered together with the 'More Is Better' myth (discussed below), 'Big' is invoked to present the classic Adam Smith case for expansionist, competitive capitalism. Its spatial-economic logic has driven international trade and transnational corporate expansion ever since, and in the easy credit, deregulatory 1980s, 'Big' spurred the worldwide migration of capital, mergers and takeovers.

The business of 'going global' was notable in the media industries as print, film, broadcast, cable, satellite, music, marketing and advertising organizations made the more interrelated universe a commercial reality and a technological fact. Although less remarked upon outside communication circles (see, for example, Bagdikian, 1989; Murdock, 1990), there has also been an escalation of ownership concentration and overlording in the media global village (e.g. Time-Warner Inc., Bertelsmann AG, News Corporation Ltd) with all their consequences for public discourse and diversity.

While the Japanese presence in Hollywood—Sony (formerly Columbia) Entertainment Industries and Matsushita MCA/Universal—provides further evidence of media globalism, it also testifies to widely shared corporate strategies of cross-national synergy, vertical integration and economies of scale (in this case, aligning video hardware and software ownership for future HDTV profit). Thus, 'Big Is Better' in the media and culture industries provides further ammunition for critiques claiming that globalization represents nothing more than corporate transnationalization at a higher level of magnitude (see, for example, Schiller, 1991).

However, what that categorical imperative overlooks is the extent of personal hubris behind corporate media expansion as the image of the global mogul took hold (e.g. Robert Maxwell, Rupert Murdoch, the Saatchi brothers). As free marketeers pursued ever wider horizons of hyperbole and investment, a symbiosis developed: the selling of globalization to the market became a part of the phenomenon itself. Thus, the myth-makers came to believe their own overextended metaphors, until their financial bubbles burst. Now as agencies and media groups juggle their debt rescheduling in the 1990s, 'Big Is Better' on a global scale may be losing some of its hold on the corporate mind.

This myth is cautionary and raises questions about the preordination of 'Big' as the foundation for economic globalization. It may be that corporate expansion on a world scale is riskier for some cultural (or material) industries than for others, just as it is clearly riskier in destabilized or rapidly changing national or regional contexts.

The Myth of 'More Is Better'

This myth firmly places a central tenet of free market economics, the universal benefits of competition, in the context of the 1980s' ethos of excess—excessive deregulation, investment and consumption. Thus, 'More Is Better' provides the cornucopia or utilitarian justification that makes 'more' a public good in and of itself: the perfect rationale for the public policies, private practices and corruptive vanities of the 'greed decade' documented in legislation, factual and fictional accounts, television and film. 'More', then, revolves around the market forces' proposition that increased competition, unfettered by ownership or trading restrictions (e.g. in airlines, telecommunications, media or finance), equals increased benefits for all: QED, increased profits, consumer choice and satisfaction.

In the wider media policy arena this myth favoured privatization and proliferation of off-air, cable and satellite television channels (and, to a lesser extent, radio) and transnational programme trade (and transcultural migration of values) to fill expanding schedules. We need only to recall how 'More' served an expansionist, deregulating broadcast industry on both sides of the Atlantic—television providers in Western Europe and cablecasters in the US.

[···]

The 'More' myth, then, sounds plausible. It fits with the globalization worldview of material and symbolic goods interdependence and with the technology of distribution, but fits less well with the cultural logic of particular media markets (e.g. where mixed economy public service broadcasting has flourished and defined itself as a service rather than a product).

The Myth of 'Time and Space Have Disappeared'

'Time and Space Have Disappeared' recalls nineteenth- as well as twentieth-century prophecy, hyperbole and inflated expectations about, respectively, the wonders of electricity and electronic media uniting the world. But the early oracles were not alone in linking communication technology to globalization.

Much 'information revolution' rhetoric from the 1970s onwards has dwelt on the facts and fantasies of communication abundance from converging computer, fibre optic, cellular, digital and satellite technology. This myth assumes their consequences are those of rendering distance in space and variance in time irrelevant: i.e. they have 'disappeared' as constraints on business or personal life. Thus, industrial policy based on information technology (IT) as the key to economic competitiveness has rationalized technology as the key to future national and corporate prosperity.

While it is true that the structural transformation of capital, information and goods markets would not have happened as it has *without* modern telecommunications and computing, the potential of IT as a force for public and private good is inflated to say the least. Especially, much 'wired societies' euphoria overlooks problems of differential access, principally North–South, to the alleged benefits and the complexity of differential impact on time–space perceptions and social experience.

The postmodernist attention paid to temporal and spatial categories as emblematic of a more globalized, transnational culture, differentiates their meaning from an earlier modernity. Claiming that classic theorists such as Weber and Marx favoured time over space, where the road to modernization was one of becoming rather than of being, Harvey (1989: 205) sees conflict: 'beneath the veneer of common-sense and seemingly "natural" ideas about space and time lie hidden areas of ambiguity, contradiction and struggle'.

Such contradictions are based on subjective as well as objective material factors. Thus, redefinitions of time and space provide a material connection between the processes of a more global cultural and political economy and the postmodern condition. But the unknown frontiers of a postmodern world create a crisis of uncertainty for Jameson (1984) wherein the 'hyperspace' of a global culture requires new 'cognitive maps' to negotiate.

Uncertainty about where and when we are in the world is at odds with the idea that technology can confer benefits of time–distance compression for all. The mobility of commerce, organizations, information and people does *not* make time and space irrelevant, rather it highlights the extent to which these areas of experience have become more, not less, multilayered, interrelated and complex. For the uprooted, the restless or the peripatetic, the business of 'living life' (family, friends, work) in three or four time zones requires new negotiating skills in a perceptual world of spatial indeterminacy and temporal recalculation, a world of 'time without time' and space without space' (Ferguson, 1990).

Neither do we know much about how shared broadcast media experience alters time–space perceptions by bringing the faraway near. Speculation, for example, as to how television may foster reproduction of political action or replication of iconic protest images from one part of the world to another, overlooks the fact that the mechanisms by which any such effects might occur remain something of a black hole in communications research. To a greater extent than other myths about globalization, 'Time and Space' typifies the extension of our horizons and problematics in the communications field.

The Myth of 'Global Cultural Homogeneity'

This myth relates to McLuhan's notions of global village shared experience and to aspects of postmodernist and media imperialist interpretations of a more culturally (and economically) intertwined world. More specifically, it relates to the inter-connectivity of the transnational organization of cultural production, distribution and consumption in the broadest sense, and, in the context of this chapter, to the export and import of media artefacts from the print, music, graphic, audiovisual and information industries.

Simply stated, then, 'Global Cultural Homogeneity' infers that the consumption of the same popular material and media products, be they Schwarzeneggar, *Cheers*, Pepsi, Big Macs, Disney Worlds, clothes, cars or architectural fashions, creates a metaculture whose collective identity is based on shared patterns of consumption, be these built on choice, emulation or manipulation.

Moreover, this myth has its nation-state and regional variants. Claims of 'national cultural integrity' or of 'regional cultural authenticity' (as manifest in, respectively, Canadian broadcasting policy goals or the EC Television Directive) typify attempts to protect or promote a national or regional collective identity based on notions of shared citizenship or sovereignty. (This notion, in the case of the EC, is under threat of extinction before it is ever realized owing to the rising pressure for wider membership.)

In fact, neither 'Global Cultural Homogeneity' nor its national or regional variants fit the emerging conflict models of the nation state, or the exclusionary imperatives of ethnic or regional entities. The first evokes a seamless web of artefact and tradition that does less than justice to the rich, global patchwork that exists, while the goals of the latter two fly in the face of dramatic, and sometimes bloody, evidence of repluralization. Paradoxically, we witness an antifederalist ethos competing with a resurgent regional economic protectionism in the EC, the North American Free Trade Area (NAFTA) and the proposed South-East Asia trading bloc.

Consequently, either this myth presumes that it is possible to argue the existence of a global cultural economy that ignores the counter-pull of localism and the rich traditions of variance, or it assumes, wrongly, that cultural identities are contained within political borders or are conferred on a transhistorical world society basis by an ethic of consumption (or exploitation).

[…]

The Myth of 'Saving Planet Earth'

If globalization as an historical process only emerged fully formed in the 1980s, now, in the 1990s, ideas about planetary interdependence embrace an ecological dimension. The one-world, Gaia philosophy at the heart of 'Saving Planet Earth' links culture and economy to perceptions of a world eco-system and its protection. Not only are we enjoined to 'think globally and act locally', but also to realize that eco-crises such as 'global warming require the rise of the global politician, buttressed by a global citizenry, whose vision extends for decades' (O'Riordan, 1990).

The utopian ideas embedded in this myth are transcultural and synchronic, displaying the power of myth to reinvent itself across space and time. In fact 'Saving Planet Earth' combines ancient (and sometimes sacred) beliefs about man's intimate relation to nature with modern ideas of eco-activism. Narratives about the environmentalist project to rescue the planet from self-destruction echo archaic myths of the 'eternal return', and such sentiments, according to Eliade (1954/1968), appeal to our primitive longings for cyclical regeneration and new beginnings.

[...]

The Myth of 'Democracy for Export via American TV'

'Democracy for Export' is an old myth that displays uniformity over space, time and sacred belief. That is to say, 'Democracy for Export via American TV' is a recycled version of seasoned ideas about the power of the mass media to influence public opinion with respect to political ends. Accordingly, it updates the technology but not the premise about direct media 'effects'.

These ideas resurfaced in a US Department of Commerce inquiry into the globalization of mass media firms (Obuchowski, 1990); the document, whose economic aims are to expand US audiovisual trade competitiveness and dominance, also envisages a politico-cultural agenda. The latter surfaces in assumptions about the effectiveness of US film and television products as exporters of US values and 'democratic ideals', notions premised on assumptions that global media can play 'an increasingly significant role in promoting free speech and fostering demands for democratic reforms internationally' (Obuchowski, 1990: 7). (A view that gains popular credence every time CNN is cited as the lingua franca of the video era by political leaders on the world stage and their media watchers.)

What this conflation of politics and economy presents, then, is 'Democracy for Export via American TV', a highly functional set of ideas for the US film and television industries (and the US President's own personal worldview, see next section). Moreover, the benign view of media products as vehicles of political enlightenment stresses their potential for political persuasion (e.g. abandoning communism for democracy) over their potential for cultural dislocation (e.g. emphasizing individualism over collectivism).

[...]

The Myth of 'The New World Order'

This, the most recent addition to globalization's mythology, demonstrates how new myths arise and old ones reappear or adapt in response to changing conditions. From the US President's first call for a 'New World Order' (NWO) during the Gulf War, this myth's core ideas have offered mixed messages, few of them clear. Therefore, we may usefully distinguish between 'world order' as the creation of order *in* the world and as an ordering *of* the world (according to a particular set of ideological conditions or economic practices). Both meanings are conflated in this myth and its ongoing revision.

Also evident from the outset was that even if the purported purposes were global, the authorship was American, and that here was an unclear vision of a New Jerusalem of world political power premised on the demise of communism and the triumph of capitalism. Before the mirage was fully formed, however, a 'new' NWO unfolded with dramatic swiftness: the Moscow 'coup' of August 1991 and the rapid disintegration of the Soviet Union that followed.

Both the old and new versions mesh with an earlier triumphalism about the end of history (Fukuyama, 1989). This thesis is essayed on the premise that 'Western liberal democracy seems at its close to be returning full circle to where it started: not to an "end of ideology" or a convergence between capitalism and socialism, as earlier predicted, but to an unabashed victory of economic and political liberalism' (Fukuyama, 1989: 3).

The notion of history having ended is connected to the end of the Enlightenment in postmodernism and to our having fallen over the edge of modernity into an uncertain void (see, for example, Gitlin, 1989; Harvey, 1989), one characterized by shifting lines of political sovereignty that exceed the bounds of the nation state (see, for example, Bauman, 1990).

[…]

MYTHOLOGY, IDEOLOGY AND TELEVISION VÉRITÉ—TOWARDS FURTHER DISCUSSION

This chapter attempts to address the problematic notion of globalization by examining the mythology within its discourse and associated problems of meaning, evidence and evaluation. Important as it is to recognize these myths, it is also important to acknowledge the empirical reality of a more interconnected world political and cultural economy.

However, this does not infer any consequences of a hegemonic global metaculture or a supranational board game controlled by powerful states or transnational corporations. Throughout I have stressed the importance of scepticism towards ideas that a 'global ecumene' is emerging on the basis of any media reductionist or technological determinist assumptions. Globalization, defined either as a journey or a destination, demands a critical approach.

Nor are any lines of cultural causality clear as to who is globalizing whom: British media barons buy New York newspapers, Hong Kong billionaires buy Vancouver's waterfront, Germans buy RCA Records and Japanese buy Radio City Music Hall. Moreover, similar kinds of questions can be posed as to who is *deglobalizing* whom, given the inconsistencies and hostilities of ethnic, religious and other forms of localism within developed and lesser developed countries alike, e.g. Spain, Canada, the former Soviet empire, Sri Lanka, India. The list is long and growing.

REFERENCES

Albrow, M. (1990) 'Introduction', in M. Albrow and E. King (eds), *Globalization, Knowledge and Society*. London: Sage. pp. 1–13.

Bagdikian, B.H. (1989) 'Lords of the global village', *The Nation*, 12 June: 805–20.

Baudrillard, J. (1985) 'Child in the bubble', *Impulse*, Winter: 12–13.

Bauman, Z. (1990) 'Modernity and ambivalence', *Theory, Culture and Society*, 7 (2/3): 143–69.

Eliade, M. (1954/1968) *Myths, Dreams and Mysteries*. London: Fontana.

Featherstone, M. (ed.) (1990) 'Global culture, nationalism, globalization and modernity', special issue of *Theory, Culture and Society*, 7 (2/3).

Featherstone, M. (1991) *Consumer Culture and Postmodernism*. London: Sage.

Ferguson, M. (1990) 'Electronic media and the redefining of time and space', in M. Ferguson (ed.), *Public Communication: The New Imperatives*. London: Sage. pp. 152–72.

Fukuyama, F. (1989) 'The end of history?', *The National Interest*, 16 (Summer): 3–18.

Gitlin, T. (1989) 'Postmodernism, roots and politics', in I. Angus and S. Jhally (eds), *Cultural Politics in Contemporary America*. New York: Routledge and Kegan Paul. pp. 347–60.

Harvey, D. (1989) *The Condition of Postmodernity*. Oxford: Blackwell.

Jameson, F. (1984) 'Postmodernism, or the cultural logic of late capitalism', *New Left Review*, 146: 53–92.

Murdock, G. (1990) 'Redrawing the map of the communications industries: concentration and ownership in the era of privatization', in M. Ferguson (ed.), *Public Communication: The New Imperatives*. London: Sage. pp. 1–15.

O'Riordan, T. (1990) 'Global warning', *Marxism Today*, July: 12–15.

Obuchowski, J. (1990) *Comprehensive Study of the Globalization of Mass Media Firms*. Washington, DC: US Department of Commerce.

Robertson, R. (1990) 'Mapping the global condition: globalization as the central concept', *Theory, Culture and Society*, 7 (2/3): 15–30.

Schiller, H. (1991) 'Not yet the post-imperialist era', *Critical Studies in Mass Communication*, 8 (1): 13–28.

Wallerstein, I. (1990) 'Societal development, or development of the world system?', in M. Albrow and E. King (eds), *Globalization, Knowledge and Society*. London: Sage. pp. 157–73.

VII

MEDIA ORGANIZATION AND PRODUCTION

From an early point in time, theorizing about mass media was based on a 'sender–content–channel–receiver' sequential model in which the 'sender' was largely identified either with a large mass media firm or organization (newspaper, radio network, etc.) or with the 'original source' (an author, spokesperson, advertiser, campaigner, etc.). Attention focused mainly on the nature of the 'content' sent, especially its 'mass' and standardized features. These were believed to stem directly or indirectly from the technology of mass distribution that characterized the typical media 'channel'. The first main deviation from this perspective, aside from some studies of certain media occupations (e.g. film-makers and journalists), occurred with the recognition that the selection and processing of content within a media organization may have as much effect in shaping content as the demands of technology. The work of media organizations is carried out in ways that systematically influence the content of what is transmitted. Varied organizational goals, work practices and the culture of the workplace have a considerable impact.

The early conceptualization of organizational impact was made in terms of the idea of a 'gatekeeper role'. This refers to the giving or denying of access through the 'gates' of the media according to some principles of organizational 'policy' or subjective ideas of what would best sell to an audience, under conditions of competition. This role was most in evidence in relation to news (see Shoemaker, Chapter 22), where editors continually select from a vast amount of available or incoming material in a very routinized and focused way. However, basically, the same model applies to the selection of books for publication, film scripts for filming, music for recording and so on. Subsequently, during the era of critical media theory, the same kind of theoretical analysis was applied to accounting for some of the alleged 'bias' of major news media in favour of authorities or the established consensus. The distinction was made between intentional ideology and propaganda, on the one hand, and, on the other hand, 'unwitting bias' arising from organizational factors that generally tended to work in favour of the status quo by applying conventional news values and procedures. These included applying market criteria (McManus, Chapter 24), relying on official, authoritative sources, neglecting minority and alternative voices, and adopting the reigning consensus in the wider framing of issues. Tuchman's (Chapter 23) classic study of news journalism vividly illustrates the way in which the nature of 'news as a form of knowledge' (the phrase used by Park [1940]) is directly shaped by constraints of time and space.

The thrust of media organizational theory is towards emphasizing not only ways of working over mass distribution technology but also the organization over the individual as a personal actor in the production process. It tends to discount the potential for individual views (unless those of the media owner) or even shared personal characteristics (such as gender, class or ethnic identity) for influencing output, unless this conforms to goals set by the organization. However, research has shown that it is not only media organizations that have alternative, even competing goals (such as profit, public service, efficiency, political influence and prestige). Established media professions are also internally diverse, according to somewhat parallel dimensions. This has been widely demonstrated in respect of news journalists (where the differences also relate to cross-cultural differences in political cultures). The occupation of producers making films for television is also differentiated in systematic ways, as shown by Muriel Cantor (Chapter 25). There are alternative orientations to the task, to colleagues, to the audience and to the employing organizations. In general, the theory supports the view that media organizations can tolerate a certain amount of diversity and even internal conflict, even if the dominant forces are towards 'mass production' and homogeneity. Media organizations are in any case under a continuous pressure to be creative and innovative as well as to conform to some supposed 'mass taste' or demand.

An important extension of ideas about the influence of media organizations was added by the concept of 'media logic', which derived from observations about the influence of technology as filtered through professional ideologies and production demands. Altheide and Snow (1976) elaborated on the concept but acknowledged their debt to Elliott (1972). Essentially, 'media logic' is the driving force in the selection and processing (or shaping) of typical content. It indicates what will maximize the benefits of a particular technology or channel. On the whole, it tends to prioritize form and presentation over substance, the concrete over the abstract, the personal over the institutional or theoretical. Media logic has been said to devalue political and other informational communication and generally replace genuine communication with spectatorship.

REFERENCES

Altheide, D.L. and Snow, R.P. (1976) *Media Logic*. Beverly Hills, CA: Sage.
Elliott, P. (1972) *The Making of a Television Documentary*. London: Constable.
Park, R. (1940) 'News as a form of knowledge', in R.H. Turner (ed.), *On Social Control and Collective Behavior*. Chicago, IL: University of Chicago Press. pp. 32–52.

22

a new gatekeeping model

PAMELA J. SHOEMAKER

Figures 22.1, 22.2 and 22.3 summarize and integrate what is known about gatekeeping, based on the theoretical approaches we have discussed. Figures 22.2 and 22.3 are not independent models but represent enlargements of portions of Figure 22.1. The overall process is shown in Figure 22.1, but without detail within communication organizations and within individual gatekeepers. Figure 22.2 shows the gatekeeping processes within a communication organization, and Figure 22.3 shows the intra-individual psychological processes within one gatekeeper. In Figure 22.1 (see Figures 22.2 and 22.3 for more detail), circles represent individual gatekeepers, vertical bars in front of gatekeepers are gates, and the arrows in front of and behind each gate represent the forces that affect a message's entrance into the gate and what happens to it afterward. The large squares are communication organizations, and small rectangles represent social and institutional factors. One or more channels lead to and from each gate and gatekeeper, each carrying one or more messages or potential messages.

The process starts with a variety of potential messages traveling through multiple channels to any of several types of communication organizations, such as a wire service, a public relations agency, a newspaper, or a television network. An organization may have multiple staff members operating in boundary role input positions, each with the power to control which potential messages actually enter the organization and the power to shape the message.

Moving to the organizational enlargement (Figure 22.2), we see that, within a complex organization, the boundary role gatekeepers in charge of inputs may channel selected messages to one or more internal gatekeepers, who may exert their own selection processes and who also may shape the message in a variety of ways. The surviving, shaped messages are then transmitted to boundary role gatekeepers for final shaping, selection, and transmission directly to the audience or to another communication organization (see Figure 22.1). As the feedback loop from organization 2 to organization 1 (and from the audience to organization 2) indicates, selection of messages for outputting is heavily influenced by the selection criteria of the receiver. As Figure 22.2 shows, the gatekeeping processes internal to the organization are embedded in the organization's communication routines and characteristics, which affect the decisions organizational gatekeepers make. Figure 22.2 also provides for the 'groupthink' phenomenon (Janis, 1983), particularly among socially cohesive groups of gatekeepers.

Figure 22.3 identifies various psychological processes and individual characteristics that can affect the gatekeeping process, including cognitive heuristics, models of thinking, socialization, second-guessing, values, attitudes, decision-making strategies, role conceptions, and type of job. Just as the broader gatekeeping model (Figure 22.1) is embedded in social system ideology and culture, and within-organization gatekeeping (Figure 22.2) is embedded in communication routines and organizational characteristics, individual-level gatekeeping processes (Figure 22.3) are embedded in the individual's life experiences.

Thus we see the complexity of the gatekeeping process. The individual gatekeeper has likes and dislikes, ideas about the nature of his or her job, ways of thinking about a problem, preferred decision-making strategies, and values that all impinge on the decision to reject or select (and shape) a message. But the gatekeeper is not

First published in *Gatekeeping*, P. Shoemaker, Sage Publications (1991), as 'A New Gatekeeping Model', pp. 70–77.

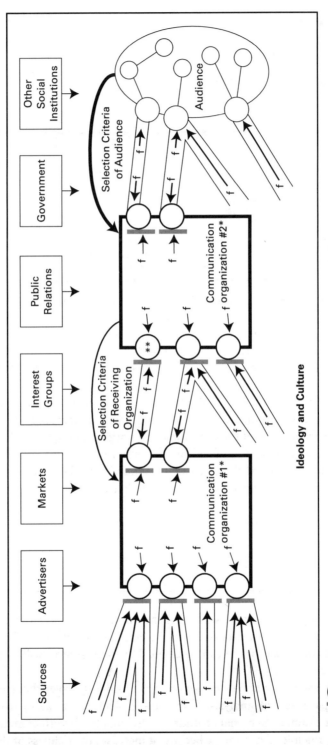

FIGURE 22.1   Gatekeeping between organizations is embedded in social system ideology
and culture and is influenced by social and institutional factors

Note: As an example, communication organizations could include wire services, public
relations agencies, television networks, or newspapers.

*See Figure 22.2 for a detailed version of gatekeeping within an organization.
**See Figure 22.3 for a detailed version of gatekeeping within an individual.

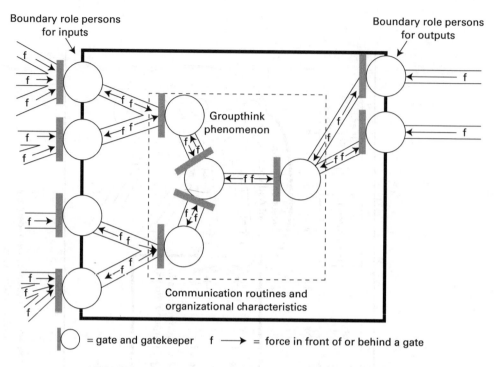

FIGURE 22.2   Gatekeeping within an organization is embedded
in communication organizational characteristics

Note: See Figure 22.3 for intra-individual gatekeeping processes.

totally free to follow a personal whim; he or she must operate within the constraints of communication routines to do things this way or that. All of this also must occur within the framework of the communication organization, which has its own priorities but also is continuously buffeted by influential forces from outside the organization. And, of course, none of these actors—the individual, the routine, the organization, or the social institution—can escape the fact that it is tied to and draws its sustenance from the social system.

FUTURE RESEARCH

Even a multiple-level model such as is shown in Figures 22.1 through 22.3 still leaves many questions unanswered. Although the gatekeeping literature covers nearly 50 years and scores of studies, more can be done. This final section will suggest directions for future studies.

First, scholars would be well advised to consider the roles that gatekeeping can play on multiple levels of analysis. Some studies include variables from more than one level—for example, personal attitudes (individual level) with communication routines; this is in principle an advantage because it increases the richness of the study. However, if variables from multiple levels are combined in one analysis, this could confuse interpretation of the results.

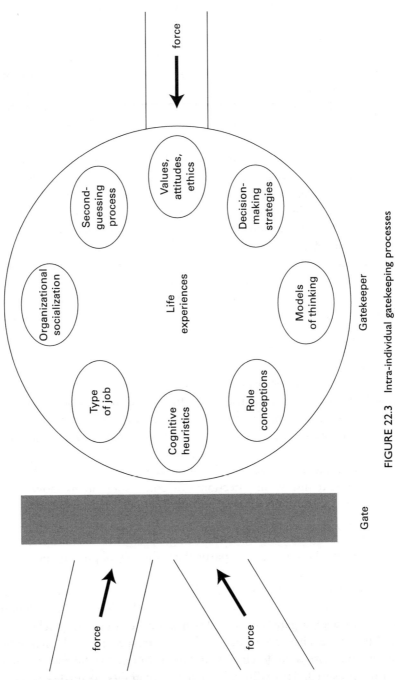

FIGURE 22.3   Intra-individual gatekeeping processes

Note: Intra-individual-level variables are embedded in life experiences.

Second, the linkages between levels could particularly benefit from study: Exactly what is the mechanism through which social system variables affect social institutions, and how do these influence communication organizations? In what ways do communication organizations and their routines influence gatekeeping processes within individuals?

Third, the relative power of the levels should be addressed. One line of thought holds that individual-level influences are least important, being effectively controlled by communication routines and influences from higher levels. As we indicated earlier, however, some studies (Sasser and Russell, 1972; Stempel, 1985) suggest that communication routines override individual influences in some circumstances but not in others. As Hirsch (1977: 21) points out, gatekeeping studies are primarily interested in 'subjective bias', and this can operate at more than the individual level of analysis. If an individual gatekeeper wants to base decisions on his or her personal attitudes, to what extent can this be done? How much autonomy and power do individual gatekeepers have to impose their own agendas on media content? What conditions would be conducive to the exercise of personal judgment over more structural constraints?

Fourth, study of the individual needs to progress beyond simple questions of attitudes or bias. We have suggested a variety of intra-individual approaches (e.g., models of thinking, cognitive heuristics, second-guessing, decision making) that could help identify the extent to which individual-level processes are important.

Fifth, the extension of gatekeeping into the higher levels of analysis allows us to use some theoretical approaches that are not generally applied to gatekeeping and presents many ideas for research. The boundary roles perspective (Adams, 1980) seems particularly fruitful, suggesting new interpretations of old studies, as suggested above. If Adams is correct, the wire services may use their own criteria to select input messages but use criteria from the receiving organizations to select outputs. This reverses the assumed causal direction in several gatekeeping studies and suggests that the media get from wire services what they want rather than what the wire services want them to have.

Sixth, studies should do more with the gates themselves and the forces surrounding them. Does the number of items in front of or behind a gate affect the polarity and strength of the force exerted? Must forces always change polarity? Is movement through a gate always unidirectional or could some items move 'backward'? What would cause them to do so? Are some gates 'lower' than others?

Seventh, the study of gatekeeping ought to be broadened beyond mere selection to the shaping, display, timing, withholding, or repetition of messages (Donohue et al., 1972). We ought to investigate particularly the role of pre- and postgate forces in these processes of nonselection.

Eighth, more can be done with characteristics of the messages. Nisbett and Ross (1980) have suggested that vivid messages would be more likely than pallid messages to pass through a gate, but this idea has not been used in gatekeeping research. We need to progress beyond a categorization of messages (e.g., human interest, economy, international issues) to develop a number of continuous dimensions on which messages can be measured. This will add much to our ability to predict whether and in what form a message will pass through a gate.

Ninth, we might compare the gatekeeping activities of various types of communication organizations, such as television networks and local stations, newspapers, radio stations, advertising agencies, public relations agencies, and magazines. How do communication routines differ? How do the differing goals of these organizations affect inputs and outputs not just in terms of selection but also in terms of how the messages are shaped?

REFERENCES

Adams, J.S. (1980) 'Interorganizational processes and organizational boundary spanning activities', in B.M. Shaw and L.L. Cummings (eds), *Research in Organizational Behavior*, Vol. 2. Greenwich, CT: JAI Press. pp. 321–55.

Donohue, G.A., Olien, C.N. and Tichenor, P.J. (1972) 'Gatekeeping: mass media systems and information control', in F.G. Kline and P.J. Tichenor (eds), *Current Perspectives on Mass Communication Research*. Beverly Hills, CA: Sage. pp. 41–70.

Donohue, G.A., Olien, C.N. and Tichenor, P.J. (1989) 'Structure and constraints on community newspaper gatekeepers', *Journalism Quarterly*, 66: 807–12, 845.

Hirsch, P.M. (1977) 'Occupational, organizational and institutional models in mass media research: towards an integrated framework', in P.M. Hirsch, P.V. Miller and F.G. Kline (eds), *Strategies for Communication Research*. Beverly Hills, CA: Sage. pp. 13–42.

Janis, I.L. (1983) *Group Think: Psychological Studies of Policy Decisions and Fiascoes*. Boston, MA: Houghton Mifflin.

Nisbett, R. and Ross, L. (1980) *Human Inference: Strategies and Shortcomings of Social Judgement*. New York: Prentice-Hall.

Sasser, E.L. and Russell, J.T. (1972) 'The fallacy of news judgement', *Journalism Quarterly*, 49: 280–4.

Stempel, G.H., III (1985) 'Gatekeeping: the mix of topics and the selection of stories', *Journalism Quarterly*, 62: 791–6, 815.

23

making news: time and typifications

GAYE TUCHMAN*

*Reprinted with the permission of The Free Press, a Division of Simon & Schuster, Inc., from MAKING NEWS: A Study in the Construction of Reality by Gaye Tuchman. Copyright © 1978 by The Free Press.

TIME AND THE GLUT OF OCCURRENCES

The news net produces more stories than can be processed. Each one of these is a potential drain upon the news organization's temporal and staff resources. For each occurrence can claim to be idiosyncratic—a particular conjunction of social, economic, political, and psychological forces that formed an occurrence into 'this particular occurrence' and not any other existing or having existed in the everyday world.

Accepting this claim for all occurrences is an organizational impossibility. Like any other complex organization, a news medium cannot process idiosyncratic phenomena. It must reduce all phenomena to known classifications, much as hospitals 'reduce' each patient to sets of symptoms or diseases, and as teachers view individual students in terms of categories pertinent to learning. Any organization that sought to process each and every phenomenon as a 'thing in itself' would be so flexible that it would be unrecognizable as a formal organization. Some means between flexibility and rigidity must be attained (March and Simon, 1958).

Concentrating reporters' working hours does not necessarily provide time to handle the idiosyncrasy of occurrences. A comparison makes this clearer. Providing more doctors than usual in a hospital's emergency room on weekend and holiday nights does not guarantee that the seriously ill and wounded will receive adequate medical treatment, even though that provision takes into account the everyday rhythm of work and recreation. (More accidents arrive in hospitals on weekends because of bar brawls and family disputes engendered by extended intensive interaction.) To facilitate adequate treatment, hospitals institute special routines. For instance, they may schedule all elective surgery before 5:00 P.M. on weekdays. Operating-room schedules also take into account the amount of time customarily required for the expected surgical procedures. What a patient sees as a personal medical emergency is thus rendered routine by the hospital so that it may plan the use of both personnel and physical resources and thus control the flow of work. When allocating resources each week, some hospitals even check lists of critical patients to estimate the kind and amount of work to be expected by the morgue's personnel (Sudnow, 1967).

Just as hospital personnel differentiate among diseases according to their demands for organizational resources, news personnel must anticipate the claims of potential occurrences upon their resources. To control work, newsworkers have developed typifications of occurrences as news stories. (Typifications are classifications arising from practical purposive action.) Anchored or embedded in the use of time, the news typifications characterize stories, much as the anchorage of the news net in space characterizes and constitutes newsworthiness.

The anchoring or embeddedness of typifications in time shares two other important characteristics with the anchoring of newsworthiness in the spatial news net. That is, both news typifications and the assignment of newsworthiness are relatively content free. We have seen that newsworthiness is a negotiated phenomenon rather than the application of independently derived objective criteria to news events. So too,

First published in *Making News: time and typification*, G. Tuchman, Free Press (1978), pp. 45–58.

typifications of kinds of news draw upon the *way* occurrences happen, not upon *what* is happening. The typifications are only relatively content free, because some sorts of occurrences are likely to happen one way while others have a different temporal rhythm. For instance, a hospital may generally preplan a specific cesarean delivery; a news organization may preplan coverage of a particular trial. Neither organization can specifically anticipate the work associated with a particular four-alarm fire.

Just as newsworkers claim that there are specific criteria of content against which news is assessed (i.e., how many people are affected by the event), so, too, newsworkers insist that their categorization of news depends upon a story's content.

NEWSWORKERS ON CATEGORIES OF NEWS

At work, reporters and editors refer to five categories of news: hard, soft, spot, developing, and continuing. Journalism texts and informants explain that these terms differentiate kinds of news content or the subject of events-as-news. Asked for definitions of their categories, newsworkers fluster, for they take these categories so much for granted that they find them difficult to define. To specify definitions, newsworkers offer examples of the stories that fall within a given category. They tend to classify the same stories in the same manner. Some stories are cited with such frequency that, viewed as prototypes, they are incorporated in the following discussion.

Hard News versus Soft News

The newsworkers' main distinction is between hard news and its antithesis, soft news. As they put it, hard news concerns occurrences potentially available to analysis or interpretation, and consists of 'factual presentations' of occurrences deemed newsworthy. When pressed, informants indicated that hard news is 'simply' the stuff of which news presentations are made. For instance, asked for a definition of hard news, a television editor offered the following catalog of basic news stories: 'Hard news is the gubernatorial message to the legislature, the State of the Union Address to Congress, the train–truck accident or the murder, the bank holdup, the legislative proposal ... and the fire tomorrow.'

This editor and other informants voluntarily contrasted hard news with soft news, also known as feature or human-interest stories (cf. Hughes, 1940). Some examples of soft-news stories are: an item about a big-city bus driver who offers a cheery 'good morning' to every passenger on his early morning run; a feature about a lonely female bear; a story about young adults who rent a billboard for a month to proclaim 'Happy Anniversary Mom and Dad.'

Newsworkers distinguish between these two lists by saying that a hard-news story is 'interesting to human beings' and a soft-news story is 'interesting because it deals with the life of human beings' (Mott, 1952: 58). Or they state that hard news concerns information people should have to be informed citizens and soft news concerns human foibles and the 'texture of our human life' (Mott, 1952: 58). Finally, newsworkers may simply summarize: Hard news concerns important matters and soft news, interesting matters.

These separate yet similar attempts to distinguish between hard and soft news present the same classificatory problem; the distinctions overlap. Frequently it is difficult, if not impossible, to decide whether an event is interesting or important or is both interesting and important. Indeed, the same event may be treated as either a hard- or a soft-news story. During a two-year period, the observed television station presented as feature stories some events that its primary television competition presented as hard news, and vice versa.

Spot News and Developing News

Difficulties also appear in the newsworkers' distinctions between spot news and developing news. The most important problem is that the newsworkers partially abandon their claim that the categories are based upon the content or subject matter of events-as-news.

Asked to discuss spot news, newsworkers replied that it is a type (subclassification) of hard news. They cited fires as a prototypical example of spot news. (Occasionally informants added a second example, such as a robbery, murder, accident, tornado, or earthquake.) The subject matter of all examples was conflict with nature, technology, or the penal code.

Asked about developing news (another subclassification of hard news), the newsworkers cited the same examples. Asked, then, to distinguish between spot and developing news, informants introduced a new element, the amount of information that they have about an event-as-news at a given moment. When they learned of an unexpected event, it was classed 'spot news.' If it took a while to learn the 'facts' associated with a 'breaking story,' it was 'developing news.' It remained 'developing news' so long as 'facts' were still emerging and being gathered. When I pointed to previous statements asserting that the subject of the story determined that story's classification, the newsworkers insisted that both statements were correct. In essence, they countered, the subject matter of certain kinds of event-as-news had a tendency to occur in specific ways (fires break out unexpectedly, whereas many demonstrations are pre-planned). And so, newsworkers happen to learn of them in certain ways.

Continuing News

Asked to define continuing news, newsworkers reverted to discussing the subject matter of an event-as-news. As the newsworkers put it, continuing news is a series of stories on the same subject based upon events occurring over a period of time. As a prototype, the newsworkers cited the legislative bill. The passage of a bill, they explained, is a complicated process occurring over a period of time. Although news of the bill's progress through the legislative maze may vary from day to day, all stories about the bill deal with the same content—the bill's provisions and whether they will be enacted. In this sense, they said, the story about the legislative bill continues as news. (Other examples cited by informants included trials, election campaigns, economics, diplomacy, and wars. Almost all examples were confrontations within or among recognized institutions, and all are produced by complex organizations.)

Then, once again, the newsworkers partially modified their statements. Maintaining that certain kinds of news content tend to fall under the rubric 'continuing news,' they added that certain kinds of content (stories about legislative bills and trials, for example) 'simply' tend to occur over an extended period of time.

TYPIFICATIONS OF NEWS

From Category to Typification

Unfortunately, the newsworkers' definitions of their categories are difficult to apply, even though the definitions, prototypical examples, and lists of stories decrease the variability of the occurrences as the raw material of news, and so reduce their idiosyncrasy. More important, discussing spot, developing, and continuing news, the newsworkers introduce a seemingly extraneous element mentioned in the comparison of hospitals and news organizations: certain kinds of event-as-news tend to happen in certain ways. And so, reporters and editors 'just happen' to be alerted to the need to process them in different ways.

The notion of news as frame, particularly the recognition that organizations perform work upon the everyday world to make sense of daily experience, enables the realization that the classificatory scheme is grounded in the rhythm of time use. Schutz's interpretive sociology suggests that the newsworkers' classifications are typifications rather than categories. 'Category' refers to the classification of objects according to one or more relevant characteristics ruled salient by the classifiers, frequently by what anthropologists term a 'formal analysis.' The use of 'category' connotes a request for definitions from informants and a sorting of those definitions along dimensions specified by the researcher. 'Typification' refers to classification in which the relevant characteristics are central to the solution of practical tasks or problems at hand and are constituted and grounded in everyday activity. The use of 'typification' connotes an attempt to place informants' classifications in their everyday context, for typifications are embedded in and take their meaning from the settings in which they are used, and the occasions that prompt their use.

Embedded in practical tasks, the newsworkers' typifications draw on the synchronization of their work with the likely schedule of potential news occurrences. As summarized in Table 23.1, the newsworkers' distinctions between hard and soft news reflect questions of scheduling. Distinctions between spot and developing news pertain to the allocation of resources across time, and vary in their application according to the technology being used. And the typification 'continuing news' is embedded in predicting the course of events-as-news.

TABLE 23.1 Practical issues in typifying news

Typification	How is event scheduled?	Is dissemination urgent?	Does technology affect perception?	Are future predictions facilitated?
Soft news	Nonscheduled	No	No	Yes
Hard news	Unscheduled and prescheduled	Yes	Sometimes	Sometimes
Spot news	Unscheduled	Yes	No	No
Developing news	Unscheduled	Yes	Yes	No
Continuing news	Prescheduled	Yes	No	Yes

Hard News: The Flow of Newswork and Scheduling

Because news is a depletable consumer product, newsworkers claim that 'quickening urgency' is the 'essence of news' (Hughes, 1940: 58; Roshco, 1975). If newsworkers do not act quickly, the hard-news story will be obsolete before it can be distributed in today's newscast or tomorrow's paper. To quote Robert Park (Park and Burgess, 1967), old news is 'mere information.'

In contrast, soft-news stories need not be 'timely.' The Sunday newspaper is padded with feature stories about occurrences earlier in the week. Concerned with 'timeliness,' newsworkers make fine distinctions. They explain that some kinds of content (hard-news stories) become obsolete more quickly than others (soft-news items). This distinction is based upon the distribution of nonscheduled, prescheduled, and unscheduled events as hard and soft news.

A *non*scheduled event-as-news is an occurrence whose date of dissemination as news is determined by the newsworkers. A *pre*scheduled event-as-news is an occurrence announced for a future date by its convenors; news of it is to be disseminated the day it occurs or the day after. An *un*scheduled event-as-news is one that occurs unexpectedly; news of it is to be disseminated that day or the day after. The type of scheduling characteristic of an event-as-news affects the organization of work.

Most hard-news stories concern prescheduled events (a debate on a legislative bill) or unscheduled events (a fire). Newsworkers do not decide when stories about prescheduled events and unscheduled events-as-news are to be disseminated. Nor do they decide when to gather 'facts' and to disseminate accounts and explanations of nonscheduled hard-news stories. Nonscheduled hard-news stories often involve investigative reporting. The publication of the *Pentagon Papers* by the *New York Times* is an example of a nonscheduled hard-news story. The *Times* held the papers for several months before it published extracts, digests, and analyses of them. Processing nonscheduled stories, the news organization copes with the timing and flow of work.

Members of the news enterprise almost always control the timing and flow of work required to process soft-news stories. Few soft-news stories concern unscheduled events, as indicated by the previous list of feature stories. Another example is the 'Man in the News' series run by the *New York Times*. Like the obituaries of famous men and women, the 'facts' can be, and often are, gathered, written up, and edited in anticipation of future dissemination. Prescheduled soft news also includes such annual 'February stories' as items appropriate for Washington's and Lincoln's birth-days and for Valentine's Day. A reporter may be assigned to these stories days in advance, and the specific information to be included in the story may be gathered, written, and edited days before its eventual dissemination.

Of course, there are exceptions to these rules. But news organizations handle those exceptions in a manner that conserves personnel and retains control of the flow of newswork. For instance, 'facts' to be used in a feature story about the atmosphere at an important trial cannot be gathered in advance. Nor can feature information about an unscheduled event, such as a fire, be gathered in advance. However, the impact of these events-as-feature stories upon the allocation of personnel is minimal. In the first case, a reporter may be assigned to write the 'feature angle' of the trial several days in advance, his name struck from the roster of reporters available to cover the fast-breaking news of the day. In the second case, the same person generally reports both the hard-news fire and its soft-news angle, so that the news organization can conserve reporters.

Spot News: Allocating Resources and Dealing with Technology

As in the case of the hospital, governing the flow of newswork involves more than scheduling. It also involves the allocation of resources and the control of work through prediction. The distinctions among spot news, developing news, and continuing news are occasioned by these practical tasks.

Spot-news events are unscheduled; they appear suddenly and must be processed quickly. The examples offered by informants indicate that spot news is the *specifically* unforeseen event-as-news. For instance, although the staff may anticipate the probability of a fire, they cannot specifically predict where and when a fire will start. This inability to make a definite prediction concerning some events affects the flow of newswork. If a three-alarm fire starts close to deadline, information must be gathered and edited more quickly than usual. If a major fire starts fifty miles from the city room, transportation problems influence the time needed to gather and process 'facts' and so influence the allocation of resources to cover the fire.

Some events that newsworkers nominate for membership in the typification 'spot news' are of such importance that newsworkers try to create a stable social arrange-ment to anticipate them—even if the probability that the event will occur is minute. The city desk of most major dailies is staffed around the clock in case a spot-news event should occur. For example, the president of the United States is covered twenty-four hours a day in case something should happen to him. Continually creating stable social arrangements such as these requires both extended allocation of resources (assigning a staff member to sit at the city desk all night) and immediate reallocation of resources (pulling a reporter off another story) if and as necessary.

The different news technologies each have their own varying time rhythms. Film can be shot, edited, and aired in an hour; print technology is more cumbersome and time consuming. Accordingly, as might be expected from the finding that technology influences the organization of work, as well as my argument that time rhythms influence typifications, a television station's allocation of resources differs from that of a newspaper. The print technology is labor intensive; electronic technology is not. At the *Seaboard City Daily* at least three of the twenty-person staff of general reporters and rewriters sat in the city room from 10:00 A.M. until midnight doing minor but necessary tasks. The observed television station had few reserve reporters and no reserve cameramen, except from 4:00 to 6:00 P.M. and from 9:30 to 11:00 P.M. At these times, reporters and cameramen, bringing their film to be processed, had generally returned from their assignments. They would wait either to cover a spot-news story or to go off shift. Should a specifically unforeseen event occur at any other time of day, the station had to: pay overtime; pull a reporter and a cameraman from a less important story they were already covering; pull a cameraman from a 'silent film story' he was covering by himself; hire a freelance cameraman; pull a staff announcer from his routine duties, such as reading station identification; or assign a newswriter to act as reporter after gaining permission from the appropriate unions. The alternative(s) chosen depended upon the specific situation—the existing dispersion of both film crews and occurrences in time and space at that moment of that day.

Developing News: Technology and the Perception of Events

Practical problems of dealing with a technology and its rhythms are so important that they even affect the newsworker's perception of a spot-news story, especially whether the typification 'developing news' will be applied to an event-as-story. In the case of developing news, technology provides a lens through which events-as-news are perceived.

Developing news concerns 'emergent situations.' A plane crashes. Although this occurrence is unexpected, there are, nonetheless, limitations on the 'facts' it can possibly contain. Editors would not expect to run a story stating that those reported dead had come to life. Nor would they expect to run a report of an official denial that a crash occurred. The 'facts' of the news story are: A plane crashed at 2:00 P.M. in Ellen Park when an engine caught fire and another went dead, killing eight people, injuring an additional fifteen persons, and damaging two houses. All else is amplification. Since this *specific* plane crash was unexpected, reporters were not present to record 'facts' 'accurately.' 'Facts' must be reconstructed, and as more information becomes known, the 'facts' will be more 'accurate.' Although the actual occurrence remains the same, the account of it changes, or, as the newsworkers put it, 'the story develops.' Ongoing changes of this sort are called 'developing news.'

Most spot-news stories are developing news. Since both present interrelated work demands, newspaper staffs tend to use the terms interchangeably. Television workers use the term 'developing news' in a more restricted sense, identifying some stories as spot news that print journalists term 'developing news.' Again, technology acts as a key in their formulations, each technology being associated with a different rhythm in the centralized services feeding the news net. The process of covering the death of Martin Luther King, an occurrence that raised different practical problems for the two New England media, illustrates this variation.

At the local newspaper, King's injury and subsequent death were labeled 'developing news.' A continual flow of updated copy needed editing and 'demanded' constant revision of the planned format. The assistant managing editor learned of the attempted assassination and plotted a format for the front page. When King's condition was reported as grave by the wire services, the editor drew another format that affected other stories above the fold on page one. When a wire-service bulletin reported King to be dead, all other stories were relegated below the fold. Every story on page one needed a new headline of different-sized type, and lead paragraphs of some stories had to be reset in smaller type. Inside pages were also affected.

The television network, with which NEWS* is affiliated, reported on King's condition as a developing story. Periodically, it interrupted programs to present bulletins. But this was a spot-news story for the local television station's personnel. Obviously, the format of the 11:00 P.M. newscast was modified early in the evening. Because of the network's bulletins, the story about King (whatever it might turn out to be) had to be the program's lead. At the newspaper, the production manager and compositors bemoaned the need to lay out the front page three times, each reset accompanying a major development in the story. All production staff worked overtime. At the television station, readjustments in production plans meant less work, not more. By pre-arrangement, the network preempted the first few minutes of the late-evening newscast to tell the story, just as it had preempted the same five minutes some months earlier to report the death of three astronauts.

Continuing News: Controlling Work through Prediction

Spot news and developing news are constituted in work arrangements intended to cope with the amount of information specifically predictable before an event occurs. This information is slight or nonexistent, because the events are unscheduled. In contrast, continuing news *facilitates* the control of work, for continuing news events are generally prescheduled. Prescheduling is implicit in the newsworkers' definition of continuing news as a 'series of stories on the same subject based upon events occurring over a period of time.' This definition implies the existence of prescheduled change. For instance, the account of the progress of a legislative bill through Congress is an account of a series of events following one another in a continual temporal sequence. An event occurring at any specific point in the sequence bears consequences for anticipated events.

Because they are prescheduled, continuing news stories help newsworkers and news organizations regulate their own activities by freeing staff to deal with the exigencies of the specifically unforeseen. Take that legislative bill. It is to be channeled through the House, the Senate, and the executive office. To cover this series of events-as-news, the reporters must be familiar with the legislative process. Such familiarity may even be viewed as part of a 'professional stock of knowledge at hand' (see Schutz, 1964: 29 ff.). The reporter knows the sentiments of pertinent committee members, as well as the

---

* NEWS is a pseudonym for the television station that was studied to provide data for this research.

distribution of power within both the various House and Senate committees and the House and the Senate themselves. In addition, the reporter also knows the progress being made by other legislative bills. With this cumulative stock of knowledge at hand, the reporter may not only predict the bill's eventual disposition, including the specific route through the legislative process (this bill will be bogged down in the House Ways and Means Committee), but may also weigh the need to cover this bill on any one day against the need to cover another bill about which there is comparable information. That 'expert' or 'professional' stock of knowledge at hand permits this reporter, other reporters and editors, and the news organization to control work activities.

The continuing news story is a boon to the reporter's ability to control his or her own work, to anticipate specifically, and so to dissipate future problems by projecting events into a routine. Indeed, newsworkers seek out continuing stories because they are predictably and readily covered. The news organization's ability to process continuing stories routinely by predicting future outcomes enables the organization to cope with unexpected events. At the very least, it enables a city editor to state, 'Joe Smith will not be available to cover spot-news stories a week from Tuesday because he will be covering the Bergman trial.'

REFERENCES

Hughes, H.M. (1940) *News and the Human Interest Story*. Chicago, IL: University of Chicago Press.

March, J. and Simon, H. (1958) *Organizations*. New York: Wiley.

Mott, F.L. (1952) *The News in America*. Cambridge, MA: Harvard University Press.

Park, R. and Burgess, E. (1967) *The City*. Chicago, IL: University of Chicago Press.

Roshco, B. (1975) *Newsmaking*. Chicago, IL: University of Chicago Press.

Schutz, A. (1964) *Collected Papers*, Vol. II: *Studies in Social Theory*. The Hague: Nijhoff.

Schutz, A. (1964) *The Phenomenology of the Social World*. Evanston, IL: Northwestern University Press.

Sudnow, D. (1967) *Passing On: The Social Organization of Death and Dying*. Englewood Cliffs, NJ: Prentice-Hall.

24

does serving the market conflict with serving the public?

JOHN H. McMANUS

A MARKET THEORY OF NEWS PRODUCTION

To the extent that the business goal of maximizing profits dominates, the analysis suggests that rational news departments should compete with each other to offer *the least expensive mix of content that protects the interests of sponsors and investors while garnering the largest audience advertisers will pay to reach*. What becomes news then depends upon a type of cost-benefit analysis at each of the three stages of production.

This is not to suggest that workers in market-driven news departments spend much of their day computing cost-benefit ratios and factoring them into algorithms that determine what becomes news. Even were news production more precise and predictable, expending such time and mental effort would be inefficient. Instead, market logic is the mold for *routines* of discovering newsworthy events, selecting some of them for coverage, and pulling information together into a report. These routines constitute the daily expression of an organizational culture—an accepted way of producing news in a particular media firm.

In any industry, routines are rational means to efficiency. In market-driven newsrooms, routines may also serve to hide the pervasiveness of the economic logic that forms them. Media firms may boast to current and prospective stockholders about how tightly organized they are for profit. But to do so to employees might raise alarm about whose interests the corporation serves.[1] In fact, disguising the economic self-interest of media firms serves management.[2] Newsworkers may be more willing to make sacrifices in salary, work hours, and personal danger (e.g., covering a riot) if they see themselves as serving the public rather than profit. Thus, although talk of making money is likely to be rare in market-driven newsrooms, the logic that drives production routines, nevertheless, is economic.[3]

If news is treated as a commodity like any other, a purely market model of news production should prevail. Such a model would be based upon anticipation within the newsroom of four attributes of any event or issue. It might look something like Table 24.1. A purely journalistic theory, Table 24.2, is simpler.

Reporters and editors estimate each predictor of coverage in the two models using simple heuristics—rules of thumb—or by reference to the organizational culture. But first let's compare the two models conceptually.

Both models share a concern for audience size. Both journalists and advertisers have legitimate reasons for wanting to reach a wide audience. But, as we saw in the previous section, the audience that each seeks may have parts that do not overlap: First among those who need to know about a particular event or issue, but are poor potential customers; and second among those who have little interest in the news, but are good potential customers.

Notice two obvious differences in the models: (1) The market approach requires bias in stories affecting the interests of the media firms' advertisers, parent corporation, and investors. In contrast, journalism requires the news be told with as little bias as humans can manage. (2) The journalistic theory contains no element of cost or payment, while the economic theory has the word 'cost' or 'pay' in three terms and cost is implied in the word 'harm' in the fourth. The journalistic model is unconcerned about what it costs to discover

---

First published in *Market-Driven Journalism: let the citizen beware*, J. H. McManus, Sage Publications (1994), pp. 85–91.

TABLE 24.1   A market theory of news production

The probability of an event/issue becoming news is:	Inversely proportional to the harm the information might cause investors or sponsors, and ...	Inversely proportional to the cost of uncovering it, and ...	Inversely proportional to the cost of reporting it, and ...	Directly proportional to the expected breadth of appeal of the story to audiences advertisers will pay to reach.

Note: For further development of these ideas, see Note 4.

TABLE 24.2   A journalistic theory of news production

The probability of an event/issue becoming news is:	Proportional to the expected consequence of the story, and ...	Proportional to the size of the audience for whom it is important.

what's happening in a community. It's equally silent about how much time or other resources might be needed to cover an issue or event. Such a standard presumes unlimited resources and is thus an ideal. This is why actual commercial news production requires some compromise of journalism ideals with business reality. Journalism that costs more to produce than it generates in revenues cannot be sustained in the marketplace.

WHERE MARKET THEORY AND JOURNALISM THEORY CONVERGE

Despite having more differences than similarities, the two theories are not always in conflict. Some events and issues that would be deemed newsworthy under journalistic norms would remain so under a market theory. A number of consequential occurrences don't threaten the interests of advertisers and investors, are inexpensive to learn of, are inexpensive to report, and promise wide appeal to a demographically 'correct' audience. Examples include tragedies such as train or airliner crashes, a fatal fire in a tenement building, and a mud-slinging debate among political candidates.

There may also be trade-offs among the terms of the business theory. A news department might spend heavily to learn of and report a story that generates unusual consumer interest. For example, the money spent investigating a sex scandal involving an important public official might justify its cost by attracting audience away from competitors. Less arousing or more complex official malfeasance, or the misbehavior of a major advertiser, however, would likely be left for some other social institution to investigate.

Ironically, market-driven news departments are at their best when times are at their worst. Events that profoundly influence the entire community served by a media firm—such as hurricanes, earthquakes, floods, riots, or the outbreak of war between the United States and another nation—raise consumers' personal stake in the news. In such cases, consumers who might routinely use news for diversion or entertainment find themselves in need of significant information—perhaps about how to cope. Crises lend greater commercial viability to informative reporting. Such market pressure for information exists regardless of whether advertisers choose to place their messages amid such coverage.[4]

Finally, note that news departments provide a *mix* of content. Newspapers, with their greater volume and random access capability, and to a lesser extent local TV newsrooms, may find it profitable to produce some normative journalism for those consumers who are more able to discern such quality and are willing to pursue it. Because such consumers are presumably those with more education and higher incomes, they are likely to attract advertiser interest. In general, the larger the metropolitan area, the larger this group of discriminating consumers is, and the more it makes sense for market-driven news departments to practice occasional normative journalism.

WHERE MARKET THEORY AND JOURNALISM THEORY CONFLICT

Principally because so few of the conditions for cooperative exchange are met in the transaction between media firms and the public, journalism and market norms conflict more than converge. If the goal of journalism is *public enlightenment*, there is potential for conflict with the business goal of maximizing benefit for investors at each stage of news production.

The First Stage of News Production

At the first stage of news production, uncovering potentially newsworthy issues and events: The most significant news is often the most expensive to discover because powerful interests want it hidden. Independent, particularly investigative, surveillance of a community is expensive. It is less costly to rely on other news providers such as wire services and on press agents to learn of community events and issues than to hire adequate staff to infiltrate the community.[5] Such passive discovery, however, creates potential for manipulation of the public agenda by sources powerful enough to hire press agents and 'manufacture' events.[6] Later we shall determine whether business or journalism norms are being followed at the stations in the study by categorizing each story aired by the investment required of the station to learn of it.

The Second Stage of News Production

At the second stage of news production, market and journalism norms may collide when important stories are dull—such as economic trends or political apportionment debates. The demands of journalism and those of the market also collide when stories about issues or events question accepted myths or prejudices, popular national policies (such as US intervention in the Persian Gulf), or popular leaders.[7]

News from a specific locality within a market causes an additional problem for regional media such as local television and metropolitan newspapers. The consequence of routine events and issues is likely to be restricted to a fraction of the circulation or broadcast signal area of a media firm. For example, news that a particular municipality is adding a sales tax, or a school district is exceeding recommended class sizes to meet a budget crisis, or a county is failing to maintain roads, may bore non-affected consumers. Although newspapers can zone editions to reduce this problem and readers can skip stories that don't pique their interest, television is likely to lose customers if it dwells too long on what's important in just a part of the market. From a market perspective, broadcasters— and to a lesser extent, newspapers[8]—are better off with more generalizable stories such as consumer-oriented features and human interest pieces that arouse emotional responses, even if the result is news that fails to help consumers make sense of current events.

Measurement here is more complex. But to preview: Each story can be rated for its level of informational importance and for its emotional appeal. Those two dimensions can be crossed because stories may be both informative and arousing. The result is a two-dimensional figure with four quadrants. Stories may be high in both emotional appeal and in informational consequence—interesting and important stories. Stories may also be just the opposite—neither important nor emotionally arousing. The last two quadrants include important but dull stories and, conversely, emotionally arousing but inconsequential stories. [This helps to show] whether news departments are more oriented toward public interest, private interest, or some compromise. The selection stage of news production is also an appropriate place to investigate the conflict between journalism's requirement that the public be fully informed and the protection market logic demands for the media firm's investors and sponsors.

The Final Stage of News Production

At the final stage of news production—reporting the story—journalism norms require selection of the most significant quotes from the most relevant sources. Journalism also requires that all sides to an issue be provided in a disinterested fashion, that dubious fact claims be checked, that conclusions not based on common knowledge be supported with evidence, and that enough context be provided for wide comprehension. Satisfying these requirements is expensive because it consumes reporters' time. If a station seeks to maximize profit, less care may be taken with information. And just as the interesting topic may replace the merely important, the interesting source and quote may replace the informative source and quote. Profit demands may also lead to truncated news reports, particularly on television. Because viewers can't pick among stories, a station might restrict the length of narratives so that few become bored enough to 'zap' the station by changing channels.

Case studies are the units of analysis here. Shadowing a reporter permits discovery of priorities in selecting story elements as well as adherence to journalistic norms of objectivity and care with information.

IS COMPROMISE VIABLE?

Both the market and journalism models are defined as extremes. If investors are willing to accept lower levels of profit—perhaps in exchange for an investment with less risk in the long term—compromises are possible. As we shall see, the profit levels of most print and broadcast media firms are high enough to accommodate greater journalistic integrity. It's also important to note that technological differences, such as those mentioned in the preceding section, make such compromises more costly for television than for newspapers.

CONCLUSION

In an ideal news market, where consumers act rationally in their self-interest, enjoy a variety of news outlets, can discern the quality of reportage, and include within their self-interest society's well-being, the same strategy that yields maximum return to investors would maximize public enlightenment. But given the actual news market, and the peculiar nature of news as a commodity, the logic of maximizing return often conflicts with the logic of maximizing public understanding.

NOTES

1   The public also may be alarmed by how media firms speak to investors. News is likely to sell better if described as a good produced, not to yield the highest return, but solely in the public interest; something that ought to be consumed if not because one wants to, then because one needs to out of obligation to the community.

2   Bagdikian, B., *The Media Monopoly* (Random House, 1990); Underwood, D., *When MBAs Rule the TV Newsrooms* (New York: Columbia University Press, 1993).

3   Matthew Ehrlich, 'The daily race to see who wins: competition, control and newswork', a paper at the Annual Convention of the Association for Education in Journalism, Kansas City, MI, 1983.

4   McManus, J.H., *Economic and Technological Influences on the Quality of Local Television News* (Unpublished doctoral dissertation, University of Stanford, 1988).

5   McManus, J.H. 'How television learns what is news', *Journalism Quarterly* (1990), 67 (4): 672–84.

6   Boorstin, D. *The Image: a guide to Pseudo-events in America* (New York: Atheneum, 1961).

7   See, for example, Cohen, S.E. 'Of time and integrity', *Columbia Journalism Review* (1989), 28 (3): 27–34; Massing, M. 'Is the most popular evening newscast the best?', *Columbia Journalism Review* (1991), 29 (6): 30–5.

8   This is because it's cheaper to produce one story for the entire press run than multiple stories, one for each zone.

25

the Hollywood TV producer

MURIEL G. CANTOR

The ways in which the producers resolve the conflict of orientation to the various groups in their environment has been the major topic discussed throughout this study. The conflicts that can emerge when one group perceives that important 'others' in the environment have norms and beliefs about mutual endeavors differing from themselves were also of concern, as well as the rewards and support the reference groups provide. The reference groups examined were those associated with the craft aspects of the occupation (writers, directors, and actors, in particular); those groups associated with the bureaucratic structure of the networks (the network censorship office and the liaison men who represent the network programming division); and, lastly, the audience who views the programs on the television screens.

In analyzing the interviews, three types of producers stand out: the film makers, the writers-producers, and the old-line producers. Each of these types relates differently to the reference groups identified in this study. In this conclusion each type is analyzed in terms of the questions asked in the study in order to understand fully the available data and to summarize the findings. However, it should be made clear again that because television series are made by 'committee,' it is possible (in fact probable) that all three types can be found on the production team and can be represented in the final product. However, the film makers are more apt to be used by the production company on the dramatic shows, westerns, and detective series. The writers-producers are usually connected with the mystery and detective stories, the more sophisticated comedies and westerns. The old-line producers are likely to be associated with simpler situation-comedy shows featuring a well-known star. Most (not all) of the producers of animated Saturday-morning shows closely resemble the old-line producers in orientation.

FILM MAKERS

While it is not possible to know if they are manipulated by the system, it is possible to know how they react to the bureaucratic structure of which they are a part. Since they think that their main role at this time is to coordinate the various parts of the film-making process, they are satisfied with their working arrangements for the most part. Of all types of producers, they have the least control over the material presented, because they had nothing to do with the original series idea and did not often rewrite material or stories that they received from the writers. Most of them state that they are using the system to enable them to become more independent and to use their creative talents someday in a more meaningful way. Their main ambition is to become a film maker of some importance. A few expressed some concern about whether they would be considered 'sellouts' by their former classmates and professors, who often express critical views about the medium generally. However, they rationalize both their high salaries and lack of creative independence in two ways: (1) They are learning to make films under more practical conditions than the conditions under which films are made in school. Several pointed to certain well-known directors (William Wyler, in particular) as examples of good directors who started in the B-movies. (2) Their high salaries enable them to accumulate part of the working capital necessary to make an independent film someday.

First published in *The Hollywood TV Producer. His work and life*, M.G. Cantor, Basic Books (1971), pp. 189–209.

They expressed few conflicts concerning the network and the production company. Because they see their function at this time as a coordinator rather than as a creator, they are less likely to view the networks as a constraining influence than the other two groups. They are also less likely to take a stand on the story content than either of the other two groups, but it did seem that they are more likely to want to try new techniques. Occasionally, this does stymie them, but it is a minor area of conflict, since it is more important for them to learn all aspects of production and especially direction and editing so they can go on to make the theater films in a more artistic way. They are holding their talent in abeyance until the time is right for them to leave series television and become movie makers. Often they look forward to directing a few of the series episodes as a further learning experience. Learning their craft is the key distinguishing ambition of this group. Since they are craft-oriented and young, they see few inconsistencies in pleasing the network officials and the production company while subordinating their own artistic values about film making.

[...]

The film makers' view of the audience was consistent with their role and with their other views. For instance, they consider themselves to have artistic tastes that are superior to those of the television audience, whom they usually regard as unsophisticated, rural, and lower-class. But since they do not think that their function is to be a taste leader or to proselytize for political or social change, they see no inconsistencies in 'giving the public what it wants to see.' Rather, they see the function of television to be entertainment, and all seem to think that television does this adequately and well for the audience to whom they are directing the content. Their own entertainment patterns and media usage are quite different from what they imagine to be those of the 'ordinary' viewer, who, as one said, 'Comes home from the factory or shop, has dinner and a beer and turns on the tube to be "tuned-out" from the problems at work.'

Although several of the film makers hoped someday to make films with a social message, these films would be for a different audience, one with tastes closer to their own. Most said that they are politically liberal and voted usually for Democratic party candidates, but here also their political views cause few if any conflicts because they view the networks as apolitical and personally do not want to use the medium as a means of political expression. Several thought that the movie personalities, both liberal and conservative, who use their popularity with the public for political action are not serving the best interests of the public.

It is not being suggested that the film makers feel no constraints or conflicts in their positions. Several verbalized that the medium does not provide freedom and that in order to produce, it is necessary to subordinate their own values, but the rewards (both actual and anticipated) of producing under the conditions described are more important than the constraints.

[...]

In any case the film makers believe that by subordinating artistic values (seen as either technological and visual skills or as more meaningful stories) at this stage of their careers, they will someday be able to do as they please and make the kind of films that will express their talent more meaningfully. This particular characteristic does seem to determine how they choose writers and how they select stories. Not only are they less apt to rewrite than other producers, but they are more apt to follow directives both from the censorship office and the production company with a minimum of struggle or conflicts. When they select writers, for instance, they seem to look for those with the greatest record of successes and are less often looking for new writers with new ideas.

Most important, although they perceive the goals of the bureaucracies involved as basically different from their ultimate or desired goals, the film makers go along with the system as it is because the rewards at present outweigh the costs.

WRITERS-PRODUCERS

This group has the most conflicts with the networks and also with their own production company because they are most committed to the ideals of their craft—principally, that the writer should have control of what he writes. The writers-producers tend to see themselves as the chief writers of series rather than as film makers. Because of this they have the most difficulties not only with the bureaucratic structure but also with their fellow writers. However, they also know more writers well and have a cadre of writers on hand who can be depended on to do blocks of episodes for the series. They are also the most interested in new ideas and in the political aspects of story writing. Yet they are also the most likely to rewrite or to change scripts that they think are not consistent with the series concept.

Most of their difficulties with the networks are covert rather than overt, because they know that unless they please the network officials, their chances to remain in production are uncertain. They think the story is the most important element in the making of a film, and they are more likely to feel that television should be used to express political views and to change the social scene. They related numerous incidents about how they were able to get a social message into a particular story. There is much reference to compromise and ideals but, especially, compromise. Many thought a primary qualification for producing was knowing how to fight the network. A good producer is one who not only fights for what he wants but also is able to give in to the authority of the networks when necessary. There is a continuous battle, one that they thought was more often lost than won. When the battle is lost, a few give up producing for a time to return when they are offered an opportunity to produce a series 'right' for them, or they give up with the hope that someday they would be able to produce a show or series that fits their value system more perfectly.

[···]

Most of the producers in this group believe either that the viewing audience is more intelligent than the networks believe it is, or that the measuring devices now used are inaccurately portraying the audience as less sophisticated and more rural than it actually is. Several show a rather well-informed knowledge about the operation of the Nielsen surveys and are also aware of some of the informed criticisms about its operation—for instance, the possible effects on the Nielsen families of the knowledge that such devices were attached to their sets.

While many of the writers-producers express feelings of impotency and constraint, few seem willing to leave the medium for other livelihoods, although this was always considered a possibility for them. The financial rewards, for one thing, keep them working in the medium, but since most of them can equal or surpass their incomes with freelance writing, the income is not the important thing that keeps them producing. Most of the writers take a genuine pleasure in their work, enjoying the excitement and the daily decisions and problems that have to be solved. Most preferred the immediacy of television production to the slow pace of moviemaking for the feature films, for instance.

However, the writer-producer does think that often he is being manipulated by the system: since they are oriented more to the content of the script and since they are well-trained and experienced in their craft, they often perceive the network's goals as in opposition to their own. The network, whom they see as willing to show anything as long as it has a high Nielsen rating, is not trying to meet its civic responsibility to show more educational series or series with a message.

The above descriptions of the writer-producer and the film maker are oversimplifications, as is always the case with heuristic types. Men, operating in a complex social setting, often have a number of motives, desires, and abilities that must be considered and that contribute to their performance and actions. However, both types do exist in the industry as does the old-line producer to be described next. The main difference between the writers-producers and film makers, on the one hand, and the old-line producers on the other, is that the former are aware of criticisms of the mass media and television and are self-critical, rationalizing their behavior to fit their self-image. The old-line producers are not.

OLD-LINE PRODUCERS

This group also has problems with the network. Since most of the men in this group have been responsible for so many successful series, they often feel that they are more aware of what will appeal to the audience than the network officials. When a series is new, the network liaison men are more likely to interfere in story selection and try to give expert advice to the producer; if a series is a success, there is less interference. When the old-line producers are involved with new series, there are battles with the networks. The conflicts are not so much value conflicts over political and social ideals, but they are often struggles over casting decisions or story ideas; the character of the hero or the direction of the series concept is often at issue. Like all the others interviewed, this producer type can only battle with the networks so far; essentially, they are also dependent on them for ultimate approval.

However, their former successes and the apolitical nature of the conflicts often makes it possible for them to win these battles. The very nature of the conflicts, of course, would make them overt in nature. Based on impressions obtained in the interviews, the conflicts are between equals rather than between those in superordinate and subordinate positions.

[...]

The old-line producer also sees the audience as unsophisticated and especially rural or semirural (small town). Most shows produced by this type are aimed directly at that audience. Producers in this group are quick to point out that while the bulk of the audience may be rural, their shows also appeal to the educated, urban audience as well. They seem to think the simple situation comedies or family-type shows have universal appeal. Mainly, however, they pitch their shows to the 'mass' audience, whom they perceive as unsophisticated and rural.

The old-line producers do not think they are subordinating their own values and beliefs by producing television because they share the networks' goals. Their political orientation varies from conservative to liberal, but this has little relevance for their roles since they separate personal politics from their job performance.

CONFLICT RECONCILIATION

The three types of producers reconcile their work values and their desire (or lack of desire) for more autonomy with the realities of the work situation. Each type of producer views the controls, constraints, and rewards differently. Of the three types, the film maker might be considered by some to be the most professionalized; his training was in film making and related fields and his work career is directed toward the goal of feature films. However, the means they are using to obtain their goals would seem to place them closer to those with a 'local' orientation rather than a 'cosmopolitan' one. Alvin Gouldner, for instance, has described academicians as locals if they are high on loyalty to the employing organization, low on commitment to specialized role skills, and likely to use an inner-reference-group orientation. On the other hand, cosmopolitans are those low on loyalty to the employing organization, high on commitment to specialized role skills, and likely to use an outer-reference-group orientation.[1]

According to these definitions, the actions of the film makers are very much in line with the goals of the organization. As pointed out, the film makers rarely have conflicts with the organization. However, the models of possible orientations to the work structure suggested by Gouldner and others seem oversimplified when applied to producers in general. Because of their mobility from studio to studio and network to network, all producers could be considered cosmopolitan; they all may be more likely to be more concerned with their discipline than with their organization.

However, it is important to emphasize that the disciplines of the various types of producers are different.

All three types of producers perform the same or similar tasks, that is, select stories for the series; help select supporting actors; have the final say about sets, directors, and related decisions; and supervise the cutting, dubbing, and the other postproduction processes. Yet all three types of producers see their occupational role differently, and consequently each reacts differently to bureaucratic controls and bureaucratic standards.

Film makers, for instance, with their training in Southern California schools and their primary work experience in television, may see film making (especially film making for television) as part of a bureaucratic enterprise, requiring a structure and organization. In any case film makers are more compatible with the system than are the writers-producers. They do not see the system as manipulating them, but view it as providing an opportunity to learn more of their 'trade' and to accumulate the funds necessary for further advancement in their chosen field.

The writers-producers are closer to the ideal of the lone creator, more similar to the artist, composer, novelist, and playwright than the other two types. Since they make up the largest group in the sample, they also may be the most important theoretically. Under Alvin Gouldner's definition of a 'cosmopolitan,' they can be definitely considered cosmopolitan rather than local. They seem to have little loyalty or sense of obligation to the network or even to the production company for which they work, but are more oriented to their discipline (script writing). Television producing is a substitute for script writing primarily because it enables them to gain control of their material.

T.H. Marshall and Lee Taylor have compared the professional to the lone artist in Western society.[2] Marshall says that the artist, like the professional, cannot work in a detached, impersonal atmosphere, 'with his eye on the clock and his mind on his cheque,' but 'must give something that is deeply rooted in his nature, something that cannot be commanded or coerced... .'[3] Those who see themselves as lone writers with something important to say must be able to reconcile the values that go with such a self-concept with the controls and commands of the organization for which they work. Their dilemma is that they have less freedom when they freelance than when they work for an organization. If they were still freelance writers, their scripts would be subject to more change and revision than is the case when they produce their own show.

Joan Moore describes the full-time television writer as having 'little or no control over any aspect of their writing except the invention of dialogue and incident. Their work is often rewritten as a matter of routine. It may be changed without their knowledge or consent by a story editor, producer, director or actor.'[4] The evidence in this study bears out Moore's contention. Producers have to worry about changes by the network, but the freelance writers have to be concerned about continuing script changes. Producers have more control, yet conflict does arise because the organizational structure makes it impossible for the writer-producer to follow his discipline without controls and constraints.

The way the writers-producers operate points out the basic dilemma in their position. They see themselves as writers with a social message to be communicated, and the medium available to them to present their message is film television. If they leave producing, which is an alternative open to them, it is unlikely that any other medium in which they might work would provide as many facilities or have the audience that television does. (In addition, they might have to give up their present style of life.) Therefore, they often feel themselves trapped. They have to give in to the bureaucratic controls, but to satisfy themselves while performing their role, they try to select stories that are 'socially significant.' They see the inconsistency in their position and verbalize the dilemma. If they satisfy themselves, they are likely to incur the displeasure of the network.

The difference in orientation between the writer-producer and the networks is basically one of standards; the networks' standards are quite different than the ideal standards of work held by the writer-producer. An example of how the networks and one writer-producer differ on what should be produced is the following:

> The network said they will 'never' do a college series. No matter how it was done they said that it has to be controversial. If it deals realistically, as I conceived the series, with the happenings on the campuses, you will be attacked for taking sides no matter which side you take or even if you try to be objective and take none. And if you take the other course and duck reality and present a fantasy college world which doesn't exist today—everybody will jump on you for obvious phoniness. The network says we can't win. And the viewing public loses... .

The quotation indicates one difference in standards. The networks operate under the assumption that all segments of the public (including the government) must not be aroused, while the writer-producer sees one of his responsibilities as informing the viewing audiences about the social realities of the world in which they live. Since it is impossible to do this overtly, such messages are hidden within other contexts so that the message is not detected by the networks. However, because of this subterfuge, timely messages are often superficial. The writer-producer, therefore, directs the series or episode primarily to the network and uses internalized standards about content, while the audience plays a secondary role.

The old-line producers react to the networks differently from the other two types of producers. They see themselves as businessmen producing entertainment as a product, and this orientation affects their relationship with the network in a special way. Since the old-line producers think they know what will sell, they often quarrel with the networks and even their own production company, but these quarrels are not value conflicts. Their fundamental aspirations are the same as the network executives and the studio heads—to be successful. They therefore have no conflicts with the present system of deciding what will stay on the air or of selecting the kind of stories. They have no desire to produce television films with a social message. The old-line producer directs the series he produces to an audience he sees primarily as simplistic, unsophisticated, and rural in outlook. For them the networks play the secondary role, although the economic realities of the situation make it impossible to ignore the network completely.

NOTES

1   Alvin Gouldner, 'Cosmopolitans and locals: towards an analysis of latent social roles – I', *Administrative Science Quarterly*, 2 (1957), p. 290.
2   T.H. Marshall, *Class, Citizenship and Social Development* (New York: Doubleday, 1964), pp. 163–4; Lee Taylor, *Occupational Sociology* (New York: Oxford University Press, 1968), pp. 425–6.
3   Marshall, p. 163.
4   Joan Moore, 'The Hollywood Writer', unpublished manuscript draft, p. 92.

VIII

MEDIA CONTENT

The theoretical positioning of the 'message' in the enduring, even if misleadingly simple, model of the 'process of mass communication' has also been subject to much change and diversification. In the beginning, so to speak, media 'content' was mainly viewed as the 'stimulus' (albeit complex and of many different kinds) that was delivered by mass distribution technology to a mass audience and achieved some kind of 'mass effect' – extensive and similar forms of behaviour, acquisition of the same limited information or adoption of the same opinions and attitudes. The first reason for the systematic study of content was to be able to describe mass media mainly in order to predict and measure their effects. This called for reliable and systematic means of classification and accounting, preferably in quantifiable form. In turn this presumed that 'meaning' could be readily and objectively attributed to the 'texts' of media by analysts, especially since the texts of mass media were supposedly simple enough for all to read and understand.

The subsequent development of content theory largely invalidated these assumptions. Linguistic theory, especially in the form of semiology (or the 'science of signs'), demonstrated that even the most apparently simple verbal or pictorial 'text' has a complex structure and a capacity for embodying alternative meanings, whether or not intended by the 'author', and leading to different interpretations of meanings. One of the early promises of semiology was that it would allow an analyst fully informed of the capacity of the 'sign system' in use in a given context to uncover hidden and potential meanings (see Barthes, Chapter 26). The approach was applied, for instance by Williamson (Chapter 27), to the analysis of the seemingly simple message of the advertisement. Semiology has also been used to some clarifying effect in film theory, where an implicit, albeit purely conventional, 'language' of imagery is routinely deployed (Monaco, 1981). While the results have been quite rewarding in uncovering complexities of meaning, semiological theory has not solved the problem of the 'objective decoding' of media texts. Not least among the many obstacles lying in the way is the multiplicity of sign systems that are used by most media, including words, sounds and visual images in many forms and combinations. Moreover, the same sign systems can convey different meanings in different contexts, cultures and media genres. Only in the case of verbal languages is there some kind of reliable guide to grammar and underlying structure. Semiological analysis is always labour-intensive and interpretative.

Despite the difficulties, there have been numerous attempts at forms of textual and 'discourse' analysis that have gone some way towards clarifying the probable 'meanings', evaluative as well as informational, given and taken, in some media texts and genres. Most attention and success probably relates to the genre of mass media news (see, for instance, van Dijk, 1983). In another tradition, based on the assumption that terms in common use also have shared and knowable evaluative meanings in a given language and social culture, the evaluative direction of news texts has been objectively measured (see van Cuilenburg et al., 1986).

The fact of multiple meanings and difficulty of objective 'decoding' has been taken by some theorists not only as a given but also as a positive step towards understanding how media work. Hall, in this selection (Chapter 28) and elsewhere, has argued that media 'messages' are encoded according to the many exigencies of the media industry, but 'decoded' according to the experience, interests and social or cultural perspectives of differently situated audience communities. The latter are open to investigation, and we can in principle make sense of media 'reception' in an intelligent albeit interpretative and qualitative manner. The meaning of content is the meaning it is given by its 'receivers' under the specific conditions of reception. This leads on to 'reception theory' (see below). Literary and film theory have both been usefully applied in the study of mass communication, especially perhaps in the analysis of different media genres. An example is provided here by Radway's (Chapter 29) description of the key characteristics of the genre of 'romantic pulp fiction'. It gains particular value by having been integrated into a study of the perceptions of women readers of the genre.

REFERENCES

Monaco, J. (1981) *How to Read a Film*. New York: Oxford University Press.
van Cuilenburg, J.J., de Ridder, J. and Kleinneijenhuis, J. (1986) 'A theory of evaluative discourse', *European Journal of Communication*, 1 (1): 65–96.
van Dijk, T. (1983) 'Discourse analysis: its development and application to the structure of news', *Journal of Communication*, 33 (3): 20–43.

26

rhetoric of the image

ROLAND BARTHES

Accotding to an ancient etymology, the word *image* should be linked to the root *imitari*. Thus we find ourselves immediately at the heart of the most important problem facing the semiology of images: can analogical representation (the 'copy') produce true systems of signs and not merely simple agglutinations of symbols? Is it possible to conceive of an analogical 'code' (as opposed to a digital one)? We know that linguists refuse the status of language to all communication by analogy – from the 'language' of bees to the 'language' of gesture – the moment such communications are not doubly articulated, are not founded on a combinatory system of digital units as phonemes are. Nor are linguists the only ones to be suspicious as to the linguistic nature of the image; general opinion too has a vague conception of the image as an area of resistance to meaning – this in the name of a certain mythical idea of Life: the image is re-presentation, which is to say ultimately resurrection, and, as we know, the intelligible is reputed antipathetic to lived experience. Thus from both sides the image is felt to be weak in respect of meaning: there are those who think that the image is an extremely rudimentary system in comparison with language and those who think that signification cannot exhaust the image's ineffable richness. Now even – and above all if – the image is in a certain manner the *limit* of meaning, it permits the consideration of a veritable onto-logy of the process of signification. How does meaning get into the image? Where does it end? And if it ends, what is there *beyond*? Such are the questions that I wish to raise by submitting the image to a spectral analysis of the messages it may contain. We will start by making it considerably easier for ourselves: we will only study the advertising image. Why? Because in advertising the signification of the image is undoubtedly inten-tional; the signifieds of the advertising message are formed *a priori* by certain attributes of the product and these signifieds have to be transmitted as clearly as possible. If the image contains signs, we can be sure that in advertising these signs are full, formed with a view to the optimum reading: the advertising image is *frank*, or at least emphatic.

THE THREE MESSAGES

Here we have a Panzani advertisement: some packets of pasta, a tin, a sachet, some toma-toes, onions, peppers, a mushroom, all emerging from a half-open string bag, in yellows and greens on a red background [1] Let us try to 'skim off' the different messages it contains.

The image immediately yields a first message whose substance is linguistic; its supports are the caption, which is marginal, and the labels, these being inserted into the natural disposition of the scene, '*en abyme*'. The code from which this message has been taken is none other than that of the French language; the only knowledge required to decipher it is a knowledge of writing and French. In fact, this message can itself be further broken down, for the sign *Panzani* gives not simply the name of the firm but also, by its asso-nance, an additional signified, that of 'Italianicity'. The linguistic message is thus twofold (at least in this particular image): denotational and connotational. Since, however, we have here only a single typical sign,[2] namely that of articulated (written) language, it will be counted as one message.

First published in *Image, Music, Text: essays selected and translated by Stephen Heath*, Roland Barthes, Fontanta (1967), as 'Rhetoric of the Image', pp. 32–45.

Putting aside the linguistic message, we are left with the pure image (even if the labels are part of it, anecdotally). This image straightaway provides a series of discontinuous signs. First (the order is unimportant as these signs are not linear), the idea that what we have in the scene represented is a return from the market. A signified which itself implies two euphoric values: that of the freshness of the products and that of the essentially domestic preparation for which they are destined. Its signifier is the half-open bag which lets the provisions spill out over the table, 'unpacked'. To read this first sign requires only a knowledge which is in some sort implanted as part of the habits of a very widespread culture where 'shopping around for oneself' is opposed to the hasty stocking up (pre-serves, refrigerators) of a more 'mechanical' civilization. A second sign is more or less equally evident; its signifier is the bringing together of the tomato, the pepper and the tricoloured hues (yellow, green, red) of the poster; its signified is Italy or rather *Italianicity*.

This sign stands in a relation of redundancy with the connoted sign of the linguistic message (the Italian assonance of the name *Panzani*) and the knowledge it draws upon is already more particular; it is a specifically 'French' knowledge (an Italian would barely perceive the connotation of the name, no more probably than he would the Italianicity of tomato and pepper), based on a familiarity with certain tourist stereotypes. Continuing to explore the image (which is not to say that it is not entirely clear at the first glance), there is no difficulty in discovering at least two other signs: in the first, the serried collection of different objects transmits the idea of a total culinary service, on the one hand as though Panzani furnished everything necessary for a carefully balanced dish and on the other as though the concentrate in the tin were equivalent to the natural produce surrounding it; in the other sign, the composition of the image, evoking the memory of innumerable alimentary paintings, sends us to an aesthetic signified: the *'nature morte'* or, as it is better expressed in other languages, the 'still life'[3]; the knowledge on which this sign depends is heavily cultural. It might be suggested that, in addition to these four signs, there is a further information pointer, that which tells us that this is an advertisement and which arises both from the place of the image in the magazine and from the emphasis of the labels (not to mention the caption). This last information, however, is co-extensive with the scene; it eludes signification insofar as the advertising nature of the image is essentially functional: to utter something is not necessarily to declare *I am speaking*, except in a deliberately reflexive system such as literature.

Thus there are four signs for this image and we will assume that they form a coherent whole (for they are all discontinuous), require a generally cultural knowledge, and refer back to signifieds each of which is global (for example, *Italianicity*), imbued with euphoric values. After the linguistic message, then, we can see a second, iconic message. Is that the end? If all these signs are removed from the image, we are still left with a certain informational matter; deprived of all knowledge, I continue to 'read' the image, to 'understand' that it assembles in a common space a number of identifiable (nameable) objects, not merely shapes and colours. The signifieds of this third message are constituted by the real objects in the scene, the signifiers by these same objects photographed, for, given that the relation between thing signified and image signifying in analogical representation is not 'arbitrary' (as it is in language), it is no longer necessary to dose the relay with a third term in the guise of the psychic image of the object. What defines the third message is precisely that the relation between signified and signifier is quasi-tautological; no doubt the photograph involves a certain arrangement of the scene (framing, reduction, flattening) but this transition is not a *transformation* (in the way a coding can be); we have here a loss of the equivalence characteristic of true sign systems and a statement of quasi-identity. In other words, the sign of this message is not drawn from an institutional stock, is not coded, and we are brought up against the paradox (to which we will return) of a *message without a code*. This peculiarity can be seen again at the level of the knowledge invested in the reading of the message; in order to 'read' this last (or first) level of the image, all that is needed is the knowledge bound up with our perception. That knowledge is not nil, for we need to know what an image is (children only learn this at about the age of four) and what a tomato, a string-bag, a packet of pasta are, but it is a matter of an almost anthropological knowledge. This message corresponds, as it were, to the letter of the image and we can agree to call it the literal message, as opposed to the previous symbolic message.

If our reading is satisfactory, the photograph analysed offers us three messages: a linguistic message, a coded iconic message, and a non-coded iconic message. The linguistic message can be readily separated from the other two, but since the latter share the same (iconic) substance, to what extent have we the right to separate them? It is certain that the distinction between the two iconic messages is not made spontaneously in ordinary reading: the viewer of the image receives *at one and the same time* the perceptual message and the cultural message, and it will be seen later that this confusion in reading corresponds to the function of the mass image (our concern here). The distinction, however, has an operational validity, analogous to that which allows the distinction in the linguistic sign of a signifier and a signified (even though in reality no one is able to separate the 'word' from its meaning except by recourse to the metalanguage of a definition). If the distinction permits us to describe the structure of the image in a simple and coherent fashion and if this description paves the way for an explanation of the role of the image in society, we will take it to be justified. The task now is thus to reconsider each type of message so as to explore it in its generality, without losing sight of our aim of understanding the overall structure of the image, the final inter-relationship of the three messages. Given that what is in question is not a 'naive' analysis but a structural description,[4] the order of the messages will be modified a little by the inversion of the cultural message and the literal message; of the two iconic messages, the first is in some sort imprinted on the second: the literal message appears as the *support* of the 'symbolic' message. Hence, knowing that a system which takes over the signs of another system in order to make them its signifiers is a system of connotation,[5] we may say immediately that the literal image is *denoted* and the symbolic image *connoted*. Successively, then, we shall look at the linguistic message, the denoted image, and the connoted image.

THE LINGUISTIC MESSAGE

Is the linguistic message constant? Is there always textual matter in, under, or around the image? In order to find images given without words, it is doubtless necessary to go back to partially illiterate societies, to a sort of pictographic state of the image. From the moment of the appearance of the book, the linking of text and image is frequent, though it seems to have been little studied from a structural point of view. What is the signifying structure of 'illustration'? Does the image duplicate certain of the informations given in the text by a phenomenon of redundancy or does the text add a fresh information to the image? The problem could be posed historically as regards the classical period with its passion for books with pictures (it was inconceivable in the eighteenth century that editions of La Fontaine's *Fables* should not be illustrated) and its authors such as Menestrier who concerned themselves with the relations between figure and discourse.[6] Today, at the level of mass communications, it appears that the linguistic message is indeed present in every image: as title, caption, accompanying press article, film dialogue, comic strip balloon. Which shows that it is not very accurate to talk of a civilization of the image – we are still, and more than ever, a civilization of writing,[7] writing and speech continuing to be the full terms of the informational structure. In fact, it is simply the presence of the linguistic message that counts, for neither its position nor its length seem to be pertinent (a long text may only comprise a single global signified, thanks to connotation, and it is this signified which is put in relation with the image). What are the functions of the linguistic message with regard to the (twofold) iconic message? There appear to be two: *anchorage* and *relay*.

As will be seen more clearly in a moment, all images are polysemous; they imply, underlying their signifiers, a 'floating chain' of signifieds, the reader able to choose some and ignore others. Polysemy poses a question of meaning and this question always comes through as a dysfunction, even if this dysfunction is recuperated by society as a tragic (silent, God provides no possibility of choosing between signs) or a poetic (the panic 'shudder of meaning' of the Ancient Greeks) game; in the cinema itself, traumatic images are bound up with an uncertainty (an anxiety) concerning the meaning of objects or attitudes. Hence in every society various techniques are developed intended to *fix* the floating chain of signifieds in such a way as to counter the terror of uncertain signs; the linguistic message is one of these techniques. At the level of the literal message, the text replies – in a more or less direct, more or less partial manner – to the question: *what is it?* The text helps to identify purely and simply the elements of the scene and the scene itself; it is a matter of a denoted description of the image (a description which is often incomplete) or, in Hjelmslev's terminology, of an *operation* (as opposed to connotation).[8] The denominative function corresponds exactly to an *anchorage* of all the possible (denoted) meanings of the object by recourse to a nomenclature. Shown a plateful of something (in an *Amieux* advertisement), I may hesitate in identifying the forms and masses; the caption ('*rice and tuna fish with mushrooms*') helps me to choose *the correct level of perception*, permits me to focus not simply my gaze but also my understanding. When it comes to the 'symbolic message', the linguistic message no longer guides identification but interpretation, constituting a kind of vice which holds the connoted meanings from proliferating, whether towards excessively individual regions (it limits, that is to say, the projective power of the image) or towards dysphoric values. An advertisement (for *d'Arcy* preserves) shows a few fruits scattered around a ladder; the caption ('*as if from your own garden*') banishes one possible signified (parsimony, the paucity of the harvest) because of its unpleasantness and orientates the reading towards a more flattering signified (the natural and personal character of fruit from a private garden); it acts here as a counter-taboo, combatting the disagreeable myth of the artificial usually associated with preserves. Of course, elsewhere than in advertising, the anchorage may be ideological and indeed this is its principal function; the text *directs* the reader through the signifieds of the image, causing him to avoid some and receive others; by means of an often subtle *dispatching*, it remote-controls him towards a meaning chosen in advance. In all these cases of anchorage, language clearly has a function of elucidation, but this elucidation is selective, a metalanguage applied not to the totality of the iconic message but only to certain of its signs. The text is indeed the creator's (and hence society's) right of inspection over the image; anchorage is a control, bearing a responsibility – in the face of the projective power of pictures – for the use of the message. With respect to the liberty of the signifieds of the image, the text has thus a *repressive* value and we can see that it is at this level that the morality and ideology of a society are above all invested.

Anchorage is the most frequent function of the linguistic message and is commonly found in press photographs and advertisements. The function of relay is less common (at least as far as the fixed image is concerned); it can be seen particularly in cartoons and comic strips. Here text (most often a snatch of dialogue) and image stand in a complementary relationship; the words, in the same way as the images, are fragments of a more general syntagm and the unity of the message is realized at a higher level, that of the story, the anecdote, the diegesis (which is ample confirmation that the diegesis must be treated as an autonomous system[9]). While rare in the fixed image, this relay-text becomes very important in film, where dialogue functions not simply as elucidation but really does advance the action by setting out, in the sequence of messages, meanings that are not to be found in the image itself. Obviously, the two functions of the linguistic message can co-exist in the one iconic whole, but the dominance of the one or the other is of consequence for the general economy of a work. When the text has the diegetic value of relay, the information is more costly, requiring as it does the learning of a digital code (the system of language); when it has a substitute value (anchorage, control), it is the image which detains the informational charge and, the image being analogical, the information is then 'lazier': in certain comic strips intended for 'quick' reading the diegesis is confided above all to the text, the image gathering the attributive informations of a paradigmatic order (the stereotyped status of the characters); the costly message and the discursive message are made to coincide so that the hurried reader may be spared the boredom of verbal 'descriptions', which are entrusted to the image, that is to say to a less 'laborious' system.

THE DENOTED IMAGE

We have seen that in the image properly speaking, the distinction between the literal message and the symbolic message is operational; we never encounter (at least in advertising) a literal image in a pure state. Even if a totally 'naive' image were to be achieved, it would immediately join the sign of naivety and be completed by a third – symbolic – message. Thus the characteristics of the literal message cannot be substantial but only relational. It is first of all, so to speak, a message by eviction, constituted by what is left in the image when the signs of connotation are mentally deleted (it would not be possible actually to remove them for they can impregnate the whole of the image, as in the case of the 'still life composition'). This evictive state naturally corresponds to a plenitude of virtualities: it is an absence of meaning full of all the meanings. Then again (and there is no contradiction with what has just been said), it is a sufficient message, since it has at least one meaning at the level of the identification of the scene represented; the letter of the image corresponds in short to the first degree of intelligibility (below which the reader would perceive only lines, forms, and colours), but this intelligibility remains virtual by reason of its very poverty, for everyone from a real society always disposes of a knowledge superior to the merely anthropological and perceives more than just the letter. Since it is both evictive and sufficient, it will be understood that from an aesthetic point of view the denoted image can appear as a kind of Edenic state of the image; cleared utopianically of its connotations, the image would become radically objective, or, in the last analysis, innocent.

This utopian character of denotation is considerably reinforced by the paradox already mentioned, that the photograph (in its literal state), by virtue of its absolutely analogical nature, seems to constitute a message without a code. Here, however, structural analysis must differentiate, for of all the kinds of image only the photograph is able to transmit the (literal) information without forming it by means of discontinuous signs and rules of transformation. The photograph, message without a code, must thus be opposed to the drawing which, even when denoted, is a coded message. The coded nature of the drawing can be seen at three levels. Firstly, to reproduce an object or a scene in a drawing requires a set of *rule-governed* transpositions; there is no essential nature of the pictorial copy and the codes of transposition are historical (notably those concerning perspective). Secondly, the operation of the drawing (the coding) immediately necessitates a certain division between the significant and the insignificant: the drawing does not reproduce *everything* (often it reproduces very little), without its ceasing, however, to be a strong message; whereas the photograph, although it can choose its subject, its point of view and its angle, cannot intervene *within* the object (except by trick effects). In other words, the denotation of the drawing is less pure than that of the photograph, for there is no drawing without style. Finally, like all codes, the drawing demands an apprenticeship (Saussure attributed a great importance to this semiological fact). Does the coding of the denoted message have consequences for the connoted message? It is certain that the coding of the literal prepares and facilitates connotation since it at once establishes a certain discontinuity in the image: the 'execution' of a drawing itself constitutes a connotation. But at the same time, insofar as the drawing displays its coding, the relationship between the two messages is profoundly modified: it is no longer the relationship between a nature and a culture (as with the photograph) but that between two cultures; the 'ethic' of the drawing is not the same as that of the photograph.

In the photograph – at least at the level of the literal message – the relationship of signifieds to signifiers is not one of 'transformation' but of 'recording', and the absence of a code clearly reinforces the myth of photographic 'naturalness': the scene *is there*, captured mechanically, not humanly (the mechanical is here a guarantee of objectivity). Man's interventions in the photograph (framing, distance, lighting, focus, speed) all effectively belong to the plane of connotation; it is as though in the beginning (even if utopian) there were a brute photograph (frontal and clear) on which man would then lay out, with the aid of various techniques, the signs drawn from a cultural code. Only the opposition of the cultural code and the natural non-code can, it seems, account for the specific character of the photograph and allow the assessment of the anthropological revolution it represents in man's history. The type of consciousness the photograph involves is indeed truly unprecedented, since it establishes not a consciousness of the *being-there* of the thing (which any copy could provoke) but an awareness of its *having-been-there*. What we have is a new space–time category: spatial immediacy and temporal anteriority, the photograph being an illogical conjunction between the *here-now* and the *there-then*. It is thus at the level of this denoted message or message without code that the *real unreality* of the photograph can be fully understood: its unreality is that of the *here-now*, for the photograph is never experienced as illusion, is in no way a *presence* (claims as to the magical character of the photographic image must be deflated); its reality that of the *having-been-there*, for in every photograph there is the always stupefying evidence of *this is how it was*, giving us, by a precious miracle, a reality from which we are sheltered. This kind of temporal equilibrium (*having-been-there*) probably diminishes the projective power of the image (very few psychological tests resort to photographs while many use drawings): the *this was so* easily defeats the *it's me*. If these remarks are at all correct, the photograph must be related to a pure spectatorial consciousness and not to the more projective, more 'magical' fictional consciousness on which film by and large depends. This would lend authority to the view that the distinction between film and photograph is not a simple difference of degree but a radical opposition. Film can no longer be seen as animated photographs: the *having-been-there* gives way before a *being-there* of the thing; which omission would explain how there can be a history of the cinema, without any real break with the previous arts of fiction, whereas the photograph can in some sense elude history (despite the evolution of the techniques and ambitions of the photographic art) and represent a 'flat' anthropological fact, at once absolutely new and definitively unsurpassable, humanity encountering for the first time in its history *messages without a code*. Hence the photograph is not the last (improved) term of the great family of images; it corresponds to a decisive mutation of informational economies.

At all events, the denoted image, to the extent to which it does not imply any code (the case with the advertising photograph), plays a special role in the general structure of the iconic message which we can begin to define (returning to this question after discussion of the third message): the denoted image naturalizes the symbolic message, it innocents the semantic artifice of connotation, which is extremely dense, especially in advertising. Although the *Panzani* poster is full of 'symbols', there nonetheless remains in the photograph, insofar as the literal message is sufficient, a kind of natural *being-there* of objects: nature seems spontaneously to produce the scene represented. A pseudo-truth is surreptitiously substituted for the simple validity of openly semantic systems; the absence of code disintellectualizes the message because it seems to found in nature the signs of culture. This is without doubt an important historical paradox: the more technology develops the diffusion of information (and notably of images), the more it provides the means of masking the constructed meaning under the appearance of the given meaning.

NOTES

1 The *description* of the photograph is given here with caution, for it already constitutes a metalanguage. The reader is asked to refer to the reproduction.

2 By *typical sign* is meant the sign of a system insofar as it is adequately defined by its substance: the verbal sign, the iconic sign, the gestural sign are so many typical signs.

3 In French, the expression *nature morte* refers to the original presence of funereal objects, such as a skull, in certain pictures.

4 'Naive' analysis is an enumeration of elements; structural description aims to grasp the relation of these elements by virtue of the principle of the solidarity holding between the terms of a structure: if one term changes, so also do the others.

5 Cf. R. Barthes, '*Éléments de sémiologie*', *Communications*, 4 (1964), p. 130. (Trans. as *Elements of Semiology* [London: 1967] and [New York: 1968], pp. 89–92.)

6 Menestrier, *L'Art des emblèmes*, 1684.

7 Images without words can certainly be found in certain cartoons, but by way of a paradox; the absence of words always covers an enigmatic intention.

8 Barthes, pp. 131–2 (trans. pp. 90–4).

9 Cf. Claude Bremond, 'Le message narratif', *Communications*, 4 (1964),

27

meaning and ideology

JUDITH WILLIAMSON

The process, then, is simply this: The product becomes a commodity, i.e. a mere moment of exchange. The commodity is transformed into exchange value. In order to equate it with itself as an exchange value, it is exchanged for a symbol which represents it as exchange value as such. As such a symbolized exchange value, it can then in turn be exchanged in definite relations for every other commodity. Because the product becomes a commodity, and the commodity becomes an exchange value, it obtains, at first only in the head, a double existence. This doubling in the idea proceeds (and must proceed) to the point where the commodity appears double in real exchange: as a natural product on one side, as exchange value on the other.

Karl Marx, *Grundrisse*

Advertisements are one of the most important cultural factors moulding and reflecting our life today. They are ubiquitous, an inevitable part of everyone's lives: even if you do not read a newspaper or watch television, the images posted over our urban surroundings are inescapable. Pervading all the media, but limited to none, advertising forms a vast superstructure with an apparently autonomous existence and an immense influence. It is not my purpose here to *measure* its influence. To do so would require sociological research and consumer data drawing on a far wider range of material than the advertisements themselves. I am simply analysing what can be *seen* in advertisements. Their very existence in more than one medium gives them a sort of independent reality that links them to our own lives: since both share a continuity they constitute a world constantly experienced as real. The ad 'world' becomes seemingly separate from the material medium—whether screen, page, etc.—which carries it. Analysing ads in their *material form* helps to avoid endowing them with a *false* materiality and letting the 'ad world' distort the real world around the screen and page.

It is this ubiquitous quality and its tenacity as a recognizable 'form' despite the fact that it functions within different technical media and despite different 'content' (that is, different messages about different products) that indicates the significance of advertising. Obviously it has a function, which is to sell things to us. But it has another function, which I believe in many ways replaces that traditionally fulfilled by art or religion. It creates structures of meaning.

For even the 'obvious' function of advertising—the definition above, 'to sell things to us'—involves a meaning process. Advertisements must take into account not only the inherent qualities and attributes of the products they are trying to sell, but also the way in which they can make those properties *mean something to us*.

In other words, advertisements have to translate statements from the world of things, for example, that a car will do so many miles per gallon, into a form that means something in terms of people. Suppose that the car did a high mpg: this could be translated into terms of thriftiness, the user being a 'clever' saver, in other words, *being a certain kind of person*. Or, if the mpg was low, the ad could appeal to the 'above money pettiness', daredevil kind of person who is too 'trendy' to be economizing. Both the statements in question could be made on the purely factual level of a 'use-value' by the simple figures of '50 mpg' and '20 mpg'. The advertisement translates these 'thing' statements to us as human statements; they are given a humanly symbolic 'exchange-value'.

First published in *Decoding Advertisements*, J. Williamson, Marion Boyars (1978), as 'Introduction: Meaning and learning', pp. 11–14.

Thus advertising is not, as might superficially be supposed, a single 'language' in the sense that a language has particular, identifiable constituent parts and its words are predetermined. The components of advertisements are variable and *not* necessarily all part of one 'language' or social discourse. Advertisements rather provide a structure that is capable of transforming the language of objects to that of people, and vice versa.

But it is too simple to say that advertising reduces people to the status of things, though clearly this is what happens when both are used symbolically. Certainly advertising sets up connections between certain types of consumers and certain products (as in the example above); and having made these links and created symbols of exchange it can use them as 'given', and so can we. For example: diamonds may be marketed by likening them to eternal love, creating a symbolism where the mineral means something not in its own terms, as a rock, but in human terms, as a sign. Thus a diamond comes to 'mean' love and endurance for us. Once the connection has been made, we begin to translate the other way and in fact to skip translating altogether: taking the sign for what it signifies, the thing for the feeling.

So in the connection of people and objects, the two do become interchangeable, as can be seen very clearly in ads of two categories. There are those where objects are made to speak—like people: 'say it with flowers'; 'a little gold says it all', etc. Conversely there are the ads where people become identified with objects: 'the *Pepsi People*' and such like. The classifications of advertisements rebound like a boomerang, as we receive them and come to use them. When 'the man' comes on in one advertisement, the TV watcher (who, it is interesting to note, sees all advertisements as one, or, rather, sees their rules as applicable to one another and thus part of an interchangeable system) *uses* the classificatory speech from *another* advertisement and directs this speech back at the screen. 'Well, he can't be a man 'cause he doesn't smoke/the same cigarettes as me'. Advertisements are selling us something else besides consumer goods: in providing us with a structure in which we, and those goods, are interchangeable, they are selling us ourselves.

And we need those selves. It is the materiality and historical context of this need which must be given as much attention as that equation of people with things. An attempt to differentiate amongst both people and products is part of the desire to classify, order, and understand the world, including one's own identity. But in our society, while the real distinctions between people are created by their role in the *process* of production, as workers, it is the *products* of their own work that are used, in the false categories invoked by advertising, to obscure the real structure of society by replacing class with the distinctions made by the consumption of particular goods. Thus instead of being identified by what they produce, people are made to identify themselves with what they consume. From this arises the false assumption that workers 'with two cars and a colour TV' are not part of the working class. We are made to feel that we can rise or fall in society through what we are able to buy, and this obscures the actual class basis that still underlies social position. The fundamental differences in our society are still class differences, but use of manufactured goods as a means of *creating* classes or groups forms an overlay on them.

This overlay is ideology. Ideology is the meaning *made necessary* by the conditions of society while helping to *perpetuate* those conditions. We feel a need to belong, to have a social 'place'; it can be hard to find. Instead we may be given an imaginary one. All of us have a genuine need for a social being, a common culture. The mass media provide this to some extent and can (potentially) fulfil a positive function in our lives.

But advertising seems to have a life of its own; it exists in and out of other media, and speaks to us in a language we can recognize but a voice we can never identify. This is because advertising has no 'subject'. Obviously people invent and produce adverts, but apart from the fact that they are unknown and faceless, the ad in any case does not claim to speak from them, it is not their speech. Thus there is a space, a gap left where the speaker should be; and one of the peculiar features of advertising is that we are drawn in to fill that gap, so that we become both listener and speaker, subject and object. This works in practice as an anonymous speech, involving a set of connections and symbols directed at us; then on receiving it, we *use* this speech, as shown in the 'diamond' example, or in the use of 'a little gold' to 'say it all'. Ultimately advertising works in a circular movement which once set in motion is self-perpetuating. It 'works' because it feeds off a genuine 'use-value'; besides needing social meaning we obviously *do need* material goods. Advertising gives those goods a social meaning so that two needs are crossed, and neither is adequately fulfilled. Material things that we need are made to represent other, non-material things we need; the point of exchange between the two is where 'meaning' is created.

[···]

The need for relationship and human meaning appropriated by advertising is one that, if only it was not diverted, could radically change the society we live in.

28

the television discourse; encoding and decoding

STUART HALL

The 'object' of production practices and structures in television is the production of a *message*: that is, a sign-vehicle, or rather sign-vehicles of a specific kind organised, like any other form of communication or language, through the operation of codes, within the syntagmatic chains of a discourse. The apparatus and structures of production issue, at a certain moment, in the form of a symbolic vehicle constituted within the rules of 'language'. It is in this 'phenomenal form' that the circulation of the 'product' takes place. Of course, the transmission of this symbolic vehicle also requires its material substratum—video-tape, film, the transmitting and receiving apparatus, etc. But it is primarily in this symbolic form that the reception of the 'product' and its distribution between different segments of the audience, takes place. Once accomplished, the translation of that message into societal structures must be made again for the communication circuit to be completed. Thus, whilst in no way wanting to limit research to 'following only those leads which emerge from content analyses',[1] we must recognise that the symbolic form of the message has a privileged position in the communicative exchange: and that the moments of 'encoding' and 'decoding', though only 'relatively autonomous' in relation to the communicative process as a whole, are *determinate* moments. The raw historical event cannot in that form be transmitted by, say, a television newscast. It can only be signified within the aural-visual forms of a televisual language. In the moment when the historical event passes under the sign of language, it is subject to all the complex formal 'rules' by which language signifies. To put it paradoxically, the event must become a 'story' before it can become a *communicative event*. In that moment of 'encoding', the formal sub-rules of language are 'in dominance', without, of course, subordinating out of existence the historical event so signified, or the historical consequences of the event having been signified in this way. The 'message-form' is the necessary form of the appearance of the event in its passage from source to receiver. Thus the transposition into and out of the 'message-form' or the meaning-dimension (or mode of exchange of the message) is not a random 'moment' that we can take up or ignore for the sake of convenience or simplicity. The 'message-form' is a determinate moment, though, at another level, it comprises the surface-movements of the communications system only, and requires, at another stage of the analysis, to be integrated into the essential relations of communication of which it forms only a part.

From this general perspective, we may crudely characterise the communicative exchange as follows. The brodcasting organisations, with their institutional structures and networks of production, their organised routines and technical infrastructures, are required to produce the programme. Production, here, initiates the message. Production and reception of the television message are not identical, but they are related: they are differentiated moments within the totality formed by the communicative process as a whole.

Though we know the television programme is not a behavioural input, like a tap on the knee-cap, it seems to have been almost impossible for researchers to conceptualise the communicative process without lapsing back into one or other variant of low-flying behaviourism. Yet, by now, it should have been firmly established, as Gerbner has remarked, that representations of violence on the TV screen 'are not violence but messages about violence'.[2]

First published in *Education and Culture* (Council of Europe), Number 25, Summer 1974, as 'The Television Discourse: encoding and decoding', pp. 8–15.

Take, for example, the simple-structure, early (and now children's) TV Western, modelled on the early Hollywood B-feature genre Western: with its clear-cut, good/bad Manichean moral universe, its clear social and moral designation of villain and hero, the clarity of its narrative line and development, its iconographical features, its clearly-registered climax in the violent shoot-out, chase, personal show-down, street or bar-room duel, etc. For long, on both British and American TV, this form constituted the predominant drama-entertainment genre. In quantitative terms, such films/programmes contained a high ratio of violent incidents, deaths, woundings, etc. Whole gangs of men, whole troops of Indians, went down nightly to their deaths. Researchers—Himmelweit among others—have, however, suggested that the structure of the early TV/B-feature Western was so clear-cut, its action so conventionalised, stylised, that most children (boys rather earlier than girls, an interesting finding in itself) soon learned to recognise and 'read' it like a 'game': a 'cowboys-and-Injuns' game. It was therefore further hypothesized that Westerns with this clarified structure were less likely to trigger the aggressive imitation of violent behaviour or other types of aggressive 'acting-out' than other types of programmes with a high violence ratio which were not stylised. But it is worth asking what this recognition of the Western as a 'symbolic game' means or implies: how does this transform our research conceptualisations and perspectives?

Conventionalizing the Western means that a set of extremely tightly coded 'rules' exist whereby stories of a certain recognisable type, content and structure can be easily encoded within the Western form. What is more, these 'rules of encoding' were so diffused, so symmetrically shared as between producer and audience, that the 'message' was likely to be decoded in a manner highly symmetrical to that in which it had been encoded. This reciprocity of codes is, indeed, precisely what is entailed in the notion of stylisation or 'conventionalisation', and the persistence of such reciprocal codes over time is, of course, what defines or makes possible the existence of a *genre*. Such an account, then, takes the encoding/decoding moments properly into account, and the case appears an unproblematic one.

The violent element or string in the narrative structure of the simple-structure Western—shoot-out, brawl, ambush, bank-raid, fist-fight, wounding, duel or massacre—like any other semantic unit in a structured discourse, cannot signify anything on its own. It can only signify in terms of the structured meanings of the message as a whole. Further, its signification depends on its relation—or the sum of the relations of similarity and difference—with other elements or units. Burgelin[3] has long ago, and definitively, reminded us that the violent or wicked acts of a villain only mean something in relation to the presence/absence of good acts.

We must now add that the meaning of the violent act or episode cannot be fixed, single and unalterable, but must be capable of signifying different values depending on how and with what it is articulated. As the signifying element, among other elements, in a discourse, it remains *polysemic*. Indeed, the way it is structured in its combination with other elements serves to delimit its meanings within that specified field, and effects a 'closure', so that a *preferred meaning* or reading is suggested. There can never be only one, single, univocal and determined meaning for such a lexical item; but, depending on how its integration within the code has been accomplished, its possible meanings will be organised within a scale that runs from *dominant* to *subordinate*. And this, of course, has consequences for the other—the reception—end of the communicative chain: there can be no law to ensure that the receiver will take the preferred or dominant meaning of an episode of violence in precisely the way in which it has been encoded by the producer.

The presence of the code has the effect of displacing the meaning of single episodes from one category to another. Thus, within the structure of the programme as a whole, the violent episode may contain a message or make a proposition, not about violence but about conduct, or even about professionalism, nor perhaps even about the relation of professionalism to character. And here we recall Robert Warshow's intuitive observation that, fundamentally, the Western is not 'about' violence but about codes of conduct.

Thus, drawing attention to the symbolic/linguistic/coded nature of communications, far from boxing us into the closed and formal universe of signs, precisely opens out into the area where cultural content, of the most resonant but 'latent' kind, is transmitted: and especially the manner in which the interplay of codes and content serves to *displace* meanings from one frame to another, and thus to bring to the surface in 'disguised' forms, the repressed contents of a culture.

Let us turn now to a different area of programming, and a different aspect of the operation of codes. The televisual sign is a peculiarly complex one, as we know. It is a visual sign with strong, supplementary aural-verbal support. It is one of the iconic signs, in Peirce's sense.

As Eco has convincingly argued, iconic signs 'look like objects in the real world', to put it crudely (e.g. the photograph or drawing of a /cow/, and the animal /cow/), because they 'reproduce the conditions of perception in the receiver'.[4] These conditions of 'recognition' in the viewer constitute some of the most fundamental perceptual codes that all culture-members share. Now, because these perceptual codes are so widely distributed, denotative visual signs probably give rise to less 'misunderstandings' than linguistic ones. A lexical inventory of the English language would throw up thousands of words that the ordinary speaker could not denotatively comprehend: but provided enough 'information' is given, culture-members would be able or be competent to decode, denotatively, a much wider range of visual signifiers. In this sense, and at the denotative level, the visual sign is probably a more universal one than the linguistic sign. Similarly, whereas, in societies like ours, linguistic competence is very unequally distributed as between different classes and segments of the population (predominantly, by the family and the education system), what we might call 'visual competence', at the denotative level, is more universally diffused. (It is worth reminding ourselves, of course, that it is not, in fact, 'universal', and that we are dealing with a spectrum: there are kinds of visual representation, short of the 'purely abstract', which create all kinds of visual puzzles for ordinary viewers: e.g. cartoons, certain kinds of diagrammatic representation, representations that employ unfamiliar conventions, types of photographic or cinematic cutting and editing, etc.) It is also true that the iconic sign may support 'mis-readings' simply because it is so 'natural', so 'transparent'. Mistakes may arise here, not because we as viewers cannot literally decode the sign (it is perfectly obvious what it is a picture of), but because we are tempted, by its very 'naturalization', to 'misread' the image for the thing it signifies.[5] With this important proviso, however, we would be surprised to find that the majority of the television audience had much difficulty in literally or denotatively identifying what the visual signs they see on the screen refer to or signify. Whereas most people require a lengthy process of education in order to become relatively competent users of the language of their speech community, they seem to pick up its visual-perceptual codes at a very early age, without formal training, and are quickly competent in its use.

The visual sign is, however, also *a connotative sign*. And it is so pre-eminently within the discourses of modern mass communication. The level of connotation of the visual sign, of its contextual reference, of its position in the various associative fields of meanings, is precisely the point where the denoted sign intersects with the deep semantic structures of a culture, and takes on an ideological dimension. In the advertising discourse, for example, we might say that there is almost no 'purely denotative' communication. Every visual sign in advertising 'connotes' a quality, situation, value or inference that is present as an implication or implied meaning, depending on the connotational reference. We are all probably familiar with Barthes' example of the /sweater/, which, in the rhetoric of advertising and fashion, always connotes, at least, 'a warm garment' or 'keeping warm', and thus by further connotative elaboration, 'the coming of winter' or 'a cold day'. In the specialized sub-codes of fashion, /sweater/ may connote 'a fashionable style of *haute couture*', or, alternatively, 'an informal style of dress'. But, set against the right background, and positioned in the romantic sub-code, it may connote 'long autumn walk in the woods'.[6] Connotational codes of this order are, clearly, structured enough to signify, but they are more 'open' or 'open-ended' than denotative codes. What is more, they clearly contract relations with the universe of ideologies in a culture, and with history and ethnography. These connotative codes are the 'linguistic' means by which the domains of social life, the segmentations of culture, power and ideology are made to signify. They refer to the 'maps of meaning' into which any culture is organised, and those 'maps of social reality' have the whole range of social meanings, practices and usages, power and interest 'written in' to them.

Literal or denotative 'errors' are relatively unproblematic. They represent a kind of noise in the channel. But 'misreadings' of a message at the connotative or contextual level are a different matter. They have, fundamentally, a societal, not a communicative, basis. They signify, at the 'message' level, the structural conflicts, contradictions and negotiations of economic, political and cultural life. The first position we want to identify is that of the *dominant or hegemonic code*. (There are, of course, many different codes and sub-codes required to produce an event within the dominant code.) When the viewer takes the connoted meaning from, say, a television newscast or current affairs programme, full and straight, and decodes the message in terms of the reference-code in which it has been coded, we might say that the viewer is operating inside the dominant code. This is the ideal-typical case of 'perfectly transparent communication', or as close as we are likely to come to it 'for all practical purposes'.

Next (here we are amplifying Parkin's model), we would want to identify the *professional code*. The professional code is 'relatively independent' of the dominant code, in that it applies criteria and operations of its own, especially those of a technico-practical nature. The professional code, however, operates within the 'hegemony' of the dominant code. The hegemonic interpretation of the politics of Northern Ireland, or the Chilean coup or the Industrial Relations Bill are given by political elites: the particular choice of presentational occasions and formats, the selection of personnel, the choice of images, the 'staging' of debates, etc. are selected by the operation of the professional code.[7] How the broadcasting professionals are able to operate with 'relatively autonomous' codes of their own, while acting in such a way as to reproduce (not without contradiction) the hegemonic signification of events is a complex matter that cannot be further spelled out here. It must suffice to say that the professionals are linked with the defining elites not only by the institutional position of broadcasting itself as an 'ideological apparatus',[8] but more intimately by the structure of *access* (i.e. the systematic 'over-accessing' of elite personnel and 'definitions of the situation' in television). It may even be said that the professional codes serve to reproduce hegemonic definitions specifically by not overtly biasing their operations in their direction: ideological reproduction therefore takes place here inadvertently, unconsciously, 'behind men's backs'. Of course, conflicts, contradictions and even 'misunderstandings' regularly take place between the dominant and the professional significations and their signifying agencies.

The third position we would identify is that of the *negotiated code*. Majority audiences probably understand quite adequately what has been dominantly defined and professionally signified. The dominant definitions, however, are hegemonic precisely because they represent definitions of situations and events which are 'in dominance' and which are *global*. Dominant definitions connect events, implicitly or explicitly, to grand totalisations, to the great syntagmatic views-of-the-world: they take 'large views' of issues: they relate events to 'the national interest' or to the level of geopolitics, even if they make these connections in truncated, inverted or mystified ways. The definition of a 'hegemonic' viewpoint is (a) that it defines within its terms the mental horizon, the universe of possible meanings of a whole society or culture; and (b) that it carries with it the stamp of legitimacy—it appears coterminous with what is 'natural', 'inevitable', 'taken for granted' about the social order. Decoding within the *negotiated version* contains a mixture of adaptive and oppositional elements: it acknowledges the legitimacy of the hegemonic definitions to make the grand significations, while, at a more restricted, situational level, it makes its own ground-rules, it operates with 'exceptions' to the rule. It accords the privileged position to the dominant definition of events, whilst reserving the right to make a more negotiated application to 'local conditions', to its own more *corporate* situation. This negotiated version of the dominant ideology is thus shot through with contradictions, though these are only on certain occasions brought to full visibility. Negotiated codes operate through what we might call particular or situated logics: and these logics arise from the differential position of those who occupy this position in the spectrum, and from their differential and unequal relation to power.

The simplest example of a negotiated code is that which governs the response of a worker to the notion of an industrial relations bill limiting the right to strike, or to arguments for a wages freeze. At the level of the national-interest economic debate, he may adopt the hegemonic definition, agreeing that 'we must all pay ourselves less in order to combat inflation', etc. This, however, may have little or no relation to his willingness to go on strike for better pay and conditions, or to oppose the industrial relations bill at the level of his shop-floor or union organisation. We suspect that the great majority of so-called 'misunderstandings' arise from the disjunctures between hegemonic-dominant encodings and negotiated-corporate decodings. It is just these mismatches in the levels which most provoke defining elites and professionals to identify a 'failure in communications'. Finally, it is possible for a viewer perfectly to understand both the literal and connotative inflection given to an event, but to determine to decode the message in a globally contrary way. He detotalises the message in the preferred code in order to retotalise the message within some alternative framework of reference. This is the case of the viewer who listens to a debate on the need to limit wages, but who 'reads' every mention of 'the national interest' as 'class interest'. He is operating with what we must call an *oppositional code*. One of the most significant political moments (they also coincide with crisis-points within the broadcasting organisations themselves for obvious reasons) is the point when events that are normally signified and decoded in a negotiated way begin to be given an oppositional reading.

The question of cultural policies now falls, awkwardly, into place. When dealing with social communications, it is extremely difficult to identify as a neutral, educational goal, the task of 'improving communications' or of 'making communications more effective', at any rate once one has passed beyond the strictly denotative level of the message. The educator or cultural policy-maker is performing one of his most partisan acts when he colludes with the resignification of real conflicts and contradictions as if they were simply kinks in the communicative chain. Denotative mistakes are not structurally significant. But connotative and contextual 'misunderstandings' are, or can be, of the highest structural significance. To interpret what are in fact essential elements in the systematic distortions of a socio-communications system as if they were merely technical faults in transmission is to misread a deep-structure process for a surface phenomenon. The decision to intervene in order to make the hegemonic codes of dominant elites more effective and transparent for the majority audience is not a technically neutral, but a political one. To 'misread' a political choice as a technical one represents a type of unconscious collusion with the dominant interests, a form of 'technological rationality' to which social science researchers are all too prone. Though the sources of such mystification are both social and structural, the actual process is greatly facilitated by the operation of discrepant codes. It would not be the first time that scientific researchers had 'unconsciously' played a part in the reproduction of hegemony, not by openly submitting to it, but simply by operating the 'professional bracket'.

NOTES

1   J.D. Halloroon, 'Understanding television', *Education and Culture*, 25: 15–20.
2   Gerbner, G., Gross, L. and Signorielli, N., *Violence in TV Drama: A Study of Trends and Symbolic Functions* (Annenberg School, Univer. of Pennsylvania 1970).
3   O. Burgelin, 'Structural analysis and mass communications', (Studies in *Broadcasting, no. 6.* (Nippon Hoso Kyokai, 1968).
4   Eco, op. cit.
5   S. Hall, 'The determination of news photos', in *The Manufacture of News* (London: *Constable*, 1972), pp. 176–90.
6   R. Barthes, 'Rhetoric of the image', in WPCS 1. CCS, B'ham (1971).
7   Cf. S. Hall, 'External/internal dialectic in broadcasting', in Fourth Symposium on Broadcasting, Dept. of Extra-Mural Studies, University of Manchester (1972).
8   Cf. L. Althusser, 'Ideological state apparatuses', in *Lenin and Philosophy, and Other Essays* (London: New Left Books, 1971), pp. 121–73.

29

the ideal romance

JANICE RADWAY

Before summarizing essential characteristics of the romantic heroine and hero, it should be pointed out that the meaning of their personalities is underscored for the reader by the presence of the secondary characters mentioned earlier. More specifically, the significance of heroine and hero as ideal feminine and masculine types is established by the existence of two abstract foils who embody those features of the female and male personalities that must be eradicated if women and men are to continue to love each other and fill one another's needs. The simple binary oppositions that are the basis for character differentiation in the romance are, therefore, a useful clue to the things women most fear as potential threats to heterosexual love and traditional marriage. Because their fears are embodied in the ideal romance in characters whose misbehavior is always explained away by their later destruction, the readers are encouraged to see those fears as unwarranted.

With its secondary characters, then, the ideal romance sketches a faint picture of male–female relationships characterized by suspicion and distrust in order to set off more effectively its later, finished portrait of the perfect union. In the act of substituting the one for the other by showing that the early hero/heroine relationship, although appearing as the former was, in reality, the latter, the romance ingeniously suggests to the reader that any evidence of worrisome traits and tendencies she finds in her own motives or those of her spouse can be reinterpreted in the most favorable light.

It can be seen from Table 29.1 that the heroine's sexual innocence, unself-conscious beauty, and desire for love are contrasted in the ideal romance with the female foil's self-interested pursuit of a comfortable social position. Because she views men as little more than tools for her own aggrandizement, the female foil is perfectly willing to manipulate them by flaunting her sexual availability. Incapable of caring for anyone other than herself, she makes demands upon the men she desires while promising nothing in return. This rival woman is the perfect incarnation of the calculating female whom the hero detests and thinks he sees hidden behind the heroine's beguiling facade. The heroine, of course, is never sure of the hero's true motives and often fears that he either loves the female foil or is taken in by her wiles.

Male rivals, on the other hand, are very shadowy figures in the ideal romance. While they do appear, they are described rather sparingly and almost never prove even momentarily attractive to the heroine. These foils are invariably of two types in the romances preferred by the Smithton women.[1] Some, like Braeger Darvey in *Ashes in the Wind*, are sensitive, expressive, and overtly appreciative of the heroine's extraordinary qualities. Men like these are used to highlight the hero's surly reserve and his obstinate refusal to be persuaded that the heroine is not a femme fatale. They are usually found lacking, however, because they are insufficiently aggressive, protective, and strong. The story suggests, in effect, that they are insufficiently masculine.

Ideal romances also employ another kind of foil, a true villain, who actually attempts to abduct the heroine from the arms of her hero. These figures are inevitably ugly, morally corrupt, and interested only in the heroine's sexual favors. They pose the constant threat of vicious rape and thus permit the author to differentiate the hero's 'love-crazed' taking of the heroine from a truly malicious wish to use her for carnal pleasure. Although the heroine initially sees no difference between these individuals and the hero,

First published in *Reading the Romance*, J. Radway, Verso (1984), as 'The Ideal Romance', pp. 131–152.

TABLE 29.1 Binary oppositions in character portrayal
at the beginning of the romantic narrative

Oppositional pair	Heroine	Female foil	Hero	Male foil	Oppositional pair	Villain
Virginal	+	−	−	Uncoded	Virginal	−
Experienced	−	+	+		Promiscuous	+
Desires love	+	−	−	+	Desires love	−
Desires wealth and position	−	+	+	−	Desires sexual pleasure	+
Unself-conscious	+	−	+	+	Unself-conscious	−
Vain	−	+	−	−	Vain	+
Beautiful	+	+	+	+	Handsome	
Plain	−	−	−	−	Ugly	+
Nurturant	+	−	−	+	Tender	−
Demanding	−	+	+	−	Indifferent	+
Independent	+	−	+	Uncoded	Honest	−
Dependent	−	+	−		Corrupt	+
Intelligent	+	Uncoded	+	−	Courageous	−
Confused (gullible)	−		−	+	Cowardly	+
Fears men	+	−	+	−	Emotionally reserved	−
Desires men	−	+	−	+	Emotionally expressive	+

their constant brutality and crude insinuations inform the reader that the hero is not cruel at all, only unskilled in the art of tender care for a woman. The presence of rival figures like Jacques Du Bonne in *Ashes in the Wind*, Thomas Hint in *The Flame and the Flower*, Louis in *The Proud Breed*, and Sir Morell in *The Black Lyon* is a constant reminder to the reader that a woman's sexuality contains the potential to do her great harm by virtue of its capacity to activate male lust and hatred of women. However, because the frequency and duration of the villains' attacks on the heroine are very carefully controlled by the authors of 'ideal' romances, the suggestion that some men see women as sexual objects is made only fleetingly in order to teach the heroine the true worth of the hero. The fear is then banished effectively by the hero because he is finally portrayed as excited by the heroine's sexuality *and* respectful of her identity as an individual. His behavior informs the reader that what she most fears from men is really only a minor threat that can be eradicated permanently by the protective care of the man who truly loves her.

It is frequently this particular threat that is not controlled effectively in 'failed' romances. In fact, villain figures run wild in these books. Moreover, they are not differentiated adequately from the hero. The happy union, then, at the romance's end is incapable of erasing the threat of violence and the fear it induces. It therefore fails to convince the reader that traditional sexual arrangements are benign.

Given the origination of this sample in actual reader selections from a large number of subgenres and publishing lines, it should not be surprising to note in turning from character to narrative that these ideal romances exhibit vide variation in superficial plot development. Nonetheless, when Vladimir Propp's method for determining the essential narrative structure of folktales is applied to these particular novels, it becomes clear that despite individual and isolated preoccupation with such things as reincarnation, adultery, amnesia, and mistaken identity, these stories are all built upon a shared narrative structure. Assuming first, as Will Wright does, that all narratives are composed of three essential stages—an initial situation, a final transformation of that situation, and an intermediary intervention that causes and explains the change—I then proceeded by trying to identify the common opening and conclusion of the romances in question. Once these had been isolated, I then looked for the most basic structure of embedded actions that could account coherently for the gradual transformation of the former into the latter. The result, a list of thirteen logically related functions, explains the heroine's transformation from an isolated, asexual, insecure adolescent who is unsure of her own identity, into a mature, sensual, and very married woman who has realized her full potential and identity as the partner of a man and as the implied mother of a child. The narrative structure of the ideal romance is summarized below:

1.   The heroine's social identity is destroyed.
2.   The heroine reacts antagonistically to an aristocratic male.
3.   The aristocratic male responds ambiguously to the heroine.
4.   The heroine interprets the hero's behavior as evidence of a purely sexual interest in her.
5.   The heroine responds to the hero's behavior with anger or coldness.
6.   The hero retaliates by punishing the heroine.
7.   The heroine and hero are physically and/or emotionally separated.
8.   The hero treats the heroine tenderly.
9.   The heroine responds warmly to the hero's act of tenderness.
10. The heroine reinterprets the hero's ambiguous behavior as the product of previous hurt.
11. The hero proposes/openly declares his love for/demonstrates his unwavering commitment to the heroine with a supreme act of tenderness.
12. The heroine responds sexually and emotionally.
13. The heroine's identity is restored.

As the initial function indicates, the ideal romance begins with its heroine's removal from a familiar, comfortable realm usually associated with her childhood and family. Heather Simmons, for example, is taken away from her guardian by an evil uncle who intends to establish her in a whorehouse; Julie Dever is hurt in a car accident in an isolated mountain pass while away on vacation; Charlotte Hungerford leaves the privacy and protection of her writer's study to go to Brighton where her single status becomes the topic of disapproving gossip; Alaina McGaren is forced to flee her family's nearly destroyed plantation during the Civil War; and Deanna Abbott goes to a ranch in Arizona to escape her parents' efforts to mold her in their own image. The details are different, but in each case the move terrifies the heroine because it strips her of her familiar supports and her sense of herself as someone with a particular place and a fixed identity. The mood of the romance's opening pages, then, is nearly always set by the heroine's emotional isolation and her profound sense of loss.

Keeping in mind what the Smithton women have said about their emotional state when they turn to romance reading, it seems possible that part of the attraction of the romance might be traced to the fact that this loss and the resulting emptiness it creates within the heroine continues and confirms a similar sense of depletion in the reader.

The reader's sense of emptiness creates the initial desire for the romance's tale of a progressing relationship because the experience of being ignored by others is an emotional state both alien to women and difficult for them to bear. Because their family histories have created in them what Nancy Chodorow has identified as a 'complex, relational self,' romance readers need to avoid such feelings of emptiness by integrating important intimates into their psychic structures who will reciprocate their interest.[2] This profound need, which Chodorow maintains is rarely filled adequately by men because they have developed asymmetrically into individuals who do not define themselves in relation, is confirmed obligingly and addressed vicariously, then, by this story that relates another woman's successful journey from isolation and its threat of annihilation to connection and the promise of a mature, fulfilled female identity.

[···]

Within this context, the possibility that there may be a correlation between *some* romance reading and the social roles of wife and mother seems less than surprising. Given the nature of the female personality as a self-in-relation, the inability of men to function as completely adequate relational partners, and the reciprocal demands made upon women by the very children they rely on to satisfy their unmet needs, it is understandable that many women derive pleasure and encouragement from repetitive indulgence in romantic fantasies. On one level, then, the romance is an account of a woman's journey to female personhood *as that particular psychic configuration is constructed and realized within patriarchal culture*. It functions as a symbolic display and explanation of a process commonly experienced by many women. At the same time, because the ideal romance symbolically represents real female needs within the story and then depicts their successful satisfaction, it ratifies or confirms the inevitability and desirability of the entire institutional structure within which those needs are created and addressed.

In returning to the narrative structure of the romance, it should now be clear that the initial function dictating the heroine's loss of connections and identity is more deeply resonant in a psychoanalytic sense than it is overtly topical. When she is plucked from her earlier relationships and thrust out into a public world, the heroine's consequent terror and feeling of emptiness most likely evokes for the reader distant memories of her initial separation from her mother and her later ambivalent attempts to establish an individual identity. At the same time, it symbolically represents in a more general sense what it feels like for a woman to be alone without the necessary relation to another. As a consequence, the romance's opening exaggerates the very feeling of emptiness and desire that sent the reader to the book in the first place. The boyish independence of the typical heroine can be reinterpreted in this context as a symbolic representation of the initial step of a young girl's journey toward individuation and subsequent connection. The heroine, in effect, employs the usual method of individuating from the mother by turning to the next most proximate individual, her father. By identifying with him specifically or more generally with traits and achievements associated with men, the heroine simultaneously justifies her impulse to separate by degrading the feminine *and* accomplishes the actual rejection itself. She is free to embark finally on her quest for a new self and new connections. In rejecting her mother, the heroine immediately locates the reader's sense of loss and emptiness within a developmental pattern that holds out the promise of its later eradication in a future, perfect union with another.

Throughout the rest of the romantic narrative, then, two initially distinct stories are progressively intertwined. In fact, the heroine's search for her identity dovetails rather quickly with the tale of her developing relationship to the hero. Chodorow's theories are especially useful in explaining the psychological import of the stories' confluence. What the heroine successfully establishes by the end of the ideal narrative is the now-familiar female self, the self-in-relation. Because she manages this relation with a man who is not only masculine but redundantly so, the romance also manages to consider the possibilities and difficulties of establishing a connection with a man who is initially incapable of satisfying a woman. Thus the romance is concerned not simply with the fact of heterosexual marriage but with the perhaps more essential issues for women—how to realize a mature self and how to achieve emotional fulfillment in a culture in which such goals must be achieved in the company of an individual whose principal preoccupation is always *elsewhere* in the public world.

The problems posed for women by characteristically masculine behavior are highlighted early in the romantic narrative by function 2 and the frightened, antagonistic response of the heroine to the mere presence of an ambiguous man. Because the hero's hard physical exterior is complemented by his imperious, distant manner, the heroine automatically assumes that he finds her uninteresting or, in some cases, intends to harm her. Still, she is troubled by that contradictory evidence of his hidden, gentle nature and she therefore feels unsure of his motives. Because she cannot seem to avoid contact with him despite her dislike, the heroine's principal activity throughout the rest of the story consists of the mental process of trying to assign particular signifieds to his overt acts. In effect, what she is trying to do in discovering the significance of his behavior by uncovering his motives is to understand what the fact of male presence and attention means for her, a woman.

It should be clear by now that romance authors raise this issue of the import of male motives for sound material and psychological reasons. In a culture that circumscribes female work within the domestic sphere by denying women full entry into the public realm, any woman who cannot attach herself to a member of the culture that is permitted to work runs the risk of poverty, if not outright annihilation.[3] At the same time, because men are parented within the culture solely by women, they tend to individuate and define themselves in explicit opposition to anything female. If this does not always result in misogyny or in its expression by violence against women, it does end at least in the repression of traits and emotional tendencies typically identified with them. Therefore, even men who are not brutal tend to relate to women on a relatively superficial emotional level just as they define them principally as sexual creatures because their physiological characteristics are the most obvious mark of their difference from men. Given the fact that a woman and any future children she might have are economically dependent on such men, it becomes absolutely essential that she learn to distinguish those who want her sexually from that special individual who is willing to pledge commitment and care in return for her sexual favor.

Male reserve and indifference also become issues in the romance because, if left untempered, they can hinder a woman from satisfying her most basic needs for relationality and emotional nurturance. Because women move out of their oedipal conflict with a triangular psychic structure intact, not only do they need to connect themselves with a member of the opposite sex, but they also continue to require an intense emotional bond with someone who is reciprocally nurturant and protective in a maternal way. The homophobic nature of the culture effectively denies them the opportunity to receive this from the hands of someone who resembles the woman responsible for their memory of it. Therefore, because direct regression through an intense relationship with an individual resembling her mother is denied a woman (as it is not denied to a man), she must learn to suppress the need entirely, to satisfy it through her relationship with a man, or to seek its fulfillment in other activities. Although the ideal romance initially admits the difficulty of relying on men for gentleness and affective intensity, thus confirming the reader's own likely experience, it also reassures her that such satisfaction is possible because men really do know how to attend to a woman's needs.

This peculiar double perspective on male behavior is achieved by a narrative structure that allows the reader greater knowledge of the hero than the heroine herself possesses. Because she is given access to his true feelings and intentions by an omniscient narration that reveals something about his past that justifies his present behavior, the reader can reinterpret the action in functions 4, 5, and 6. For example, where the heroine believes the hero's behavior is merely ambiguous (function 3), the reader knows that his unreadable actions are the product of emotional turmoil prompted by his feelings for the heroine. Similarly, when the hero appears to punish the heroine (function 6), the reader can tell herself that such punishment is the result of hurt and disappointment at the heroine's supposed infidelity or lack of interest in him. It is, then, a sign of his love for her, not of his distaste. The double perspective on the hero's behavior thus allows the reader to have it both ways. She can identify with the heroine's point of view and therefore with her anger and fear. The act of reading, in that case, provides her with an imaginative space to express her reservations and negative feelings about men. On the other hand, she can rely on the greater knowledge accorded to her by the narration and enjoy the reassurance it provides that, in fact, men do not threaten women or function as obstacles to their fulfillment. In the safe realm of the imaginary, then, the romance reader is allowed to indulge in the expression of very real fears that she is permitted to control simultaneously by overruling them with the voice of her greater knowledge.

[···]

Thus the romance originates in the female push toward individuation and actualization of the self, but because it is written by women who have been engendered within a patriarchal family characterized by exclusively female 'mothering,' that drive is embodied within the language and forms created and prescribed by patriarchy. Consequently, to achieve *female* selfhood in the romance, which is an expression of patriarchal culture, is to realize an identity in relation not merely to one but to two important others. The romance does deny the worth of complete autonomy. In doing so, however, it is not obliterating the female self completely. Rather, it is constructing a particular kind of female self, the self-in-relation demanded by patriarchal parenting arrangements.

It is obvious, then, why the romance must also concern itself with the nature of masculinity and its implications for women. The stories are written from a perspective that is well aware of the difficulties posed by male autonomy and reticence and, as a result, they are exercises in the imaginative transformation of masculinity to conform with female standards. This is precisely what occurs when the emotional standoff between hero and heroine is partially broken in the ideal romance by the hero's act of tenderness (function 8). What makes this so interesting, however, is not the fact that it occurs. This is, after all, a woman's fantasy and, as such, it fulfills desires and satisfies wishes that are basic to her psychological construction. Function 8 of the ideal romance is intriguing precisely because it is *not structurally explained* by the narrative *at the time that it occurs*. No action on the part of the hero or, for that matter, on the part of any other character can be said to cause or explain the magic transformation of his cruelty and indifference into tender care. The abrupt transformation simply takes place.

Although the hero's punishment of the heroine results in his separation from her, the separation is never connected explicitly *at this point in the story* with his ensuing act of kindness. Because the hero does not indicate overtly either in his thoughts or in conversation that this separation causes him to recognize his dependence upon the heroine, function 7 is not presented as the effective agent in the transformation of function 6 into function 8. The separation simply occurs and then the hero demonstrates miraculously that he can be tender with the heroine. Of course, the fact that this transformation has been prepared for surreptitiously by earlier descriptions of the hero, which contain a clue to the underlying softness hiding behind his impassive facade, makes the shift palatable to the reader. But in relying on the reader's greater knowledge, the romance author avoids having the hero openly declare his dependence on a woman. He continues to be seen as a supreme example of unchallenged, autonomous masculinity. Later in the text when hero and heroine are finally united, he confesses that it was the prospect of losing her that frightened him and prompted his decision to woo her with tenderness. In falling back on this kind of retroactive interpretation, however, the romance avoids considering the problem of the contradiction between admission of dependency and relationality and the usual definition of masculinity as total autonomy. The hero is permitted simply to graft tenderness onto his unaltered male character. The addition of the one, the romance implies, need not transform the other. Consequently, the genre fails to show that if the emotional repression and independence that characterize men are actually to be reversed, the entire notion of what it is to be male will have to be changed.

The romance inadvertently tells its reader, then, that she will receive the kind of care she desires only if she can find a man who is *already* tender and nurturant. This hole in the romance's explanatory logic is precisely the point at which a potential argument for change is transformed into a representation and recommendation of the status quo. The reader is not shown how to find a nurturant man nor how to hold a distant one responsible for altering his lack of emotional availability. Neither is she encouraged to believe that male indifference and independence really can be altered. What she is encouraged to do is to latch on to whatever expressions of thoughtfulness he might display, no matter how few, and to consider them, rather than his more obvious and frequent disinterest, as evidence of his true character. In learning *how to read* a man properly, the romance tells its reader, she will reinforce his better instincts, break down his reserve, and lead him to respond to her as she wishes. Once she has set the process in motion by responding warmly to his rare demonstrations of affection (function 9), she will further see that his previous impassivity was the result of a former hurt (function 10). If she can recognize that, she will understand, as the romantic heroine always does, that her man really loves her and that he is dependent on her even if neither of them wishes to admit it openly.

The romantic narrative demonstrates that a woman must learn to trust her man and to believe that he loves her deeply even in the face of massive evidence to the contrary. The fantasy's conclusion suggests that when she manages such trust, he will reciprocate with declarations of his commitment to her (function 11). That commitment, the romance further insists, which also implies his need for her, is the condition for her free and uninhibited response (function 12). Once she responds to his passion with her own, she will feel as the heroine does, both emotionally complete and sexually satisfied. In short, she will have established successfully an external connection with a man whose behavior she now knows how to read correctly. The romance's conclusion promises her that if she learns to read male behavior successfully, she will find that her needs for fatherly protection, motherly care, and passionate adult love will be satisfied perfectly. The explanatory structure of this argument is represented in Figure 29.1.

Clifford Geertz has observed that in attending a cockfight, the young Balinese receives from this essential art form of his culture 'a kind of sentimental education.'[4] 'What he learns there,' Geertz writes, 'is what his culture's ethos and his private sensibility ... look like when spelled out externally in a collective text.'[5] The experience of reading the romance is little different for the Smithton women. In effect, they are instructed about the nature of patriarchy and its meaning for them as women, that is, as individuals who do not possess power in a society dominated by men. Not only does the romantic drama evoke the material consequences of refusal to mold oneself in the image of femininity prescribed by the culture but it also displays the remarkable benefits of conformity.

Equally significant, however, the romance also provides a symbolic portrait of the womanly sensibility that is created and required by patriarchal marriage and its sexual division of labor. By showing that the heroine finds someone who is intensely and exclusively interested in her and in her needs, the romance confirms the validity of the reader's desire for tender nurture and legitimizes her pre-oedipal wish to recover the primary love of her initial caretaker. Simultaneously, by witnessing her connection with an autonomous and powerful male, it also confirms her longing to be protected, provided for, and sexually desired. The romance legitimizes her own heterosexuality and decision to marry by providing the heroine with a spectacularly masculine partner and a perfect marriage. In thus symbolically reproducing the triangular object configuration that characterizes female personality development through the heroine's relationships, the romance underscores and shores up the very psychological structure that guarantees women's continuing commitment to marriage and motherhood. It manages to do so, finally, because it also includes a set of very usable instructions which guarantee that *she* will not reject her current partner or hold out for the precise combination of tenderness and power that the heroine discovers in the hero. Because the romance provides its reader with the strategy and ability to reinterpret her own relationship, it insures patriarchal culture against the possibility that she might demand to have both her need for nurturance and adult heterosexual love met by a single individual.

The romance thematizes the activity of interpretation and reinterpretation for a very good reason, then. In suggesting that the cruelty and indifference that the hero exhibits

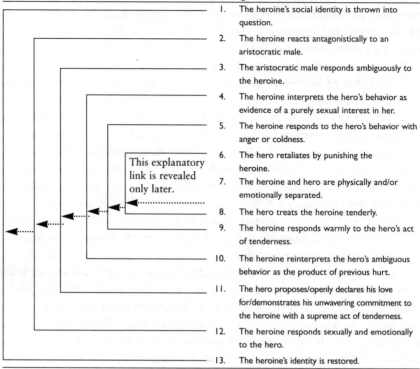

FIGURE 29.1   The narrative logic of the romance

1.	The heroine's social identity is thrown into question.
2.	The heroine reacts antagonistically to an aristocratic male.
3.	The aristocratic male responds ambiguously to the heroine.
4.	The heroine interprets the hero's behavior as evidence of a purely sexual interest in her.
5.	The heroine responds to the hero's behavior with anger or coldness.
6.	The hero retaliates by punishing the heroine.
7.	The heroine and hero are physically and/or emotionally separated.
8.	The hero treats the heroine tenderly.
9.	The heroine responds warmly to the hero's act of tenderness.
10.	The heroine reinterprets the hero's ambiguous behavior as the product of previous hurt.
11.	The hero proposes/openly declares his love for/demonstrates his unwavering commitment to the heroine with a supreme act of tenderness.
12.	The heroine responds sexually and emotionally to the hero.
13.	The heroine's identity is restored.

This explanatory link is revealed only later.

toward the heroine in the early part of the novel are really of no consequence because they *actually* originated in love and affection, the romance effectively asserts that there are other signs for these two emotions than the traditional ones of physical caresses, oral professions of commitment, and thoughtful care. When the heroine retroactively reinterprets the hero's offensive behavior as equivalent expressions of his basic feeling for her, the reader is encouraged to engage in the same rereading process in order to understand properly what she is offered daily in her own relationship. The romance perpetuates the illusion that, like water into wine, brusque indifference can be transformed into unwavering devotion. Its value derives from its offer of a set of procedures that will accomplish the transformation. In learning how to read male behavior from the romance, a woman insulates herself from the need to demand that such behavior change. As Geertz has said of quartets, still lifes, and cockfights, the romance is not merely the analogical representation of a preexisting sensibility but a positive agent in its creation and perpetuation.[6]

As a coda to the argument presented in this chapter that some romance fiction is as much about recovering motherly nurturance and affection as it is about the need to be found desirable by men, I would like to point out that romances vary considerably in the explicitness with which they acknowledge and represent this persistent desire to merge with a wholly attentive, gentle other. Kathleen Woodiwiss, for instance, places heavy emphasis on the nurturing abilities of her heroes but does not concern herself overtly with the heroine/mother relationship. Elisabeth Barr, on the other hand, parallels her love story with another tale about the heroine's efforts to recover her lost identity and her real mother. Despite such internal variation within the genre, however, all popular romantic fiction originates in the failure of patriarchal culture to satisfy its female members. Consequently, the romance functions always as a utopian wish-fulfillment fantasy through which women try to imagine themselves as they often are not in day-to-day existence, that is, as happy and content. Some writers are simply more successful than others at refusing the language of desire and satisfaction offered to them by their culture. A few have managed to retain a semblance of a more independent voice in order to say that it is not hardness, indifference, and emotional cruelty that women want but an exclusive and intense emotional relationship with a tender, life-giving individual. This longing, born of relational poverty, is implicit in all romantic fiction; only occasionally does it manage to forge for itself a language of forms capable of giving it fuller expression.

NOTES

1 Smithton is the pseudonym of the town that provided the location for the study of women readers reported here.
2 N. Chodorow, *The Reproduction of Mothering: Psychoanalysis and the Sociology of Gender* (Berkeley: University of California Press, 1978), pp. 169–70.
3 For an extended discussion of the connection between patriarchy and the sexual division of labour that denies women access to arenas of production in the public sphere, see R. McDonough and R. Harrison, 'Patriarchy and relations of production', in A. Kuhn and A. Wolpe (eds), *Feminism and Materialism: Women and Modes of Production* (London: Routledge and Kegan Paul, 1978), pp. 11–41.
4 C. Geertz, 'Deep play: notes on the Balinese cockfight', in *The Authority of Interpretative Communities*, pp. 412–53 (New York: Basic Books, 1973), p. 449.
5 Ibid.
6 Ibid.

IX

THE MEDIA AUDIENCE

The developments of theory described in the General Introduction have all made their mark on audience research, especially in leading towards a view of the audience experience as variable and negotiable, rather than closely managed by the media industry and predictable in its significance (see Alasuutari, Chapter 30). Nevertheless, certain 'facts' about the audience are both predictable up to a point and also 'knowable' after the event. For the most part, these are the facts that most interest media managers, since they relate to numbers and demographic composition. These are the stuff of the audience constructed as a 'commodity' (Ang, Chapter 31), and the collection and analysis of such facts continues unabated and uninformed by theory, troubled only by the increasing complexity of the measurement task, as channels multiply and 'being in the audience' becomes a more uncertain state. The 'administrative' attitude towards the audience has long been criticized by theorists who connect it with manipulation and exploitation, especially where the goal is not just to reach more people with a 'message' but to deliver (and sell) the time and attention of the audience to advertisers. According to Dallas Smythe (1977), the main product of the media is the audience, and, in effect, audiences for commercial media are working for the advertisers.

The sociological approach to audiences generally adopted the premise that people are not obliged to attend to the mass media and that media use behaviour should thus be open to rational explanation according to the needs, interests and pleasures expected on the part of the audience. These would also be mediated according to more fundamental social and cultural background and circumstances. The resulting theory has generally been described as the 'uses and gratifications' approach, although there are several distinct variants (see Blumler and Katz, 1974). Numerous accounts of audience experience and perceptions of media-related functions and needs have ensued, an example provided here by Celia von Feilitzen's outline of children's use of media (Chapter 33).

Audience reception theory in the cultural studies tradition has played an important part in feminist media theory and research (and vice versa). Numerous studies have been made of the appeal and significance of different media genres, taking account of the 'interpretative community' to which the audience belongs. The work of Janice Radway, whose analysis of romantic fiction is excerpted in Part VIII (Chapter 29), provides an example.

Joli Jensen's (Chapter 32) contribution to this reader reminds us of the potential richness and intensity of the audience experience, which can be more active and participant than is envisaged in the plans of media managers, accounted for in formal analysis of audience interests or as conceived by critics of commodification. 'Fandom' is a special kind of 'audiencehood' that is widely understood but not very well theorized. The work of Liebes and Katz (1990) represents another branch of the interpretative tradition, which demonstrates multiplicity of meanings and explicates some of the ways in which audiences apprehend the representations they encounter in media, whatever their cultural origin. The final excerpt (Neuman, Chapter 34) tackles the now increasingly pressing issue of the future of the mass audience (and thus of mass media) under conditions of changing technology, connecting with some of the matters raised in Part IV.

REFERENCES

Blumler J.G. and Katz, E. (eds) (1974) *The Uses of Mass Communications*. Beverly Hills, CA: Sage.

Liebes, T. and Katz, E. (1990) *The Export of Meaning: Cross-cultural Readings of* Dallas. Oxford: Oxford University Press.

Smythe, Dallas W. (1977) 'Communications: the blind spot of Western Marxism', *Canadian Journal of Political and Social Theory*, 1: 120–7.

30

three phases of reception studies

PERTTI ALASUUTARI

The key idea of this chapter is to argue that a 'third generation' of reception studies and audience ethnography is presently taking shape and will establish itself in the near future. However, the division of the development of reception studies and audience research into three 'generations' outlined in here must not be taken matter-of-factly. Rather, the outline of the suggested division should be seen as a way of pointing out an emergent trend, a direction audience research could take. There are elements in the present research that already lead the way to the new agenda that future research should, in my view, address, but a solid body of research tackling the new field of research is yet to be done. I hope that this chapter can help in addressing the new questions and outline the basic dimensions of the new field.

The role of this chapter is in other words, to act as a midwife: to suggest a 'story line' in cultural media research, a way to read its history in such a way that it points to the emergent trend outlined here. This of course means that the history of the 'three generations' told here is a retrospective view, a history of the present (as Foucault says histories always are) or of an anticipated future. Because media audience and reception research has been a rich and many-faceted field, there would be many other ways to tell its history. Other stories would take up other aspects in the development of the field, and would thus imply different worthwhile future trends. The future is always open, and there will most probably be several future trends in the field. As long as future developments are solutions to problems perceived in past and present research, they will affect history-writing.

The 'three generations' talked about here must be understood metaphorically also in the sense that the tradition of cultural media research is at most a loose 'school' and has throughout the years since its inception incorporated research undertaken in other fields as influential parts of the 'tradition'. In that sense, its histories can only be told retrospectively, from the viewpoint of the present and future rather than the perspective of the motives of the researchers counted as part of that 'tradition'. The influences of James Lull's (1980a, 1980b) and Janice Radway's (1984) studies serve as good examples of this.

To recapitulate, the history of cultural media research told here is not the only possible line of development that could be discerned in the field. However, that does not mean that it is totally unsubstantiated. Instead, I argue that many researchers in the field perceive the history in the way it is outlined here. The 'inscribed audience' trend of media research is taking its shape. To draw an outline of the emergent agenda, of the questions addressed within it, let us first discuss the three phases of cultural media research.

THE FIRST GENERATION: RECEPTION RESEARCH

The birth of reception studies in mass communication research is typically dated back to Stuart Hall's (1974) *Encoding and Decoding in the Television Discourse*, which in its earliest version came out as a 'Stencilled Occasional Paper', No. 7 in the Media Series of the Centre for Contemporary Cultural Studies. What became known as reception research in media studies was from the very beginning associated with

First published in *Rethinking the Media Audience*, P. Alasuutari, Sage Publications (1999), as 'Three Phases of Reception Studies', pp. 1–8.

cultural studies and the Birmingham Centre, although it has later been pointed out that reception theory also has other roots. First, in a sense it carried on and readdressed the themes already raised in what was known as the 'uses and gratifications' paradigm. Second, reception studies in mass communication research was historically preceded and later influenced by German reception theory developed in late 1960s literary criticism.[1]

Despite other roots and influences, Hall's encoding/decoding article laid the foundation for and articulated the problems to be addressed in the 'reception paradigm' of what became known as 'media studies'. Media studies was understood as a branch of the broader intellectual movement called cultural studies. Hall's article really presents a fairly simple model, but it was partly just because of its elegant simplicity that it gained a reputation as a key text.

When compared to earlier communication models (e.g. Gerbner, 1956; Lasswell, 1948; Shannon and Weaver, 1963), Hall's encoding/decoding model is actually not a very radical change. Like the older models, it approaches (mass) communication as a process whereby certain messages are sent and then received with certain effects. For instance, it does not approach television and other mass media in themselves as part of modern society and its structures, and neither does it address the fact that the media are constitutive of or at least affect the communicated events. However, the reception paradigm Hall promoted did involve a shift from a technical to a semiotic approach to messages. A message was no longer understood as some kind of a package or a ball that the sender throws to the receiver. Instead, the idea that a message is encoded by a programme producer and then decoded (and made sense of) by the receivers means that the sent and received messages are not necessarily identical, and different audiences may also decode a programme differently. Hall does not altogether dismiss the assumption that a message may have an effect, but the semiotic framework he introduces means that one moves away from a behaviouristic stimulus–response model to an interpretive framework, where all effects depend on an interpretation of media messages.

> At a certain point [...] the broadcasting structures must yield an encoded message in the form of a meaningful discourse. The institution–societal relations of production must pass into and through the modes of a language for its products to be 'realized'. This initiates a further differentiated moment, in which the formal rules of discourse and language operate. Before this message can have an 'effect' (however defined), or satisfy a 'need' or be put to a 'use', it must first be perceived as a meaningful discourse and meaningfully de-coded. It is this set of de-coded meanings which 'have an effect', influence, entertain, instruct or persuade, with very complex perceptual, cognitive, emotional, ideological or behavioural consequences. (Hall, 1974: 3)

With this linguistic or semiotic turn that Hall proposes, the arguments about effects are effectively swallowed up or at least made dependent upon people's interpretations or thought processes. This turn could have led directly to a kind of radical phenomenology where everything – including, say, the 'structures of production' Hall talks about – is conceived as a social and linguistic construct. Instead of such a big leap, Hall concentrates on applying the semiotic perspective to what he calls the 'determinate moments' of first 'encoding' and then 'decoding'.

> In the moment when the historical event passes under the sign of language, it is subject to all the complex 'rules' by which language signifies. To put it paradoxically, the event must become a 'story' before it can become a *communicative event*. In that moment, the formal sub-rules of language are 'in dominance', without, of course, subordinating out of existence the historical event so signified, or the historical consequences of the event having been signified in this way. (Hall, 1974: 2)

Questions about the role of language and signification are a can of worms in social sciences. Keeping the can firmly closed leads to a mechanistic and simplistic understanding of social phenomena, but once you open it there is the danger that the worms will eat the whole theoretical structure and notion of society. Hall's solution to just peek into the can is clever: he is able to take the role of rhetoric into account to some extent, but otherwise – for instance as far as his notion of social structures is concerned – he sticks to a realistic conception of language.

However, this solution led to an obsession with 'determinate moments', especially the moment of 'decoding', in reception research. From the perspective of the encoding/decoding model it appears that the ideological effects of programming are dependent on the particular strategic moment when the encoded media message enters the brain of an individual viewer.

Hall (1974) suggests that there are four 'ideal-type' positions from which decodings of mass communication by the audience can be made: within the *dominant or hegemonic code* the connotative level of the messages is decoded in terms of the dominant of preferred meanings; the *professional code* is what the professional broadcasters employ when transmitting a message that has already been signified in a hegemonic manner; the *negotiated code* contains a mixture of adaptive and oppositional elements; and finally the *oppositional code* is the position where a viewer perfectly understands both the literal and connotative inflection given to an event, but determines to decode the message 'in a globally contrary way'.

The encoding/decoding model suggested by Hall created a series of empirical studies about the reception of television programmes by different audiences, the first one of which was David Morley's *The Nationwide Audience* (1980).[2] By selecting different groups of people and showing them the *Nationwide* public affairs television programme, Morley could more or less confirm and develop Hall's idea about the four codes discussed above. For instance, the art students whose reception of the programme Morley studied more or less represented the 'professional code'. An innovative, schematic theory had led to the beginning of an empirical project to be carried on by an enthusiastic group of new researchers.

THE SECOND GENERATION: AUDIENCE ETHNOGRAPHY

Morley's seminal study was soon followed by studies about the reception of, especially, romantic serials (Ang, 1985; Hobson, 1982; Katz and Liebes, 1984; Liebes, 1984; Liebes and Katz, 1990). What became known as qualitative audience reception studies meant that one analyses a programme and studies its reception among a particular audience by conducting 'in-depth' interviews of its viewers. However, along with an increasing number of empirical reception studies, there occurred a series of gradual shifts in the whole reception paradigm, so that we could say that a new *audience ethnography* paradigm was created.

First, there was a move away from an interest in conventional politics to identity politics, particularly to questions about gender. This can be seen, for instance, in the fact that a slackening interest in the reception of public affairs programmes was balanced out by a growing interest in fictional programmes, particularly romantic serials. These studies concentrated on the politics of gender, on the discourses within which gender is dealt with in the programmes, and how women viewers interpret and make use of the offered readings against the background of their everyday life and experiences. Feminist scholarship especially has had an important role here in breaking new ground and addressing new questions in reception research.

Second, at the expense of a diminishing interest in programme contents, much more emphasis was laid on the functions of the medium, as is the case with, for instance, James Lull's (1980a, 1980b) analyses of the social uses of television or David Morley's *Family Television* (1986). The growing interest in the functions of television in the family could be seen partly as a rebirth of the older American uses and gratifications paradigm. However, unlike the old paradigm, in the new audience ethnography one focuses on television as a social resource for conversation or on the way in which television use reflects and reproduces (gendered) relations of power in family life. A large project about the role of information and communication technologies in the home also reflected the increased interest in the social uses of television and other media (Silverstone, 1991; Silverstone et al., 1991).

Third, even when the studies of this second generation dealt with a particular programme or serial, researchers started to look at reception from the audience's end of the chain. One does not try to explain a reception of a programme by probing into an 'interpretive community' (Fish, 1979). Instead, one studies the everyday life of a group, and relates the use of (a reception of) a programme or a medium to it. One studies the role of the media in everyday life, not the impact (or meaning) of everyday life on the reception of a programme (e.g. Gray, 1992; Hermes, 1995).

People representing the second generation of reception studies like to emphasize that they are doing or that one should do proper ethnographic case studies of 'interpretive communities'. One even talks about an 'ethnographic turn' quite comparable to the previous 'linguistic turn'. Like classic anthropologists such as Malinowski (1922/1961), it has been argued that a proper ethnographic study in audience ethnography entails at least several months' stay in the 'field' (Drotner, 1992) – a demand which, strangely enough, is presented at a time when anthropologists and qualitative sociologists are increasingly questioning the whole notion of a 'field' (Gupta and Ferguson, 1997). On the other hand, what is called an 'ethnographic study' often simply amounts to qualitative 'in-depth' interviews of a group of people, which is of course quite understandable as one bears in mind that most television or video viewing takes place in very small and private settings. There are restrictions to an ethnographer's possibilities of doing a long-term participant observation study in a home.

THE THIRD GENERATION: A CONSTRUCTIONIST VIEW

The starting point for the new agenda of cultural audience studies could be dated back to the late 1980s, when a number of writers began to question and discuss the premises of audience ethnography (Allor, 1988; Ang, 1989, 1990; Fiske, 1988, 1990; Grossberg, 1988; Lull, 1988; Radway, 1988). For instance, Allor (1988), Grossberg (1988) and Radway (1988) emphasized that there isn't really such a thing as the 'audience' out there; one must bear in mind that audience is, most of all, a discursive construct produced by a particular analytic gaze. As Grossberg puts it, 'media audiences are shifting constellations, located within varying multiple discourses which are never entirely outside of the media discourse themselves' (1988: 386). Radway (1988) emphasized that, instead of one particular circuit of producer, text and audience, people's daily lives must be the point of departure and object of research. Traditional ethnography was heavily criticized. On the other hand, other researchers, such as Lull (1988), were concerned with a development whereby some cultural studies theorists were enthusiastic about the impossibility of doing empirical work, although (or because) they had never even tried it.

We must not, however, conceive of the third generation as a clear-cut paradigm with a definite time of birth, let alone a list of studies or researchers representing it. It is an emergent trend, evident not only in the critical discussion outlined above but also in the 'discussion' parts of many 'second generation' studies, where researchers place their study in a larger framework.

This wave of critique and self-reflection meant a thorough rethinking of the place of the media in everyday life, the concept of 'audience' and, along with that, the place of media research itself in the whole picture. As a consequence, a new agenda or third generation of cultural audience studies emerged, although many of its implications are still to be spelled out.

The third generation entails a broadened frame within which one conceives of the media and media use. One does not necessarily abandon ethnographic case studies of audiences or analyses of individual programmes, but the main focus is not restricted to finding out about the reception or 'reading' of a programme by a particular audience. Rather, the objective is to get a grasp of our contemporary 'media culture', particularly as it can be seen in the role of the media in everyday life, both as a topic and as an activity structured by and structuring the discourses within which it is discussed. One is interested in the discourses within which we conceive of our roles as the public and the audience, and how notions of programmes-with-an-audience or messages-with-an-audience are inscribed in both media messages and assessments about news events and about what is going on in the 'world'. The third generation resumes an interest in programmes and programming, but not as texts studied in isolation from their usage as an element of everyday life. Furthermore, it adds a neglected layer of reflexivity to the research on the 'reception' of media messages by addressing the audience's notions of themselves as the 'audience'.

The second generation of reception studies involved a move away from the media to 'interpretive communities' of the everyday, even to the extent that, for instance, Jensen argued that 'the central object of analysis of mass communication research lies outside the media, in the cultures and communities of which media and audiences are constituents' (1990: 14). As Schrøder puts it, 'this development towards ethnography and the everyday is now threatening to write the media, as the focus of research, out of existence' (1994: 338). The third generation brings the media back to media studies, but conceives of the media and media messages in a broader sense than just as an encoded text to then be decoded by a particular 'interpretive community'. A study may start out from such a research design, but the big picture one wants to shed light on, or the big question to pursue, is the cultural place of the media in the contemporary world. It may entail questions about the meaning and use of particular programmes to particular groups of people, but it also includes questions about the frames within which we conceive of the media and their contents as reality and as representations – or distortions – of reality. And how are these frames or discourses about the programmes and about viewing and audiences inscribed in the programmes themselves? What are the cultural concerns that surround media use and media messages? This big research programme also includes questioning the role of media research itself. How are these concerns inscribed in the theoretical models of mass communication research? What is the place of expert knowledge produced by media researchers in enhancing or quieting down public concerns, and in reproducing or transforming the frames within which the media and 'audiencing' (that is, being in the position of the audience, see Fiske [1993]) are perceived?

This does not mean that everything should be attempted in any single study. Neither does it imply that we should return to a macro-level investigation of the function of the media, and forget about 'audience ethnographies'. Rather, in a way the new agenda of audience research reclaims the meaning of ethnography. Among anthropologists ethnography means something like 'social and cultural analysis in a particular setting, based on extensive first-hand research'. Ethnography and 'fieldwork' vary considerably from researcher to researcher, and they also depend on the society being studied, but they often include the gamut from surveys and interviews to naturalistic observations. During recent years anthropologists themselves have begun to question the meaning of 'field' and fieldwork in what is now often called our 'postmodern' world. Traditionally even anthropologists studying highly developed and urbanized societies have selected a remote rural community, typically a village, to do their fieldwork, but urban and multiple-method ethnography is becoming much more common. And even if anthropologists have selected a particular community as an empirical starting point, they have made use of all the data and statistics available about a country and cultural area they are trying to get a grasp of. Anthropologists are increasingly aware of the difficulties in defining the Other, the object of research. How does an anthropologist, for instance, relate to 'native' social researchers: should the anthropologist assume that he or she can outwit the native informant simply because of an outsider's view, weighed against the native's years and years of 'participant observation' and a lifelong 'field experience'? Or how should an emigrant who has returned to study his country of origin conceive of the 'native' or 'Other' in himself, as John Stewart (1989) questions in his study? Or does an American show on local television represent the 'Other' or a 'foreign' element in the everyday life of a people?

As social researchers studying our own culture and society we are quite comparable to anthropologists studying 'other' cultures. Compared with anthropologists, who often have a cultural distance that enables them to see the forest for the trees, we have the disadvantage of being insiders. That is why we have to work hard, develop theoretical perspectives and methods that will better enable us to take distance, to see the bigger picture and ourselves in it too. On the other hand, we have the advantage of a very long, personal field experience. We know a lot about the culture, and we possess what Clifford Geertz (1983) calls 'local knowledge': we master in practice many of the rules and discourses we are trying to make our objects of reflection and questioning. In light of our abundant field experience, it is ridiculous to think of a media ethnography in terms of so-and-so many months of participant observation: 'fieldwork' has actually started years before we knew anything about a particular site we are going to study. Similarly, the duration of participant observation or any active part of data gathering depends on the particular study in mind.

NOTES

1   More precisely, that paradigm can be dated back to 1969, when Hans Robert Jauss published his essay 'Paradigmawechsel in der Literaturwissenschaft'. In that essay, Jauss himself characterizes the ideas he presents as a paradigm shift in literary criticism, and he was not mistaken in that. Instead of studying authors' biographies, German literary critics began to study the social conditions accounting for the reception of a work (Holub, 1984).
2   It was the second part of a research project which started with Brunsdon and Morley's (1978) analysis of the *Nationwide* programme itself.

REFERENCES

Allor, M. (1988) 'Relocating the site of the audience', *Critical Studies in Mass Communication*, 5: 217–33.

Ang, I. (1985) *Watching Dallas: Soap Opera and the Melodramatic Imagination*. London: Methuen.

Ang, I. (1989) 'Beyond self-reflexivity', *Journal of Communication Inquiry*, 13 (2): 27–9.

Ang, I. (1990) 'Culture and communication: towards an ethnography of media consumption', *European Journal of Communication*, 5, 239–60.

Brunsdon, C. and Morley, D. (1978) *Everyday Television: 'Nationwide'*. London: British Film Institute.

Drotner, K. (1992) 'What is "the everyday" in media ethnography?' Paper presented to the Mass Media and the Ethnography of Everyday Life seminar, Holbaek, Denmark, November.

Fish, S. (1979) *Is there a Text in this Class? The Authority of Interpretive Communities*. Cambridge, MA: Harvard University Press.

Fiske, J. (1988) 'Meaningful moments', *Critical Studies in Mass Communication*, 5: 246–51.

Fiske, J. (1990) 'Ethnosemiotics: some personal and theoretical reflections', *Cultural Studies*, 4 (1): 85–99.

Fiske, J. (1993) 'Audiencing: cultural practice and cultural studies', in Norman Denzin (ed.), *Handbook of Qualitative Research*. Thousand Oaks, CA: Sage. pp. 189–98.

Geertz, C. (1983) *Local Knowledge: Further Essays in Interpretive Anthropology*. New York: Basic Books.

Gerbner, G. (1956) 'Towards a general model of communication', *Audio Visual Communication Review*, 4 (3): 171–99.

Gray, A. (1992) *Video Playtime: The Gendering of a Leisure Technology*. London: Routledge.

Grossberg, L. (1988) 'Wandering audiences, nomadic critics', *Cultural Studies*, 2 (3): 377–92.

Gupta, A. and Ferguson, J. (eds) (1997) *Anthropological Locations: Boundaries and Grounds of a Field Science*. Berkeley: University of California Press.

Hall, S. (1974) *Encoding and Decoding in the Television Discourse*. Centre for Contemporary Cultural Studies, Stencilled Occasional Paper No. 7. Birmingham: University of Birmingham.

Hermes, J. (1995) *Reading Women's Magazines: An Analysis of Everyday Media Use*. Cambridge: Polity Press.

Hobson, D. (1982) Crossroads: *The Drama of a Soap Opera*. London: Methuen.

Hulub, R. (1984) Reception Theory: A Critical Introduction. London: Methuen.

Jauss, H. (1969) 'Paradigmawechsel in der Literaturwissenschaft', *Linguistische Berichte* 3: 44–56.

Jensen, K.B. (1990) 'Television futures: a social action methodology for studying interpretive communities', *Critical Studies in Mass Communication*, 7 (2): 1–18.

Katz, E. and Liebes, T. (1984) 'Once upon a time, in *Dallas*', *Intermedia*, 12: 28–32.

Lasswell, H.D. (1948) 'The structure and function of communication in society', in L. Bryson (ed.), *The Communication of Ideas*. New York: Institute for Religious and Social Studies. pp. 243–78.

Liebes, T. (1984) 'Ethnocriticism: Israelis of Moroccan ethnicity negotiate the meaning of *Dallas*', *Studies in Visual Communication*, 10 (3): 46–72.

Liebes, T. and Katz, E. (1990) *The Export of Meaning: Cross-Cultural Readings of* Dallas. New York: Oxford University Press.

Lull, J. (1980a) 'The social uses of television', *Human Communication Research*, 6: 197–209.

Lull, J. (1980b) 'Family communication patterns and the social uses of television', *Communication Research*, 7 (3): 319–34.

Lull, J. (1988) 'The audience as nuisance', *Critical Studies in Mass Communication*, 5: 239–42.

Malinowski, B. (1922/1961) *Argonauts of the Western Pacific*. New York: E.P. Dutton.

Morley, D. (1980) *The Nationwide Audience*. London: British Film Institute.

Morley, D. (1986) *Family Television: Cultural Power and Domestic Leisure*. London: Comedia.

Radway, J.A. (1984) *Reading the Romance: Women, Patriarchy, and Popular Literature*. Chapel Hill: University of North Carolina Press.

Radway, J.A. (1988) 'Reception study: ethnography and the problems of dispersed audiences and nomadic subjects', *Cultural Studies*, 2 (3): 359–76.

Schrøder, K.C. (1994) 'Audience semiotics, interpretive communities and the "ethnographic turn" in media research', *Media, Culture & Society*, 16: 337–47.

Shannon, C.E. and Weaver, W. (1963) *The Mathematical Theory of Communication*. Urbana: University of Illinois Press.

Silverstone, R. (1991) 'From audiences to consumers: the household and the consumption of communication and information technologies', *European Journal of Communication*, 6: 135–54.

Silverstone, R., Hirsch, E. and Morley, D. (1991) 'Listening to a long conversation: an ethnographic approach to the study of information and communication technologies in the home', *Cultural Studies*, 5 (2): 204–27.

Stewart, J.O. (1989) *Drinkers, Drummers, and Decent Folk: Ethnographic Narratives of Village Trinidad*. New York: State University of New York Press.

31

streamlining 'television audience'

IEN ANG

Ratings discourse's object of knowledge, 'television audience', is not the transparent representation of pregiven actual audiences. In and through the descriptions made by ratings discourse a certain profile of 'television audience' takes shape – a profile that does not exist outside or beyond those descriptions but is produced by them. In this sense, 'television audience', as it is constructed in ratings discourse, is a fictive entity. This does not mean, of course, that ratings dream the audience into existence. They are based on actual data on how many and who are watching what. The knowledge produced by ratings is therefore neither false nor untrue. On the contrary, ratings are powerful precisely because of their ability to define a certain field of empirical truth. That regime of truth is fictive, however, because the very terms with which it covers empirical reality inevitably result in a description of the audience that foregrounds certain characteristics but suppresses others. The category of 'television audience' as such already implies a highly selective delineation of the real, and the very fact that we tend to regard 'television audience' as a taxonomic collective having a definite and defineable size and composition is a 'reality effect' of ratings discourse (Hall, 1982).

For one thing, to perceive the audience as something that *can* be measured is already a rather peculiar move. It is an assumption originating in the general idea of the 'measurability of markets' quintessential to the parameters of marketing thought as it began to be developed in the early 1920s (Beniger, 1986). The emphasis on size leads to a representation of the audience as a calculable entity, a taxonomic collective consisting of the sum of individual, serialized units, defined as households or persons. The attention given to demographic composition of the audience does not alter this in any essential sense: it only breaks down the total audience into separate slices of audience that are, each of them, in turn imagined as countable entities (often called segments). The units of those entities only matter insofar as they can be added up: in the imagination of ratings discourse, all households of the total audience are, by projection, principally the same; all people belonging to one demographic segment basically equivalent and equal. In other words, in ratings discourse the individual units of the audience, the 'audience members', are ultimately devoid of personal identity and history, of idiosyncratic subjectivity.

But 'television audience' as constructed by ratings discourse is not only characterized by objective, thing-like figures such as size and composition. A subjective, human dimension is inevitably comprised in it, simply because ratings are assumed to measure something done by human beings. Awareness of this subjective dimension can be found in a certain ambivalence within everyday industry language: although the role of the audience in the institutional set-up of the television industry is structurally that of commodified object, it is often spoken about as if it were a huge, living subject. Industry people are often heard saying things like, 'the audience wants comedy', 'the audience won't understand this show', or 'they don't like soap ads'. Such attribution of preference or competence invests the concept of 'television audience' with human qualities, although strictly speaking 'television audience', being a category that owes its existence to its position as 'passive' target of corporate practices, cannot want or understand something. Only people, invested with subjectivity, can. The 'slip of the tongue' is not meaningless. It indicates

First published in Desperately Seeking the Audience, I. Ang, Routledge (1991), as 'Streamlining television audience', pp. 60–67.

that however object-ified 'television audience' as a categorical entity is, its construction is related to the subjective moment of actual people watching television.

The notion that the television audience is a taxonomic collective in which viewers are aggregated undergirds ratings discourse. This notion brings together the idea of the whole (television audience) and that of separate units (audience members) which make up that whole. Thus, 'television audience' as constructed in audience measurement is an object that is made up of subjects. This leads to a fundamental instability of the category. As an object made up of subjects, 'television audience' is not a static, stone-like object whose characteristics can be described once and for all, but is a continually changing, dynamic object that always seems to elude definitive description. The fact that the production of ratings is an ongoing, never-ending practice testifies to this slipperiness: even the most factual, objective characteristics of 'television audience', its size and its composition, cannot be assumed constant, and have to be re-established again and again, day after day. Ratings are very fleeting products: they become obsolete almost instantly.

As has been remarked before, individuals watching television (gathered in households) are taken to be the basic units of audience measurement data. But individuals are concrete social subjects and because they are situated in concrete everyday contexts and circumstances, the way they watch television will be subjective too, formed by and associated with those concrete contexts and circumstances. However, taking this into account would make the production of ratings, which seeks to arrive at a generalized construct of 'television audience', utterly unmanageable. Therefore audience measurement, as is the general rule in quantifying social science, tends to abstract from the detailed singularities in experience and practice. In other words, in order to construct an object-ive 'television audience', it has to mould the subject-ive into wieldy, measurable forms. As a result, the subjective practices and experiences of actual audiences are objectified in audience measurement in the easily identifiable and verifiable concept of 'viewing behaviour'.

Behaviourism marks the convenient marriage between the objective and the subjective in ratings discourse: individual television viewers are typically 'captured' and measured in ratings discourse in terms of their externally observable behaviour, excluding more intractable subjective dimensions such as the psychical (e.g. viewers' internal, mental states or orientations), or the cultural (e.g. the specific social uses people make of television in various contexts, or the various ways in which viewers interpret television material). In short, the subjective is 'domesticated' and 'purified' in ratings discourse by breaking it down to measurable behavioural variables.

The technologies of audience measurement testify to this tendency toward reductionist behaviourism. For example, the electronic setmeter can register nothing more than whether the set is on or off. In this case, viewing behaviour is defined as a simple, one-dimensional and purely mechanical act. As Gitlin (1983: 54) has rightly remarked, 'the numbers only sample sets tuned in, not necessarily shows watched, let alone grasped, remembered, loved, learned from, deeply anticipated, or mildly tolerated'. Thus, what audience measurement tends to erase from its field of discernment is any specific consideration of the meanings, saliences or impacts of television for people, the 'lived reality behind the ratings' (Jensen, 1987: 25). In standard ratings discourse watching television is reduced to the observable behaviour of having the TV set on: it is done by subjects but is devoid of subjective dimensions. Human subjects here are thus merely relevant for their bodies: strictly speaking, they appear in the logic of ratings discourse only in so far as they are agents of the physical act of tuning-in. As a result, the problem for the industry facing the subjectivity of viewers is funneled into one simple but obsessive question: how do we get them tuned in?

It would make no sense to simply condemn this lack of sensitivity for the subjective dimension of viewer practices in audience measurement. Nor is it to the point to criticize it for its faulty epistemology, in terms of a lack of conceptual validity or methodological adequacy. After all, audience measurement is not social science, but social technology: its purpose is the systematic accumulation of strategic knowledge. Knowledge about the audience is only interesting for the industry when it is useful for their commercial purposes, and too much awareness about the heterogeneous and contradictory responses of actual audiences to television is just not practical for the industry. Industry people need a kind of knowledge that allows them to act, not paralyze them – a convenient kind of knowledge that enables the industry to concoct its relation to the audience in a simple, clear-cut, and manageable way. Ratings discourse offers this knowledge because it puts together a streamlined map of 'television audience'.

The streamlined audience is a 'disciplined' audience. It is constructed by ratings discourse through a smoothening out of problematic subjectivity and translating it into ordered and regular instances of viewing behaviour. This is achieved through the quantifying perspective of audience measurement, which inevitably leads to emphasizing averages, regularities and generalizable patterns rather than idiosyncracies and surprising exceptions (cf. Anderson, 1987). As a result, a streamlined profile of 'television audience' comes into being that reduces the individual viewer to a 'typical' audience member who can be objectively classified. In the discursive map of the streamlined audience, each viewer can ideally be assigned an exact place in a comprehensive table of knowledge, formed by the central axes of size and demographic composition on the one hand, and the variables of 'viewing behaviour' on the other hand.

This procedure of streamlining can be clarified by having a closer look at the logic of demographics. The matching of factors such as age, sex, race, income, occupation, education and area of residence with viewing behaviour variables (e.g. amount of viewing and programme choice) results in the statistical determination of relatively stable 'viewing habits' – a set of imputed behavioural routines that form a perfect merger of the objective and the subjective. Thus, in an article aptly entitled 'The World According to Nielsen', it is observed that '[V]iewing may vary by age, sex, region, and income, but within those categories the vast TV audience has surprisingly predictable habits' (Traub, 1985: 26). This, then, is the streamlined audience: an objectified category in which the stable is foregrounded over the erratic, the likely over the extraordinary, the consistent over the inconsistent. Through demographics 'television audience' is streamlined by neatly slicing it up in substantive 'segments', each of which consists of presumably well-organized, serialized viewers displaying dependable viewing behaviour. Sometimes, typical characteristics are assigned to each segment which conjure up nicely contained subjectivities, formalized in so-called 'psychographics'. For example, in 'The World According to Nielsen' the viewing habits of a typical member of the 'Men 55+' category, 'George', are described:

> Over the years George's tastes have grown oddly similar to Ruth's [his wife]. He still likes sports (though now he prefers golf to football), but he can no longer watch without flinching those death 'n destruction shows like *A Team*. ... Nowadays he sits around with Ruth to watch the likes of *Dallas*. ... Perhaps he's surrendering his own fantasies for his wife's. (Traub, 1985: 71)

In this portrait, 'George' is a type, an exemplar of 'later-middle-aged, married men', not a personalized, situated individual. In such psychographic profiles ratings data are combined with projections about the category's typical 'life style', as a result of which it is possible to 'freeze' the viewing practices of later-middle-aged, married men into some fixed habits, even comprising some peculiar psychological and behavioural inclinations. As Traub sums up, 'older men are in the living room more, but they get tired early'.

Of course, users of demographic and psychographic information know perfectly well that such descriptions are generalizations and that all statistical generalizations are conditional, but the patterns emerging from that information still enable broadcasters and advertisers to develop simple practical truths, such as that women 18 to 49 (one of the most desirable demographic segments for advertisers) are more changeable than over-50 viewers and thus more easily introduced to new programmes, that women aged 18 to 35 are in their early married years and like to try out all kinds of new products and make major purchasing decisions on home furnishings and appliances, and so on (Tyler Eastman et al., 1981). Such profiles provide an extreme example of what streamlining the audience amounts to: in the end, it conjures up the utopia of a neatly ordered world inhabited by perfectly predictable people.

Again, the streamlined audience is not a false representation of people's concrete ways of relating to television, but rather a certain structuring mould imposed upon the multifaceted activities of television viewers. As a result, whatever contingent routines actual audiences create in their everyday engagements with television cannot be expected to coincide with the predictable 'viewing habits' invented by audience measurement. The latter are conceivable only because ratings discourse describes individual viewers, and the differences between and among them, exclusively in terms of a small number of generalized and standardized viewing behaviour variables. All other bases of identity and difference are considered irrelevant and are therefore deliberately ignored.

Streamlining, then, is a discursive procedure that results in the construction of a representation of 'television audience' consisting of a finite and limited set of parameters. This mapping of the virtual 'audience field' leads to the establishment of a more or less comprehensive classificatory system over which all viewers (as projected from the sample) can be distributed and arranged. However, this cannot be known once and for all: the mapping has to be repeated every day because it is not certain how viewers will actually respond to the television programmes that are intended to attract them. That is, every day the viewing behaviour of each viewer (or his or her representative in the sample) needs to be regauged: this is the one element that ratings discourse cannot determine in advance, but must confirm and reconfirm empirically. After all, it is the relative success or failure of the broadcasters' efforts to attract audiences that is the ultimate rationale for audience measurement. What the streamlining procedure does, in fact, is the calculating of that success or failure (i.e. of 'audience response') in compliance with a prefabricated formal structure. As a result, all too big surprises are not likely to occur: uncertainty about audience response is reduced to uncertainty about the number of viewers in each parcel of the map. Empirically-found variations within the streamlined audience are conveniently contained in 'types' and 'patterns'; developments over time are straightened out in terms of 'trends'. This is the core productivity of the streamlining procedure: it purifies, through a kind of filtering process, people's concrete viewing activities by representing them in a smooth, totalized but adaptable map.

The map of the streamlined audience then is characterized by variation in regularity, regularity in variation – stable enough to guarantee continuity, malleable enough to allow for responsiveness to temporal fluctuations. The map is very handy indeed for the industry: it supplies both broadcasters and advertisers with neatly arranged and easily manageable information, a form of knowledge that almost cannot fail to provide a sense of provisional certainty, as maps generally do. For example, the ranking of programmes according to their ratings performance constitutes a weekly flow chart which is used as a reliable and agreed-upon indicator of 'popularity', and thus of the value of the audience commodity.

But such discursively constructed 'facts' are not only indispensable guidelines for both broadcasters and advertisers in their economic negotiations; they are also made to serve as cultural clues for the networks to develop and commission new programmes. This use of ratings is made possible by the construction of the 'hit show' for instance. It is a peculiar oddity indeed that while the networks know perfectly well, thanks to ratings discourse, which programmes have been 'successful', they do not know why they have been and which new ones will be. There is no way to foretell the ratings performance of a new programme. Therefore, the use of past 'successes' in the constant search for future ones remains a gamble. As one network programmer, Donald Grant of CBS, has said: 'When I originally picked out *Dallas*, I didn't know it was going to be a hit – it was only after it was on that it sparked *Knot's Landing* and *Dynasty*. Hits create trends, not the other way around' (Wilner, 1987: 44). Even so, although ratings and demographics are estimates about audience size and composition for a past situation, the regularities highlighted by ratings discourse allow the industry to take decisions that do affect the future. These regularities furnish a sense of predictability and, as a consequence, the (imagined) power to anticipate and act upon it, in an attempt to bring the variable element in the streamlined audience under control.

The impact of this power to anticipate is reflected in the iron repetitiveness that characterizes television scheduling and programming on American network television. A programme that proves to be a ratings winner is likely to set the tone for a whole number of other programmes, either in the form of spin-offs or of copies. As a consequence, a kind of streamlining of television programming itself is achieved, a form of what Gitlin (1983) has called 'recombinant culture'. The construction of the streamlined audience then goes hand in hand with the streamlining of television's output: the categorization and structuring of programmes in terms of formulaic genres, the segmentation of time in regular units, the placing of programmes in fixed time slots, and their sequencing into a smooth flow – these are all strategies developed by the networks to match the streamlined audience with an equally streamlined television 'supertext' (Browne, 1984).

The idea of 'prime time', for example, is essentially a construct of the regularity that was found in the fluctuations of audience size evening after evening: continuous audience measurement has demonstrated that as a rule it is between 8.00 p.m. and 11.00 p.m. that the number of households having their television sets on is the largest. Now the concept of prime time has acquired an entrenched, institutionalized status within the industry: programming and scheduling are geared to it; advertising rates are determined accordingly.

To sum up, we can conclude that audience measurement's discursive object-ification of 'television audience' necessarily involves the serialization of television viewers as 'audience members'. But actual television viewers are always more than just audience members; their identities as television viewers are more complex than their being part of the audience. In other words, when people watch television they of course inevitably occupy the position of audience members, but they also simul-taneously inhabit a myriad of other subject positions such as parent, critic, fan, democrat, cook or whatever – culturally specific subject positions whose inter-dependent meanings elude the symbolic world constructed by ratings discourse. As a consequence, ratings discourse, and the audience facts mapped by it, always inevitably stand in a strained relationship with what actual audiences are up to. The mould never quite fits, as it were.

By itself, however, this epistemological gap between the map of the streamlined audience and the world of actual audiences does not constitute a problem for the industry. As long as the map works, the industry will not bother to look for more 'real-istic' maps. In other words, the concrete practices and experiences of actual audiences are irrelevant for the industry so long as the information delivered by audience mea-surement is uncontested and perceived to be adequate. Therefore, the gap will only be problematized when the streamlining process tends to slacken; that is, when it no longer seems possible to establish fixed viewing habits, unambiguous behavioural variables, and so on, by which viewers can be unproblematically typified and classified. At such moments, the existing streamlining procedures themselves will be questioned, and a lack of validity or reliability in the ratings services will be perceived in industry circles. Suddenly, elements of the subjective world of actual audiences do matter and help to disturb the consensus over the existing map of the streamlined audience. Then, a reconstruction of the streamlining process is called for in order to come to a new, more satisfying map: a struggle over the very question of how to streamline the audience will be fought out. Then, audience measurement is in crisis. In fact, such a crisis has been unfolding in the American television industry throughout the 1980s.

REFERENCES

Anderson, J.A. (1987) *Communication Research: Issues and Methods*. New York: McGraw-Hill.
Beniger, J.R. (1986) *The Control Revolution*. Cambridge, MA: Harvard University Press.
Browne, N. (1984) 'The political economy of the television (super) text', *Quarterly Review of Film Studies*, 9 (3): 174–82.

Gitlin, T. (1978) 'Media sociology: the dominant paradigm', *Theory and Society*, 6 (2): 205–53.

Gitlin, T. (1983) *Inside Prime Time*. New York: Pantheon.

Hall, S. (1982) 'The rediscovery of "ideology": return of the oppressed in media studies', in M. Gurevitch, T. Bennett, J. Curran and J. Woollacott (eds), *Culture, Society and the Media*. London: Methuen. pp. 56–90.

Jensen, K.B. (1987) 'Qualitative audience research: towards an integrative approach to reception', *Critical Studies in Mass Communication*, 4 (1): 21–36.

Traub, J. (1985) 'The world according to Nielsen', *Channels of Communication*, January/February.

Tyler Eastman, S., Head, S.W. and Klein, L. (1981) *Broadcast Programming: Strategies for Winning Television and Radio Audiences*. Belmont, CA: Wadsworth Publishing.

Wilner, P. (1987) 'Are new forces imposing changes in web TV strategy?', *Television/Radio Age*, 27 April.

32

fandom as pathology: the consequences of characterization

JOLI JENSEN

The literature on fandom is haunted by images of deviance. The fan is consistently characterized (referencing the term's origins) as a potential fanatic. This means that fandom is seen as excessive, bordering on deranged, behavior. This essay explores how and why the concept of fan involves images of social and psychological pathology.

In the following pages I describe two fan types – the obsessed individual and the hysterical crowd. I show how these types appear in popular as well as scholarly accounts of fans and fandom. I consider why these two particular characterizations predominate – what explains this tendency to define fans as, at least potentially, obsessed and/or hysterical fanatics?

I suggest here that these two images of fans are based in an implicit critique of modern life. Fandom is seen as a psychological symptom of a presumed social dysfunction; the two fan types are based in an unacknowledged critique of modernity. Once fans are characterized as deviant, they can be treated as disreputable, even dangerous 'others.'

Fans, when insistently characterized as 'them,' can be distinguished from 'people like us' (students, professors and social critics) as well as from (the more reputable) patrons or aficionados or collectors. But these respectable social types could also be defined as 'fans' in that they display interest, affection and attachment, especially for figures in, or aspects of, their chosen field.

But the habits and practices of, say, scholars and critics are not deemed fandom, and are not considered to be potentially deviant or dangerous. Why? My conclusion claims that the characterization of fandom as pathology is based in, supports, and justifies elitist and disrespectful beliefs about our common life.

CHARACTERIZING THE FAN

The literature on fandom as a social and cultural phenomenon is relatively sparse. What has been written is usually in relationship to discussions of celebrity or fame. The fan is understood to be, at least implicitly, a result of celebrity – the fan is defined as a *response* to the star system. This means that passivity is ascribed to the fan – he or she is seen as being brought into (enthralled) existence by the modern celebrity system, via the mass media.

This linking of fandom, celebrity and the mass media is an unexamined constant in commentary on fandom. In a *People Weekly* article on the killing of TV actress Rebecca Schaeffer by an obsessive fan, a psychologist is quoted as saying:

> The cult of celebrity provides archetypes and icons with which alienated souls can identify. On top of that, this country has been embarking for a long time on a field experiment in the use of violence on TV. It is commonplace to watch people getting blown away. We've given the losers in life or sex a rare chance to express their dominance.[1]

First published in *The Adoring Audience*, Lisa A. Lewis, Routledge (1992), as 'Fandom as Pathology: the consequences of characterization', pp. 9–23.

In one brief statement, cults, alienation, violence, TV, losers and domination (themes that consistently recur in the fandom literature) are invoked. A security guard, also quoted in the article, blames media influence for fan obsessions: 'It's because of the emphasis on the personal lives of media figures, especially on television. And this has blurred the line between appropriate and inappropriate behavior.'[2]

In newspaper accounts, mental health experts offer descriptions of psychic dysfunctions like 'erotomania' and 'Othello's Syndrome,' and suggest that the increase in fan attacks on celebrities may be due to 'an increasingly narcissistic society or maybe the fantasy life we see on television.'[3]

This same blending of fandom, celebrity and presumed media influence in relation to pathological behavior can be found in more scholarly accounts. Caughey describes how, in a media addicted age, celebrities function as role models for fans who engage in 'artificial social relations' with them. He discusses fans who pattern their lives after fantasy celebrity figures, and describes at some length an adolescent girl, 'A,' who in 1947 shot Chicago Cubs first baseman Eddie Waitkus. He argues that her behavior cannot simply be dismissed as pathological, because up to a point her fan activity resembled that of other passionate fans. The model of fandom Caughey develops is one in which pathological fandom is simply a more intense, developed version of more common, less dangerous, fan passion.[4]

This is also Schickel's explicit claim. He ends his book on the culture of celebrity by comparing deranged fans and serial killers to 'us.' He concludes that we 'dare not turn too quickly away' from 'these creatures' who lead 'mad existences' because 'the forces that move them also move within ourselves in some much milder measure.'[5] These academically-oriented accounts develop an image of the pathological fan who is a deranged version of 'us.'

One model of the pathological fan is that of the obsessed loner, who (under the influence of the media) has entered into an intense fantasy relationship with a celebrity figure. These individuals achieve public notoriety by stalking or threatening or killing the celebrity. Former 'crazed' acts are referenced in current news stories of 'obsessive' fans: Mark David Chapman's killing of ex-Beatle John Lennon, and John Hinckley's attempted assassination of President Ronald Reagan (to gain and keep the attention of actress Jodie Foster) are frequently brought up as iconic examples of the obsessed loner type.

This loner characterization can be contrasted with another version of fan pathology: the image of a frenzied or hysterical member of a crowd. This is the screaming, weeping teen at the airport glimpsing a rock star, or the roaring, maniacal sports fan rioting at a soccer game. This image of the frenzied fan predominates in discussions of music fans and sports fans.

Since the 1950s, images of teens, rock 'n' roll and out-of-control crowds have been intertwined. In press coverage, the dangers of violence, drink, drugs, sexual and racial mingling are connected to music popular with young people. Of particular concern are the influences of the music's supposedly licentious lyrics and barbaric rhythms. Crowds of teen music fans have been depicted as animalistic and depraved, under the spell of their chosen musical form. Heavy Metal is the most recent genre of youth music to evoke this frightening description of seductive power: Metal fans are characterized, especially by concerned parents, as vulnerable youngsters who have become 'twisted' in response to the brutal and Satanic influence of the music.[6]

The press coverage of rock concerts almost automatically engages these images of a crazed and frantic mob, of surging crowds that stampede out of control in an animalistic frenzy. When 11 teenagers were crushed to death in Cincinnati's Riverfront Coliseum (before a 1979 concert by The Who) press coverage was instantly condemnatory of the ruthless behavior of the frenzied mob. In his Chicago-based syndicated column, Mike Royko vilified the participants as 'barbarians' who 'stomped 11 persons to death [after] having numbed their brains on weeds, chemicals and Southern Comfort.'[7]

Yet, after investigation, the cause of the tragic incident was ascribed not to a panic or a stampede of selfish, drug-crazed fans, but instead to structural inadequacies of the site, in combination with inadequate communication between police, building workers and ticket-takers. Apparently, most crowd members were unsuccessfully (but often heroically) trying to help each other escape from the crush, a crush caused by too few doors into the arena being opened to accommodate a surge of people pressing forward, unaware of the fatal consequences at the front of the crowd.

In other words, the immediately circulated image of mass fan pathology (a crazed and depraved crowd climbing over dead bodies to get close to their idols) was absolutely untrue. As Johnson concludes, 'the evidence ... is more than sufficient to discount popular interpretations of "The Who Concert Stampede" which focus on the hedonistic attributes of young people and the hypnotic effects of rock music.'[8] Nonetheless, the 'hedonistic and hypnotic' interpretation was widely made, an interpretation consistent with the iconic fans-in-a-frenzy image historically developed in connection with musical performances.

Concern over fan violence in crowds also appears in relation to sports. There is an academic literature, for example, on football hooliganism.[9] This literature explores the reasons for violence at (mostly) soccer games, where 'hard-core hooligans' engage in violent and destructive acts, often against the opposing teams' fans. These incidents have become cause for social concern, and have been researched in some depth, especially in Britain. Even though, obviously, not all soccer fans engage in spectator violence, the association between fandom and violent, irrational mob behavior is assumed. In this literature, fans are characterized as easily roused into violent and destructive behavior, once assembled into a crowd and attending competitive sports events.[10]

To summarize, there is very little literature that explores fandom as a normal, everyday cultural or social phenomenon. Instead, the fan is characterized as (at least potentially) an obsessed loner, suffering from a disease of isolation, or a frenzied crowd member, suffering from a disease of contagion. In either case, the fan is seen as being irrational, out of control, and prey to a number of external forces. The influence of the media, a narcissistic society, hypnotic rock music, and crowd contagion are invoked to explain how fans become victims of their fandom, and so act in deviant and destructive ways.

FANS AS SOCIALLY SYMPTOMATIC

What explains these two iconic images? One possibility is that they genuinely embody two different aspects of the fan/celebrity interaction – individual obsessions, privately elaborated, and public hysteria, mobilized by crowd contagion. But *do* these models accurately or adequately describe the ways in which fandom is manifested in contemporary life? *Are* they appropriate representations of fandom? Do fans *really* risk becoming obsessed assassins or hysterical mobs? Do they (we) too easily 'cross the line' into pathological behavior, as Schickel suggests, because 'we suffer to some degree from the same confusion of realms that brings them, finally, to tragedy?'[11]

I suspect not, and the crux of my argument here is that these particular pathological portrayals exist in relation to different, unacknowledged issues and concerns. I believe that these two images tell us more about what we want to believe about modern society, and our connection to it, than they do about actual fan–celebrity relations.[12]

What is assumed to be true of fans – that they are potentially deviant, as loners or as members of a mob – can be connected with deeper, and more diffuse, assumptions about modern life. Each fan type mobilizes related assumptions about modern individuals: the obsessed loner invokes the image of the alienated, atomized 'mass man'; the frenzied crowd member invokes the image of the vulnerable, irrational victim of mass persuasion. These assumptions – about alienation, atomization, vulnerability and irrationality – are central aspects of twentieth-century beliefs about modernity.

Scholars as well as everyday people characterize modern life as fundamentally different from pre-modern life. Basically, the present is seen as being materially advanced but spiritually threatened. Modernity has brought technological progress but social, cultural and moral decay. The modernity critique is both nostalgic and romantic, because it locates lost virtues in the past, and believes in the possibility of their return.

In the early twentieth century, mass society terms (like alienation and atomization) took on added resonance in the urbanizing and industrializing United States, where the inevitable beneficence of progress (celebrated by technocrats and industrialists) was being increasingly questioned by intellectuals and social critics. Two aspects were of particular concern to American critics – the decline of community, and the increasing power of the mass media.

These concerns are related. Communities are envisioned as supportive and protective, they are believed to offer identity and connection in relation to traditional bonds, including race, religion and ethnicity. As these communal bonds are loosened, or discarded, the individual is perceived as vulnerable – he or she is 'unstuck from the cake of custom' and has no solid, reliable orientation in the world.

The absence of stable identity and connection is seen as leaving the individual open to irrational appeals. With the refinement of advertising and public relations campaigns in the early twentieth century, along with the success of wartime propaganda and the dramatic rise in the popularity of film and radio, fears of the immense and inescapable powers of propaganda techniques grew. It seemed that 'mass man' could all too easily become a victim of 'mass persuasion.' And under the spell of propaganda, emotions could be whipped into frenzies, publics could become crowds and crowds could become mobs.

This conceptual heritage, which defines modernity as a fragmented, disjointed mass society, is mobilized in the two images of the pathological fan. The obsessed loner is the image of the isolated, alienated 'mass man.' He or she is cut off from family, friends and community. His or her life becomes increasingly dominated by an irrational fixation on a celebrity figure, a perverse attachment that dominates his or her otherwise unrewarding existence. The vulnerable, lonely modern man or woman, seduced by the mass media into fantasy communion with celebrities, eventually crosses the line into pathology, and threatens, maims or kills the object of his or her desire.

The frenzied fan in a crowd is also perceived to be vulnerable, but this time to irrational loyalties sparked by sports teams or celebrity figures. As a member of a crowd, the fan becomes irrational, and thus easily influenced. If she is female, the image includes sobbing and screaming and fainting, and assumes that an uncontrollable erotic energy is sparked by the chance to see or touch a male idol. If he is male, the image is of drunken destructiveness, a rampage of uncontrollable masculine passion that is unleashed in response to a sports victory or defeat.

Dark assumptions underlie the two images of fan pathology, and they haunt the literature on fans and fandom. They are referenced but not acknowledged in the relentless retelling of particular examples of violent or deranged fan behavior. Fans are seen as displaying symptoms of a wider social dysfunction – modernity – that threatens all of 'us.'

FANDOM AS PSYCHOLOGICAL COMPENSATION

The modernity critique, with its associated imagery of the atomized individual and the faceless crowd, is mostly social theory – it does not directly develop assumptions about individual psychology. Nonetheless, it implies a connection between social and psychological conditions – a fragmented and incomplete modern society yields a fragmented and incomplete modern self. What we find, in the literature of fan–celebrity relationships, is a psychologized version of the mass society critique. Fandom, especially 'excessive' fandom, is defined as a form of psychological compensation, an attempt to make up for all that modern life lacks.

In 1956, Horton and Wohl characterized the media–audience relationship as a form of 'para-social interaction.'[13] They see fandom as a surrogate relationship, one that inadequately imitates normal relationships. They characterize the media mode of address as a 'simulacrum of conversation' and demonstrate how it tries to replicate the virtues of face-to-face interaction.

They also examine the structure and strategies of celebrity public relations, noting how they function to create what they call the celebrity 'persona.' They suggest that 'given the prolonged intimacy of para-social relations ... it is not surprising that many members of the audience become dissatisfied and attempt to establish actual contact. ... One would suppose that contact with, and recognition by, the persona transfers some of his prestige and influence to the active fan.' This implies that the fan, unable to consummate his desired social relations 'normally,' seeks celebrity contact in the hope of gaining the prestige and influence he or she psychologically needs, but cannot achieve in anonymous, fragmented modern society.

This statement is followed by commentary on a letter written to Ann Landers by a female fan (another 'Miss A.'), who says she has 'fallen head over heels in love with a local television star' and now can't sleep, finds other men to be 'childish,' and is bored by her modeling job. Miss A. is said to reveal in this letter 'how narrow the line often is between the more ordinary forms of social interaction and those which characterize relations with the persona.' Even worse, 'persona' relations are deemed to have 'invaded' Miss A.'s life, 'so much so that, without control, it will warp or destroy her relations with the opposite sex' (Horton and Wohl, 1956: 206).

Horton and Wohl suggest, however, that 'it is only when the para-social relationship becomes a substitute for autonomous social participation, when it proceeds in absolute defiance of objective reality, that it can be regarded as pathological' (1956: 200). These extreme forms of fandom, they claim, are mostly characteristic of the socially isolated, the socially inept, the aged and invalid, the timid and rejected. For these and similarly deprived groups, para-social interaction is an attempt by the socially excluded (and thus psychologically needy) to compensate for the absence of 'authentic' relationships in their lives.

Schickel suggests that celebrities act to fulfil our own dreams of autonomy (the famous appear to have no permanent allegiances) and dreams of intimacy (the famous appear to belong to a celebrity community). The psychopathic fan-turned-assassin, he implies, similarly uses mediated celebrities to form an identity, although he kills in order to share their power and fame. To be a fan, Schickel and others imply, is to attempt to live vicariously, through the perceived lives of the famous. Fandom is conceived of as a chronic attempt to compensate for a perceived personal lack of autonomy, absence of community, incomplete identity, lack of power and lack of recognition.

These vague claims, bolstered by various strains of social and psychological research, parallel, strikingly, the claims made about the reasons for fanaticism. Milgram defines a fanatic as 'someone who goes to extremes in beliefs, feelings and actions.'[14] He suggests that fanatics use belief systems as a 'therapeutic crutch ... staving off a collapse of self worth.' Any challenge to the fanatic's belief system is seen as a 'threat to his self-esteem,' and thus to his 'ego-defensive system.'

Interestingly, deviants are also seen by researchers as lacking in self-worth, or as having weak 'ego-boundaries.'[15] This characteristic may even be linked to 'role engulf-ment,' where the identity of deviance becomes a way to organize a 'concept of self.'[16] Thus in all three concepts (fan, fanatic and deviant) a psychological portrait of fundamental inadequacy, and attempted compensation, is developed.

The inadequate fan is defined as someone who is making up for some inherent lack. He or she seeks identity, connection and meaning via celebrities and team loyalties. Like the fanatic and the deviant, the fan has fragile self-esteem, weak or non-existent social alliances, a dull and monotonous 'real' existence. The mass media provide (the argument goes) ways for these inadequate people to bolster, organize and enliven their unsatisfying lives.

Fandom, however, is seen as a risky, even dangerous, compensatory mechanism. The fan-as-pathology model implies that there is a thin line between 'normal' and excessive fandom. This line is crossed if and when the distinctions between reality and fantasy break down. These are the two realms that must remain separated if the fan is to remain safe and normal.[17]

The literature implies that 'normal' fans are constantly in danger of becoming 'obsessive loners' or 'frenzied crowd members.' Ann Lander's curt response to Miss A.

('you are flunking the course of common sense') is figuratively given to all fans – as long as the fan shows 'good common sense,' remains 'rational' and 'in control,' then he or she will be spared. But if the fan ceases to distinguish the real from the imaginary, and lets emotion overwhelm reason and somehow gets 'out of control,' then there are terrible consequences. These consequences are referenced in the cautionary tales of fans who go 'over the edge' into fanaticism, and thus pathology.

AFICIONADOS AS FANS

The literature on fandom, celebrity and media influence tells us that: fans suffer from psychological inadequacy, and are particularly vulnerable to media influence and crowd contagion. They seek contact with famous people in order to compensate for their own inadequate lives. Because modern life is alienated and atomized, fans develop loyalties to celebrities and sports teams to bask in reflected glory, and attend rock concerts and sports events to feel an illusory sense of community.

But what happens if we change the objects of this description from fans to, say, professors? What if we describe the loyalties that scholars feel to academic disciplines rather than to team sports, and attendance at scholarly conferences, rather than Who concerts and soccer matches? What if we describe opera buffs and operas? Antique collectors and auctions? Trout fishermen and angling contests? Gardeners and horti-culture shows? Do the assumptions about inadequacy, deviance and danger still apply?

I think not. The paragraph makes sense only if it is believed to describe recognizable but nebulous 'others' who live in some world different from our own. Fandom, it seems, is not readily conceptualized as a general or shared trait, as a form of loyalty or attachment, as a mode of 'enacted affinity.' Fandom, instead, is what 'they' do; 'we,' on the other hand, have tastes and preferences, and select worthy people, beliefs and activities for our admiration and esteem. Furthermore, what 'they' do is deviant, and therefore dangerous, while what 'we' do is normal, and therefore safe.

What is the basis for these differences between fans like 'them' and aficionados like 'us'? There appear to be two crucial aspects – the objects of desire, and the modes of enactment. The objects of an aficionado's desire are usually deemed high culture: Eliot (George or T.S.) not Elvis; paintings not posters; the *New York Review of Books* not the *National Enquirer*. Apparently, if the object of desire is popular with the lower or middle class, relatively inexpensive and widely available, it is fandom (or a harmless hobby); if it is popular with the wealthy and well educated, expensive and rare, it is preference, interest or expertise.

Am I suggesting, then, that a Barry Manilow fan be compared with, for example, a Joyce scholar? The mind may reel at the comparison, but why? The Manilow fan knows intimately every recording (and every version) of Barry's songs; the Joyce scholar knows intimately every volume (and every version) of Joyce's *oeuvre*. The relationship between Manilow's real life and his music is explored in detail in star biographies and fan maga-zines; the relationship between Dublin, Bloomsday and Joyce's actual experiences are explored in detail in biographies and scholarly monographs.

Yes, you may say, there are indeed these surface similarities. But what about the fans who are obsessed with Barry, who organize their life around him?[18] Surely no Joyce scholar would become equally obsessive? But the uproar over the definitive edition of *Ulysses*[19] suggests that the participant Joyceans are fully obsessed, and have indeed organized their life (even their 'identity' and 'community') around Joyce.

But is a scholar, collector, aficionado 'in love' with the object of his or her desire? Is it the existence of passion that defines the distinction between fan and aficionado, between dangerous and benign, between deviance and normalcy?

So far we have established that one aspect of the distinction between 'them' and 'us' involves a cultural hierarchy. At least one key difference, then, is that it is normal and therefore safe to be attached to elite, prestige-conferring objects (aficionado-hood), but it can be abnormal and therefore dangerous to be attached to popular, mass-mediated objects (fandom).

But there is another key distinction being made between the fan and the aficionado. Fans are believed to be obsessed with their objects, in love with celebrity figures, willing to die for their team. Fandom involves an ascription of excess, and emotional display – hysterics at rock concerts, hooliganism at soccer matches, autograph seeking at celebrity sites. Affinity, on the other hand, is deemed to involve rational evaluation, and is displayed in more measured ways – applause and a few polite 'Bravos!' after concerts; crowd murmurs at polo matches; attendance of 'big-name' sessions at academic conferences.

This valuation of the genteel over the rowdy is based in status (and thus class) distinctions. It has been described in nineteenth-century parades,[20] public cultural performances,[21] and turn of the century newspaper styles.[22] Unemotional, detached, 'cool' behavior is seen as more worthy and admirable than emotional, passionate, 'hot' behavior. 'Good' parades are orderly and sequential and serious (not rowdy, chaotic or lighthearted); 'good' audiences are passive and quiet and respectful (not active, vocal or critical); 'good' newspapers are neutral, objective and gray (not passionate, subjective and colorful). Congruently, then, 'good' affinities are expressed in a subdued, undisruptive manner, while 'bad' affinities (fandom) are expressed in dramatic and disruptive ways.

The division between worthy and unworthy is based in an assumed dichotomy between reason and emotion. The reason–emotion dichotomy has many aspects. It describes a presumed difference between the educated and uneducated, as well as between the upper and lower classes. It is a deeply rooted opposition, one that the ascription of intrinsic differences between high and low culture automatically obscures.

Apparently, the real dividing line between aficionado and fan involves issues of status and class, as they inform vernacular cultural and social theory. Furthermore, the Joyce scholar and the Barry Manilow fan, the antique collector and the beer can collector, the opera buff and the Heavy Metal fan are differentiated not only on the basis of the status of their desired object, but also on the supposed nature of their attachment. The obsession of a fan is deemed emotional (low-class, uneducated), and therefore dangerous, while the obsession of the aficionado is rational (high-class, educated), and therefore benign, even worthy.

These culturally-loaded categories engage Enlightenment-originated ideas based on rationality. Reason is associated with the objective apprehending of reality, while emotion is associated with the subjective, the imaginative, and the irrational. Emotions, by this logic, lead to a dangerous blurring of the line between fantasy and reality, while rational obsession, apparently, does not. But does this reason–emotion dichotomy, complete with dividing line, hold up? Let me give you some examples from my own life to suggest that the line is inevitably and constantly crossed, without pathological consequences, by respectable professorial types like me.

Anyone in academia, especially those who have written theses or dissertations, can attest to the emotional components of supposedly rational activity. A figure or topic can become the focal point of one's life; anything even remotely connected to one's research interests can have tremendous impact and obsessive appeal. For example, while I was writing my dissertation (on the commercialization of country music in the 1950s), the chance to touch Patsy Cline's mascara wand, retrieved from the site of her 1963 plane crash, gave me chills.

Similarly (but far more respectably), the handling of a coffee cup made by William Morris was deeply moving. I have also envied a colleague who once owned a desk that had been used by John Dewey, and I display a framed copy of a drawing of William James in my office. I would be thrilled if I could own any memorabilia associated with Lewis Mumford, to whom I regret not having written a letter of appreciation before he died.

Am I, then, a fan of Patsy Cline, William Morris, William James, John Dewey and Lewis Mumford? Or of country music, the pre-Raphaelites, the pragmatists and iconoclastic social critics? Yes, of course I am, if fandom is defined as an interest in, and an attachment to, a particular figure or form. Would I write a fan letter to these figures? Yes, if fan letter includes (as it does, in academic circles) review essays or appreciative quotation. Would I read a fanzine? Again yes, but in the scholarly versions – heavily footnoted biographies and eloquent critical appreciations. Would I seek autographs? Yes, if I could do so without losing face, via auctions or books or scholarly correspondence. Would I collect memorabilia? Well, I confess here to having at least one version of all 100 of Patsy Cline's recordings; calendars and a piece of cloth designed by Morris; and as many books as I can afford to purchase by James, Dewey and Mumford, along with miscellaneous biographies, reviews and commentaries.[23]

Would I defend my 'team,' the pragmatists, against the attacks on them by, say, Hegelians, neo-Marxists and/or poststructuralists? You bet. Would I do so in a rowdy, rambunctious or violent way? Of course not. I would respond instead with respectable rowdiness (acerbic asides in scholarly articles) and acceptable violence (the controlled, intellectual aggression often witnessed in conference presentations).

Would I claim to be 'in love' with any of these individuals, would I offer to die for any of these preferences? Not likely, and certainly not in public. I would lose the respect of my peers. Instead, I will say that I 'admire' William James, I 'read with interest' Lewis Mumford, I 'enjoy' pre-Raphaelite design and 'am drawn to' aspects of pragmatism. In short, I will display aficionado-hood, with a vengeance. But, as I hope my confessions have made obvious, my aficionado-hood is really disguised, and thereby legitimated, fandom.

The pejorative connotations of fans and fandom prevent me from employing those terms to describe and explore my attachments. While my particular affinities may be somewhat idiosyncratic, everyone I've ever met has comparable ones. Most of us seem to have deep, and personal, interests, and we enact our affinities by investing time, money and 'ourselves' in them. I have even been fortunate enough to make a living in relation to my interests. Does that mean I am truly 'obsessed' by them? Am I, perhaps, even more dysfunctional than most because I force others (like students) to listen, even temporarily to participate, in my predilections?

Were I to call myself a fan, I would imply that I am emotionally engaged with unworthy cultural figures and forms, and that I was risking obsession, with dangerous consequences. I would imply that I was a psychologically incomplete person, trying to compensate for my inadequate life through the reflected glory of these figures and forms. My unstable and fragile identity needs them, they are a 'therapeutic crutch,' a form of 'para-social relations,' functioning as 'personae' in my life. I must have these relationships because my lonely, marginal existence requires that I prop myself up with these fantasy attachments to famous dead people, and these alliances with abstract, imaginary communities.

Obviously, I find these ascriptions of dysfunction, based on my affinities, to be misguided and muddleheaded, as well as extraordinarily insulting. I assume that others would, too, whether they call themselves aficionados or fans. The pejorative association of fandom with pathology is stunningly disrespectful when it is applied to 'us' rather than 'them.'

NOTES

1 Marilyn Robinette Marx, quoted in Axthelm (1989).
2 Gavin de Becker is described in Axthelm (1989: 66) as 'an L.A. security expert who helps stars ward off unwanted attentions'.
3 Jack Pott, Assistant Clinical Director of Psychiatry for Maricopa County Health Services, quoted in Rosenblum (1989), an *Arizona Daily Star* article kindly provided to me by Lisa Lewis.
4 Caughey (1978a). See also Caughey (1978b).
5 Schickel (1985). See especially the final pages.
6 See Miller (1988).
7 Quoted in Johnson (1987).
8 Ibid.
9 See, for example: Ingham (1978), Lee (1985); and Marsh et al. (1978).
10 See Dunning et al. (1986: 221), where they say that many fans are 'drawn into hooligan incidents – fans who did not set out for the match with disruptive intent ... [by contact with] hard-core hooligans'.
11 Schickel (1985: 285).
12 The argument in this essay draws on my belief that vernacular social theory is accessible through the analysis of the narrative strategies of popular and scholarly accounts. I develop this belief, as well as the associated notion of the displacement of ambivalence, or scapegoating, in Jensen (1990).
13 Horton and Wohl (1956). Subsequently reprinted in Gumpert and Cathcart (1982).
14 Milgram (1977).
15 See, for example, the model developed by Shoham (1976).

16 See the brief summary of this and other claims in Schur (1971).

17 The mass media, in conjunction with modern society, are believed somehow to blur this necessary distinction. The media are defined as dangerous precisely because they are believed to disrupt people's ability consistently and reliably to separate fantasy from reality. This account of media influence is pervasive, but fails to recognize the historical presence of narrativity in cultures, and that the insistence on distinctions between 'objective' fact and 'subjective' fiction is an historically recent development.

18 Vermorel (1985).

19 Probably best recorded in the *New York Review of Books* letters in 1988 and 1989.

20 See Davis (1986).

21 Levine (1988).

22 Schudson (1978).

23 In the case of William James, my fandom extends to an interest in his parents and siblings, and I wish I knew something about his descendants. I have considered taking a vacation that would include visits to places he lived and worked. I disagree with some of the interpretations of some of his biographers, and am infuriated by Leon Edel's 'unfair' portrayal of William in his biography of Henry James.

REFERENCES

Axthelm, Pete (1989) 'An innocent life, a heartbreaking death', *People Weekly*, 32 (5): 60–6.

Caughey, John L. (1978a) 'Artificial social relations in modern America', *American Quarterly*, 30 (1).

Caughey, John L. (1978b) 'Media mentors', *Psychology Today*, 12 (4): 44–9.

Davis, Susan (1986) *Parades and Power: Street Theatre in Nineteenth-Century Philadelphia*. Philadelphia, PA: Temple University Press.

Dunning, Eric, Murphy, Patrick and Williams, John (1986) 'Spectator violence at football matches: towards a sociological explanation', *British Journal of Sociology*, 37 (2).

Gumpert, Gary and Cathcart, Robert (eds) (1982) *Inter/Media: Interpersonal Communication in a Media World*, 2nd edn. New York: Oxford University Press.

Horton, David and Wohl, R. Richard (1956) 'Mass communication and para-social interaction: observation on intimacy at a distance', *Psychiatry*, 19 (3): 188–211.

Ingham, Roger (ed.) (1978) *Football Hooliganism: The Wider Context*. London: Inter-Action.

Jensen, Joli (1990) *Redeeming Modernity: Contradictions in Media Criticism*. Beverly Hills, CA: Sage.

Johnson, Norris R. (1987) 'Panic at "The Who stampede": an empirical assessment', *Social Problems*, 34 (4): 362.

Lee, Martin J. (1985) 'From rivalry to hostility among sports fans', *Quest*, 37 (1): 38–49.

Levine, Lawrence W. (1988) *Highbrow/Lowbrow: The Emergence of Cultural Hierarchy in America*. Boston, MA: Harvard University Press.

Marsh, Peter, Rosser, Elizabeth and Harré, Rom (1978) *The Rules of Disorder*. London: Routledge & Kegan Paul.

Milgram, Stanley (1977) 'The social meaning of fanaticism', *Et Cetera*, 34 (1): 58–61.

Miller, Dale (1988) 'Youth, Popular Music and Cultural Controversy: The Case of Heavy Metal', PhD thesis, University of Texas at Austin.

Rosenblum, Keith (1989) 'Psychiatrists analyze fantasies, fixations that lead to crimes against celebrities', *Arizona Daily Star*, 21 July, Section A: 2.

Schickel, Richard (1985) 'Coherent strangers', in *Intimate Strangers: The Culture of Celebrity*. Garden City, NY: Doubleday.

Schudson, Michael (1978) *Discovering the News: A Social History of American Newspapers*. New York: Basic Books.

Schur, Edwin M. (1971) New York: Harper & Row.

Shoham, S. Giora (1976) *Social Deviance*. New York: Gardner Press.

Vermorel, Fred and Judy (1985) *Starlust: The Secret Fantasies of Fans*. London: W.H. Allen.

33

needs as an explanatory factor of television viewing

CELIA VON FEILITZEN

Trying to explain why children watch television is, it seems, like opening a Chinese box, only to find that it contains another box, and that this in its turn contains yet another. It is possible—and this indeed is what characterizes most research—to go on indefinitely, continually eliciting new factors. We are forced, ultimately, to realize that instead of lining up more and more individual explanatory factors, we should start at the other end. We must assume that the total situation plays a role, and consider the interplay or the tensions existing between *all* factors. Then we should assess the importance of different factors in relation to each other. We should recall that the reason for trying to explain children's television viewing by means of these individual factors—and, similarly, their cinema going, or comic reading—was not *primarily* to explain their TV viewing as such, but rather to establish under what circumstances and for which children the media have 'positive' and 'negative' effects. The fundamental question was thus: 'What do the mass media do with the individual?'

Parallel, however, with this research into effects, another approach in mass communications research has asserted itself, although to a markedly lesser degree. With this approach, the question is rather: 'What does the individual do with the mass media?' This is a converse approach in which the active role is assigned to the individual, and not to the mass media. Investigations of this kind have been dubbed 'uses and gratifications' studies, in that they are based on the assumption that the individual, by his use of the mass media, obtains a reward in the form of needs gratification. The individual is selective and chooses (more or less consciously) mass medium and mass medium content on the basis of the functions, or the meaning, which the medium and the content have for him, and the availability of functional alternatives. The functions are steered by the individual's needs, which are dependent in their turn upon both psychological factors existing in the individual (e.g. sex, age, development, personality, intelligence, experience and interests) and the more social factors (e.g. place of domicile, socio-economic status, relationships with family and peers, living habits, leisure activities and the society's system of norms and values). Thus mass media effects do not occur unless the individual himself chooses to use the mass media in a certain way (Edelstein, 1966; Klapper, 1963; Maletzke, 1963).

The first uses and gratifications studies were performed in the 1940s, and the approach has been adopted in a number of investigations of children. Schramm et al. (1961), for example, formulated this approach in their study of children and television. They rejected 'the favourite image of children as helpless victims to be attacked by television', believing a more adequate picture to be that of television as a 'great and shiny cafeteria from which children select what they want at the moment. ... A child comes to television seeking to satisfy some need. He finds something there, and uses it.' It should be added that the child not only chooses between different television programmes, but also between television and other activities, the functional alternatives, which may meet his needs as adequately. It is possible that the child will enter instead the adjoining restaurant or go to the ice-cream stall outside.

The picture of the independent, active child is undeniably attractive. But the studies on children in England and Sweden that have applied the uses and gratifications model in recent years have used the model in a more differentiated way. The research results reported above are sufficient for us to understand that the child cannot, in all reason,

First published in *Children and Television*, R. Brown, Collier-Macmillan (1975), as 'The Functions Served by the Media', pp. 94–105.

be so fully active and rational. The influence of the family, for example, on the child's viewing was mentioned as a restricting factor. And, if we considered the picture at large, the type of society also played a role here. Other essential factors that we have hardly touched upon relate to the structure and content of the mass media, i.e. broadcasting times, the division into channels, type of programmes and so on. What is shown on television constitutes, after all, a limited supply, and it reflects a biased selection of norms and values, depending on the more or less conscious policy of the producer, and the organization within which he works. Content analyses have shown, for example, the existence of large 'white areas on the map' in the world commented upon by news programmes (Nordström and Thorén, 1972–3). Similarly, we know that many entertainment programmes present a stereotyped picture of people as regards occupational roles, sex roles and minority groups (Huston Stein, 1972). Finally, our own experience tells us that children's access to different mass media and their actual opportunities to meet friends and pursue other leisure activities are often limited.

The conclusion is thus that the uses and gratifications model admittedly offers an advantage, in that it does assume that the total situation plays a role. Since the needs of the individual are assumed to be shaped by all his psychological and social characteristics, we can also assume that by studying his needs we will already have allowed for the various circumstances that influence children's television viewing and the relative importance of these circumstances. In this way, we have roped in, as it were, the many separate explanatory factors. But at the same time, we must not accord excessive emphasis to the individual's needs. That the psychological and social factors, including the mass media system, and type of society, are channelled through the needs structure of the child implies, after all, that the child does not have unlimited freedom of choice. The child is selective, admittedly, but it is a selectivity that operates *within the framework* of all these conditions. For example, certain needs must be seen as having been created by the television output. Why a child watches television is thus to some extent a question of the interplay between supply and demand.

The needs structure of the child and the functions of the mass media are consequently dynamic phenomena; they can be altered if other factors, for example, the programmes, change character. The meanings of mass media for the individual must thus be seen in an ongoing process; they vary at different times, in different environments, and with different mass communication systems.

It is also important to point out that the future goal of uses and gratifications studies should not be limited to exploration of the functions of the mass media, but should include the consequences of the use of the mass media and their functions to the individual, to his social groups and to the society at large. For the uses and gratifications model to be meaningful in the long term, the question that it must ultimately answer must, as with the traditional effect models, relate to the influence of mass media (Klapper, 1963).

THE FUNCTIONS SERVED FOR CHILDREN BY THE MASS MEDIA

With this more differentiated picture of the uses and gratifications model in mind, we shall now consider a selection of results obtained in a Swedish survey of what needs the mass media satisfy in the case of children. The survey thus tries to answer the question 'Why is it so?' in the alternative manner described above. It does not, however, offer a complete answer. The intention was to plot the general functions of all the mass media—i.e. TV, radio, cinema, books, newspapers, magazines, comics and records—for three- to fifteen-year-olds in Sweden.[1] The question of what needs television satisfies among different groups of children was also studied to some extent. On the other hand, the survey does not tell us what needs are satisfied by different mass media *contents*. Nor was it the intention to deal with effects, i.e. to say what effects the mass media have on children for whom the media satisfy different needs. Examples of the questions considered are: 'What do children get out of watching television?', 'What is more important for young people listening to the radio: that the programmes are good, or that radio provides an opportunity to withdraw for a while?', 'Which mass media compete with each other in the sense of being functionally similar?', and 'Does television serve similar functions for both children who are heavily exposed to it and those who are infrequent viewers?'

It would be beyond the scope of this article to consider in any detail the different ways in which one can delimit and measure needs/functions. We will simply note that uses and gratifications studies delimit functions by applying a subjective definition.[2] What are reported here are, therefore, the functions that children experience the mass media as having, or the needs they experience them as satisfying.[3] In order to measure needs/functions the survey applied the theory of motivation.[4] If, for example, one of the motives for viewing is that 'you get information about what is happening in the world', then television has an informative function. All motives incorporated in the survey have been formulated by children, and consist of words and expressions that children actually use and understand.[5]

THE FUNCTIONS THAT CHILDREN EXPERIENCE TELEVISION AS HAVING

The first striking result obtained by the study is that the mass media have more than thirty different functions for children. For the sake of clarity, we shall group them under five headings. At the same time, we shall consider how far they are valid in the case of television. In the public debate mass media are often said to have two functions: to entertain and to inform. These two expressions, however, proved irrelevant to children. And even if we have allowed ourselves to incorporate them in two of the headings, we are aware that they are both diffuse and schematic concepts. The terms 'entertainment' and 'information' cover a whole succession of subsidiary aspects.

Entertaining or Emotional Functions

Three motives for viewing emerge as being by far the most important and were mentioned by practically every three- to fifteen-year-old in Sweden: I watch television because 'the programmes are good', 'the programmes are fun', and 'the programmes are exciting'. These motives show a high internal correlation. A further three functions come into this group: I watch because 'it's a bit of relaxation', 'I don't have anything else to do for the moment', and 'you can see things that don't happen for real'. Apart from programmes being *good, amusing* and *exciting*, television viewing can thus mean *relaxation, passing the time* and *fantasy orientation*. And indeed not only can mean, but usually does mean, since these functions are reported by a large majority of children.

Informative or Cognitive Functions

Even if children on average place television's entertaining functions in the foremost place, television meets informative needs with almost equal frequency. The majority of both younger and older children (three to six and seven to fifteen years of age respectively) give all of the following functions: 'you see things that happen in real life', 'you learn a lot', 'you find out what is happening in the world', and 'you get new thoughts and ideas'. Almost equally often they say they watch because 'you learn how to do things', 'TV shows what is right and what is wrong', and 'I want to try everything'.

The informative needs that television satisfies for children can be described as *reality orientation, general knowledge, information on current events* and *stimulation of fantasy*. They can also be the needs for *practical information and advice, norms* and *curiosity*.

Social Functions

In addition to TV's entertaining and informative functions, there emerges a group that is often of equal importance: television meets a large number of social needs on the part of children. The children actually report eleven such motives. Four are mentioned by the majority of both younger and older children. They watch because 'you "get inside" people and events', 'You get to be a sort of friend with some of the people on the screen', 'I'm used to it', and 'you talk about the programmes with other people'.

Television's most important social functions are thus that one can *identify* with and obtain *an almost real contact* with people on television (an idea that was discussed by Horton and Wohl [1956], and which they labelled 'para-social interaction'), that viewing has become a well-established *habit*, and that the programmes provide *topics of conversation*.

Two functions are mentioned by a majority of the older children: 'I want to know as much as other people', and 'you get the feeling you want to talk about the injustices of the world'. These functions could be termed *status* and *social commitment*. The remaining five fit certain children, but less than half of either the younger or the older group. These are, in the order given: I watch because 'you meet other people at the same time', 'it makes me feel calm and secure', 'it feels as if you were really doing something', 'I feel alone', and 'it makes you feel older'. Television thus sometimes makes possible: *contact with others in the actual viewing situation, security, performance, distraction from loneliness* and yet another form of *status*.

Non-social or Escapist Functions

The fourth group of functions is by no means as prominent. It contains only two motives, and these are mentioned by a minority of both younger and older children: I watch because 'you dream yourself away', and 'you can be in peace then'. Television can thus from time to time, but not particularly often, meet a need for *escapism*, and a need to *get away from the people around*. It is reasonable perhaps to call both motives escapism. While the first is related primarily to the programmes, the second relates more to the actual act of viewing.

In connection not only with escapism but all the functions listed above, it is important to emphasize that while some have to do with the actual *content* of the mass medium, others have to do with the *act* of viewing, listening and/or reading.

Mode of Consumption or Medium Level Functions

It is not always easy to decide whether some functions are associated with a particular type of programme or with the act of watching television. There is, however, a clearly defined group of functions which are associated with the mode of consumption and the non-content characteristics of the medium. These functions are connected with the form of the mass medium in question, both in terms of its technical properties and the context of use. For example, must the child watch, listen or read? Is it possible to do something else whilst using the medium? Can the medium be used at any time, or only during defined periods? Can the medium be used anywhere, or only in a special environment? And is it possible for the child to re-use specific content at will, or must it be accepted when given? As will be seen, this category of function is often extremely influential in determining which medium the child turns to at any particular time. In the case of television, the majority of children say they choose it because: 'TV's got both picture and sound' and 'you can watch TV at home'.

Summarizing Comments

Five main groups of needs satisfied in children by the mass media have emerged: entertaining (or emotional) functions, informative (or cognitive) functions, social functions, non-social (or escapist) functions, and mode of consumption (or medium level) functions. Apart from the interest of each individual function *per se*, the results obtained provide a basis for *inter alia* a more general argument.

On average, children consider the most important functions of television to be its 'entertaining' functions, closely followed by the 'informative' functions. One may have been led to believe that it is television's 'entertainment programmes' that meet the need for 'entertainment', and its 'informative programmes' the need for 'information'. This, however, is far too simple a conclusion. In the light of what we know about children's interest in different programmes, the informative functions would then have come very much farther down the list, at least in the case of the older children. And, after all, if it were that easy to link a specific function to a specific type of programme, research into the functions would be unnecessary.

One of the reasons for this sort of conclusion may be the common conception of entertainment and information as opposing poles. But it is more reasonable to suppose that every programme and every message in a communication contains, basically, a certain measure of information that is more or less entertaining, depending on the manner of presentation. With such an approach, one can understand why children tie the motive 'the programmes are good' to 'the programmes are fun' and 'exciting'. It does not necessarily follow that children think informative programmes are poor, but rather that children are positive about what is communicated in an entertaining manner. In this context it is worth noting that television, in spite of the children's comprehensive consumption of entertainment programmes, is the mass medium that constitutes their most important source of knowledge. In the long run, learning is in this way 'indirect', i.e. it is primarily the adult entertainment programmes that broaden children's sphere of experience. The information they acquire from television is not simply an acquaintance with current events, but is perhaps more a sort of 'reality orientation' in the adult world. Television's contribution to this reality orientation has been shown to relate less to the family and peers, with whom the child is anyway familiar, and more to values and concepts concerning occupations, status, and people's roles outside the home and the schools (Capecchi and Livolsi, 1973; Himmelweit et al., 1958).

In the light of empirical evidence the assumption that particular forms of content are monofunctional—entertainment programmes serving solely to entertain, information programmes to inform—can no longer be maintained. For example, in spite of the fact that adults view news broadcasts with great interest, the audience member's understanding of news is often exiguous, but functional studies have shown that for many viewers, and especially those who are alienated, the primary function of news is not informational. The news broadcast, apparently, is more closely related to habit; it also affords the individual feelings of security and social contact (Nordenstreng, 1969).

If we consider for a moment the earlier studies of children and mass media functions conducted in other countries, we find that they have often concentrated, apart from on entertainment and information, on children's need for escapism. In fact, the uses and gratifications studies had their historical origins in precisely this line of thinking. Attempts were made to test the assumption that a high degree of attention to such entertaining content in the mass media as affords an unrealistic picture of the world, implied escapism on the part of the individual. It was assumed that this in its turn could lead, for example, to an impaired capacity to deal with the problems of real life, and to physical, mental and social passivity. Over the years frequent voices have also been raised in the public debate to warn us that children's interest in stereotyped television entertainment serves an escapist need.

The results of the Swedish study among children, however, do not support this assumption in respect of television. The non-social or escapist functions are the group that children, in relation to television, mention least frequently of all. It is possible that we are faced here with discrepancies of definition. Escapism, as indeed entertainment and information, is a vague and overused concept (Katz and Foulkes, 1962). If one gives the term a very wide interpretation and assumes that it covers, in addition to flight from reality, such factors as relaxation, passing time, identification and contact with people on the screen, then it will apply, as shown above, to the majority of children. But if one means escapism in the sense it is used here, to denote social with-drawal, then it actually applies only to a minority of children. A possible objection that the children in the study have not mentioned escapism for reasons of language or pres-tige can easily be met. As we shall see later, children mention the escapist functions fairly frequently in regard to certain other mass media. And, ignoring the mass media entirely, the great majority admit a tendency to escapism from time to time. In addi-tion, recent research in England and Japan indicates that television viewing by children does not usually involve escapism (Brown et al., 1974; Furu, 1971).

Instead of putting the emphasis, perhaps too one-sidedly, on children's need for TV escapism, one should therefore adopt a perspective corresponding to that applied in the studies on adults and news programmes quoted above. We should look in the other direction and focus on what has so far attracted relatively little attention in research and debate, namely the many-faceted social functions that television has for children. It is this group that the children themselves experience as the third most important. When one looks at the social functions a bit more closely, they fall into one of two cat-egories. First, it seems as if television viewing can mean a social relationship *per se* (cf., for example, the findings that television permits identification, contact with television personalities, distraction from loneliness, and security). Second, children consider television as a source of information on the social environment, or of information that they can use in their social environment (cf. that TV means topics of conversation and social commitment, that viewing signifies status and performance).

One should remember that mass communication is a form of communication, an interaction between two or more persons. And one can therefore ask whether the social functions of mass media are not in fact the most fundamental of all. If this assumption is correct, then the argument pursued in the last few pages could be summed up as follows: why do children watch television? Children want information from television, preferably presented in an entertaining manner, because they want social contact *per se*, and because they want in various ways to improve their real social contacts. Sometimes, but not in the majority of cases, this is coupled with escapism.

NOTES

1   Data were collected in 1970 by a mail questionnaire sent to a sample of some 1800 children, representative of all three- to fifteen-year-olds in Sweden. Non-response was *c.* 5 percent. Parents answered the questionnaire on behalf of the three- to seven-year-olds, while the eight- to fifteen-year-olds completed their own questionnaires during school hours.
2   'The functions of the mass media are the specific meaning the media have for the individual as an acting and experiencing subject' (Maletzke, 1963). Some authors have tried to make a list of needs or functions on the basis of an objec-tive approach (e.g. Merton, 1957; Wright, 1960). These lists inevitably vary according to the researcher's premises. It would seem more reasonable to describe that approach as normative.

3 We must therefore be more cautious when interpreting the results obtained in respect of the younger children, in that we are here obliged to rely on information from the parents.

4 The behaviour of the individual is a constant attempt to satisfy his needs. When a need is directed, by means of learning, towards a given goal, a motive arises that activates and steers the individual's behaviour. Achievement of the goal entails a reward in the form of needs-gratification. The functions are thus defined as motives (need + goal) for a certain action. For the sake of simplicity, however, the terms 'TV's functions for the individual', 'the individual's motive for viewing' and 'the individual's need to watch television' are used here as equivalent.

5 These wordings emerged in a previous pilot study, in which children produced answers to open-ended questions on their mass media and other leisure activities. In the main study, the children were asked to consider the same motives for each mass medium, each motive representing a function. Thus, the motives incorporated in the main study covered functions that are not associated primarily with the mass media, but excluded those which were never associated with media in the pilot study.

REFERENCES

Brown, J.R., Cramond, J.K. and Wilde, R. (1974) 'Displacement effects and the child's functional orientation to television', in J.G. Blumler and E. Katz (eds) *The Uses of Mass Communication: Current Perspectives on Gratification Research*. Beverly Hills, CA: Sage.

Capecchi, V. and Livolsi, M. (1973) *The Socialization Process in Pre-Adolescent Children*. Rome: RAI, Servizio Opinioni.

Edelstein, A.S. (1966) *Perspectives in Mass Communication*. Copenhagen: Einar Harcks Forlag.

Furu, T. (1971) *The Function of Television for Children and Adolescents*. Tokyo: Sophia University Press.

Himmelweit, H.T., Oppenheim, A.N. and Vince, P. (1958) *Television and the Child*. London: Oxford University Press.

Horton, D. and Wohl, R. (1956) 'Mass communication and para-social interaction', *Psychiatry*, 19(3): 215–9.

Huston Stein, A. (1972) 'Mass media and young children's development', in I.J. Gordon (ed.), *Early Childhood Education*, Vol. II. Chicago, IL: University of Chicago Press.

Katz, E. and Foulkes, D. (1962) 'On the use of mass media as "escape": clarification of a concept', *Public Opinion Quarterly*, XXVI: 377–88.

Klapper, J.T. (1963) 'Mass communication research: an old road resurveyed', *Public Opinion Quarterly*, 27: 515–27.

Maletzke, G. (1963) *Psychologie der Massenkommunikation*. Hamburg: Hans Bredow Institut.

Nordenstreng, K. (1969) 'Consumption of mass media in Finland', *Gazette*, 15: 249–59.

Nordström, B. and Thorén, S. (1972–3) *Studier Kring nyhetstbudet vid Sveriges Radio* [Studies of the Content of Swedish News on Television and Radio]. Stockholm: Audience and Programme Research Department.

Schramm, W., Lyle, J. and Parker, E.B. (1961) *Television in the Lives of Our Children*. Stanford, CA: Stanford University Press.

34

the future of the mass audience

W. RUSSELL NEUMAN

What are we to make of this technological juggernaut of the new media? On the one hand, we have been warned that these technologies pose an ominous threat to privacy and provide a tempting tool for the manipulation of a helpless mass public. On the other, we have heard of unprecedented opportunities for electronic participation, education, and communication. Lest the reader grow weary of this polarity or become suspicious that a pair of straw men lurk in the background, it may be appropriate to review how such a polarization of views arose in the first place and how we ought to respond to it.

First, such a polarity is a predictable outcome of the efforts of authors to attract attention to their views. In making the case that the structure and technology of communications are important to society, analysts tend to slide into pro or con views emphasizing threat or opportunity. Second, there is a natural tension between those who believe they stand to lose and those who expect to benefit from the developments in new, competing media. The most articulate champions of new media usually are investors and salesmen, who stand to profit directly. Their opposites, the Luddites, take their name from the frustrated workers of the early industrial revolution who calculated, quite correctly, that the new machines would threaten their traditional livelihood. Indeed, a number of forceful and sophisticated critiques of the new media have been written by those who continue to work for the old (Greenberger, 1985; Noam, 1985). Third, such contrapuntal worldviews frequently are tied to the prospect of disruptive and dramatic social change. The two sides in such debates concur that life will be very different. Change is more interesting that continuity. Tönnies predicted that the new technologies would lead to new forms of social organization, emphasizing market rather than personal relationships. Marx argued that history marches inevitably and irreversibly from capitalism to socialism. Weber characterized the modern age as moving toward rationalized, bureaucratic social organization. It would be counter-intuitive to conclude that fundamental changes in the technology of communications would not have equally fundamental effects on the flow of public information. But that, in large measure, is what the evidence indicates.

The shift to reliance on new means of communication will be evolutionary rather than revolutionary. The anticipated impacts of the new media are neither inevitable nor self-evident. It is not that our analysis leads to a prediction of no effects or no change. Far from it. Perhaps the appropriate analogy is a tug-of-war: On the two ends of a sturdy rope are powerful forces in tension. When new technologies conducive to increasingly diverse and smaller-scale mass communications emerge, commercial market forces and deeply ingrained media habits pull back hard in the other direction. If the rope moves only slowly in one direction or another, that should not be mistaken for evidence that the forces involved are not strong and significant.

But there is a further point. This process of change, although infused with conflicting, vested political and economic interests, is still subject to our collective control. The key to controlling it is to understand the nature of these forces in tension. We stand at a historic threshold. A new electronic infrastructure is about to be built. How it is to be designed and used should be the subject of a self-conscious inquiry. Moving away

First published in *The Future of the Mass Audience*, W.R. Neumann, Cambridge University Press (1991), as 'The Future of the Mass Audience', pp. 164–171.

from the mystique of historical inevitability and determinism can only be a step in the right direction.

THEORIES OF TECHNOLOGICAL EFFECTS

Some say that it is foolhardy to try to predict how the new technologies of communications will take shape, let alone to speculate on their social and political impacts. But the analysis here points to a clear-cut bottom line. The properties of digital electronics are convergent; they facilitate human calculations and communications. Getting a message to a large audience or to a select few will be cheaper and easier, in fact, dramatically so.

Given this conclusion about technological properties, how do we derive such a modest prediction about technological impacts? The answer is that although mediated political and cultural communications will change, the motivation to communicate will not. Communications are already remarkably inexpensive and convenient. It costs but a few dollars to make several telephone calls, write letters, or photocopy a newsletter. One can communicate with one's fellow citizens if moved to, but few are so moved. If there is an issue of great public concern, there are plentiful opportunities for the modern Thomas Paine to try to raise the consciousness of his fellow citizens. But such individuals are rare. Equally important, most citizens are not inclined to pay much attention (Neuman, 1986).

Perhaps the lesson of Mancur Olson's analysis of the costs and benefits of direct participation in politics is most apt (Olson, 1965): Who will participate in politics and how much effort they will put into it will depend on what they expect to get out of it. There is an informal but nonetheless rational set of ongoing calculations for individuals concerning whether or not political participation (like other forms of public activity) is worth the effort (Downs, 1957). These insights have been reinforced by subsequent research, including that of Gamson (1975) and DeNardo (1985) on protest behavior and the work of Verba and his colleagues on political participation and voting (Schlozman and Verba, 1979; Verba and Nie, 1972). If many citizens are ill-informed, misinformed, or ambivalent about their civic duties, it is not because the price of a newspaper is too high or because television news is scheduled at an inconvenient time. Such public attitudes and behaviors are not the beginning of a new and ominous trend; they are political constants, the backdrop against which all new technologies are introduced.

Christopher Arterton (1987), in a study parallel to this, examined 20 demonstration projects in which new communications technologies were used to facilitate public participation in policy-making. The enthusiasm and energy, as well as the technical resources, invested in those diverse projects were impressive. Congressmen participated in computer conferences with their constituents; community groups were brought together by two-way cable; satellite technology connected remote villages; electronic town meetings included debates, polls, and plebiscites. The findings were the same in almost every case: The enthusiastic initiators of those projects embraced the new technological means to an idealistically democratic end. Sometimes, with great effort, they succeeded in attracting public attention and stimulating thought, debate, and participation. Sometimes, despite the considerable talents and resources of the organizers, the inertia of a semiattentive political process seemed unaffected. In every case but one, however, as soon as the demonstration project was completed, the initiative was dropped. Reports were written up, and people moved on to other projects. The technologies were dismantled or sat idle. The one activity that did continue under its own power involved a mayor and community groups that had a taste and a talent for using community cable television for public discussion. The mayor believed, probably correctly so, that there were political benefits from the activity, and she was pleased to continue it. Therein lies the key to the communications 'revolution': It is less the push of the new media than the pull of the political cultures that may choose to use these technologies.

PLURALIST VERSUS MASS SOCIETY

A central question is whether or not the proliferation of new communications channels will lead to fragmentation of the mass audience. Over the past 30 years, a number of mass-audience magazines have gone into decline and apparently been replaced by smaller, special-interest publications. Cable television channels have sprung up, providing specialized information for different interest and ethnic groups. The share of the viewing audience captured by the three national networks has declined dramatically. Economic pressures have raised the possibility that the networks may have to cut back on national news coverage. As a result, concern has arisen that the common cultural and political identity of Americans, traditionally reinforced by the mass media, may be eroding.

My approach to addressing this matter has been to identify it not as a new issue but rather as a continuing and central problematic of political communications. The key issue is that of balance: balance between the center and the periphery, between different interest factions, between competing elites, between an efficient and effective central authority and the conflicting demands of the broader electorate.

My strategy has been to draw on two theoretical traditions that emerged at the close of World War II – mass society theory and communications/development theory – and explore whether or not the questions they raise can provide a common framework for analysis. Mass society theory warned that an overly strong central authority in control of the communications media could debilitate local authority and participation. Communications/development theory pointed out the appropriately central role of the media in defining and maintaining a sense of national identity and collective interest.

The two traditions converge in their emphasis on two concepts: community and pluralism. A national identity is not the sum of a series of rational calculations of individual self-interest. A sense of community and belonging meets fundamental human needs that transcend self-interest calculations. It is, after all, somewhat difficult to imagine people engaging in wartime heroics or political mass movements, or even mass participation in elections, simply on the basis of hardheaded cost-benefit calculations.

Some national identities and political cultures emphasize obedience to authority and homogeneity. Others emphasize individual initiative and pluralism. The key to the

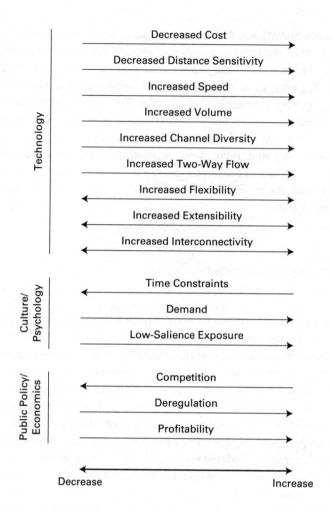

FIGURE 34.1   Pressures on communications volume

future of the mass audience lies in the subtle interplay of cultural and political norms and the structures of the media that convey them. What might we expect from the interaction between the new media and the American political culture?

There are, as outlined earlier, three sets of factors: (1) the character of the technology, (2) the mass psychology of habitual audience behavior, and (3) the political economy of the communications industries. Some factors are more critical than others, and some are more amenable to change. Some mechanisms operate at the aggregate level, and others at the level of individual behavior; so it is difficult simply to add them together. But for the purposes of overview, it may be helpful to array the factors we have analyzed in terms of the general direction of the expected effects. In doing so, we are led to two predictions: a clear increase in communications volume, but not a corresponding increase in communications diversity.

These patterns are summarized in Figures 34.1 and 34.2. Figure 34.1 outlines the forces that tend to increase the volume of public communications. Virtually all of the

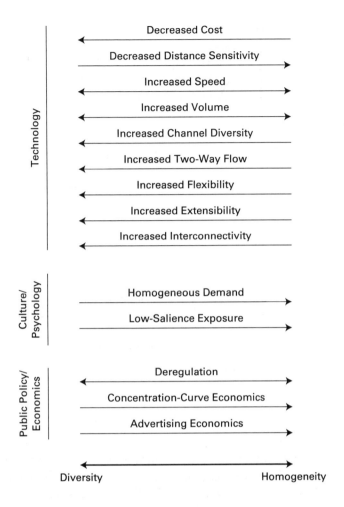

FIGURE 34.2 Pressures on communications homogeneity

technological factors have at least some component that is weighted toward greater communications volume. In the case of two-way interactive communications and the citizen's increased ability to electronically filter and scan the flow of information, it is not yet clear whether or not large segments of the public will exercise that control to decrease their exposure to news and public information. That is an important question for further research. The analysis of media psychology indicates, so far at least, a hearty appetite for the mass media, limited only by the simple constraint of available time. Exposure to broadcast media continues to climb, and the print media and even theatrical motion pictures appear to have held their own. The pattern of low-salience exposure means that people are not always highly attentive, but that leads to an increase rather than a decrease in overall communications volume. And finally, despite the constraints of market competition, the movement toward deregulation and the continuing profitability of the industry lead to an increased communications volume.

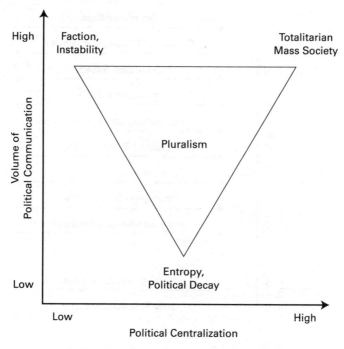

FIGURE 34.3 The equilibrium model revisited

But increased volume, as we have noted, does not guarantee increased diversity. In fact, unless significant changes in the cultural norms or economics of mass communications evolve, the forces pushing in the direction of communications homogeneity appear to be as strong as ever. Figure 34.2 summarizes the technological effects. They would appear to be about evenly balanced in terms of homogeneity of content. Both media habits and media economics, however, continue to involve strong incentives toward common-denominator mass-audience content. These structures and incentives are subject to change, but the pressure for change is not necessarily evident in the character of digital electronics.

We might turn at this point to the equilibrium model introduced earlier. If mass society theory and communications/development theory settle on a common ideal of community and national identity, balanced against political and cultural pluralism, how is such an ideal to be achieved? Figure 34.3 reproduces the basic dimensions of the equilibrium model, but now from the point of view of the individual citizen, rather than the working of the political system as a whole. It emphasizes not just what is made available to the individual, but how individual choices in an open market-place of information and media, in turn, can influence the direction of the market. Individuals do develop a sense of national identity and of civic duty. The mass media, as well as family and local institutions, are part of that process. Most individuals want to have a sense that they know what is going on in the world around them. Few are so alienated as to seek isolation from this flow of public information. Given the electronic ability to cut themselves off from public life, to bury themselves in highly specialized hobbies or escapist entertainment, some will exercise it, but probably no more than those who have done so before perhaps by means of science-fiction novels or stamp collecting.

There is ample evidence that people are distrustful of overly centralized media. Studies of the domestic propaganda machine in Nazi Germany, as well as media behavior in modern totalitarian regimes, indicate that, on the whole, people seek out confirming information from other sources. When information ministries routinely exaggerate, people learn to discount the reports they are fed. Furthermore, when the hubbub of conflicting voices gets to be extreme, people retreat and seek solace in the common norms of national identity.

Thus, in terms of Figure 34.3, we might expect the center of gravity to move upward, toward higher levels of communications volume. But unless we have an emergence of political forces as yet unforeseen that are entirely independent of the technological developments, the horizontal equilibrium will remain in balance.

When Gutenberg developed his printing press in the 1450s, he began a complex historical process that enhanced the ability of humans to communicate with each other across space and time. That process is still under way. Gutenberg, it can be presumed, had little trouble in deciding what book to print. It would be the Bible, of course. Much has changed as we stand on the threshold of the third millennium. The diversity of information available to us has increased manyfold. The satellite and optical fiber allow us to communicate text, voice, or moving images over thousands of miles almost effortlessly. One can imagine Gutenberg suddenly transported to our age and puzzling over the diversity of communications media at hand: People have so many books and other media available to them, he muses. What single book is most often found nowadays in the American home? It is the Bible, of course. Sometimes history moves at less than a revolutionary pace.

THE CRITICAL EPOCH

Although we have seen that the pressures of the new communications technologies are unlikely to bring a revolution in national politics, we are not led by the foregoing analysis to conclude that these new developments will be without effects. In fact, they offer intriguing opportunities for experimentation.

The bulk of the data and research reported here draws on the recent American experience with publishing and cable and broadcast television. The two central themes are the nature of the media habit of the mass audience and the incentives of the commercial marketplace for the media elite. The two, in interaction, indicate a pattern of common-denominator and politically centrist mass communications. The new media will not change this, in the main. But what about changes at the margins?

The media habit is subject to gradual change. We have a habit of watching television passively that is, in part, a product of the television technology that evolved in the 1940s. As the number of channels grows and the ability to interact with them expands, new opportunities will arise. Most new experiments, as Arterton (1987) has demonstrated, will likely fail. But if the norms and expectations of public communications begin to change at the margin, we would be remiss not to follow these issues closely.

The odd fit, at this historical epoch, concerns the market economics of commercially supported mass communications. Our media have valuable qualities, but the fundamental conservatism of advertiser-supported media limits experimentation. If it takes a decade for the new, pluralistic, niche markets for cultural and political communications to evolve and define themselves, which is not an unreasonable expectation, we shall find few entrepreneurs willing to take the losses necessary to see the decade through. The commercial media need not be replaced or constrained, but they could be complemented by a diversity of administrative structures to match the diversity of new technological potentials.

The evolution of public broadcasting out of a virtually moribund system of educational broadcasting in 1967 represented an exciting step forward. Public broadcasting continues to counterprogram to complement the commercial broadcasting entities. At this point we need to assess where the new media are and where they are headed in the commercial sphere, in order to see if the time may have come again to add new structures and new voices as an experiment in testing the potential of the new media.

Narrowcast Media

We have gotten used to the mass character of the mass media: newspapers with circulations in the tens of thousands, national magazines with hundreds of thousands of subscribers, and, of course, network television audiences in the tens of millions. New digital network technologies, however, will open up whole new domains of special-interest and special-purpose communications, narrowcasting rather than broadcasting. The outlook for a vibrant and dynamic cultural and political life in the United States is indeed positive.

Political theorists frequently remark on the importance of 'issue publics,' the virtual communities of like-minded individuals within a metropolitan area or around the country who will band together and speak out spontaneously in response to a public concern or event – an issue of religious or moral concern, or issues of self-interest among veterans, older citizens, or Hispanic-Americans. That was the essence of the vigorous citizen-based democracy that so impressed Alexis de Tocqueville when he toured the United States in the 1830s and wrote his classic *Democracy in America* (1836). What made that possible then was an extensive communications network within the small village. What may make it possible in the future for an urbanized, postindustrial society will be the rebirth of minimedia, the electronic soapbox, Thomas Paine on a computer network. We are seeing some evidence of that already.

Until recently, the natural separation between the telephone network and the broadcast networks led to a dichotomous choice between interpersonal communications or microcommunications and traditional mass communications. User-controlled, spontaneous, small-group communications, mixtures of a newsletter and a town meeting, create a new alternative: minicommunication.

Transactional Services

There is another capacity of an advanced network that is just now being explored: transactional services. We are all familiar with the primitive forms of telephone transactions for the residential customer: We see a product advertised on late-night television and order it by telephone with a credit card, or perhaps order an item from a direct-mail catalog by touch-tone telephone. Sometimes that proves to be convenient and productive, and sometimes not. The irony of these primitive versions of transactional services is that they carry with them all of the limiting and negative features of the advertising-based mass media; that is, all the information at hand is supplied by the seller. One sees the advertising stimulus and has only the options to resist or respond. What intelligent, two-way systems will permit is instantaneous inquiry for other information resources by the consumer while the transaction is in process: Is the firm reliable? Is the product well designed? What are the ecological effects of using this product? Is it offered elsewhere at a lower price? These may seem like minor issues, and with respect to a single purchase they may well be. But blurring the distinction between a broadcast information network, with its ads and newscasts, and an electronic marketplace, where individuals can register their requests for a particular bundle of goods, may well have significant effects on how the market for things and the market for ideas operate. The integrated network will allow for more interconnection between the two markets, and that is likely to have beneficial effects.

In an earlier study (Neuman, 1986), I described typical voters who had limited interest in and knowledge of politics, but who for reasons of good intentions and some social pressure found themselves in a voting booth: For whom should one vote? The names are vaguely familiar, but which one is which? I describe such voters as staring at their shoes in vain hope of some clue. Preceding any election there are debates, speeches, pamphlets, and numerous media reports and analyses of positions on the issues and candidate competencies, and from such a hubbub one may derive a vague sense of who the candidates are and who may best serve one's individual interests and those of the polity at large. But it is not easy. Well-paid media specialists in political campaigning continue to embellish the views and capacities of the candidate paying their bill, and to distort the views of the opponent.

Economists examining such a political marketplace might describe its operation as suboptimal. What would the economists and public-choice theorists suggest? Allow each consumer/voter to determine what criteria are of particular relevance to them. Allow them to gather information on those criteria from trusted independent sources. Allow them to gather this information at the time they need it, when a decision must be made.

The evolving integrated network will make it easier for information markets and product markets to approach such an ideal. It will take time because cultural expectations and technical capacities interact in delicate chemistry. Some citizens will decline to take advantage of all the information resources offered to them, as do a great many people today. But even if only a few people do, imagine the consequences.

REFERENCES

Arterton, F.C. (1987) 'Campaign organizations confront the media-political environment', in J.D. Barber (ed.), *Race for the Presidency*. Englewood Cliffs, NJ: Prentice-Hall.

Arterton, F.C. (1987) *Teledemocracy: Can Technology Protect Democracy...?* Newbury Park, CA: Sage.

DeNardo, J. (1985) *Power in Numbers: The Political Strategy of Protest and Rebellion*. Princeton, NJ: Princeton University Press.

Downs, A. (1957) *An Economic Theory of Democracy*. New York: Harper & Row.

Gamson, W.A. (1975) *The Strategy of Social Protest*. Chicago, IL: Dorsey Press.

Greenberger, M. (ed.) (1985) *Electronic Publishing Plus: Media for a Technological Future*. White Plains, NY: Knowledge Industries Press.

Neuman, W.R. (1986) *The Paradox of Mass Protest*. Cambridge, MA: Harvard University Press.

Noam, E.M. (ed.) (1985) *Video Media Competition: Regulation, Economics and Technology*. New York: Columbia University Press.

Olson, M. (1965) *The Logic of Collective Action: Public Goods and the Theory of Groups*. Cambridge, MA: Harvard University Press.

Schlozman, K.L. and Verba, S. (1979) *Injury to Insult: Unemployment, Class and Political Participation*. Cambridge, MA: Harvard University Press.

Verba, S. and Nie, N.H. (1972) *Participation in America: Political Democracy and Social Democracy*. New York: Harper & Row.

MASS MEDIA EFFECTS

The first chapter in this book (Gitlin, Chapter 1) sets out the classic sociological view of how mass media effects occur, and it also heavily criticizes the comforting supposition that we are protected from the unwanted power and influence of mass media by our social environment and the networks of social contact to which we generally belong. Subsequent chapters by Herman (Chapter 4) and Mills (Chapter 5) present the case for powerful media operating largely in the interests of the 'established power'. Theory of media effect has continually veered between stressing and relativizing the power of mass media, providing no clear conclusion, not surprisingly in the light of continuing change in the mass media themselves and in their relation to the surrounding environment. But progress has been made in identifying a number of the conditions under which effects are more or less likely and which can be examined in specific circumstances.

There has typically been a quasi-monopolistic representation of the 'social reality' that lies beyond personal experiences, that most of us cannot easily resist (lacking motivation or alternative information resources). The 'cultivation' theory of Gerbner and associates (see Signorielli and Morgan, 1990) is the most developed exposition of this view. Our chapter by Katz (Chapter 35) deals with some of the issues of public opinion, more or less within the same set of assumptions about society and the mass media. This chapter also examines the 'spiral of silence' theory of Elisabeth Noelle-Neumann (1984) that figured centrally in her 'return to the concept of powerful mass media'.

Another of the chapters below (Entman, Chapter 36) deals with one quite well-documented aspect of the influence of mass media news by way of the process of 'framing'. The theoretical formulation is plausible and testable and offers useful critical insights into contemporary informational processes. The third chapter (Wartella et al., Chapter 37) briefly but succinctly summarizes key theoretical insights into one of the most extensively studied aspects of the potential effects of mass media – that of the portrayal of violence. The fourth chapter (Zillmann, Chapter 38) is a reminder that the 'effects' of mass media are not confined to behavioural (doing, buying, voting, etc.) or cognitive matters (learning and opinion formation), nor are they mainly negative. They are more often affective and emotional, and are positively sought out by audiences. Research based on media gratification theory has produced much evidence that media use is motivated by emotional needs of many kinds and the search for various personal pleasures. We know this from personal experience, although it has not figured much in the dominant theoretical paradigm. The various 'pleasures' of media use have often been described within the cultural studies tradition, but, as our chapter shows, they can also be treated as aspects of individual behaviour.

The way media seem to be developing offers no escape from a continued preoccupation with the issue of 'effects', notwithstanding the supposed 'demassification' as a result of new media. In respect of politics they have become, if anything, more important as the platform for political expression, and the link between political elites and events and the 'people' has developed. The 'media logic' referred to in Part VII has been said to exert a strong and malign influence on the way democratic politics is played out by way of mass media, diminishing its substance and sapping its vitality. As institutional actors in an 'information society', media firms have more financial power than in the past, as well as global reach, and the old spectre of the media magnate pulling political strings is not just fanciful. New media forms pose a challenge for reconceptualizing media 'power' in more relevant ways than as either dominant 'message systems' or 'gatekeepers'.

REFERENCES

Noelle-Neumann, E. (1984) *The Spiral of Silence*. Chicago, IL: University of Chicago Press.
Signorielli, N. and Morgan, M. (eds) (1990) *Cultivation Analysis*. Newbury Park, CA: Sage.

35

publicity and pluralistic ignorance: notes on 'the spiral of silence'

ELIHU KATZ

It is strange, but true, that public opinion research, mass communications research and public opinion theory have become disconnected. It is difficult even to explain how any one of these can exist without the others, and yet the fact is that each has wandered off on its own. It is to the great credit of Elisabeth Noelle-Neumann that she has taken the lead in trying to bring them together again.[1] Beginning with her call for a 'return to a theory of powerful mass media', Noelle-Neumann has been trying to show how the dynamics of media production and the dynamics of opinion formation interact, and how the process of this interaction can be described empirically by means of creative polling techniques.[2] There may be room for debate over her inferences from the data, but nobody can underestimate the importance of her attempt to put the whole together.

If I may be permitted to summarize this effort impressionistically, drawing on a number of papers all at once,[3] I would state her argument as follows: (1) Individuals have opinions; (2) Fearing isolation, individuals will not express their opinions if they perceive themselves unsupported by others; (3) A 'quasi-statistical sense' is employed by individuals to scan the environment for signs of support; (4) Mass media constitute the major source of reference for information about the distribution of opinion and thus for the climate of support/nonsupport; (5) So do other reference groups (but the relative importance of these is not clear, on which see below – EK); (6) The media tend to speak in one voice, almost monopolistically; (7) The media tend to distort the distribution of opinion in society, biased as they are by the (leftist) views of journalists; (8) Perceiving themselves unsupported, groups of individuals – who may, at times, even constitute a majority – will lose confidence and withdraw from public debate, thus speeding the demise of their position through the self-fulfilling spiral of silence. They may not change their own minds, but they stop recruitment of others and abandon the fight; (9) Society is manipulated and impoverished thereby (for the absence of dialogue and/or the repression of truth – these inferences are not spelled out by Noelle-Neumann). Thus the 'powerful effect' assigned to mass communication is a subtle one. The media are not perceived as agents of direct influence, but rather as reporters on the distribution of (acceptable) opinion. The media are used by individuals as indicators to determine who may speak and who should remain silent. The extreme case – illustrated in two recent German elections – is one of 'pluralistic ignorance' in which individual supporters of one of the major political parties believed their cause to be doomed because they inferred from the media that 'everyone' believed the other side would win, and began to believe so themselves.

Assuming that this exposition of the 'spiral of silence' is reasonably accurate, I should now like to comment on a number of aspects of the thesis. My object is not to evaluate findings – indeed, I shall not consider empirical findings at all – but to discuss underlying assumptions, raise questions about certain elements of the theory, attempt to relate it to ongoing work of myself and others, and to explore its implications for our image of modern society and its future. For lack of an integrated theory of my own, I shall do this in the form of notes and comments, in no formal order, for which I ask the reader's indulgence. Specifically, I would like (1) to compare the role of communication in Noelle-Neumman's thesis to the 'liberating' role of publicity implicit in the traditional treatment of pluralistic ignorance, by which individuals learn what they

First published in *Public Opinion and Social Change: for Elisabeth Noelle-Neumann*, H. Baier, H.M. Kepplinger and K. Reumann, Wiesbaden: Westdeutscher Verlag, as 'Publicity and Pluralistic Ignorance: notes on the spiral of silence', pp. 28–38.

had not known before, namely that others think as they do; (2) to raise the question of the conditions under which individuals might be expected to break a spiral of silence; (3) to consider a case at the opposite extreme where 'everybody knows' something and 'everybody knows that everybody knows', and thus where publicity might be expected to be merely redundant; (4) to relate Noelle Neumann's image of powerful media to similar claims by others.

PUBLICITY AND PLURALISTIC IGNORANCE

Floyd Allport's concept of pluralistic ignorance has been used by social psychologists to explain ostensibly rapid social change.[4] When everybody believes that he is the only one who thinks something, and does not talk about his opinion for fear of violating a moral taboo or an authoritarian ruler, or of just being unpopular, it sometimes happens that a wave of publicity will sweep through the community, informing people that everybody else (or many others) think as they do. In such cases, what appears to be revolutionary change – say, the uprising in Poland in 1956, or the changed status of homosexuals following publication of the *Kinsey Report* – may not be the product of a basic change in attitude but, rather, the result of changed perception of the distribution of opinion. In this view, communication is perceived as liberating. The Emperor's New Clothes, of course, is the classic example. The tailors duped the vain Emperor into believing that only wise men could see his golden-threaded suit. Nobles and officials believed it, too, or at least they acted as if they did, for fear of betraying their incompetence. So did the common people, perhaps out of fear. Only the child – with nothing to lose – declared publicly that the Emperor was naked.

Silence, it appears, is a reaction to taboo, fear and shame – for those who think differently than what they perceive others to be thinking. Asch finds that some people actually begin to *see* things as they think the others do.[5] Most people, however, continue to think as they thought, deferring to the majority either out of self-doubt or self-protection. Even a single truth-teller is enough to wipe out the effect on the naive subject of a large majority.[6] The experimental literature has focussed only rarely on this enlightening function of interpersonal communication. Most laboratory research has examined only the pressures toward conformity exerted by groups on their members. By comparison with such studies of small groups, communications theory and research has focussed as much on the enlightening, as on the repressive, role of communication. Of course the media propound false consciousness! But in democratic societies, where the media may speak out against authority, or where journalistic norms require balance, something close to truth is often to be seen and heard, or at least inferred.[7] Truth-telling liberates people from their reticence to reveal their true thoughts to others, thus reviving a social network that has become atomized or atrophied by perceptions of the consensus, true or false.

Noelle-Neumann wants us to consider the dark side of mass communication. Even in the democracies, media – like interpersonal communication – can impose acquiescence and silence, in defiance of the free flow of information. People will become disconnected from each other, warns Noelle-Neumann, if the media practice misrepresentation and monopolization. People, searching for support, will scan their environments in vain if the distribution of opinions is misrepresented and if the media arbitrarily shut out the plurality of voices. Such monopolization (Noelle-Neumann calls it 'consonance') offers no basis for selectivity, and one readily finds oneself outside the ostensible consensus. Noelle-Neumann feels that the communications literature has underestimated this state of affairs and the powerful media that sustain it. Lazarsfeld and Merton noted that monopolization of the media does, indeed, produce more powerful effects, but they do not associate media monopolization with Western democracy.[8] Noelle-Neumann does, thus ironically joining forces with the critical school, from the other side of the political spectrum. There is 'consonance' in media, and it is on the right, say the Frankfurt school and their descendants. Noelle-Neumann sees it on the left, and brings data to bear.

Has the concentration of media ownership, and the professionalization of journalism, really led to a narrowing of the range of opinion offered to the public? Is the narrowing, if there is one, biased towards the left, in spite of the economic and political interests of those who control the media?[9] Does television news typically reflect the ideological leanings of its editors and reporters? *Should* the press be expected to mirror – in news and editorials – the gamut of opinion in the population? Should reality, as reported by journalists, be expected to coincide with the reality of, say, the Central Bureau of Statistics or of opinion polls?[10] Noelle-Neumann appears to be saying yes to all of these questions and it remains for the rest of us to join in the debate.

BREAKING THE SILENCE

When will individuals speak out against a consensus? Asch found certain of his subjects self-confident and fiercely dedicated to the independence of their own observations; some were independent but withdrawn; some maintained their independence because of their commitment to carrying out the assigned task.[11] Reviewing the experimental literature on conformity, Kretch et al. suggest that individuals are more independent when status in the group is less important to them, or when they can expect to be rewarded by an outsider for non-conformity, as when a prize is offered for being right or for being independent.[12] A recent paper by James Coleman takes us a step further.[13] Like the laboratory experimenters, Coleman assumes that individuals are motivated by self-interest; this may sometimes lead to action that takes no account of the group or action that is contingent on what the others do. Such contingent behavior, however, may be similar or opposite to the others' actions. (Unlike Coleman, Noelle-Neumann appears to assume that self-interest is regularly expressed in terms of conformity.) Coleman asks us to consider the conditions under which a rational individual, calculating his self-interest, will make his behavior or his thought contingent on that of others, or in Coleman's words, will invest in others the authority to determine his own behavior. Among his illustrations from collective behavior, Coleman tells us of some individuals, trapped with a crowd in a fire, who will run for the exit under any circumstances, while some will run only if others do. People *closer* to the door are more likely to run first, says Coleman, since they have most to gain by running: those who make their running contingent on whether others run have less to gain by running.

These same dynamics, suggests Coleman, can help explain the phenomenon of milling crowds who seem suddenly to erupt in revolution or in dissidence. Typically, in such situations discontented people gather around some symbolic target. They do not act at first because they (1) know that the police, or some other agency of enforcement, will punish them for illegal action, and (2) they are not certain about how others in the crowd think. In such circumstances, members of the crowd continue to circulate, keeping one eye on the police and another on the crowd. If somebody acts, however, others will quickly follow. The actor is, typically, somebody who has little to gain from obedient behavior, and/or who is perceptive enough to know that the others are with him. Once he has acted, the *ratio* of possible loss to possible gain changes. That is, each successive actor is less likely to be caught and punished as the crowd overwhelms the police and the attractions of expressive or revolutionary action increasingly outweigh its dangers. This takes us a step beyond Noelle-Neumann's assertion that 'at the beginning and toward the end of changes in the climate of opinion, minorities – avant garde and hard core – are more willing to stand up for their opinion than the majority, while during the hot phase, when the new opinion actually begins to prevail, those who think that they are, or soon will be, the majority, are more willing to do so.'[14]

But in most of the statements of Noelle-Neumann the emphasis is on conformity rather than independence. People seek affiliation and thus celebrate the unity of their shared perceptions; those who feel outside this consensus fall silent. Noelle-Neumann's majorities are social beings; the minorities speak only to each other and, gradually, to no one at all. She has very little to say about independents, or about those who have more distant reference groups. Ostensibly, the independents are the heroes of democracy. They not only stand up for their opinions, but in situations of pluralistic ignorance, they ignite the process of rapid social change. But it is evident – consider Coleman's example of the rioting crowd – that pluralistic ignorance may sometimes keep passion in check. It is sometimes a functional fiction – not only for the society, but for the individual as well – to assume that one's fellows do not share one's baser feelings and prejudices. A liberating communication – an independent voice spreading knowledge of shared passions – may also shatter a society. It is no wonder that advocates of free speech prefer also to assume that their fellows are reasonable.

PUBLICITY AS COMMITMENT

Communication may be liberating, we have seen, or it may be an agent of repression. It may stimulate further communication, or it may cause silence to spread. In the one case, communication may be seen to correct a false impression; it permits 'true consciousness' to prevail. In the opposite case, communication is the agent of pluralistic ignorance, or of false consciousness, causing people to misperceive what their similarly-situated fellows think or believe. In both cases, communication is used to transmit information about what relevant others are thinking or doing. It is obvious that when people want to know what others think, communication of such information will have an effect. But consider the curious case where everybody knows something, and everybody knows that everybody knows, and yet communication of that piece of information will have an effect nevertheless. The history of the State of Israel provides a number of case-studies of this phenomenon.[15] In the 1950s, for example, Jewish immigrants were permitted to leave Poland for Israel. This fact was never publicly acknowledged, either in Poland or in

Israel, and strict censorship on this matter was imposed on the Israeli press. Yet, it is almost certain that everybody who mattered – Poland, Israel, the United States, the Soviet Union – all knew, and each knew that the others knew. The very same dynamics are evident in the imposition of censorship on publication of the primary source from which Israel received its oil in the 1950s and 1960s. In this case, too, it is likely that all relevant actors knew, and knew that the others knew. Certainly informed public opinion in Israel knew, and it is likely that decision-makers in Iran, the Arab states, as well as the US and Russia all knew, and were aware that the others knew. Then why the taboo on publication? What difference would such information make?

That it would make a difference is evident from the reaction to the adoption by the Knesset of the Law of Jerusalem in the Summer of 1980. The Law declares Jerusalem the capital of Israel, thus reiterating officially a situation that had existed *de facto* and perhaps even *de jure*. Foreign embassies that had been located in Jerusalem since the establishment of the State in 1948 – attesting to the widespread recognition that everybody knew, and that everybody knew that everybody knew – felt constrained to leave the capital. A related example comes from the Eastern bloc: a 'new economic order' was established in one of the Eastern European countries and everybody, including government, acted in accord with it. But there was a strict taboo on mention of this in the press, and when the first violation did occur, repercussions were drastic. Entire nations may collectively misrepresent themselves with full knowledge that they are living schizophrenically.

One could multiply examples from both the public and the private spheres. Many cities have acknowledged pockets of violation or deviance. So-called blue-laws which require shops to remain closed on the Sabbath in certain American cities are often violated, with the knowledge and tacit consent of buyers, police and municipalities. Similarly, the existence and location of red-light districts is often well-known. Yet a letter to the editor of a newspaper, or a speech in Parliament – even when they do not add any information at all, since everybody knows and everybody knows that everybody knows – will cause authorities to enforce the norm. In the private sphere, it is not unusual for all parties involved in a case of adultery – even the 'deceived' spouse – to know and to know that everybody knows, and yet to wish to keep the matter unpublicized. The knowledgeable spouse may even insist that he doesn't 'want to know'. A gossip columnist can change all that. Similar dynamics are involved in social change. Persons favoring legalized abortion or homosexual practice, for example, may purposely insist on publicizing what is already known in order to challenge the norm. Their object, paradoxically, is to publish what is already known by all to be the case – not to add information, but to make it 'public' or 'official'.

The classic literature of communication is aware of this norm-enforcing role of communication.[16] Exposing deviance and thus rallying society to reinforce a norm is a familiar function of mass communication. But the assumption is that the journalist has exposed something 'new'. Why should exposing something 'old' – something that everybody already knows – make such a difference? It is true that there will always be somebody who doesn't know, and it is equally true that there will always be somebody who didn't know that the other knew – but let us assume, for the moment, that there are no such people. Let us assume that everybody knows and everybody knows that everybody knows and ask how it is that publication matters. The symbolic-interactionist will answer in terms of the idea of negotiated reality.[17] So long as the information is not published – that is, so long as it is not 'public' – there is flexibility open to all concerned in the assignment of meaning. 'This shop isn't open on Sundays; we are just doing some repair work.' But if Poland or Iran or the Blue Laws are mentioned by name, if the red-light district is signposted, it leaves no room for ambiguity.

More specifically, publication of a violation – even one about which all know – calls for a reaction of our public selves. While we can tolerate a certain form of deviance privately and unofficially, we cannot allow ourselves to do so publicly and officially. Publicly, the norm must either be upheld or defied: there is no room for ambiguity. It follows that we can probably tolerate a higher level of dissonance privately than publicly. Our public selves are more consistent. Thus, publication – even in a situation where everybody knows, and everybody knows that everybody knows – has consequences because it forces people to *take account* of the fact that the others know. Prior to publication, an actor may act *as if* only he knew – because he does not have to acknowledge that the others know as well. (Note that this is the very opposite of the case of pluralistic ignorance where each person believes that he is the only one who knows. In the present case, all know that the others know. But in both cases one acts as if the others think differently.)

When news of the broken norm is published, however, one can no longer act as if the others do not know. In this 'public' situation, where the norm-violator has to take account of his audience, he must decide whether to retreat into consonance, or publicly declare that he is *committed* to the violation, that is, to some new norm. In other words, the fact of publication of an act of norm-violation forces the violator to face up to the demands of the norm-upholders or to defy them openly. In choosing defiance, he may well base his decision on his perception of the extent to which those who have tacitly concurred in his deviance will now give him open support. Whereas the stone-thrower in Coleman's crowd, or the would-be charismatic leader, must employ his refined quasi-statistical sense to judge whether the crowd agrees with him and will follow him, the norm-violator in the present instance already knows that the others agree privately. His problem is whether they will agree *publicly*, or in other words, whether they will follow him in public. A community cannot tolerate the public flaunting of immorality/illegality, as if to say 'I really mean it'. Even despots – who sense that the people support them – sometimes do not make public their horrific actions and do not make them into laws for fear that *public* opinion will not tolerate them.[18]

PUBLICITY, FALSE CONSCIOUSNESS, SILENCE, MASS SOCIETY

Noelle-Neumann's spiral of silence theory brings us back to theories of the mass society. The essentials of these theories, from which the earliest models of mass communication were derived, consist of atomized individuals, on the one hand, and powerful agencies of remote social control, on the other. The more the media speak in one voice, and the more people are disconnected from each other, from intermediate organizations (church, trade union, political party, voluntary organizations, etc.) and from their past, the more absolute is the rule of the media and their masters. Empirical research on mass communication beginning in the late 1930s argued that this model did not seem to apply. Mass media campaigns were less effective than was expected because the voice of the media was not monolithic; people belonged to organizations and to primary groups, and their exposure to media influence was mediated by two important filters: (1) selectivity which protects prior opinions and attitudes from being overwhelmed, and (2) interpersonal relations which are forums for pre-testing, forming and changing opinions and attitudes. Subsequent models of mass communication are based on transferring to the people some part of the power originally attributed to the media.[19]

The current call for a return to theories of powerful media – of which Noelle-Neumann's is a major representative – must show that the mediating processes of selectivity and interpersonal relations were inapplicable when they were originally enunciated or are inapplicable now. In his critique of *Personal Influence*, Gitlin claims they were inapplicable then.[20] Interpersonal communication, he says, is only a conduit through which media influence is relayed and has no real relevance therefore, except to distract public attention from the omnipotent media. Moreover, says Gitlin, personal influence was the primary source for only 48 percent of *political* decisions (as compared with much higher proportions for decisions in the fields of marketing, fashions and movie-going) and thus its role in politics is misrepresented in Katz and Lazarsfeld. The mass society has long been with us, says Gitlin.

Not so, say Gerbner and Gross,[21] or, indeed, Noelle-Neumann. These authors, and others, are saying that the theories of mass society of 50 years ago are now (again?) becoming truly applicable to the modern, democratic societies of the West. They think that things have changed. They believe, first of all, that television is different from its predecessors. Viewing television is a more 'total' experience, appealing, as it does, to eyes and ears, providing information, entertainment, and companionship – in short, a symbolic environment in place of the real world outside. Noelle-Neumann has data to show that television owners lose interest in their jobs, apparently preferring to stay home.[22] Gerbner and Gross argue that the image of urban violence as augmented by television helps to keep people home, and thus disconnected from the larger society.

As was noted above, the effect of television viewing for Noelle-Neumann is an indirect one: by portraying the (false) climate of opinion, TV causes people to perceive a reality different from the one that surrounds them. Similarly, Gerbner et al. argue that reality as perceived by heavy television viewers is a reflection of what they have seen and heard on television and not in the real world. Thus, a vicious circle is at work in which people fear the world portrayed by television because of its violence (Gerbner and Gross) or its misrepresentation of the climate of opinion (Noelle-Neumann), causing people to feel lonely, retreat into their nuclear cells to watch television, talking neither to neighbor nor spouse, but to be satisfied, apparently, with their many hours of viewing. Cut off as they are from work and other affiliations, they are all the more vulnerable to manipulation by the media. Moreover, says Noelle-Neumann, the message of the media is monopolistic, due to the journalists' professional proclivity to peek over each other's shoulders and to their shared ideological leanings. Thus, selectivity and interpersonal communication are neutralized as mediating factors, and the media of mass communication may indeed be described as 'powerful'.

It is extremely interesting that Gitlin, Gerbner and Gross, and Noelle-Neumann, despite their very different theoretical and ideological orientations, share the idea that the media are active agents of false consciousness, constraining people to misperceive their environment and their own place in it. Following in the steps of the Frankfurt school, Gitlin argues that the media suppress opposition and reinforce existing authority by making things look much better than they are. Gerbner and Gross agree that the media reinforce the status quo, by depoliticizing people, by teaching them their proper place in the status system, and by inculcating fear of social interaction. For a different set of reasons, already reviewed, Noelle-Neumann also notes a withdrawal from social interaction and political activity (along with an overall increase in political interest) but she sees the media as agents for undermining establishments rather than as agents for their glorification.

In a general way, these more subtle, more sociological definitions of effect are familiar from the theoretical writings of critics of mass communication and mass society. They are anchored in the belief that the media can 'construct reality' and impose their construction on defenseless minds. The innovation in the work of this generation of critics – of whom Noelle-Neumann and Gerbner and Gross are leading representatives – is in their painstaking efforts to spell out the processes – social and psychological – through which these effects are thought to take place and to put empirical tests to some of the steps in the process. Such theorizing also constrains those who disagree to be precise! In the last few years, the work of the Gerbner team has engendered such reactions, and a sharp but focussed debate is presently in progress between Gerbner and Gross and certain critics.[23] Noelle-Neumann's data have not yet been subject to such criticism, at least not in English-language journals. The progress of science clearly warrants such debate. In a word, one must ask whether we are entering a new era of mass society? Are modern media reducing the political choices offered to citizens of Western democracies? Are the media serving as substitutes for reference and membership groups? Are individuals less involved and less active in their organizational affiliations? Is there a retreat from interpersonal communication on public affairs? Are people becoming more silent? I will not attempt to answer these questions, since I have not set out to criticize the available data or to marshall new data of my own. I would like to elaborate on only one of the above questions which seems to me a key to the others: Are mass media usurping the place of reference groups?[24]

Central to Noelle-Neumann's thesis is the notion that the media have come to substitute for reference groups. It is strongly implicit in the Noelle-Neumann papers that people decide whether or not to be silent on the basis of the distribution of opinion reported (often incorrectly) by the media. But Noelle-Neumann herself is ambivalent in her presentation of this point. The spiral of silence theory itself cannot so easily dismiss the direct influence of actual membership and reference groups. Consider two examples: (1) In discussing the data on recall of how one voted, Noelle-Neumann points out that recall is distorted not so much by national or even regional election results as by the distribution of votes within demographic and social groupings with which respondents are identified. (2) When groups retreat into silence, or when conflict polarizes opinion, Noelle-Neumann tells us that one's membership group becomes more salient as a reference group. In such circumstances, individuals are likely to misperceive the world not because they use the media as reference but because they have their own proximate groups to which they refer. In these two examples, and elsewhere, Noelle-Neumann reminds us of the importance of real-life reference groups, contact with whom is not, typically, mediated by mass communications. This is not just a minor point. It is basic to our entire perspective on society whether the media are usurping and monopolizing the role of reference groups. If reference groups are alive and well, individuals will not so quickly fall silent in the face of mass-communicated information about the opinion attributed by journalists to some vaguely defined majority, or by journalists to themselves. And discussion can continue.

If reference groups are declining and people becoming more victimized by pluralistic ignorance and fear of isolation, we are in trouble, indeed.

NOTES

1 Tamar Liebes assisted me in exploring the interrelations among the ideas of Elisabeth Noelle-Neumann and those of James Coleman, Todd Gitlin, George Gerbner and others noted below. I also wish to thank Professor Marc Galanter who is interested in pluralistic ignorance from the point of view of the law, as well as Professor and Mrs David Weiss-Halivni, Professor Ruth Katz, Dr Yvette Biro and Pierre Motyl who contributed and clarified in various ways. Members of the faculty-student interdepartmental seminar in social psychology at the Hebrew University, under the leadership of Professor Shalom Schwartz, helpfully reacted to an earlier version of the chapter.

2 Elisabeth Noelle-Neumann, 'Return to the concept of powerful mass media', in H. Eguchi and K. Sata (eds), *Studies of Broadcasting*, No. 9, NHK (Tokyo: 1973), pp. 67–112.

3 In addition to the 1973 paper, ibid., I draw on the following writings of Elisabeth Noelle-Neumann: 'Spiral of silence: a theory of public opinion', *Journal of Communication*, 24 (1974), pp. 43–51; 'Turbulences in the climate of opinion: methodological applications of the spiral of silence theory', *Public Opinion Quarterly*, 41 (1977), pp. 143–58; and 'Mass media and social change in developed societies', in Elihu Katz and Tamas Szecsko (eds), *Mass Media and Social Change* (London: Sage, 1981), pp. 119–42.

4 Textbook discussions of the concept of 'pluralistic ignorance' can be found in Theodore Newcomb, *Social Psychology* (New York: Dryden, 1950), and in David Kretch, Richard S. Crutchfield and Egerton L. Ballachey, *Individual in Society* (New York: McGraw-Hill, 1972).

5 Solomon E. Asch, 'Effects of group pressure upon the modification and distortion of judgments', in E. Maccoby, T. Newcomb and P. Hartley (eds), *Readings in Social Psychology*, 3rd edn (New York: Holt, 1958). See also the Crutchfield technique as described in Kretch et al., *Individual in Society*, op. cit., pp. 509–12.

6 Ibid.

7 In this connection see the recent reviews by J.G. Blumler of research paradigms in American and European communication studies and the democratic contexts in which they are pursued, 'Mass communications research – a transatlantic perspective', *Journalism Quarterly*, 55 (1978), pp. 219–30 and 'Mass communication research in Europe', *Media, Culture and Society*, 2 (1980), pp. 367–76, especially pp. 373–5.

8 Paul F. Lazarsfeld and Robert K. Merton, 'Mass communication, popular taste and organized social action' (1948), reprinted in Wilbur Schramm and Donald Roberts (eds), *Process and Effects of Mass Communication* (Urbana: University of Illinois Press, 1971).

9 A sophisticated discussion of this problem is Alvin Gouldner, *Dialectics of Ideology and Technology* (London: Macmillan, 1976).

10 This is an assumption in such recent works as Glasgow University Media Group, *Bad News* (London: Routledge and Kegan Paul, 1976), where official statistics of man-days lost in strikes are compared with extent of media coverage of the same strikes.

11 Asch, 'Effects of group presure', op. cit.

12 Kretch et al., *Individual in Society,* op. cit., pp. 512 ff.

13 James S. Coleman, 'Authority systems', *Public Opinion Quarterly,* 44 (1980), pp. 143–63.

14 Noelle-Neumann, 'Turbulences', op. cit., p. 151.

15 These cases are discussed in Dina Goren, *Secrecy and the Right to Know* (Tel Aviv: Turtledove Press, 1979).

16 See Lazarsfeld and Merton, 'Mass communication, popular taste', op. cit.

17 See Anselm Strauss, *Negotiations* (San Francisco, CA: Josey-Bass, 1978).

18 Interpreting the despotism of Pharaoh toward the Hebrews, the 13th century biblical commentator, Rabbi Moses ben Nahman (Nahmanides) anticipated this point. When Pharaoh says to his advisers, 'Let us outwit them' (Exodus 1:10), Nahmanides observes that the king feared that an open attack upon the Hebrews would cause defections in the army ('in the face of an arbitrary attack on a people who had come to Egypt at the invitation of a former king') and, moreover, that *'the people would not give permission to the king* to act so unjustly. ... Pharaoh's order to act deviously [was] so that the Israelites would not realize that he was acting against them out of hate.' Ironically, when Moses made public Pharaoh's scheming, the Israelites turned against Moses in anger. By putting Pharaoh's conspiracy into the open (i.e. now that everybody knows), 'the Egyptians will increase their hatred of us and libel us by saying that we are rebelling against the throne. They will no longer have to resort to trickery; they will kill us.' Free translation, paraphrasing, underlining and parentheses are mine – E.K.

19 For a discussion of these models, see Elihu Katz, 'On conceptualizing media effects', in Thelma McCormack (ed.), *Studies in Communication,* Vol. I (Bridgeport, CT: JAI Press, 1980).

20 See Todd Gitlin, 'Media sociology: the dominant paradigm', *Theory and Society,* 6 (1978), pp. 205–53. This paper is in sharp criticism of Elihu Katz and Paul Lazarsfeld, *Personal Influence* (Glencoe, IL: The Free Press, 1956).

21 See George Gerbner and Larry Gross, 'Living with television: the violence profile', *Journal of Communication,* 26 (1976), pp. 173–99, and a series of subsequent papers by these authors and their associates, in the same journal, in succeeding years.

22 Noelle-Neumann, Mass media and social change', op. cit.

23 See Paul M. Hirsch, 'The "scary world" of the nonviewer and other anomalies: a reanalysis of Gerbner et al.'s findings on cultivation analysis, part I and part II', *Communication Research,* 7 (1980), pp. 403–56, and 8 (1981); Michael Hughes, 'The fruits of cultivation analysis: a reexamination of some effects of television watching', *Public Opinion Quarterly,* 44 (1980), pp. 287–302; J.M. Wober, 'Televised violence and paranoid perception: the view from Great Britain', *Public Opinion Quarterly,* 42 (1978), pp. 315–21. A detailed reply appears in George Gerbner, Larry Gross, Michael Morgan and Nancy Signorielli, 'A curious journey into the scary world of Paul Hirsch', *Communication Research,* 8 (1981), pp. 3–38, 39–72.

24 The classic discussion of this concept is Robert K. Merton and Alice Kitt, 'Contributions to the theory of reference group behavior', in R.K. Merton and P.F. Lazarsfeld (eds), *Studies in the Scope and Method of the American Soldier* (Glencoe, IL: Free Press, 1950), pp. 40–105. See also continued discussions of this topic in the several recent editions of R.K. Merton, *Social Theory and Social Structure* (New York: Macmillan-Free Press, 1958.) Pioneer of this field is Herbert H. Hyman, 'The psychology of status', *Archives of Psychology,* 269 (1942).

36

framing: towards clarification of a fractured paradigm

ROBERT M. ENTMAN

In response to the proposition that communication lacks disciplinary status because of deficient core knowledge, I propose that we turn an ostensible weakness into a strength. We should identify our mission as bringing together insights and theories that would otherwise remain scattered in other disciplines. Because of the lack of interchange among the disciplines, hypotheses thoroughly discredited in one field may receive wide acceptance in another. Potential research paradigms remain fractured, with pieces here and there but no comprehensive statement to guide research. By bringing ideas together in one location, communication can aspire to become a master discipline that synthesizes related theories and concepts and exposes them to the most rigorous, comprehensive statement and exploration. Reaching this goal would require a more self-conscious determination by communication scholars to plumb other fields and feed back their studies to outside researchers. At the same time, such an enterprise would enhance the theoretical rigor of communication scholarship proper.

The idea of 'framing' offers a case study of just the kind of scattered conceptualization I have identified. Despite its omnipresence across the social sciences and humanities, nowhere is there a general statement of framing theory that shows exactly how frames become embedded within and make themselves manifest in a text, or how framing influences thinking. Analysis of this concept suggests how the discipline of communication might contribute something unique: synthesizing a key concept's disparate uses, showing how they invariably involve communication, and constructing a coherent theory from them.

Whatever its specific use, the concept of framing consistently offers a way to describe the power of a communicating text. Analysis of frames illuminates the precise way in which influence over a human consciousness is exerted by the transfer (or communication) of information from one location—such as a speech, utterance, news report, or novel—to that consciousness. (A representative list of classic and recent citations would include: Edelman, 1993; Entman and Rojecki, 1993; Fiske and Taylor, 1991; Gamson, 1992; Goffman, 1974; Graber, 1988; Iyengar, 1991; Kahneman and Tversky, 1984; Pan and Kosicki, 1993; Riker, 1986; Snow and Benford, 1988; Tuchman, 1978; White, 1987; Zaller, 1992.) A literature review suggests that framing is often defined casually, with much left to an assumed tacit understanding of reader and researcher. After all, the words *frame, framing*, and *framework* are common outside of formal scholarly discourse, and their connotation there is roughly the same. The goal here is to identify and make explicit common tendencies among the various uses of the terms and to suggest a more precise and universal understanding of them.

OF FRAMES AND FRAMING

Framing essentially involves *selection* and *salience*. To frame is to *select some aspects of a perceived reality and make them more salient in a communicating text, in such a way as to promote a particular problem definition, causal interpretation, moral evaluation, and/or treatment recommendation* for the item described. Typically frames diag-

First published in *Journal of Communication, 43*, 4, Oxford University Press, as 'Framing Towards Clarification of a Fractured Paradigm', pp. 51–58.

nose, evaluate, and prescribe, a point explored most thoroughly by Gamson (1992). An example is the 'cold war' frame that dominated US news of foreign affairs until recently. The cold war frame highlighted certain foreign events—say, civil wars—as problems, identified their source (communist rebels), offered moral judgments (atheistic aggression), and commended particular solutions (US support for the other side).

Frames, then, *define problems*—determine what a causal agent is doing with what costs and benefits, usually measured in terms of common cultural values; *diagnose causes*—identify the forces creating the problem; *make moral judgments*—evaluate causal agents and their effects; and *suggest remedies*—offer and justify treatments for the problems and predict their likely effects. A single sentence may perform more than one of these four framing functions, although many sentences in a text may perform none of them. And a frame in any particular text may not necessarily include all four functions.

The cold war example also suggests that frames have at least four locations in the communication process: the communicator, the text, the receiver, and the culture. *Communicators* make conscious or unconscious framing judgments in deciding what to say, guided by frames (often called schemata) that organize their belief systems. The *text* contains frames, which are manifested by the presence or absence of certain keywords, stock phrases, stereotyped images, sources of information, and sentences that provide thematically reinforcing clusters of facts or judgments. The frames that guide the *receiver's* thinking and conclusion may or may not reflect the frames in the text and the framing intention of the communicator. The *culture* is the stock of commonly invoked frames; in fact, culture might be defined as the empirically demonstrable set of common frames exhibited in the discourse and thinking of most people in a social grouping. Framing in all four locations includes similar functions: selection and highlighting, and use of the highlighted elements to construct an argument about problems and their causation, evaluation, and/or solution.

HOW FRAMES WORK

Frames highlight some bits of information about an item that is the subject of a communication, thereby elevating them in salience. The word *salience* itself needs to be defined: It means making a piece of information more noticeable, meaningful, or memorable to audiences. An increase in salience enhances the probability that receivers will perceive the information, discern meaning and thus process it, and store it in memory (see Fiske and Taylor, 1991).

Texts can make bits of information more salient by placement or repetition, or by associating them with culturally familiar symbols. However, even a single unillustrated appearance of a notion in an obscure part of the text can be highly salient, if it comports with the existing schemata in a receiver's belief systems. By the same token, an idea emphasized in a text can be difficult for receivers to notice, interpret, or remember because of their existing schemata. For our purposes, schemata and closely related concepts such as categories, scripts, or stereotypes connote mentally stored clusters of ideas that guide individuals' processing of information (see, e.g., Graber, 1988).

Because salience is a product of the interaction of texts and receivers, the presence of frames in the text, as detected by researchers, does not guarantee their influence in audience thinking (Entman, 1989; Graber, 1988).

Kahneman and Tversky (1984) offer perhaps the most widely cited recent example of the power of framing and the way it operates by selecting and highlighting some features of reality while omitting others. The authors asked experimental subjects the following:

> Imagine that the U.S. is preparing for the outbreak of an unusual Asian disease, which is expected to kill 600 people. Two alternative programs to combat the disease have been proposed. Assume that the exact scientific estimates of the consequences of the programs are as follows: If Program A is adopted, 200 people will be saved. If Program B is adopted, there is a one-third probability that 600 people will be saved and a two-thirds probability that no people will be saved. Which of the two programs would you favor? (1984: 343)

In this experiment, 72 percent of subjects chose Program A; 28 percent chose Program B. In the next experiment, *identical options* to treating the same described situation were offered, but framed in terms of likely deaths rather than likely lives saved: 'If Program C is adopted, 400 people will die. If Program D is adopted, there is a one-third probability that nobody will die and a two-thirds probability that 600 people will die' (Kahneman and Tversky, 1984: 343). The percentages choosing the options were reversed by the framing. Program C was chosen by 22 percent, though its twin Program A was selected by 72 percent; and Program D garnered 78 percent, while the identical Program B received only 28 percent.

As this example vividly illustrates, the frame determines whether most people notice and how they understand and remember a problem, as well as how they evaluate and choose to act upon it. The notion of framing thus implies that the frame has a common effect on large portions of the receiving audience, though it is not likely to have a universal effect on all.

Kahneman and Tversky's experiments demonstrate that frames select and call attention to particular aspects of the reality described, which logically means that frames simultaneously direct attention away from other aspects. Most frames are defined by what they omit as well as include, and the omissions of potential problem definitions, explanations, evaluations, and recommendations may be as critical as the inclusions in guiding the audience.

Edelman highlights the way frames exert their power through the selective description and omission of the features of a situation:

> The character, causes, and consequences of any phenomenon become radically different as changes are made in what is prominently displayed, what is repressed and especially in how observations are classified. ... [T]he social world is ... a kaleidoscope of potential realities, any of which can be readily evoked by altering the ways in which observations are framed and categorized. (1993: 232)

Receivers' responses are clearly affected if they perceive and process information about one interpretation and possess little or incommensurable data about alternatives. This is why exclusion of interpretations by frames is as significant to outcomes as inclusion.

Sniderman et al. (1991: 52) provide a clear instance of the power of presence and absence in framing:

The effect of framing is to prime values differentially, establishing the salience of the one or the other. [Thus] ... a majority of the public supports the rights of persons with AIDS when the issue is framed [in a survey question] to accentuate civil liberties considerations—and supports ... mandatory testing when the issue is framed to accentuate public health considerations.

The text of the survey question supplies most people with the considerations they use when they respond to the issue of AIDS testing (Zaller, 1992). Often a potential counterframing of the subject is mostly or wholly absent from a text, although, to use this instance, an audience member with a strong civil liberties philosophy might reject mandatory testing even if the poll framed AIDS strictly in public health terms.

Frames in Political News

This portrait of framing has important implications for political communication. Frames call attention to some aspects of reality while obscuring other elements, which might lead audiences to have different reactions. Politicians seeking support are thus compelled to compete with each other and with journalists over news frames (Entman, 1989; Riker, 1986). Framing in this light plays a major role in the exertion of political power, and the frame in a news text is really the imprint of power—it registers the identity of actors or interests that competed to dominate the text.

Reflecting the play of power and boundaries of discourse over an issue, many news texts exhibit homogeneous framing at one level of analysis, yet competing frames at another. Thus, in the pre-war debate over US policy toward Iraq, there was a tacit consensus among US elites not to argue for such options as negotiation between Iraq and Kuwait. The news frame included only two remedies, war now or sanctions now with war (likely) later, while problem definitions, causal analyses, and moral evaluations were homogeneous. Between the selected remedies, however, framing was contested by elites, and news coverage offered different sets of facts and evaluations. The Iraq example reveals that the power of news frames can be self-reinforcing. During the pre-war debate, any critique transcending the remedies inside the frame (war soon versus more time for sanctions) breached the bounds of acceptable discourse, hence was unlikely to influence policy. By conventional journalistic standards, such views were not newsworthy (Entman and Page, 1994). Unpublicized, the views could gain few adherents and generate little perceived or actual effect on public opinion, which meant elites felt no pressure to expand the frame so it included other treatments for Iraqi aggression, such as negotiation. Relatedly, Gamson (1992) observes that a frame can exert great social power when encoded in a term like *affirmative action*. Once a term is widely accepted, to use another is to risk that target audiences will perceive the communicator as lacking credibility—or will even fail to understand what the communicator is talking about. Thus the power of a frame can be as great as that of language itself.

BENEFITS OF A CONSISTENT CONCEPT OF FRAMING

An understanding of frames helps illuminate many empirical and normative controversies, most importantly because the concept of framing directs our attention to the details of just how a communicated text exerts its power. The example of mass communication explored here suggests how a common understanding might help constitute framing as a *research paradigm*. A research paradigm is defined here as a general theory that informs most scholarship on the operation and outcomes of any particular system of thought and action. The framing paradigm could be applied with similar benefits to the study of public opinion and voting behavior in political science; to cognitive studies in social psychology; or to class, gender, and race research in cultural studies and sociology, to name a few. Here are some illustrations of theoretical debates in the study of mass communication that would benefit from an explicit and common understanding of the concept of frames.

1. Audience Autonomy

The concept of framing provides an operational definition for the notion of *dominant meaning* that is so central to debates about polysemy and audience independence in decoding media texts (Fiske, 1987). From a framing perspective, dominant meaning consists of the problem, causal, evaluative, and treatment interpretations with the highest probability of being noticed, processed, and accepted by the most people. To identify a meaning as dominant or preferred is to suggest a particular framing of the situation that is most heavily supported by the text and is congruent with the most common audience schemata.

A framing paradigm cautions researchers not to take fugitive components of the message and show how they *might* be interpreted in ways that oppose the dominant meaning. If the text frame emphasizes in a variety of mutually reinforcing ways that the glass is half full, the evidence of social science suggests that relatively few in the audience will conclude it is half empty. To argue that the polysemic properties of the message conduce to such counterframing, researchers must show that real-world audiences reframe the message, and that this reframing is not a by-product of the research conditions—for example, a focus group discussion in which one participant can lead the rest, or a highly suggestive interview protocol (Budd et al., 1990).

Certainly people can recall their own facts, forge linkages not made explicitly in the text, or retrieve from memory a causal explanation or cure that is completely absent from the text. In essence, this is just what professors encourage their students to do habitually. But Zaller (1992), Kahneman and Tversky (1984), and Iyengar (1991), among others, suggest that on most matters of social or political interest, people are not generally so well-informed and cognitively active, and that framing therefore heavily influences their responses to communications, although Gamson (1992) describes conditions that can mitigate this influence.

2. Journalistic Objectivity

Journalists may follow the rules for 'objective' reporting and yet convey a dominant framing of the news text that prevents most audience members from making a balanced assessment of a situation. Now, because they lack a common understanding of framing, journalists frequently allow the most skillful media manipulators to impose their dominant frames on the news (Entman, 1989; Entman and Page, 1994; Entman and Rojecki, 1993). If educated to understand the difference between including scattered oppositional facts and challenging a dominant frame, journalists might be better equipped to construct news that makes equally salient—equally accessible to the average, inattentive, and marginally informed audience—two or more interpretations of problems. This task would require a far more active and sophisticated role for reporters than they now take, resulting in more balanced reporting than that which the formulaic norm of objectivity produces (Tuchman, 1978).

3. Content Analysis

The major task of determining textual meaning should be to identify and describe frames; content analysis informed by a theory of framing would avoid treating all negative or positive terms or utterances as equally salient and influential. Often, coders simply tote up all messages they judge as positive and negative and draw conclusions about the dominant meanings. They neglect to measure the salience of elements in the text, and fail to gauge the relationships of the most salient clusters of messages—the frames—to the audience's schemata. Unguided by a framing paradigm, content analysis may often yield data that misrepresent the media messages that most audience members are actually picking up.

4. Public Opinion and Normative Democratic Theory

In Zaller's (1992) account, framing appears to be a central power in the democratic process, for political elites control the framing of issues. These frames can determine just what 'public opinion' is—a different frame, according to Zaller, and survey evidence and even voting can indicate a different public opinion. His theory, along with that of Kahneman and Tversky, seems to raise radical doubts about democracy itself. If by shaping frames elites can determine the major manifestations of 'true' public opinion that are available to government (via polls or voting), what can true public opinion be? How can even sincere democratic representatives respond correctly to public opinion when empirical evidence of it appears to be so malleable, so vulnerable to framing effects?

Say there are three ways to frame an issue and one generates 40 percent approval, the others 50 percent and 60 percent, respectively. Approving the option with 60 percent support is not axiomatically the most democratic response because of the cyclical majority problem (Riker, 1986), which makes majority rule among several complex options mathematically impossible. Just as important, attempting to determine which of the differently framed opinions is the closest to the public's 'real' sentiments appears futile, because it would require agreement among contending elites and citizens on which frame was most accurate, fair, complete, and so forth. A framing paradigm can illuminate, if not solve, such central puzzles in normative democratic theory.

Indeed, the concept of framing is important enough in the many fields of inquiry that use it to merit a book-length essay. The present effort, constrained by space limitations, offers not the definitive word on frames but a preliminary contribution. Equally important, this chapter exemplifies how the field of communication might develop from its wide ambit and eclectic approaches a core of knowledge that could translate into research paradigms contributing to social theory in the largest sense.

REFERENCES

Budd, M., Entman, R.M. and Steinman, C. (1990) 'The affirmative character of U.S. cultural studies', *Critical Studies in Mass Communication*, 7: 169–84.

Edelman, M.J. (1993) 'Contestable categories and public opinion'. *Political Communication*, 10 (3): 231–42.

Entman, R.M. (1989) *Democracy Without Citizens: Media and the Decay of American Politics*. New York: Oxford University Press.

Entman, R.M. and Page, B.I. (1994) 'The news before the storm: the Iraqi war debate and the limits to media independence', in W.L. Bennett and D.L. Paletz (eds), *Taken by Storm: The Media, Public Opinion and U.S. Foreign Policy in the Gulf War*. Chicago, IL: University of Chicago Press.

Entman, R.M. and Rojecki, A. (1993) 'Freezing out the public: elite and media framing of the U.S. anti-nuclear movement', *Political Communication*, 10 (2): 151–67.

Fiske, J. (1987) *Television Culture*. New York: Routledge.

Fiske, S.T. and Taylor, S.E. (1991) *Social Cognition*. New York: McGraw-Hill.

Gamson, W. (1992) *Talking Politics*. New York: Cambridge University Press.

Goffman, E. (1974) *Frame Analysis*. New York: Free Press.

Graber, D.A. (1988) *Processing the News: How People Tame the Information Tide*, 2nd edn. New York: Longman.

Iyengar, S. (1991) *Is Anyone Responsible?* Chicago, IL: University of Chicago Press.

Kahneman, D. and Tversky, A. (1984) 'Choice, values, and frames', *American Psychologist*, 39: 341–50.

Pan, Z. and Kosicki, G.M. (1993) 'Framing analysis: an approach to news discourse', *Political Communication*, 10 (1): 55–76.

Riker, W.H. (1986) *The Art of Political Manipulation*. New Haven, CT: Yale University Press.

Sniderman, P.M., Brody, R.A. and Tetlock, P.E. (1991) *Reasoning and Choice: Explorations in Political Psychology*. Cambridge: Cambridge University Press.

Snow, D.A. and Benford, R.D. (1988) 'Ideology, frame resonance, and participation mobilization', *International Social Movement Research*, 1: 197–217.

Tuchman, G. (1978) *Making News*. New York: Free Press.

White, H. (1987) *The Content of the Form*. Baltimore. MD: Johns Hopkins University Press.

Zaller, J.R. (1992) *The Nature and Origins of Mass Opinion*. New York: Cambridge University Press.

37

children and television violence in the United States

ELLEN WARTELLA, ADRIANA OLIVAREZ
AND NANCY JENNINGS

Americans live in a violent society. Alarming statistics reveal changes in US society as the result of increased violence. According to a report issued by the American Psychological Association (American Psychological Association, 1993), guns are involved in more than 75 percent of adolescent killings. Firearm-related violent crimes have been on the rise in the 1990s. Research indicates a 75.6 percent increase in firearm-related aggravated assault from 1985 to 1994 (Federal Bureau of Investigation, 1996). Americans have the highest murder rate of any nation in the world. But the numbers that tell the most tragic story concern children and adolescents:

- Among young people in the age group 15–24 years old, homicide is the second leading cause of death and for African American youth murder is number one.
- Adolescents account for 24 percent of all violent crimes leading to arrest. The rate has increased over time for those in the 12–19-year-old age group, while it is down in the 35 and older age group. According to the Federal reports on crime in 1995, juvenile arrests for weapon violations have increased 11.3 percent nationwide between the years 1985 and 1994.
- Every five minutes a child is arrested in America for committing a violent crime and gun-related violence takes the life of an American child every three hours.
- A child growing up in Washington, DC, or Chicago is 15 times more likely to be murdered than a child in Northern Ireland.

What could account for this? Most of us generally accept the notion that violent behavior is a complex, multivariable problem, formed of many influences. Racism, poverty, drug abuse, child abuse, alcoholism, illiteracy, gangs, guns, mental illness, a decline in family cohesion, a lack of deterrents, the failure of positive role models ... all interact to affect antisocial behavior. As Rowell Huesmann has argued, aggression is a syndrome, an enduring pattern of behavior that can persist through childhood into adulthood.

In simple terms, one given specific act of violence may be less mysterious than some think. We only suggest this rhetorically for, of course, we have few doubts that violence is nothing if not insidious and intractable in many ways. But consider the context not of one act of violence, but of the persistent fact of violence. Clearly a number of factors contribute to violence in American society, but to ignore television violence would be a grave oversight. Violence tears across the television screen through many types of programs from music videos and entertainment shows to reality programming and the evening news. By the time the average American child graduates from elementary school, he or she will have seen over 8000 murders and more than 100,000 other assorted acts of violence (Huston et al., 1992). Even though viewing media violence may not be the *sole* contributor to violent behavior, nor does it have the same effect on all who watch it, more than 40 years of research *does* indicate a relationship between exposure to media violence and aggressive behavior.

Moreover, the United States is a very heavy television using country: 98 percent of the 95 million American homes have television sets and nearly three quarters have more than one set; two-thirds have cable TV and four-fifths have VCRs. The television

First published in *Children and Media Violence*, Yearbook from the UNESCO Clearinghouse on Children and Media Violence on the Screen, E. Wartella, A. Olivarez and N. Jennings, NORDICOM: Goteborg University (1998), as 'Children and Television Violence in the United States, pp. 57–61.

set is on more than seven hours per day in the average American home (*Broadcasting and Cable Yearbook*, 1996).

Most importantly, the television Americans watch – and increasingly the television programming transported around the world via American and other multinational television conglomerates – is very violent programming. Since 1994 we have been involved in the largest-ever study of portrayals of violence on American television, the National Television Violence Study, which came about as a consequence of American public and political concern about the relationship between television violence and real world violence.

THE NATIONAL TELEVISION VIOLENCE STUDY

The NTVS reports on how violence is portrayed on cable and broadcast television in each of three years, 1996, 1997 and 1998, and it makes recommendations to policy-makers, the industry and to parents. Our first report in February 1996 reported on television programming from the 1994–95 television season, and the latest report released in March 1997 reported on programming from the 1995–96 season.

The content analysis of television was of a constructed sample week (collected over more than two dozen weeks from October through June) of programming from 6 a.m. to 11 p.m. on 23 channels; these channels included the major broadcast networks, three independent stations, public broadcasting, 12 of the most popular basic cable networks and three premium cable channels – HBO, Cinemax and Showtime. In all, about 3200 programs were sampled each year and about 2700 were content analyzed for their depictions of violence.

We found very little change from year one to year two of our studies. The majority of American television shows have at least one act of violence in them; the context in which most violence is presented is sanitized; violence is rarely punished in the immediate context in which it occurs; and it rarely results in observable harm to the victims. For instance, in both years, we found that perpetrators of violence go unpunished in more than 70 percent of all violent scenes – although they may be punished by the end of the program. Moreover, the negative consequences of violence – harm to the victims, their families, as well as the psychological, if not actual physical harm to the perpetrators of violence – are not often portrayed. For example, nearly half of all violent interactions show no harm to the victims and more than half show no pain. And very infrequently, in less than one-fifth of all violent programming, are the long-term negative repercussions of violence, such as psychological, financial or emotional harm, ever portrayed. Weapons (such as handguns) appear in about one quarter of all violent programs and very few programs (we estimate 4 percent in each year) have anti-violent themes. On the good side, with the exception of movies on television, television violence is not usually explicit or graphic. And there are differences across television channels (American public television being the least violent and premium cable channels being the most likely to have violent programs), and across programming genres (again movies on cable are most likely to show violence). Overall, however, the NTVS has demonstrated a striking amount of consistency in the presentation of violence on American television over the first two years of the study. American television is indeed a violent medium.

RESEARCH ON THE INFLUENCES OF TELEVISION VIOLENCE

Over the past 40-plus years more than 3500 research studies of the effects of television violence on viewers have been conducted in the United States, and during the 1990s there have been several extensive reviews of this literature, including the 1991 report of the Centers for Disease Control, which declared television violence a public health hazard; the 1993 study of violence in American life from the National Academy of Science, which implicated media along with other social and psychological contributors to violence; and the American Psychological Association's 1992 study, which also implicated media violence. All three of these reviews supported the conclusion that mass media contribute to aggressive behavior and attitudes as well as leading to desensitization and fear effects. No study claims that viewing media violence is the *only*, nor even the most important, contributor to violent behavior. Furthermore, it is not every act of violence in the media that raises concern, nor every child or adult who is affected. Yet, there is clear evidence that exposure to media violence contributes in significant ways to real world violence. Each of the three major effects of watching media violence, with specific concerns for child viewers, will be considered: the social learning effect, the desensitization effect and the fear effect.

SOCIAL LEARNING

The 1993 report of the American Psychological Association concluded that: 'there is absolutely no doubt that those who are heavy viewers of this violence demonstrate increased acceptance of aggressive attitudes and increased aggressive behaviour' (American Psychological Association, 1993). This conclusion is based on the examination of hundreds of experimental and longitudinal studies which support this position. Moreover, field studies and cross-national studies indicate that the viewing of television aggression increases subsequent aggression and that such behavior can become part of a lasting behavioral pattern.

Three basic theoretical models have been proposed to describe the process by which such learning and imitation of television violence occurs: social learning theory, priming effects theory and a social developmental model of learning.

Social learning theory, first proposed by Albert Bandura in the 1960s, is perhaps the best known theoretical account of violence effects. Bandura asserts that through observing television models, viewers come to learn behaviors that are appropriate; that is, which behaviors will be rewarded and which will be punished. In this way, viewers seek to attain rewards and therefore want to imitate these media models. When both children and adults are shown an aggressive model who is either rewarded or punished for their aggressive behavior, models who are positively reinforced influence imitation among the viewers. Even research in the field has demonstrated that aggression is learned at a young age and becomes more impervious to change as the child grows older. In a longitudinal study to examine the long-term effects of television violence on aggression and criminal behavior, Huesmann et al. (1984) studied a group of youths across 22 years, at ages 8, 18 and 30. For boys (and to a lesser, though still significant, extent for girls), early television violence viewing correlated with self-reported aggression at age 30 and added significantly to the prediction of serious criminal arrests accumulated by age 30. These researchers find a longitudinal relationship between habitual childhood exposure to television violence and adult crime and suggest that approximately 10 percent of the variability in later criminal behavior can be attributed to television violence.

Priming effects theory serves to augment the more traditional social learning theory account of television violence effects. In the work of Leonard Berkowitz and his colleagues, this theoretical account asserts that many media effects are immediate, transitory and short (Berkowitz, 1984). Berkowitz suggests that when people watch television violence, it activates or 'primes' other semantically related thoughts that may influence how the person responds to the violence on TV: viewers who identify with the actors on television may imagine themselves like that character carrying out the aggressive actions of the character on television, and research evidence suggests that exposure to media aggression does indeed 'prime' other aggressive thoughts, evaluations and even behaviors such that violence-viewers report a greater willingness to use violence in interpersonal situations.

Only Rowell Huesmann's (1986) theoretical formulation of the social developmental model of violence effects offers a true reciprocal theoretical account of how viewers' interest in media violence, attention to such violence and individual viewer characteristics may interact in a theory of media violence effects. Using ideas from social cognition theory he develops an elaborate cognitive mapping or script model. He argues that social behavior is controlled by 'programs' for behavior which are established during childhood. These 'programs' or 'scripts' are stored in memory and are used as guides to social behavior and problem solving. Huesmann and Miller (1994) submit that 'a script suggests what events are to happen in the environment, how the person should behave in response to these events, and what the likely outcome to those behaviors would be'. Violence from television is 'encoded' in the cognitive map of viewers, and subsequent viewing of television violence helps to maintain these aggressive thoughts, ideas and behaviors. Over time such continuing attention to television violence thus can influence people's attitudes toward violence and their maintenance and elaboration of aggressive scripts.

This theory suggests that while viewing violence may not cause aggressive behavior, it certainly has an impact on the formation of cognitive scripts for mapping how to behave in response to a violent event and what the outcome is most likely to be. Television portrayals, then, are among the media and personal sources that provide the text for the script which is maintained and expanded upon by continued exposure to scripts of violence.

Huesmann has demonstrated that there are key factors that are particularly important in maintaining the television viewing-aggression relationship for children: the child's intellectual achievement level, social popularity, identification with television characters, belief in the realism of the TV violence and the amount of fantasizing about aggression. According to Huesmann, a heavy diet of television violence sets into motion a sequence of processes, based on these personal and interpersonal factors, that results in many viewers becoming not only more aggressive but also developing increased interest in seeing more television violence.

Variations by Portrayals and Viewers

Clearly, not all violent depictions should be treated equally, nor all viewers. The NTVS has identified several contextual factors within a representation that may influence audience reactions to media violence including: 1) the nature of the perpetrator, 2) the nature of the target, 3) the reason for the violence, 4) the presence of weapons, 5) the extent and graphicness of the violence, 6) the degree of realism of the violence, 7) whether the violence is rewarded or punished, 8) the consequences of violence, and 9) whether humor is involved in violence (Wilson et al., 1996).

In addition, research indicates that certain factors may be processed differently by young viewers. First, young children have more difficulty distinguishing reality from fantasy and often imitate superheros with magical powers such as the *Power Rangers* (Boyatzis et al., 1995). Second, young children may have difficulty connecting scenes and drawing inferences from the plot. Timing of punishments and rewards becomes important in this instance. In many programs, the crime or violent behavior may go unpunished until the end of the program. Young children may have difficulty connecting the ending punishment with the initial violent act and may, therefore, believe that the violence went unpunished (Wilson et al., 1996). Thus, learning of aggressive attitudes and behaviors from television varies by both the nature of the portrayals and the nature of the viewers. The presence of contextual factors in the portrayals which may inhibit young children's social learning of aggression decreases the negative consequences of such portrayals and should be encouraged. Not all violent portrayals are the same and the context of violence is clearly quite important. Similarly, young children, those under the age of seven or eight, may be particularly susceptible to learning from exposure to television violence because of differences in how they make sense of television compared to adults.

Desensitization and Fear

Two other effects of television violence viewing have been identified in the research literature: the desensitization and the fear effect. These effects may influence even those viewers who do not themselves behave violently or who have positive attitudes toward using violence.

Research has demonstrated that prolonged viewing of media violence can lead to emotional desensitization toward real world violence and the victims of violence which in turn can lead to callous attitudes toward violence directed at others and a decreased likelihood to take action on behalf of the victim when violence occurs (e.g., Donnerstein et al., 1994; for further references and discussion, see Wilson et al., 1996). Over time, even those viewers who initially react with horror at media violence may become habituated to it or more psychologically comfortable such that they view any given act of violence as less severe and they may evaluate media violence more favorably. Desensitization can affect all viewers over time.

A third likely effect of viewing television violence which has been studied extensively by George Gerbner and his colleagues (Gerbner et al., 1986) demonstrates that heavy viewers of television violence become fearful of the world, afraid of becoming a victim of violence and over time engage in more self-protective behaviors and show more mistrust of others. To the extent that viewers equate the fictional world of television with its overrepresentation of violence as the same as the real world they live in, then such heavy viewers tend to see their world as a fearful and crime-ridden place. It is likely that both fictional and reality programs (including crime-saturated television news) contribute to this fear-inducing effect among viewers.

TELEVISION VIOLENCE IN A GLOBAL CONTEXT

The substantial research in the United States over the past more than 40 years has been reviewed and found persuasive among the American public and politicians. It was reviews and conclusions such as those presented here which encouraged Senator Simon's and the US Congress's considerable policy initiatives against television violence in the last four years. Children as an audience for such violence have been of considerable concern, and indeed, the V-chip blocking device is thought to be a reasonable remedy for parents to use to protect their children from violent television programming.

Whether the magnitude of the effects of television violence in comparison with other causes of American violence and our violent society is small or large is not at all clear. Many European critics of the American violence literature have pointed out that neither television outside of the US is as violent as our television, nor are the other underlying factors such as poverty and the easy access to guns as prevalent, and therefore this literature is not applicable to other countries and other cultures. To the extent that the global nature of television and film and the dominance of American popular culture is moving across the privatized television environments of Europe and elsewhere, then perhaps American television programming and its effects will foreshadow concerns about television violence effects in other countries. It is clear that where children and television violence is concerned, the question that remains is not whether media violence has an effect, but rather how important that effect is in comparison with other factors in bringing about the current level of crime in the US and other industrialized nations. Future research should also aim to establish who precisely is most susceptible to media violence, and, most importantly, what sorts of intervention might help diminish its influence. In the meantime, any interventions that help establish policies and practices to reduce the socially inappropriate ways of portraying violence and increase the socially responsible ways (such as using violence to assert anti-violence messages) should be encouraged as well. Children and television violence is a public issue that is not going away and should engage all who are concerned with children's welfare.

REFERENCES

American Psychological Association (1993) *Violence and Youth: Psychology's Response*, Vol. 1. Summary Report of the American Psychological Association Commission on Violence and Youth. Washington, DC: American Psychological Association.

Berkowitz, Leonard (1984) 'Some effects of thoughts on anti- and prosocial influences of media events: a cognitive neoassociationistic analysis', *Psychological Bulletin*, 95 (3): 410–27.

Boyatzis, Chris, Matillo, Gina, Nesbitt, Kristen and Cathey, Gina (1995) 'Effects of "the Mighty Morphin Power Rangers" on children's aggression and pro-social behavior', Presented at the Society for Research in Child Development, Indianapolis, IN.

Broadcasting and Cable Yearbook (1996) New Providence, NJ: R.R. Bowker.

Center for Communication and Social Policy, University of California, Santa Barbara (1997) *National Television Violence Study 2*. Thousand Oaks, CA: Sage.

Donnerstein, Ed, Slaby, Ron and Eron, Leonard (1994) 'The mass media and youth violence', in J. Murray, E. Rubinstein and G. Comstock (eds), *Violence and Youth: Psychology's Response*, Vol. 2. Washington, DC: American Psychological Association. pp. 219–50.

Federal Bureau of Investigation (1996) *Uniform Crime Reports for the United States, 1995*. Washington, DC: US Government Printing Office.

Gerbner, G., Gross, L., Morgan, M. and Signorielli, N. (1986) 'Living with television: the dynamics of the cultivation process', in J. Bryant and D. Zillmann (eds), *Media Effects*. Hillsdale, NJ: Lawrence Erlbaum. pp. 17–41.

Huesmann, L. Rowell (1986) 'Psychological processes promoting the relation between exposure to media violence and aggressive behavior by the viewer', *Journal of Social Issues*, 42 (3): 125–40.

Huesmann, L. Rowell and Miller, Laurie (1994) 'Long-term effects of repeated exposure to media violence in childhood', in L.R. Huesmann (ed.), *Aggressive Behavior*. New York: Plenum. pp. 153–86.

Huesmann, L. Rowell, Eron, L.D. Lefkowitz, M.M. and Walder, L.O. (1984) 'The stability of aggression over time and generations', *Developmental Psychology*, 20 (6): 1120–34.

Huston, Aletha, Donnerstein, Edward, Fairchild, Halford, Feshbach, Norma, Katz, Phyllis, Murray, John, Rubinstein, Eli, Wilcox, Brian and Luckerman, Diana (1992) *Big World, Small Screen: The Role of Television in American Society*. Lincoln: University of Nebraska Press.

Wartella, Ellen (1995) 'Media and problem behaviours in young people', in M. Rutter and D. Smith (eds), *Psychosocial Disorders in Young People: Time Trends and Their Origins*. Chichester: Wiley. pp. 293–323.

Whitney, Charles, Wartella, Ellen, Lasorsa, Dominic, Danielson, Wayne, Olivarez, Adriana, Lopez, Rafael and Klijn, Marlies (1996) Part II: 'Television violence in "reality" programming', University of Texas, Austin, in *National Television Violence Study*, Vol. 1. Thousand Oaks, CA: Sage. pp. 269–360.

Wilson, Barbara, Kunkel, Dale, Linz, Dan, Potter, James, Donnerstein, Ed, Smith, Stacy, Blumenthal, Eva and Gray, Timothy (1996) Part I: 'Violence in television programming overall', University of California, Santa Barbara, in *National Television Violence Study*, Vol. 1. Thousand Oaks, CA: Sage. pp. 1–268.

38

entertainment as media effect

DOLF ZILLMANN AND JENNINGS BRYANT

ENJOYMENT OF ENTERTAINMENT

Quite obviously, mass media entertainment does not merely serve the regulation of arousal and associated affect or produce a contagion with merriment for persons in need of overcoming the blahs. Entertaining messages are capable of gratifying respondents because of unique intrinsic properties, along with the respondents' idiosyncratic appraisals of these properties. But what are these properties? What are the ingredients of good entertainment? And what properties spoil enjoyment?

The enjoyment of drama, comedy, and sports is influenced by a multitude of variables, many of which have received considerable attention (e.g., Goldstein, 1979; Jauss, 1982). But none seem to control enjoyment as strongly and as universally as do affective dispositions toward interacting parties, especially parties confronted with problems, conflict, and aversive conditions. The exhibition of human conflict in the raw has often been singled out as the stuff of which all good drama is made (e.g., Smiley, 1971). The focus on conflict constitutes only a starting point, however. The dramatic portrayal of intense conflict, in and of itself, does not with any degree of regularity, certainly not by necessity, lead to enjoyment reactions in the audience. Enjoyment depends not so much on conflict as on its resolution and on what the resolution means to the parties involved. It depends on how much those who come out on top are liked and loved and on how much those who come out on the short end are disliked and hated. Good drama, then, relies on positive and negative sentiments toward the parties in conflict and on the extent to which a resolution can be accepted by the audience. Indifference toward protagonists and antagonists is the antidote to good drama. Positive and negative affective dispositions toward the agents in drama are vital and must be created if drama is to evoke strong emotions, enjoyment included. There need be beloved heroes (regardless of how their definition might change over the years), and there need be villains whom the audience can love to hate.

Dispositions and Affective Reactions

The response side of what is commonly referred to as 'character development' is affect. The portrayal of goodness in protagonists is to make them likable and lovable. Analogously, the portrayal of evil in antagonists is to make them dislikable and hateable. To the extent that any intended character development works, it produces positive and negative dispositions toward the agents of a play.

Character development is effective, generally speaking, because respondents bring empathy and, more important, moral considerations to the screen. What the agents in a play do matters the most. It is the basis for the audience's approval or disapproval of conduct. Such approval or disapproval is a moral verdict, of course. The fact that this is not generally recognized by respondents (and those who study their behavior) does not alter that circumstance. Approval of conduct is assumed to promote liking;

First published in Media Effects, J. Bryant and D. Zillmann, Hillsdale, NJ: Erlbaum (1994) as 'Entertainment as a Media Effect', pp. 447–459.

disapproval is assumed to promote disliking. Affective dispositions toward protagonists and antagonists derive in large measure from moral considerations (cf. Zillmann, 1991c).

Once an audience has thus placed its sentiments pro and con particular characters, enjoyment of conflict and its resolution in drama depends on the ultimate outcome for the loved and hated parties. Positive affective dispositions inspire hopes of positive outcomes and fears of negative ones. Protagonists are deemed deserving of good fortunes and utterly undeserving of bad ones. Negative affective dispositions, on the other hand, activate the opposite inclinations: fear of positive outcomes and hopes for negative ones. Antagonists are deemed utterly undeserving of good fortunes and deserving of bad ones. Such hopes and fears are obviously mediated by moral considerations.

These hopes and fears lead respondents to empathize with the emotions displayed by protagonists. The joys as well as the suffering of liked characters tend to evoke concordant affect in the audience. Positive and negative affect is said to be 'shared.' In contrast, these hopes and fears prompt counterempathetic reactions to the emotions experienced by antagonists. The villains' joy is the audience's distress, and their suffering, their being brought to justice, and their getting their comeuppance is the audience's delight (cf. Zillmann, 1991a). These basic dynamics of affect in spectators are summarized in Figure 38.1.

Although these dynamics of affect have been outlined in dichotomous terms, they should not be construed as merely dichotomous. They should be thought of as a dichotomous system underneath which continuous variables exist. Liking and disliking of characters are clearly matters of degree, and the projection of consequences for the enjoyment of events and final outcomes must take this into account. In more formal terms, the following predictions can be stated (cf. Zillmann, 1980):

1. Enjoyment deriving from witnessing the debasement, failure, or defeat of a party, agent, or object increases with the intensity of negative sentiment and decreases with the intensity of positive sentiment toward these entities.
2. Enjoyment deriving from witnessing the enhancement, success, or victory of a party, agent, or object decreases with the intensity of negative sentiment and increases with the intensity of positive sentiment toward these entities.
3. Annoyance deriving from witnessing the debasement, failure, or defeat of a party, agent, or object decreases with the intensity of negative sentiment and increases with the intensity of positive sentiment toward these entities.
4. Annoyance deriving from witnessing the enhancement, success, or victory of a party, agent, or object increases with the intensity of negative sentiment and decreases with the intensity of positive sentiment toward these entities.
5. Propositions 1 through 4 apply jointly. Consequently, all contributions to enjoyment and/or annoyance combine in total enjoyment or annoyance. In this integration of contributions, annoyance is conceived of as negative enjoyment, and contributions to enjoyment and to annoyance are assumed to combine in an additive fashion.

Predictions from this disposition model have been confirmed not only for the enjoyment of drama, but also for humor appreciation and the enjoyment of sports (Zillmann and Bryant, 1991; Zillmann and Cantor, 1976; Zillmann et al., 1979). Comedy can of course be construed as a form of drama that differs from drama proper only in that

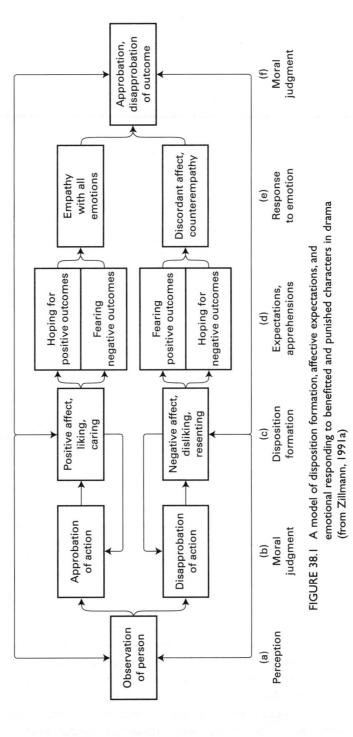

FIGURE 38.1 A model of disposition formation, affective expectations, and emotional responding to benefitted and punished characters in drama (from Zillmann, 1991a)

cues abound that signal that things are not to be taken too seriously (McGhee, 1979). Most tendentious jokes (i.e., hostile and/or sexual ones in which somebody is victimized) can also be construed as dramatic episodes – miniaturized ones, to be sure – in which there is conflict that is resolved in favor of a deserving party and to the detriment of a victim who had it coming. Setting someone up for the punch line is nothing other than making him or her deserving of the humorous knockdown.

The dispositional mechanics of enjoyment are most obvious in sports spectatorship. Sports fans have favorite players and teams. They also have players and teams that they detest with considerable intensity. Seeing a beloved competing party humble and humiliate a resented one obviously constitutes the ultimate in sports enjoyment. And the reverse outcome is the kind of event that can make grown men cry. It is clear, in addition, that indifference toward persons or teams in a contest is the kind of condition under which excitement and intense enjoyment cannot materialize. Hirt et al. (1992) provided compelling evidence for these mechanics and showed that the projected emotions transcend enjoyment or dispair proper. Enjoyment from seeing a beloved team win was found to elevate the fans' self-esteem and enhance confidence in their physical, mental, and social abilities and skills. Despair from seeing their beloved team defeated, in contrast, deflated self-esteem and diminished confidence in their own talents. Surely, in the enjoyment of athletic events, there are many other factors that must be considered (Zillmann et al., 1979). But the dispositional mechanics seem of overriding significance in the enjoyment of dramatic confrontations of any kind.

On Thrills and Suspense

Upon cursory inspection, the enjoyment of suspenseful drama may strike one as being contradictory, even paradoxical. Such drama tends to be enjoyed despite the fact that for most of its duration the protagonist or protagonists (i.e., those dear to the audience) are seen in duress and in peril; they appear to be doomed (Zillmann, 1980, 1991c). Over considerable periods of time, the heroes are tormented and about to be overpowered and destroyed by evil forces or extraordinary dangers. Dreaded, disastrous happenings are imminent – repeatedly, frequently, and in the latest action-packed raids on the audience, almost continually. How can anybody, under these circumstances, enjoy drama? The dominant affective experience should be one of empathetic distress. Surely, such distress is relieved at times when the feared and seemingly imminent events fail to materialize and, especially in the resolution, when in the grandest of fashions and usually against all odds, the protagonists overcome the dangers that threatened them and destroy the evil forces manifesting these dangers, too. At times, of course, the resolution is less full-fledged, and the protagonists merely get away with dear life (e.g., the survivors of typical disaster movies). Contemporary horror movies tend to take that format also, as tormented ladies barely escape the chainsaws, and the villains are spared for the sequel. But even in these resolutions that do not feature the annihilation of evil forces, there is cause for jubilation, and the resolution can be deemed satisfying.

Generally speaking, then, suspenseful drama exhibits much of the condition describable as 'hero in peril,' but it also offers a resolution that is satisfying, if only minimally so. The indicated paradox consists of the fact that such drama should evoke more empathetic distress than euphoria, at least in terms of time. It should be suffered more – or more accurately, longer – than it should be enjoyed. How can this formula work for nonmasochistic audiences?

One explanation is that the persons attracted to such drama are sufficiently under-stimulated and bored to appreciate any shake-up of their excitatory state (Tannenbaum, 1980; Zillmann, 1991b; Zuckerman, 1979). If arousal levels are sub-normal, excitatory reactions – even those derived from distress – can help return arousal to more pleasantly experienced levels. The safety and convenience of the exposure situation make it unlikely that levels rise to uncomfortable heights. Still, the immediate affective experience associated with any arousal kicks tends to be construed as negative in valence, and this seems to favor a more elaborate explanation.

According to the alternative account, residues of excitation from empathetic distress and/or from the response to the threatening stimuli persist through resolutions and intensify the euphoric experience that is evoked by these resolutions. Because the magnitude of residual excitation is greater the more intense the distressful experience, it follows that the enjoyment of satisfying resolutions will be the more intensified the greater (and more immediate) the preceding distress reaction. The simple consequence of this is that suspenseful drama will be the more enjoyable, the more the audience is initially made to suffer, through empathy with the endangered protagonists and/or any duress induced by those dangers with which the protagonists struggled. Great enjoyment rides the back of great distress. Evidence for this relationship has been provided by numerous experimental investigations of suspenseful drama (Zillmann, 1980, 1991c).

The intensification of the enjoyment of favorable final outcomes by residual excitation from preceding uncertainty and distress should apply to the appreciation of athletic performances, too. A liked team's victory after a close, tense game should be more enjoyable than a similar victory that was decided early in the contest (Sapolsky, 1980). A recent investigation by Bryant et al. (1992) supported this contention experimentally. A high school football game was videotaped with multiple cameras, edited, and embellished with different versions of play-by-play and color commentary. Conditions were created under which viewers of the various versions of the game saw play in which the outcome was decided either early in the game or on the very last play of the game – a field goal. Enjoyment of the game was more pronounced when the outcome was decided as the clock expired.

Tragic Events and Bad News

The phenomenon that is most puzzling in the projection of enjoyment from the discussed disposition model is the apparent appeal of tragedy and news reports about disasters and the like. The persons who are witnessed suffering misfortunes and grievous occurrences are, as a rule, not resented and not considered deserving of tragic happenings. However, despite the fact that fiction often entails circumstances that make a tragic outcome more acceptable (e.g., the hero's so-called tragic flaw), it need not be assumed that the immediate affective reactions to the portrayal of tragic events are in any way positive. In all probability, these immediate reactions are negative, even intensely so. Tearjerkers are, after all, known to jerk tears, and negative affect in response to newscasts on tragic events is not in doubt (Veitch and Griffitt, 1976). This makes the fascination with seeing the victimization of parties that are neither disliked nor deemed deserving of what happens to them all the more bewildering. Granted that tragic drama is not exactly the main course of popular drama, it does enjoy a considerable following that needs to be explained. The same applies, outside fiction, to the appeal of bad news in print and broadcast journalism, which is said to be ubiquitous and growing in popularity (Haskins, 1981). Even acutely annoyed men, who would emotionally benefit from exposure to good or affectively neutral news, cannot resist the lure of bad news about misfortunes, mayhem, and disasters (Biswas et al., in press). What needs might be satisfied by exposure to tragic happenings? And how can such exposure be gratifying, if it is gratifying in some way?

Some have postulated that the fascination with tragic events reflects morbid curiosity (Haskins, 1981). Others have suggested that responding sadly to the sadness of suffering people affords respondents an opportunity to celebrate their own emotional sensitivity (Smith, 1759/1971). Sobbing through a tearjerker is proof to oneself that a valued social skill is abundantly present. Yet others have emphasized that exposure to tragic events invites social comparison, that respondents contrast their own situation with that of the suffering parties they witness, and that this contrasting eventually produces a form of satisfaction (Aust, 1984). Seeing misfortunes befall others and seeing them suffering from them thus may make viewers cognizant and appreciative of how good they have it. And as such positive feelings accrue to seeing tragedy strike, in reality or in fiction, tragedy becomes appealing despite the negative affect that is initially associated with it.

All these explanatory efforts remain conjecture at present. Research has failed to elucidate the response to the exhibition of tragedy in people's lives. Not only does it remain unclear why respondents are initially drawn to watching truly tragic events, but it remains particularly puzzling why exposure is sought repeatedly, as it seems likely that immediate responses were noxious and noxious experiences are generally avoided. Understanding tragedy and, in particular, the popularity of bad news thus poses a formidable challenge to entertainment research.

Audience Influences

Much of the consumption of entertaining messages occurs in particular social situations. Going to the movies is an event that usually involves friends or that happens in the context of dating (Mendelsohn, 1966). Going to see an athletic contest similarly tends to involve well-known others. Television fare is also consumed in the company of such others, but with one big difference: The television audience is limited to comparatively small numbers, in contrast to the backdrop of large audiences composed of unknown others at the movies or, especially, at athletic events.

Given these social circumstances, it should not be surprising to find that a considerable amount of speculation exists that deals with the consequences of specific social conditions for the enjoyment of the entertaining event, even with the consequences of the entertaining event for cohesion in the audience and for affective inclinations among members of that audience. Regarding the latter effect, Ovid (*Ars Amatoria*) (1947) was one of the first to propose that audience members' romantic passions might be enhanced by arousing, potentially violent, and bloody entertaining events. His intuition has actually received experimental support in recent years (e.g., White et al., 1981). But many other socially relevant effects on the audience have remained unexplored, in spite of the fact that they are highly obtrusive on occasion. For instance, winning an Olympic hockey match against a powerful nation, especially when the victory comes unexpectedly, seems to have the capacity for uniting – for a limited period – a nation in some not so tangible way. In a similar vein, entire communities become high-spirited cities of champions when they have a winning team or fall into gloom if their athletic entertainers fail to defeat the out-of-towners. Effects of this kind have received little attention by researchers. Rigorous exploration is difficult and, presumably for this reason, virtually nonexistent (Schwarz et al., 1987; Schweitzer et al., 1992).

The exploration of the effects of social conditions of consumption on the enjoyment of entertaining events has met with greater success, but is quite incomplete nonetheless. The best documented phenomenon of this kind is the facilitative influence of others' laughter on the laughter of respondents (e.g., Chapman, 1973b; Chapman and Wright, 1976; Fuller and Sheehy-Skeffington, 1974; Smyth and Fuller, 1972). Even the canned laughter that accompanies comedy and humorous situations has been found to enhance laughter in child and adult audiences; moreover, it has been found to increase enjoyment in many, though not in all, instances (e.g., Chapman, 1973a; Cupchik and Leventhal, 1974; Leventhal and Cupchik, 1975; Leventhal and Mace, 1970). Persons responding to humor appear to take the reactions of others as a cue that signals the extent to which the events before them are laughable and, ultimately, enjoyable. The facilitative effect of others' laughter on laughter and enjoyment, then, seems to derive from the informational utility of the reactions of others rather than from a mechanical contagion that produces laughter, which, through self-monitoring, eventually leads to a distorted appraisal of enjoyment. Such an interpretation is suggested by the finding that a model's laughter in response to particular stimuli tends to enhance an observer's laughter to these stimuli at a later time; that is, laughter is enhanced in the absence of the laughter of others that could function as an immediate stimulus for laughter in observers and thus serve contagion (Brown et al., 1980, 1981).

Applause in response to musical performances functions analogously. As others' laughter makes humor appear funnier, others' applause makes music seem better. Hocking et al. (1977), for instance, succeeded in planting numerous confederates into a nightclub, and members of the audience later evaluated the quality of the band and its music. This quality was deemed higher on nights when the confederates showed delight by applauding enthusiastically than on nights when they failed to do so.

Oddly enough, where the social facilitation of enjoyment is thought to be least in doubt – namely, in the cheering, quasi-hysterical crowds at athletic events – research has failed us, and we must continue to trust journalistic assertions (Hocking, 1982). Research on the effects of the social conditions under which athletic contests are watched on television has proven similarly uninformative. Audience size, for instance, could not be shown to exert an appreciable degree of influence on the enjoyment of a game (Sapolsky and Zillmann, 1978).

Audience size, in and of itself, may not have the impact that many feel it has. What people in the audience do, in contrast, seems to matter greatly. In many instances, the expression of particular emotions may well affect similar emotions in those amidst an expressive audience. The effects can be far more complicated, however, than any model of empathetic contagion and escalation would suggest.

A specific kind of influence of a companion's behavior on the enjoyment of drama has been demonstrated for horror movies. In an investigation by Zillmann et al. (1984), participants saw terrifying events from the latest horror flicks in the presence of an opposite-gender confederate who gave ample indication of being terrified in a distress condition, gave no indication of affective responsiveness in a neutral condition, or gave clear signs of taking things with the greatest of ease in a mastery condition. Following exposure to the materials, participants reported their enjoyment.

Could their enjoyment be affected by these audience conditions and, if so, in what way? Those who believe in affective contagion might expect the terrified companion to enhance similar reactions in the participants and, because the object of horror movies is to terrify the audience, the film is deemed scarier and, hence, better and, hence, more enjoyable, at least in retrospect. It could also be conjectured that seeing horror with a terrified companion enhances enjoyment in those who enjoy being scared and/or seeing others scared and that it diminishes enjoyment in those who detest being scared and/or seeing others scared. But the findings are consistent with another model that is somewhat more elaborate, yet also more obvious.

On the premise that in our own and in most other societies young men are expected to master fear-arousing situations and, if scared, to deny such a response, whereas young women are allowed, if not encouraged, to express their distress freely, it can be argued that horror films, for better or worse, are a significant socializing institution. The horror genre provides a forum in which persons can confront terrifying happenings such as gruesome maimings and killings, and they can do so safely (i.e., without suffering bodily harm). Respondents can gauge their emotional reactions and in case these reactions should become overly intense, they can curb them by discounting the disturbing events as mere fiction. The reactions are thus always bearable, and thanks to excitatory habituation (cf. Zillmann, 1982), they should grow smaller with repeated exposure to similar stimuli.

Boys and young men apparently benefit most from such habituation. As their distress reactions diminish, they can more readily pretend not to be distressed at all. In fact, they should become proficient in denying any distress by expressing amusement or by similarly belittling the terrifying events before them. How better to exhibit mastery of terror than by waving it off with a smile? And what better companion for showing off this mastery than an apparently terrified female? The presence of such a female, compared to a less expressive one or, worst of all, one that exhibits mastery herself, should make the male feel great because (a) the movie is obviously scary, and (b) he is so cool about it that he could virtually comfort his disturbed companion. Young women, on the other hand, are not burdened with acculturation pressures toward callousness. They can live through and express their dismay. But as they do, an equally frightened male companion renders little comfort. He who effectively pretends not to be disturbed about the terrifying happenings is the one who radiates security, and a terrified female should feel inclined to seek comfort with him rather than with his more sensitive (or less callous) counterparts. The frightened maiden's desire to snuggle up on the macho companion is a cliché for horror movies. If there is any truth to it, we can see why boys want to master, why girls want to scream, and why both parties want to go to such movies in the first place. We can see the implications of entertainment consumption for falling in love. But what about enjoyment of the movies themselves? Here it may be assumed that persons do not fully comprehend what it is that gives them pleasure. They do not neatly identify the sources of their enjoyment and trace different contributions. Rather, they are likely to come to a global assessment of how much they enjoyed a particular movie. Enjoyment that derives from the social circumstances of consumption tends to go unrecognized and is usually misattributed to the entertaining message.

According to this, young men should enjoy horror more in the company of an apparently frightened female companion than in the company of an unexpressive or mastering female. Young women, on the other hand, should enjoy horror more in the company of a mastering male companion than in the company of an unexpressive or distressed male. The experimental investigation (Zillmann et al., 1984) confirmed just that very strongly.

CONCLUDING REMARK

This brief introduction to research into the entertainment experience is necessarily incomplete. The interested reader is referred to the various cited summaries of research in particular domains (i.e., the exploration of enjoyment from suspense, comedy, horror, sports, etc.). But granted incompleteness, this exposition should make the point that it is most meaningful to treat the entertainment experience as an effect. It is, in fact, *the* effect of entertainment consumption. It is the primary effect that is sought out and pursued for the benefits that it entails – benefits such as being distracted from acute grievances, having boredom removed, being cheered up, being given great excitement, being helped to calm down, or being fed pacifying messages. Surely, many media analysts might be inclined to label the attainment of these benefits *escapism*. Heavy consumption of entertainment is indeed likely to be maladaptive in the sense that problems that could be resolved by appropriate action remain unresolved and may grow to calamity levels. The consumption of much entertainment does not fit such an account, however. Consumption is often not only not maladaptive; it can be highly adaptive. This is the case when consumption serves to improve on prevailing moods, affects, and emotions, shifting them from bad to good or from good to better, under conditions in which undesirable states cannot be eliminated and altered through well-targeted action. What should an individual who comes home exhausted from a long day's work in a steel mill or, for that matter, in an executive office do about this undesirable situation? And what can a woman with premenstrual pains do about the pain-inducing conditions? If entertainment consumption manages to calm them down, cheer them up, and get them ready for the next similarly trying day, is it fair to condemn such benefit as escapism? Would it not be more reasonable to accept such effects on mood and emotional well-being as recreational success?

But regardless of how media analysts might elect to characterize the effects in question, the fact remains that much entertainment is consumed to alter moods, affects, and emotions in the specified fashion; moreover, the fact remains that the desired effects come about with considerable regularity. De facto, then, the consumption of much entertainment has beneficial consequences. It is adaptive, recreational, restorative, and in this sense, therapeutic. This is not to say that all of entertainment necessarily has these effects or that massive consumption has benefits. Quite obviously, numerous highly undesirable side-effects exist. It is to say, however, that entertainment provided by the so-called mass media can provide highly beneficial emotional experiences that are truly recreational and that may be uplifting. These effects of entertainment, presumably because of the ready condemnation of entertainment as cheap escapism, have received very little attention from researchers. We feel that some reevaluation is in order, and we hope that the exploration of the entertainment experience with its consequences for the emotional welfare of the consumers of entertaining fare will receive the attention that it deserves.

REFERENCES

Aust, C.F. (1984) 'The effect of bad news on respondents' satisfaction with their own situation', unpublished master's thesis, Indiana University, Bloomington.

Biswas, R., Riffe, D. and Zillmann, D. (in press) 'Mood influence on the appeal of bad news', *Journalism Quarterly*,

Brown, G.E., Brown, D. and Ramos, J. (1981) 'Effects of a laughing versus a nonlaughing model on humor responses in college students', *Psychological Reports*, 48: 35–40.

Brown, G.E., Wheeler, K.J. and Case, M. (1980) 'The effects of a laughing versus a nonlaughing model on humor responses in preschool children', *Journal of Experimental Child Psychology*, 29: 334–9.

Bryant, J. and Zillmann, D. (1984) 'Using television to alleviate boredom and stress: selective exposure as a function of induced excitational states', *Journal of Broadcasting*, 28 (1): 1–20.

Bryant, J., Rockwell, S.C., and Owens, J.W. (1992) 'Degree of suspense and outcome resolution as factors in the enjoyment of a televised football game', unpublished manuscript, University of Alabama, Tuscaloosa, AL.

Chapman, A.J. (1973a) 'Funniness of jokes, canned laughter and recall performance', *Sociometry*, 36: 569–78.

Chapman, A.J. (1973b) 'Social facilitation of laughter in children', *Journal of Experimental Social Psychology*, 9: 528–41.

Chapman, A.J. and Wright, D.S. (1976) 'Social enhancement of laughter: an experimental analysis of some companion variables', *Journal of Experimental Child Psychology*, 21: 201–18.

Cupchik, G.C. and Leventhal, H. (1974) 'Consistency between expressive behavior and the evaluation of humorous stimuli: the role of sex and self-observation', *Journal of Personality and Social Psychology*, 30: 429–42.

Fuller, R.G.C. and Sheehy-Skeffington, A. (1974) 'Effects of group laughter on response to humorous material: a replication and extension', *Psychological Reports*, 35: 531–4.

Goldstein, J.H. (ed.) (1979) *Sports, Games, and Play: Social and Psychological Viewpoints*. Hillsdale, NJ: Lawrence Erlbaum Associates.

Haskins, J.B. (1981) 'The trouble with bad news', *Newspaper Research Journal*, 2 (2): 3–16.

Hirt, E.R., Zillmann, D., Erickson, G.A. and Kennedy, C. (1992) 'Costs and benefits of allegiance: changes in fans' self-ascribed competencies after team victory versus defeat', *Journal of Personality and Social Psychology*, 63 (5): 724–38.

Hocking, J.E. (1982) 'Sports and spectators: intra-audience effects', *Journal of Communication*, 32 (1): 100–8.

Hocking, J.E., Margreiter, D.G. and Hylton, C. (1977) 'Intra-audience effects: a field text', *Human Communication Research*, 3 (3): 243–9.

Jauss, H.R. (1982) *Aesthetic Experience and Literary Hermenutics*, Vol. 3: *Theory and History of Literature* (trans. M. Shaw). Minneapolis: University of Minnesota Press.

Leventhal, H. and Cupchik, G.C. (1975) 'The informational and facilitative effects of an audience upon expression and evaluation of humorous stimuli', *Journal of Experimental Social Psychology*, 11: 363–80.

Leventhal, H. and Mace, W. (1970) 'The effect of laughter on evaluation of a slapstick movie', *Journal of Personality*, 38: 16–30.

McGhee, P.E. (1979) *Humor: Its Origin and Development*. San Francisco, CA: Freeman.

Mendelsohn, H. (1966) *Mass Entertainment*. New Haven, CT: College & University Press.

Ovid (1947) *The Art of Love and Other Poems* (trans. J.H. Mozley). Cambridge, MA: Harvard University Press.

Sapolsky, B.S. (1980) 'The effect of spectator disposition and suspense on the enjoyment of sport contests', *International Journal of Sport Psychology*, 11 (1): 1–10.

Sapolsky, B.S. and Zillmann, D. (1978) 'Enjoyment of a televised sport contest under different social conditions of viewing', *Perceptual and Motor Skills*, 46: 29–30.

Schwarz, N., Strack, F., Kommer, D. and Wagner, D. (1987) 'Soccer, rooms, and the quality of your life: mood effects on judgments of satisfaction with life in general and with specific domains', *European Journal of Social Psychology*, 17: 69–79.

Schweitzer, K., Zillmann, D., Weaver, J.B. and Luttrell, E.S. (1992) 'Perception of threatening events in the emotional aftermath of a televised college football game', *Journal of Broadcasting and Electronic Media*, 36: 75–82.

Smiley, S. (1971) *Playwriting: The Structure of Action* . Englewood Cliffs, NJ: Prentice-Hall.

Smith, A. (1759/1971) *The Theory of Moral Sentiments*. New York: Garland.

Smyth, M.M. and Fuller, R.G.C. (1972) 'Effects of group laughter on responses to humorous material', *Psychological Reports*, 30: 132–4.

Tannenbaum, P.H. (1980) 'An unstructured introduction to an amorphous area', in P.H. Tannenbaum (ed.), *The Entertainment Functions of Television*. Hillsdale, NJ: Lawrence Erlbaum Associates. pp. 1–12.

Veitch, R. and Griffitt, W. (1976) 'Good news-bad news: affective and interpersonal effects', *Journal of Applied Social Psychology*, 6: 69–75.

White, G.L., Fishbein, S. and Rutstein, J. (1981) 'Passionate love and the misattribution of arousal', *Journal of Personality and Social Psychology*, 41: 56–62

Zillmann, D. (1977) 'Humor and communication', in A.J. Chapman and H.C. Foot (eds), *It's a Funny Thing, Humor*. Oxford: Pergamon. pp. 291–301.

Zillmann, D. (1980) 'Anatomy of suspense', in P.H. Tannenbaum (ed.), *The Entertainment Functions of Television*. Hillsdale, NJ: Lawrence Erlbaum Associates. pp. 133–63.

Zillmann, D. (1982) 'Television viewing and arousal', in D. Pearl, L. Bouthilet and J. Lazar (eds), *Television and Behavior: Ten Years of Scientific Progress and Implications for the Eighties*, Vol: 2: *Technical Reviews*. Washington, DC: US Government Printing Office. pp. 53–67.

Zillmann, D. (1991a) 'Empathy: affect from bearing witness to the emotions of others', in J. Bryant and D. Zillmann (eds), *Responding to the Screen: Reception and Reaction Processes*. Hillsdale, NJ: Lawrence Erlbaum Associates. pp. 135–67.

Zillmann, D. (1991b) 'Television viewing and physiological arousal', in J. Bryant and D. Zillmann (eds), *Responding to the Screen: Reception and Reaction Processes*. Hillsdale, NJ: Lawrence Erlbaum Associates. pp. 103–33.

Zillmann, D. (1991c) 'The logic of suspense and mystery', in J. Bryant and D. Zillmann (eds), *Responding to the Screen: Reception and Reaction Processes*. Hillsdale, NJ: Lawrence Erlbaum Associates. pp. 281–303.

Zillmann, D. and Bryant, J. (1991) 'Responding to comedy: the sense and nonsense of humor', in J. Bryant and D. Zillmann (eds), *Responding to the Screen: Reception and Reaction Processes*. Hillsdale, NJ: Lawrence Erlbaum Associates. pp. 261–79.

Zillmann, D. and Cantor, J.R. (1976) 'A disposition theory of humour and mirth', in A.J. Chapman and H.C. Foot (eds), *Humour and Laughter: Theory, Research, and Applications*. London: Wiley. pp. 93–115.

Zillmann, D., Bryant, J. and Sapolsky, B.S. (1979) 'The enjoyment of watching sport contests', in J.H. Goldstein (ed.), *Sports, Games, and Play: Social and Psychological Viewpoints*. Hillsdale, NJ: Lawrence Erlbaum Associates. pp. 297–335.

Zillmann, D., Weaver, J., Mundorf, N. and Aust, C.F. (1984) 'Companion effects on the enjoyment of horror', unpublished manuscript, Indiana University, Bloomington.

Zuckerman, M. (1979) *Sensation Seeking: Beyond the Optimal Level of Arousal*. Hillsdale, NJ: Lawrence Erlbaum Associates.